THE SEXUAL SUBJECT

The Sexual Subject: A Screen *Reader in Sexuality* brings together writing on sexuality which has appeared in *Screen* over the past two decades. It reflects the journal's continuing engagement with questions of sexuality and signification in the cinema, an engagement which has had a profound influence on both the development of academic study of film and on alternative film and video practice.

The collection opens with Laura Mulvey's classic 'Visual Pleasure and Narrative Cinema' with its conjunction of semiotics and psychoanalysis, the critical approach most closely associated with *Screen*'s rise to international prominence. The Reader then goes on to explore the particular questions and debates which that conjunction provoked: arguments around pornography and the representation of the body; questions around the representation of femininity and masculinity, the female spectator, and the social subject.

Many of the writings in this Reader have become indispensable texts within the study of film. The purpose of the Reader is not only to make the articles available to a wider readership, and to a new generation, but also to pose fresh conjunctions, making connections in one volume between debates and enquiries which have spanned two crucial decades of film theory.

The Sexual Subject is intended not only for all those with a particular interest in film and film theory, but for anyone with a serious commitment to cultural theory, theories of representation, and questions of sexuality and gender.

* * *

Screen is the leading international journal of film and television theory. It started as an educational journal in the 1950s under the auspices of the Society for Education in Film and Television, and rose to international pre-eminence in the 1970s with its pioneering work on theories of the subject in cinema. With the disbandment of SEFT in 1989, editorship passed to the John Logie Baird Centre at the University of Glasgow.

Managing editors for the Reader are John Caughie and Annette Kuhn, both of whom teach Film and Television Studies at the University of Glasgow and are editors of *Screen*.

Mandy Merck, who selected the material, was editor of *Screen* from 1982 to 1989. She was series editor of the Channel 4 series 'Out on Tuesday' (Abseil Productions). Barbara Creed, who wrote the introductions, lectures in Cinema Studies at La Trobe University, Melbourne.

The contributors: Homi K. Bhabha, Edward Buscombe, Mary Ann Doane, Richard Dyer, John Ellis, Christine Gledhill, Stephen Heath, Claire Johnston, Annette Kuhn, Alan Lovell, Laura Mulvey, Steve Neale, Claire Pajaczkowska, Griselda Pollock, Jackie Stacey, Lesley Stern, Paul Willemen, Christopher Williams, and Dugald Williamson.

THE SEXUAL SUBJECT

A *Screen* Reader in Sexuality

Screen

London and New York

First published 1992
by Routledge
11 New Fetter Lane, London EC4P 4EE

Simultaneously published in the USA and Canada
by Routledge
29 West 35th Street, New York, NY 10001

Reprinted 1995, 1996, 1998, 1999

Typeset in 10 on 12 point Times by
Florencetype Ltd, Kewstoke, Avon
Printed in Great Britain by
Butler & Tanner Ltd, Frome and London

British Library Cataloguing in Publication Data
The sexual subject : a *Screen* reader in sexuality.
791.430909353

Library of Congress Cataloguing in Publication Data
The Sexual subject : a *Screen* reader in sexuality / *Screen*.
p.   cm.
1. Sex in motion pictures. I. *Screen* (London, England)
PN1995.9.S45S485   1992
791.43'6538 — dc20   91–40140

ISBN 0–415–07466–5 (hbk)   ISBN 0–415–07467–3 (pbk)

CONTENTS

Notes on contributors   vii
General Introduction   1

Part I Psychoanalysis and Subjectivity

Introduction   15

1 VISUAL PLEASURE AND NARRATIVE CINEMA   22
Laura Mulvey

2 PSYCHOANALYSIS AND FILM   35
Edward Buscombe, Christine Gledhill, Alan Lovell,
Christopher Williams

3 DIFFERENCE   47
Stephen Heath

4 LANGUAGE AND SEXUAL DIFFERENCE   107
Dugald Williamson

Part II Pornography

Introduction   129

5 WHAT'S WRONG WITH 'IMAGES OF WOMEN'?   135
Griselda Pollock

6 ON PORNOGRAPHY   146
John Ellis

7 LETTER TO JOHN   171
Paul Willemen

8 THE HETEROSEXUAL PRESUMPTION   184
Claire Pajaczkowska

9 THE BODY AS EVIDENCE   197
Lesley Stern

CONTENTS

Part III The Female Spectator

Introduction   223

10 FILM AND THE MASQUERADE: THEORIZING THE
    FEMALE SPECTATOR   227
    Mary Ann Doane

11 DESPERATELY SEEKING DIFFERENCE   244
    Jackie Stacey

Part IV Images of Men

Introduction   261

12 DON'T LOOK NOW: THE MALE PIN-UP   265
    Richard Dyer

13 MASCULINITY AS SPECTACLE   277
    Steve Neale

Part V The Social Subject

Introduction   291

14 THE SUBJECT OF FEMINIST FILM THEORY/PRACTICE   295
    Claire Johnston

15 WOMEN'S GENRES   301
    Annette Kuhn

16 THE OTHER QUESTION: THE STEREOTYPE AND
    COLONIAL DISCOURSE   312
    Homi K. Bhabha

Index   332

CONTRIBUTORS

Homi K. Bhabha teaches Literature at the University of Sussex and is the author of *The Location of Culture*, forthcoming

Edward Buscombe is Head of Trade Publishing at he British Film Institute. His most recent publication is *The British Film Institute Companion to the Western* (1990).

Mary Ann Doane is Professor and Director of Modern Culture and Media at Brown University. She is the author of *The Desire to Desire: Women's Films of the 1940s*, (1988) and *Femmes Fatales: Feminism, Film Theory, Psychoanalysis* (1991).

Richard Dyer teaches Film Studies at the University of Warwick. His publications include *Now You See It* (1990) and *Only Entertainment* (1992).

John Ellis is a television producer and partner in the independent company Large Door Ltd. He is the author of *Visible Fictions: Cinema*, and *Television, Video* (1990).

Christine Gledhill is Senior Lecturer in Media and Cultural Studies at Stafford University.

Stephen Heath was a member of the *Screen* editorial board from 1972 to 1982.

Claire Johnston pioneered feminist film theory. She served on the *Screen* editorial board and worked with the Edinburgh Film Festival in the 1970s. She died in 1987.

Annette Kuhn is an editor of *Screen*, and Reader in Film and Television Studies at the University of Glasgow.

Alan Lovell is a freelance filmmaker and lecturer.

Laura Mulvey is a freelance lecturer, writer and filmmaker.

Steve Neale is Senior Lecturer in Film Studies at the University of Kent, and co-author of *Popular Film and Television Comedy* (1990). He is a regular contributor to *Screen*.

Claire Pajaczkowska is Senior Lecturer in Cultural Studies at Middlesex Polytechnic. Her doctoral thesis, 'Before Language', was on the prelinguistic in history and theory.

Griselda Pollock is Professor of the Social and Critical Histories of Art, and Director of the Centre for Cultural Studies at the University of Leeds.

Jackie Stacey lectures in Film Studies and Women's Studies in the Department of Sociology at Lancaster University. She is author of a forthcoming study of Hollywood stars and female spectatorship, *With Stars in Their Eyes*.

Lesley Stern teaches in the Department of Theatre and Film Studies at the University of New South Wales, Sydney. She has written widely in the areas of cinema, performance and cultural studies.

Paul Willemen worked with *Screen* and the Edinburgh Film Festival in the 1970s, edited *Framework* in the 1980s, and is currently employed as an editor at the British Film Institute.

Christopher Williams is Senior Lecturer in Film at the Polytechnic of Central London.

Dugald Williamson is Senior Lecturer in the Division of Humanities at Griffith University, Brisbane, and co-editor of *On Pornography: Literature Sexuality and Obscenity Law*, forthcoming.

GENERAL INTRODUCTION

There is a scene in *Aliens* in which a female paratrooper is doing press-ups on a bar. Her hair is short, her body muscular, lithe, powerful, her skin black. This image of female muscularity threatens boundaries of race, gender, colour. By way of offering an insult, a white male paratrooper (not nearly as virile) says: 'Hey, Vasquez! You ever been mistaken for a man?' She eyes him calmly and replies – with just the right hint of menace – 'No! Have you?' The phrase 'sexual subject', with its emphasis on 'subject' rather than the already determined categories of 'female' and 'male' invites us – like Vasquez – to adopt a flexible response to the question of sexual subjectivity. Is she a man? Is he a woman? A not-woman? Or a he-woman? An object? A subject? Bisexual? Homosexual? Asexual? Nothing?

Lacanian theories of the subject have emphasized the importance of subjectivity and sexual identity as a state of 'being' and 'becoming' – of risk and instability. Constituted during the mirror phase, the period when image takes precedence over language, the 'subject' is forever after haunted by images – ideal image, ego ideal, self-image, copy, imago, double, *alter ego*. Later, the 'outline' of the subject is filled in through the agency of words – through language, words whose meanings pre-exist the individual subject. Subjectivity is a construct, Lacan argues, which can cease to function, even disappear altogether. The subject is assigned a place in language, a gender identity which, in western and all other patriarchal societies of the late twentieth century, is organized around dichotomies of active/masculine and passive/feminine. How important are Lacanian theories of subjectivity to the cinema? How is the subject 'sexed' or made 'sexual'? What is the relationship of gender to subjectivity? Is gender identity as precarious as subjectivity? Can we even separate the two? How important is sexual preference? For instance, prior to the advent of psychoanalysis in the late nineteenth century, sexual preference was seen only as a part of one's identity. The terms 'homosexual' and later 'heterosexual' were coined to describe the relatively new idea that sexual preference profoundly altered the nature of subjectivity. Until then the homosexual was called an 'invert'. Can gender identity, like subjectivity,

1

also change direction, fragment, cease to function, disappear? What is the relation of the sexual subject to representation, the gaze, power, sociality, class, race? What are femininity and masculinity? How is the sexual subject represented in the cinema? These are some of the issues that the chapters in this volume explore.

By bringing together a collection of key articles written between 1975 and 1987 on these issues, *The Sexual Subject* aims not only to document the key developments in this area but also to provide a focus for ongoing discussion. During the period covered film debates were strongly influenced by the discourses of structuralism, semiotics, ideology, feminism and psychoanalysis. The previous two *Screen* readers – the first *Cinema/Ideology/Politics* (1977) and the second, *Cinema and Semiotics* (1981) – focused on two crucial aspects of these debates: ideology and semiotics. *The Sexual Subject*, with its emphasis on psychoanalysis and subjectivity, completes this important work. Prior to *Screen*'s interest in promoting these new areas, film theory was dominated by an impressionistic approach to criticism which did not address textual construction or the screen–spectator relationship. Historical and political developments, particularly after the political upheavals in France in 1968, brought about dramatic changes in French theory which exerted a profound influence on the course of film studies in Britain and eventually on the rest of the international film community.

The introduction of these new ideas, however, was not a monolithic or harmonious enterprise. First, the new areas themselves were quite different in emphasis and direction; for instance, whereas the structuralist critics examined the text as an autonomous, self-contained entity in which meaning existed according to a set of already existing rules, other writers began to argue that meaning is created in the *encounter* between text and reader. While both approaches shared a common interest in the relationship between text and ideology, structuralism charted this relationship in terms of the internal workings of the text while its critics sought to introduce a subjective dimension. In exploring the screen–spectator relationship, film theorists turned their attention to a number of diverse areas: ideology; the nature of the 'classic realist' text; point-of-view; suture; theories of the look, psychoanalysis, subjectivity and gender. *The Sexual Subject*, as the title indicates, is about the sexual and subjective dimension of the screen–spectator relationship.

Written over a twelve-year period, the various articles trace the debates which surrounded the introduction of theories of the sexual subject into film studies. The five sections have been organized around areas of interest which gradually emerged as central to these debates. Over this period we can see a gradual change in the emphasis accorded to the importance of psychoanalytic theory and to the spectating subject seen as an effect of the text. While the opening chapter, Laura Mulvey's now famous 'Visual

Pleasure and Narrative Cinema', called for the use of psychoanalytic theory as a 'political weapon' for studying the film text, chapters in the final section by Claire Johnston and Annette Kuhn accept the importance of psychoanalytic theory but caution that its use must also be related to the world outside the filmic discourse – the world of political, social and economic formations.

The development of theories about the sexual subject and its relationship to the cinema has taken a number of directions and been subject to different influences. At least four different but related approaches were explored during the period we are discussing: a psychoanalytic approach which draws primarily on Lacan's theory of the Symbolic and sees subjectivity as male and phallic; a related Lacanian approach which emphasizes the constitution of the subject as split and places emphasis on subjectivity as imaginary; the fantasy view of subjectivity which is based on Freud's theory of the primal fantasies and defines subjectivity as fluid, mobile and dispersed; difference theory which argues that patriarchal ideology constructs different subjectivities – based on race, sex, class, colour, sexual preference – as 'other' in order to control and silence their voices. I have not specified a separate feminist position as, in varying degrees, all of the above have been strongly influenced by a feminist critique of the cinema. Nor am I suggesting that these four approaches represent discrete positions; they are all interconnected although their emphases are different. Here, I plan to discuss each of these notions of the sexual subject with specific reference to a number of the chapters contained in this collection.

The most original and controversial analysis of the sexual subject comes from Laura Mulvey's highly influential article, 'Visual Pleasure and Narrative Cinema'. It was this article which inaugurated the debates around subjectivity and sexual difference which were to span the following decade and beyond. Mulvey's aim was to use psychoanalytic theory to demonstrate 'the way the unconscious of patriarchal society has structured film form'. She used Lacan's rereading of Freud's theory of the unconscious to explore the representation of subjectivity in the cinema. She presents her analysis from a feminist perspective in which subjectivity is seen as the work of representation. In classic narrative cinema subjectivity is active, male, phallic. Prior to the publication of Mulvey's article, feminist analyses of the cinema tended to speak of the representation of subjectivity – male and female – as a *reflection* of gender relations in the real world. In the Autumn 1975 edition of *Screen*, Claire Johnston, in her invaluable review article 'Feminist Politics and Film History', presented a comprehensive and critical account of these early feminist approaches to the cinema. She presented her critique in relation to three early feminist books: Molly Haskell's *From Reverence to Rape*; Majorie Rosen's *Popcorn Venus*; and Joan Mellen's *Women and Their Sexuality in the New Film*.

Unlike this early feminist approach to film and subjectivity, Mulvey presents subjectivity as a construction, a representation produced through semiotic activity in response to the workings of the unconscious of patriarchal society. This became the dominant aim of cinematic theories about the sexual subject – to see subjectivity as a construction rather than as a reflection of a biological given existing in the real world. Theories of the sexual subject equally emphasized the importance of the relationship between the subject, male and female, on the screen and the spectator in the auditorium. In her article, 'Women's Cinema and Feminist Film Criticism', also included in the Autumn 1975 edition of *Screen*, Annette Kuhn presented a critique of purely text-based criticisms of the cinema. She drew attention to the crucial importance of the screen–spectator relationship, and the tendency of much critical work to take this relationship for granted. Her call for more attention to this area anticipated the direction of emerging debates on spectatorship.

THE PHALLIC SUBJECT

Mulvey commences her article with a discussion of the Lacanian concept of the 'subject' and its constitution in the mirror phase. It is this notion of the subject, as constituted in a moment of recognition and misrecognition, which was central to film debates of the period. The latter part of her analysis is primarily concerned with the nature of male subjectivity. She states that little is known or stated about the nature of the female unconscious in phallocentric theory – a point I shall discuss shortly. In Mulvey's view, the sexual *subject*, that is, the one whom the film is addressing and constructing in an active position, both in the diegetic world of the film and in the auditorium, is the ideal male spectator. Male subjectivity is seen as active, controlling, desiring. Woman is not accorded a place as a desiring sexual subject – only as an object of desire, caught up in a dominant male discourse. 'Woman's desire is subjected to her image as bearer of the bleeding wound, she can exist only in relation to castration and cannot transcend it.'[1] The female subject, in so far as she is a 'subject' at all, represents lack and difference. The male accepts her difference either by re-establishing her 'castration' and punishing her accordingly or by disavowing her castration by setting up a fetish in place of her 'lack'. In this scenario male subjectivity represents aggressivity and sadism: female subjectivity represents passivity and masochism. The assumption is that the male derives pleasure from his dominance over woman.

Although Mulvey argued that mainstream narrative cinema presents the male as the subject of desire, she also saw the representation of male sexuality as highly problematic, produced as it is in relation to Oedipal desire and castration anxiety. In order to deal with this problem, the cinematic machine is compelled to adopt a number of strategies which point to the workings of ideology at the level of the subtext: objectification

4

of the female image in relation to the controlling male gaze; highly coded and fetishized images of the female face and form; cyclical narrative processes which restore a conservative status quo; destruction of female characters who threaten the patriarchal order; denial of aberrant forms of desire, particularly homosexual desire. Influenced by Mulvey's theory, feminist critics sought to expose the workings of ideology by 'reading against the grain'. These readings in a sense produced a notion of the sexual subject as a construction-in-crisis. This view was of course re-inforced by Lacan's theory of the constitution of subjectivity in which the subject, male and female, is seen as marked by castration and lack from birth. Despite an emphasis on reading against the grain in order to find contradictions and gaps in the representation of male subjectivity, the male was still positioned – by both the text and the reading – as the subject of desire, woman as its object. The assumption that the male, as represented in the text and positioned in the audience, experienced sadistic pleasure as a result of his renewed encounter with and control of woman as castration threat was rarely questioned.

Mulvey's view of man as subject and woman as non-subject exerted a profound influence on critical debates, particularly feminist debates, of the following decade. At their worst, critical readings of specific texts applied Mulvey's ideas about male and female subjectivity in a reductive and uncritical manner. Other writers were careful not to use Mulvey's ideas reductively and produced readings which saw masculinity, as well as femininity, as a problematic concept. The filmic text might appear to construct the male as sexual subject, signifier of the law, but frequently this was only brought about through a series of repressions – particularly the repression of homosexual desire. Richard Dyer and Steve Neale, whose articles are included in part IV, questioned the assumption that the male is never sexually objectified within the signifying practices of the text. They sought to problematize the notion that the male protagonist in the text is always represented as in control of the gaze, the looker rather than the object of the look. Neale argues for the existence of the voyeuristic and fetishistic gaze directed at male characters by other males within the diegetic world of the western and the epic film. Dyer finds evidence of sexual objectification of the male in which the male body is posed in such a way as to suggest the power of the phallus. This is not simply to applaud male power but rather to disguise the fact that the penis can never live up to the promise of the phallus.

Similarly an examination of pornography revealed that the male is not always represented in a position of power. Some pornographic texts play to the masochistic desires of the male spectator by representing the male as victim of the dominant sadistic woman who subjects his body and penis to a series of sadistic attacks. Interestingly, Deleuze's work on male maso-chism[2] argues that the masochist is, in fact, the *subject* of the interaction

5

because it is in accordance with his desires that he is humiliated and punished. In this context, the male masochist assumes the seemingly contradictory positions of object and subject. The question of whether woman might also take up a similar position as object and subject of the male gaze has also been raised, not in relation to pornography but in relation to the gaze. To what extent does woman as object of the look also control the look? Only recently have theorists turned their full attention to the notion of male sexuality as problematic and begun to discuss masculinity in relation to areas usually associated with femininity – areas such as male masochism and male hysteria.

THE CASTRATED SUBJECT

In an important contribution to debates about the sexual subject, 'Masochism and Subjectivity',[3] Kaja Silverman further unsettles the notion of a coherent, phallic masculinity. She is interested in the 'insufficiency of the male subject' and the way in which the mechanism of the sadistic, 'male' gaze is employed by classic narrative to project male inadequacy on to the female subject. I would include other operations of the classic text here such as fetishization and narrative recuperation. Silverman argues that the notion of the 'male gaze' should be seen primarily in terms of a structure, a controlling point from which the look originates, a look that is open to both male and female subjects. It is worth recapitulating her argument here as it further undermines the assumption that the male is always the controlling subject, the woman the passive object. First, Silverman draws on Lacan's theory that the subject, whether male or female, is constituted through a series of splittings, separations and misrecognitions. Second, she draws on Lacan's argument, based on his reading of Freud's famous *fort/da* game, that the human experience of pleasure is based on the repetition of those *painful* instances when the subject experienced those moments of separation and loss through which her/his subjectivity was constituted in the first place. However, she does not agree with Freud that this pleasure is derived from an experience of mastery; on the contrary she proposes that what is at stake is 'the pleasure of passivity, of subjection'.

She argues that texts 'provide pleasure to the degree that they reposition us culturally; to the extent that they oblige us to re-enact those moments of loss and false recovery by which we are constituted as subjects; in so far as they master us'.[4] Silverman points out, however, that it is the female character who usually enacts the narrative of loss and recovery. In other words, it is woman who is required to re-experience this drama on behalf of *both* female and male subjects – presumably because it is more acceptable within the dictates of patriarchal ideology for a woman to play the role of the masochistic victim. In Silverman's view it is woman-as-victim who is the real centre of attention. The 'fascination of the sadistic point of view is merely that it provides the best vantage point from which to watch the masochistic story unfold'.[5]

Silverman's view of the role of masochism in the workings of pleasure opens up Mulvey's theory of spectatorship to permit a more fluid positioning of male and female characters within the diegesis and of spectators within the auditorium. In this context male and female characters can take up the masochistic position as well as the position of the spectating subject, although the workings of a sexist ideology dictate that the active position is more likely to be aligned with the male subject and the passive position with the female. Silverman argues that because 'the inadequacy of the male subject must never be acknowledged' the female subject is made to bear his burden which is 'endlessly perpetuated through displacement' on to scenarios which depict the female subject as castrated. In other words, woman is made to bear, for both sexes, the castrations or separations on which subjectivity is constituted. Silverman elaborates further on the nature of the masochistic scenario with reference to Freud's theory of dreams. The spectator's relationship to the film text resembles her/his relationship to the dream. Because of the way in which displacement and condensation work, the ego can be represented in this scenario in an infinite number of positions. Forms of identification are varied, mobile and fluid. Silverman's reference to Freud's work on identification in dreams anticipated the development of writings on the importance of fantasy to theories of the viewing subject, which I will discuss shortly.

The notion of the female subject as castrated can be understood in two contexts. First, like male subjectivity, female subjectivity is also constituted in lack and separation – as discussed above. Second, the male subject imagines woman is castrated in a moment of fright and misrecognition and continues to perpetuate this notion within phallocentric discourse both consciously and unconsciously. It is this latter account that was central to Mulvey's theory and to debates of the period. However, although Mulvey was primarily concerned with male subjectivity, her analysis raises, if indirectly, a series of questions about female subjectivity. Represented only as object in a male discourse, in what sense is woman a subject? Does woman experience the separations of infancy (birth, weaning, etc.) in the same way as man? What is her relationship to the mother? Can woman speak in her own voice in texts presented from the perspective of the male subject?

In Mulvey's view, the entire area of female subjectivity and issues related to the female unconscious are hardly relevant to phallocentric theory. She does, however, draw attention to three areas she considers crucial: the constitution of the female child as sexual subject and her relationship to the Symbolic; definitions of woman as sexual subject which do not depend on her social and biological role as mother; a definition of the maternal subject which does not necessarily depend on notions of the

7

vagina and phallus, that is, sexual difference. In other words, she is interested in the meaning of woman as subject in terms of her socially constructed roles as young girl, non-mother, mother. The contexts in which woman is constructed as a sexual subject outside her maternal, reproductive functions were analysed in a number of key articles on femininity during this period, particularly in relation to the *femme fatale* of *film noir*.[6] Such a woman was almost always positioned as phallic in so far as she sought to take the place of the male, to become the phallus herself.

Interestingly, the majority of articles on sexual difference focused primarily on woman's image as castrated, wounded 'other' rather than her image as the menstruating, castrating female figure of dread. This imbalance is also present in the writings of Freud and Lacan. For instance, Lacan's 1972–3 seminar 'Encore', devoted to Freud's notorious question 'What does woman want?', takes as the object of its discourse Bernini's famous statue of Saint Teresa in which the nun is depicted during a moment of religious/sexual ecstasy. Saint Teresa is displayed before the gaze of the (male) spectator. Head thrown back, eyes closed, lips suggestively parted, body arched backwards, Saint Teresa awaits the moment of penetration by the angel's arrow. Everything about her signals passivity, powerlessness, castration as she surrenders to the power of the Other. Lacan decides she is coming – 'no doubt about it' he says almost defiantly – although her pose suggests rather that she is *waiting* for the moment, hoping/wanting to come. Like the heroines of other soap operas, Saint Teresa was probably disappointed. Lacan, however, is convinced the moment has already arrived or is arriving just when *he* is looking. The gaze coincides with the pleasure of the other as if conditional upon, made possible by, the act of looking. The thought that she is coming – that the phallus still works – no doubt appeals to his vanity. It certainly makes for a less interesting story. In a later seminar when Lacan is again discussing woman, he seizes upon an altogether different image. 'Queen Victoria, there's a woman . . . when one encounters a toothed vagina of such exceptional size.'[7] Interestingly, this view in which woman is represented as the *castrating* other is relegated to a footnote. However, it is the image of woman as castrated that dominated debates about female subjectivity until the early 1980s.

One of the first attempts to question the notion of woman as castrated was presented by Susan Lurie in her important article, 'The Construction of the "Castrated Woman" in Psychoanalysis and Cinema'.[8] Lurie challenges the Freudian notion that men fear woman because she appears to be castrated. On the contrary, Lurie claims, men are comforted by the idea that women are castrated. The real reason woman inspires terror is *'that she is not castrated* despite the fact that she has no penis . . .'. Woman further inspires terror because the male imagines she might castrate him during intercourse – not only does her vagina look like a devouring mouth but his experience of detumescence feels like a form of castration. It is because woman is not castrated, Lurie argues, that the male unconscious constructs woman as castrated within the signifying practices of the cinema. This is carried out by a variety of means: on the one hand woman is symbolically castrated by being positioned as a helpless child, undermined in her role as mother, or punished for speaking her desire; while on the other hand she is literally castrated in those films where she is wounded, mutilated and murdered. Lurie applied her theory to a close analysis of the construction of the castrated 'other' in Hitchcock's *The Birds*. It is probably indicative of the period, so heavily influenced by Lacanian psychoanalytic theory, that Lurie chose to analyse the representation of woman as castrated rather than as castrator. Only recently have feminists turned their attention to woman as castrating 'other', particularly in horror and science fiction cinema.

The image of woman as sexual subject has been explored by a number of theorists included in this Reader. In her article, 'Film and the Masquerade' (chapter 10), Mary Ann Doane also emphasizes the importance of seeing woman's so-called castration as a construction, an enactment or masquerade of femininity. She concludes that the female spectator can relate to the cinematic image of woman in one of three ways: adoption of a masculine position as theorized by Laura Mulvey in her article on *Duel in the Sun*; masochistic over-identification with the image; or a deliberate distancing from the image in order to stand back and read the image. Doane argues that the last perspective becomes possible if the female spectator acknowledges that femininity is a masquerade, a performance, something faked. Jackie Stacey (chapter 11) also attempts to find a way around the theorization of the spectator only in terms of the male gaze. She explores the possibility of an erotic exchange of looks between women in a number of texts.

SUBJECTS IN FANTASY

The question of fantasy became central to discussions of spectatorship during the early 1980s. Lesley Stern takes up this issue in her discussion of pornography (chapter 9), and Homi K. Bhabha in his analysis of the colonial subject (chapter 16). Writers interested in fantasy theory hoped to find another way of theorizing spectatorship which did not draw on the binarism of male subject as controller of the look and woman as its passive object. Drawing on Freud's theories of the three primal fantasies, fantasy theory offers a way of opening up multiple positions of identification for the female and male viewer. This means that the viewing subject is also free to take up a variety of subject positions regardless of gender. The three primal fantasies elaborated by Freud are: the fantasy of the primal scene; the seduction fantasy; and the fantasy of castration. Each of these fantasies deals with the question of the subject's origins: its origin in its parents' lovemaking; the origin of desire; and the origin of sexual difference. It is interesting, and perhaps predictable given the interest in gender, that the fantasy of castration has dominated theories of the subject. Yet the other two fantasies are also central to the representation of sexual difference in film. One of the first and most significant analyses was Elizabeth Cowie's 'Fantasia', in which she explored the multiplicity of subject positions opened up in relation to fantasy.[9]

In the act of fantasizing, or viewing the representation of a primal fantasy in film, the individual is free to take up any position she or he wishes. According to Victor Burgin: 'the subject may be represented as an observer, as actor, even in the very *form* of an utterance.'[10] From this we can see that fantasy theory represents subjectivity as fluid, mobile and not necessarily constrained by gender, although not all would agree with this. It has also been argued that in viewing film a subject is not as 'free' as fantasy theory might otherwise hold;[11] the filmic strategies of identification, such as the point-of-view shot, may well influence the spectator and must also be considered. *Screen* has published a number of articles which explore fantasy theory and its relationship to subjectivity. One of the most interesting is Donald Greig's 'The Sexual Differentiation of the Hitchcock Text'.[12] Greig is critical of Bellour's influential analysis of Hitchcock's films, particularly his reduction of the narrative to a male Oedipal scenario. Bellour's analysis yet again reinforces the view that the female subject is defined only in relation to the phallus. Greig argues that Bellour ignores other dimensions of the text such as female Oedipality and the representation of various primal scenes. In her discussion of the pornographic text, a privileged site of the primal fantasy, Lesley Stern presents an interesting analysis of fantasy in relation to fiction and the way in which the activity of fantasizing works to disperse sexual identity. Homi K. Bhabha looks at the way in which racial stereotypes draw on primal fantasies of origin.

SUBJECTIVITY AND DIFFERENCE THEORY

Psychoanalytic interpretations of the classic realist text hold that the classic narrative constructs an impression of plenitude and coherence to cover over the underlying reality of lack, separation and difference. Similarly, the ideal subject of classic narrative is given a unified, coherent but illusory identity. The notion of the lack at the centre of being is denied in the signifying practices of the classic narrative. The patriarchal subject is represented as an imaginary unity – lack is displaced on to the 'Other'. In narratives of sexual difference the male subject represents unity and coherence, the female lack and difference. Subjects who represent other forms of difference – based on race, class, colour, sexual preference – are almost always constructed as the 'Other' whose presence threatens to disturb the boundaries of civilization and rationality. 'Difference' is thus transformed into 'otherness' and repressed within the signifying practices of the text.

The representation of sexual difference is the area which has been most analysed and discussed. In her excellent discussion of these debates, 'Difference and Its Discontents',[13] Mandy Merck charts the course of these debates and the profound influence that sexual difference theory exerted on cultural studies between 1975 and 1987. In particular she discusses 'the rush to Lacan' and the consequent problems which arose from an often uncritical acceptance of his ideas. One of the major problems has been the tendency to rely exclusively on psychoanalytic theories of subjectivity which define the feminine always in terms of 'lack' and 'absence'. Phallocentric theories of the sexual subject, unable to break free from the tyranny of the phallic signifier, also tend to define homosexuality simply as a disavowal of difference. More recent work explores difference in other contexts such as race, class, colour, age and sexual preference. Writers stress the importance of also defining subjectivity in its social and historical context. Bhabha discusses subjectivity and race, Stacey considers erotic desire between women, and Johnston and Kuhn stress the importance of the historical and social order in the formation of subjectivity. *The Sexual Subject* charts the progress of these debates while also offering ideas about future directions.

NOTES

1 Laura Mulvey, 'Visual Pleasure and Narrative Cinema', chapter 1 in this volume, p. 22.
2 Gilles Deleuze, *Masochism*, New York, Zone Books, 1989.
3 Kaja Silverman, 'Masochism and Subjectivity', *Framework*, 1980, no. 12, pp. 2–9.
4 ibid., p. 3.
5 ibid., p. 5.
6 See the essays in E. Ann Kaplan, *Women in Film Noir*, London, BFI Publishing, 1980.
7 Quoted in Stephen Heath, 'Difference', chapter 3 in this volume, p. 56.
8 Susan Lurie, 'The Construction of the "Castrated Woman" in Psychoanalysis and Cinema', *Discourse*, Winter 1981–2, no. 4, pp. 52–74.
9 Elizabeth Cowie, 'Fantasia', *m/f*, 1984, no. 9, pp. 71–105.
10 Victor Burgin, 'Diderot, Barthes, *Vertigo*', *The End of Art Theory*, London, Macmillan, 1986, p. 128.
11 Barbara Creed, 'A Journey Through *Blue Velvet*: Film, Fantasy and the Female Spectator', *New Formations*, Winter 1988, no. 6, pp. 97–117.
12 Donald Greig, 'The Sexual Differentiation of the Hitchcock Text', *Screen*, Winter 1987, vol. 28, no. 1, pp. 28–46.
13 Mandy Merck, 'Introduction – Difference and Its Discontents', *Screen*, Winter 1987, vol. 28, no. 1, pp. 2–9.

Part I

PSYCHOANALYSIS AND SUBJECTIVITY

INTRODUCTION

Looking back over the debates of the 1970s, it might appear as if the new developments in film theory, often referred to as poststructuralist, were relatively straightforward. A closer study of the period, however, reveals important differences and numerous shifts of direction. One of the most crucial was the introduction of psychoanalytic theory – specifically Jacques Lacan's theories of subjectivity, which developed from his rereading of Freud. In general terms this shift could be seen as moving from studies of the film text as autonomous and discrete to studies which concentrated on the text–reader relationship. The former approach, based on the disciplines of structuralism and semiotics, argued that meaning resides in the text, whereas the latter argued that meaning is constructed in the act of reading. This new development, which increasingly came to dominate film studies, explored the text–reader relationship through a number of related areas: point-of-view, classic realism, the Althusserian view of ideology. One of the most important of these areas, psychoanalysis, gave rise to a number of interesting theories designed to help explain the relationship between text and reader. These included: suture, notions of identification, the male gaze.

Lacanian psychoanalysis, particularly its theory that the subject is constituted in lack and separation in relation to the Symbolic order, exerted a profound influence on ideas about subjectivity and the text–spectator relationship. Gradually, however, psychoanalytic approaches to subjectivity and film viewing came under increasing attack. First, critics argued that the notion of the viewing subject that emerges is ultimately nothing more than a generalized abstraction. The Lacanian theory of the subject ignores important factors such as the individual's own history as well as factors such as class, race and age. The final part of this book, 'The Social Subject', contains articles which address this issue. Defenders of the psychoanalytic approach argue that it does make sense to talk of an abstract notion of the subject outside of these empirical realities, in that the text does position the viewing subject in certain ways through the workings of its more formal mechanisms such as suture and the voyeuristic gaze.

This does not mean that the viewing subject is or should be reduced to a passive object of the text's formal operations; the viewing subject also contributes to the way in which meaning is constructed. If we ignore the formal operations of the text in the construction of meaning, we are left with the argument that the spectator is free to construct any meaning she or he wishes.

On the one hand, the psychoanalytic approach seeks to construct a meaning which is true for all viewers while, on the other hand, the sociocultural approach posits an infinite number of possible meanings. To avoid the abstraction of the former and the extreme pluralism of the latter one needs to explore ways in which the two approaches interact. A second major criticism of the Lacanian theory of subjectivity is that, because of a confusion which arises over the distinction between phallus and penis, it posits man as fullness and woman as lack in relation to the Symbolic order. It is this debate which is central to the chapters contained in this part.

Laura Mulvey's 'Visual Pleasure and Narrative Cinema', first published in *Screen* in 1975, has probably generated more debate, both in the pages of *Screen* and elsewhere, than any other single article in the history of contemporary film theory. Drawing on Freudian and Lacanian theory from a feminist perspective, Mulvey set out the parameters of what was to become an ongoing debate about the nature of the screen–spectator relationship, with particular emphasis on the filmic constructions of femininity and masculinity as conceived within a phallocentric discourse. Her article has variously been supported, extended, debated, opposed and applauded. Regardless of the stand different theorists have taken towards her theory of spectatorship, probably all would agree that it had a revolutionary impact on existing film theory debates. Almost all of the articles in this collection refer at some point to Mulvey's argument.

Mulvey argues that popular narrative film is primarily addressed to the male protagonist in the diegesis and by extension to the male spectator in the audience. She holds that in narrative film woman is represented as the passive object of the active male gaze. On the one hand woman as icon plays to male desire but on the other hand her image threatens to awaken man's unconscious castration anxieties. The male unconscious can escape the threat of castration through one of two avenues: voyeurism or fetishistic scopophilia. Mulvey's argument that woman functions as image and man as bearer of the look appeared to make immediate sense of the way sexual difference was represented in mainstream cinema, specifically the way it reflected the values of 'a world ordered by sexual imbalance'. Analysing the films of Sternberg and Hitchcock, Mulvey considered various ways in which the figure of woman could signify 'trouble' within the classic text.

Unhappy with the binarism of Mulvey's argument, various critics challenged the fixed positions Mulvey assigned to the representation of masculinity and femininity. They demonstrated that masculinity is not always equated with activity and the controlling gaze, nor is femininity necessarily aligned with passivity: two of these refutations, by Steve Neale and by Richard Dyer, are published in part IV, 'Images of Men'. Crucial to Mulvey's argument is the theory of the castration complex which feminist theorists gradually began to question, particularly its alleged universality as well as the position allocated to the female child. Despite the various criticisms, and Mulvey's own reconsideration of femininity as set out in her article on *Duel in the Sun*,[1] contemporary debates continue to be influenced by the issues raised in her article – the use of psychoanalysis as a radical tool for analysis, the importance of the look to narrative cinema, the mechanisms of voyeurism and fetishism, the workings of desire. Mulvey also argued that film theorists should lay bare the mechanisms by which cinematic pleasure is constructed and that filmmakers should attempt to expose these mechanisms even if that meant destroying pleasure itself.

The Winter 1975 edition of *Screen* included an article entitled 'Statement: Psychoanalysis and Film' in which some members of the editorial board voiced their criticism of the journal's growing involvement in a psychoanalytic approach to film. They did not oppose the use of psychoanalytic theory altogether; rather they were critical of the way in which it was being used by some contributors to *Screen*. Their article (chapter 2) sets out a number of reservations: first, that some writers assumed on the basis of dubious evidence that psychoanalysis was a science; second, that the Lacanian version of psychoanalysis being used was notoriously inaccessible; and third, that an interpretive method based on clinical analysis is not necessarily applicable to a film text. These criticisms were also shared by others in the wider film community, and at the time *Screen*'s growing involvement with psychoanalysis aroused heated debate.

The authors of the 'statement' drew attention to the area of the screen–spectator relationship where they believed the use of psychoanalysis had been both 'substantial and distinctive' but nevertheless problematic. They argued that many of the psychoanalytic concepts employed, such as the mirror phase, the castration complex, voyeurism and fetishism, were not used consistently. They also voiced concern about the Freudian account of women and the lack of theorization about the female spectator in Mulvey's article. Interestingly, it is this subject which became central to feminist debates in the 1980s and continues to provide a focus for contemporary debates about the cinema. Two important articles on this subject are included in part III, 'The Female Spectator'. Although the authors of the 'statement' clearly held strong reservations about the use of psychoanalytic theory as it appeared in *Screen* during the mid-1970s, they were not opposed to its use altogether, but urged that psychoanalytic theory should be approached more critically.

Stephen Heath's 'Difference' (chapter 3) critically examines the representation of sexual difference in psychoanalytic theory, specifically in Jacques Lacan's 1972–3 seminar, 'Encore', which set out to explore Freud's question, 'What does woman want?' Heath writes from a feminist perspective, although he is conscious of the problem that this poses – the problem of his gender: the difficulty 'for me, for me not a woman'. Heath's interrogation begins with Lacan's discussion of Bernini's famous statue of Saint Teresa. He first examines the nature of Lacan's address, that is, the kind of audience Lacan has in mind, and concludes that from the beginning Lacan fails to take into account the problem of sexual difference; his discourse therefore reflects the sexist biases of a patriarchal order. Heath's detailed attention to language, and its enunciation, is characteristic of his approach throughout.

In particular, Heath is critical of what he sees as a tendency towards essentialism in Lacan's theory of sexual difference – an essentialism which is attached to Lacan's use of the terms 'penis' and 'phallus'. Although Lacan claims that the phallus is not an object, not the penis, but a signifier only, Heath sees this claim as a 'pure analogical rationalization'. He is particularly critical of the way in which Freud and Lacan both construct a theory of castration around the dynamics of sight, seeing, the visible. Woman's sex is unseeable; man's sex is strikingly visible. It is an appeal to the visible which is used to explain and justify the theory of woman's imaginary castration. As Heath rightly points out, 'The vision, any vision, is constructed, not given . . .'. In Heath's view, Lacan goes against the approach to psychoanalysis he himself developed, resorting instead to an appeal to the mythical and 'natural' in order to explain sexual difference.

Heath also draws attention to the feminist work on the pre-Symbolic or Imaginary period in the subject's life. It is interesting to note the attention he devotes to this area, particularly as feminist work on the pre-Symbolic and the mother–daughter relationship was to become central to feminist writings of the 1980s. Heath views attempts to link woman to the pre-Symbolic with some concern, not only because of the way in which patriarchal ideology stresses relations between woman, duality and narcissism, but also because of its representation of woman as having a special relationship to the specular, the domain of images, the cinema. There is a fine line, frequently traversed, between arguing that woman is outside the Symbolic because of her essential nature and outside because of the nature of patriarchy.

In his concluding discussion, Heath reiterates his earlier assessment of psychoanalysis. He sees it as 'an institution of represention'.[2] 'It is not the woman who is not-all but psychoanalysis, which is what the latter has been so generally unwilling to grasp.'[3] In Heath's view, psychoanalysis understands the unstable nature of subjectivity and gender, but continues to produce a theory of sexual difference based on the phallus as the sign of the symbolic construction of sexual difference because the phallus is something which man has and woman lacks. Difference is asserted through the processes of representation – but a 'difference' grounded in inequality. In Heath's view, Lacanian psychoanalytic theory perpetuates male power at the expense of other sexual subjectivities. Not all feminists, however, are happy with the way in which Heath presents his critique. In her witty discussion of Lacan's seminar, Jane Gallop subjects Heath's critique of Lacan to a similar critique and finds him wanting.[4]

Dugald Williamson continues the debate on the usefulness of Lacanian psychoanalytic theory for the cinema in 'Language and Sexual Difference' (chapter 4). Like Heath, he is also concerned with the conflation of the penis/phallus in Lacan's theory: however he tackles the problem from a different perspective. He argues that it is essential for Lacanian theory to refer to the phallus as *both* signifier and organ if the theory is to make sense. This is because a number of forms of reasoning, or discursive figures, used by Lacan to demonstrate his theory of subject formation and sexual difference are problematic.

Lacan draws on the Saussurean notion of the sign in which linguistic elements are defined in terms of their rule-governed relations. The signifier is not the servant of the signified but has its own principles of organization. This view of language criticizes the idea that the signifier exists only 'to represent the signified or to serve a meaning that somehow exists outside language in an ideal world of intention or spirit'.[5] For Lacan, meaning exists in the chain of the signifier. Language pre-exists the subject who must take up her or his assigned place in society and culture. The subject does not know the pre-existing structure of language, that is, the conditions which make speech possible, as these exist outside consciousness. Williamson argues that in Lacanian theory 'the structure is defined as an ideal form existing in a dialectical relation to the subject who must realize the potential effects of the structure at the level of experience'. Thus the subject's personal experience also plays an important role in understanding language. Williamson points out that the structure is seen as an *ideal* form while an *empiricist* view of learning is upheld.

Williamson illustrates what he believes is a confusion at the heart of Lacan's theory of subjectivity and sexual difference with reference to his notion of the phallus. He draws attention to Lacan's insistence that the phallus is a signifier only; it is the indicator of the Symbolic, not the biological, setting out of sexual difference. Williamson then raises the question of how the subject comes to understand the meaning of the phallus, that is, sexual difference if the phallus is a signifier only, if the subject can have no understanding of the term at the level of experience. Access to the Symbolic is brought about by the recognition of sexual difference. But how 'does the subject, defined initially in the Imaginary, "recognize" difference?' In the Imaginary, representation involves a notion of unity which is somehow experienced autonomously; in the Symbolic, it involves rules and grammar which exist regardless of the

19

subject – the two concepts of language involved are in opposition. In his view, Lacan's theory *must* refer to the phallus as both signifier and object to explain how it is that the infant comes to recognize the meaning of sexual difference in the first place. Whereas the usual criticism levelled at Lacan is that he conflates penis and phallus, Williamson argues that Lacan is actually *compelled* to refer to the phallus in both contexts if his theory is to make sense. Lacan's theory is only logical if we assume that the subject's awareness of systemic difference is *joined with* an observed or empirical perception of difference. 'Either the subject is already in the Symbolic' or it possesses in the Imaginary 'a pre-discursive capacity to experience difference in a form which is appropriate to all subsequent codings.'

If we place Heath's and Williamson's critiques alongside each other we can see that the meaning of the phallus, particularly its conflation with the penis, constitutes a central problem for a number of critics and for a variety of reasons. It is possible that the main reason the meaning of the phallus is so problematic is due to Lacan's refusal to define exactly what he meant by the terms Symbolic and symbol. According to Roger Kennedy,[6] Lacan refused to provide a clear definition of the Symbolic because, in his desire to avoid being reductive, Lacan refused to agree that a signifier could be tied permanently to a signified. To hold to the opposite position would run counter to everything in which Lacan believed.

Feminist theorists, on the one hand, have been particularly interested in Lacan's attempt to free notions of psychosexual development from biology, that is, to avoid reductionism by arguing that psychosexuality is constituted in language, that is, in *the signifier*, the phallus, which in Lacanian theory is not attached to a signified. The conflation of penis and phallus, on the other hand, has meant for some critics that Lacan's theory itself is grounded in phallocentrism – as argued by Heath. Despite this, and despite the sometimes uncritical use of Lacanian theory, his concept of psychosexual development has been important for an understanding of the representation of sexual difference in film. This is largely because its emphasis on the crucial role played by language in the constitution of gender has helped focus attention more sharply on the *constructed* nature of gender representations in the film text as a signifying practice. The psychoanalytic approach has also proven useful for an understanding of the sexual subject in so far as it reveals the unspoken of a text, that which is repressed in the interest of dominant notions of what constitutes 'proper' forms of sexuality.

NOTES

1 Laura Mulvey, 'Afterthoughts on "Visual Pleasure and Narrative Cinema" inspired by *Duel in the Sun*', in *Visual and Other Pleasures*, London, Macmillan, 1989, pp. 29–39.

2 Stephen Heath, 'Difference', chapter 3 in this volume, p. 97.
3 ibid., p. 55.
4 Jane Gallop, *Feminism and Psychoanalysis – The Daughter's Seduction*, London, Macmillan, 1982, pp. 43–55.
5 Dugald Williamson, 'Language and Sexual Difference', chapter 4 in this volume, p. 108.
6 Bicc Benvenuto and Roger Kennedy, *The Works of Jacques Lacan*, London, Free Association Books, 1986, p. 102.

1

VISUAL PLEASURE AND NARRATIVE CINEMA

Laura Mulvey

I INTRODUCTION

A A political use of psychoanalysis

This paper intends to use psychoanalysis to discover where and how the fascination of film is reinforced by pre-existing patterns of fascination already at work within the individual subject and the social formations that have moulded him. It takes as starting point the way film reflects, reveals and even plays on the straight, socially established interpretation of sexual difference which controls images, erotic ways of looking and spectacle. It is helpful to understand what the cinema has been, how its magic has worked in the past, while attempting a theory and a practice which will challenge this cinema of the past. Psychoanalytic theory is thus appropriated here as a political weapon, demonstrating the way the unconscious of patriarchal society has structured film form.

The paradox of phallocentrism in all its manifestations is that it depends on the image of the castrated woman to give order and meaning to its world. An idea of woman stands as linchpin to the system: it is her lack that produces the phallus as a symbolic presence, it is her desire to make good the lack that the phallus signifies. Recent writing in *Screen* about psycho-analysis and the cinema has not sufficiently brought out the importance of the representation of the female form in a symbolic order in which, in the last resort, it speaks castration and nothing else. To summarize briefly: the function of woman in forming the patriarchal unconscious is twofold, she first symbolizes the castration threat by her real absence of a penis and second thereby raises her child into the Symbolic. Once this has been achieved, her meaning in the process is at an end, it does not last into the world of law and language except as a memory which oscillates between memory of maternal plenitude and memory of lack. Both are posited on nature (or on anatomy in Freud's famous phrase). Woman's desire is subjected to her image as bearer of the bleeding wound, she can exist only in relation to castration and cannot transcend it. She turns her child into the signifier of her own desire to possess a penis (the condition, she

22

imagines, of entry into the Symbolic). Either she must gracefully give way to the word, the Name of the Father and the Law, or else struggle to keep her child down with her in the half-light of the Imaginary. Woman then stands in patriarchal culture as signifier for the male other, bound by a symbolic order in which man can live out his phantasies and obsessions through linguistic command by imposing them on the silent image of woman still tied to her place as bearer of meaning, not maker of meaning.

There is an obvious interest in this analysis for feminists, a beauty in its exact rendering of the frustration experienced under the phallocentric order. It gets us nearer to the roots of our oppression, it brings an articulation of the problem closer, it faces us with the ultimate challenge: how to fight the unconscious structured like a language (formed critically at the moment of arrival of language) while still caught within the language of the patriarchy. There is no way in which we can produce an alternative out of the blue, but we can begin to make a break by examining patriarchy with the tools it provides, of which psychoanalysis is not the only but an important one. We are still separated by a great gap from important issues for the female unconscious which are scarcely relevant to phallocentric theory: the sexing of the female infant and her relationship to the Symbolic, the sexually mature woman as non-mother, maternity outside the signification of the phallus, the vagina. . . . But, at this point, psycho-analytic theory as it now stands can at least advance our understanding of the status quo, of the patriarchal order in which we are caught.

B   Destruction of pleasure as a radical weapon

As an advanced representation system, the cinema poses questions of the ways the unconscious (formed by the dominant order) structures ways of seeing and pleasure in looking. Cinema has changed over the last few decades. It is no longer the monolithic system based on large capital investment exemplified at its best by Hollywood in the 1930s, 1940s and 1950s. Technological advances (16mm, etc.) have changed the economic conditions of cinematic production, which can now be artisanal as well as capitalist. Thus it has been possible for an alternative cinema to develop. However self-conscious and ironic Hollywood managed to be, it always restricted itself to a formal *mise-en-scène* reflecting the dominant ideological concept of the cinema. The alternative cinema provides a space for a cinema to be born which is radical in both a political and an aesthetic sense and challenges the basic assumptions of the mainstream film. This is not to reject the latter moralistically, but to highlight the ways in which its formal preoccupations reflect the psychical obsessions of the society which produced it, and, further, to stress that the alternative cinema must start specifically by reacting against these obsessions and assumptions. A politically and aesthetically avant-garde cinema is now possible, but it can still only exist as a counterpoint.

The magic of the Hollywood style at its best (and of all the cinema which fell within its sphere of influence) arose, not exclusively, but in one important aspect, from its skilled and satisfying manipulation of visual pleasure. Unchallenged, mainstream film coded the erotic into the language of the dominant patriarchal order. In the highly developed Hollywood cinema it was only through these codes that the alienated subject, torn in his imaginary memory by a sense of loss, by the terror of potential lack in phantasy, came near to finding a glimpse of satisfaction: through its formal beauty and its play on his own formative obsessions. This article will discuss the interweaving of that erotic pleasure in film, its meaning, and in particular the central place of the image of woman. It is said that analysing pleasure, or beauty, destroys it. That is the intention of this article. The satisfaction and reinforcement of the ego that represent the high point of film history hitherto must be attacked. Not in favour of a reconstructed new pleasure, which cannot exist in the abstract, nor of intellectualized unpleasure, but to make way for a total negation of the ease and plenitude of the narrative fiction film. The alternative is the thrill that comes from leaving the past behind without rejecting it, transcending outworn or oppressive forms, or daring to break with normal pleasurable expectations in order to conceive a new language of desire.

II PLEASURE IN LOOKING/FASCINATION WITH THE HUMAN FORM

A.   The cinema offers a number of possible pleasures. One is scopophilia. There are circumstances in which looking itself is a source of pleasure, just as, in the reverse formation, there is pleasure in being looked at. Originally, in his 'Three Essays on the Theory of Sexuality', Freud isolated scopophilia as one of the component instincts of sexuality which exist as drives quite independently of the erotogenic zones. At this point he associated scopophilia with taking other people as objects, subjecting them to a controlling and curious gaze. His particular examples centre around the voyeuristic activities of children, their desire to see and make sure of the private and the forbidden (curiosity about other people's genital and bodily functions, about the presence or absence of the penis and, retrospectively, about the primal scene). In this analysis scopophilia is essentially active. (Later, in 'Instincts and their Vicissitudes', Freud developed his theory of scopophilia further, attaching it initially to pre-genital auto-eroticism, after which the pleasure of the look is transferred to others by analogy. There is a close working here of the relationship between the active instinct and its further development in a narcissistic form.) Although the instinct is modified by other factors, in particular the constitution of the ego, it continues to exist as the erotic basis for pleasure in looking at another person as object. At the extreme, it can become fixated into a perversion, producing obsessive voyeurs and Peeping Toms, whose only sexual satisfaction can come from watching, in an active controlling sense, an objectified other.

At first glance, the cinema would seem to be remote from the under-cover world of the surreptitious observation of an unknowing and unwilling victim. What is seen of the screen is so manifestly shown. But the mass of mainstream film, and the conventions within which it has consciously evolved, portray a hermetically sealed world which unwinds magically, indifferent to the presence of the audience, producing for them a sense of separation and playing on their voyeuristic phantasy. Moreover, the extreme contrast between the darkness in the auditorium (which also isolates the spectators from one another) and the brilliance of the shifting patterns of light and shade on the screen helps to promote the illusion of voyeuristic separation. Although the film is really being shown, is there to be seen, conditions of screening and narrative conventions give the specta-tor an illusion of looking in on a private world. Among other things, the position of the spectators in the cinema is blatantly one of repression of their exhibitionism and projection of the repressed desire on to the performer.

B. The cinema satisfies a primordial wish for pleasurable looking, but it also goes further, developing scopophilia in its narcissistic aspect. The conventions of mainstream film focus attention on the human form. Scale, space, stories are all anthropomorphic. Here, curiosity and the wish to look intermingle with a fascination with likeness and recognition: the human face, the human body, the relationship between the human form and its surroundings, the visible presence of the person in the world. Jacques Lacan has described how the moment when a child recognizes its own image in the mirror is crucial for the constitution of the ego. Several aspects of this analysis are relevant here. The mirror phase occurs at a time when the child's physical ambitions outstrip his motor capacity, with the result that his recognition of himself is joyous in that he imagines his mirror image to be more complete, more perfect than he experiences his own body. Recognition is thus overlaid with mis-recognition: the image recog-nized is conceived as the reflected body of the self, but its misrecognition as superior projects this body outside itself as an ideal ego, the alienated subject, which, re-introjected as an ego ideal, gives rise to the future generation of identification with others. This mirror moment predates language for the child.

Important for this article is the fact that it is an image that constitutes the matrix of the imaginary, of recognition/misrecognition and identification, and hence of the first articulation of the 'I', of subjectivity. This is a moment when an older fascination with looking (at the mother's face, for an obvious example) collides with the initial inklings of self-awareness. Hence it is the birth of the long love affair/despair between image and

25

self-image which has found such intensity of expression in film and such joyous recognition in the cinema audience. Quite apart from the extraneous similarities between screen and mirror (the framing of the human form in its surroundings, for instance), the cinema has structures of fascination strong enough to allow temporary loss of ego while simultaneously reinforcing the ego. The sense of forgetting the world as the ego has subsequently come to perceive it (I forgot who I am and where I was) is nostalgically reminiscent of that pre-subjective moment of image recognition. At the same time the cinema has distinguished itself in the production of ego ideals as expressed in particular in the star system, the stars centring both screen presence and screen story as they act out a complex process of likeness and difference (the glamorous impersonates the ordinary).

C.   Sections II. A and B have set out two contradictory aspects of the pleasurable structures of looking in the conventional cinematic situation. The first, scopophilic, arises from pleasure in using another person as an object of sexual stimulation through sight. The second, developed through narcissism and the constitution of the ego, comes from identification with the image seen. Thus, in film terms, one implies a separation of the erotic identity of the subject from the object on the screen (active scopophilia), the other demands identification of the ego with the object on the screen through the spectator's fascination with and recognition of his like. The first is a function of the sexual instincts, the second of ego libido. This dichotomy was crucial for Freud. Although he saw the two as interacting and overlaying each other, the tension between instinctual drives and self-preservation continues to be a dramatic polarization in terms of pleasure. Both are formative structures, mechanisms not meaning. In themselves they have no signification, they have to be attached to an idealization. Both pursue aims in indifference to perceptual reality, creating the imagized, eroticized concept of the world that forms the perception of the subject and makes a mockery of empirical objectivity.

During its history, the cinema seems to have evolved a particular illusion of reality in which this contradiction between libido and ego has found a beautifully complementary phantasy world. In *reality* the phantasy world of the screen is subject to the law which produces it. Sexual instincts and identification processes have a meaning within the symbolic order which articulates desire. Desire, born with language, allows the possibility of transcending the instinctual and the imaginary, but its point of reference continually returns to the traumatic moment of its birth: the castration complex. Hence the look, pleasurable in form, can be threatening in content, and it is woman as representation/image that crystallizes this paradox.

III   WOMAN AS IMAGE, MAN AS BEARER OF THE LOOK

A.   In a world ordered by sexual imbalance, pleasure in looking has been split between active/male and passive/female. The determining male gaze projects its phantasy on to the female figure which is styled accordingly. In their traditional exhibitionist role women are simultaneously looked at and displayed, with their appearance coded for strong visual and erotic impact so that they can be said to connote *to-be-looked-at-ness*. Woman displayed as sexual object is the leitmotif of erotic spectacle: from pin-ups to strip-tease, from Ziegfeld to Busby Berkeley, she holds the look, plays to and signifies male desire. Mainstream film neatly combined spectacle and narrative. (Note, however, how in the musical song-and-dance numbers break the flow of the diegesis.) The presence of woman is an indispensable element of spectacle in normal narrative film, yet her visual presence tends to work against the development of a story line, to freeze the flow of action in moments of erotic contemplation. This alien presence then has to be integrated into cohesion with the narrative. As Budd Boetticher has put it:

> What counts is what the heroine provokes, or rather what she rep-resents. She is the one, or rather the love or fear she inspires in the hero, or else the concern he feels for her, who makes him act the way he does. In herself the woman has not the slightest importance.

(A recent tendency in narrative film has been to dispense with this problem altogether; hence the development of what Molly Haskell has called the 'buddy movie', in which the active homosexual eroticism of the central male figures can carry the story without distraction.) Traditionally, the woman displayed has functioned on two levels: as erotic object for the characters within the screen story, and as erotic object for the spectator within the auditorium, with a shifting tension between the looks on either side of the screen. For instance, the device of the showgirl allows the two looks to be unified technically without any apparent break in the diegesis. A woman performs within the narrative: the gaze of the spectator and that of the male characters in the film are neatly combined without breaking narrative verisimi-litude. For a moment the sexual impact of the performing woman takes the film into a no man's land outside its own time and space. Thus Marilyn Monroe's first appearance in *The River of No Return* and Lauren Bacall's songs in *To Have or Have Not*. Similarly, conventional close-ups of legs (Dietrich, for instance) or a face (Garbo) integrate into the narrative a different mode of eroticism. One part of a fragmented body destroys the Renaissance space, the illusion of depth demanded by the narrative, it gives flatness, the quality of a cutout or icon rather than verisimilitude to the screen.

B.   An active/passive heterosexual division of labour has similarly con-trolled narrative structure. According to the principles of the ruling ideology and the psychical structures that back it up, the male figure cannot bear the burden of sexual objectification. Man is reluctant to gaze at his exhibitionist like. Hence the split between spectacle and narrative supports the man's role as the active one of forwarding the story, making things happen. The man controls the film phantasy and also emerges as the representative of power in a further sense: as the bearer of the look of the spectator, transferring it behind the screen to neutralize the extra-diegetic tendencies represented by woman as spectacle. This is made possible through the processes set in motion by structuring the film around a main controlling figure with whom the spectator can identify. As the spectator identifies with the main male[1] protagonist, he projects his look on to that of his like, his screen surrogate, so that the power of the male protagonist as he controls events coincides with the active power of the erotic look, both giving a satisfying sense of omnipotence. A male movie star's glamorous characteristics are thus not those of the erotic object of the gaze, but those of the more perfect, more complete, more powerful ideal ego conceived in the original moment of recognition in front of the mirror. The character in the story can make things happen and control events better than the subject/spectator, just as the image in the mirror was more in control of motor co-ordination. In contrast to woman as icon, the active male figure (the ego ideal of the identification process) demands a three-dimensional space corresponding to that of the mirror-recognition in which the alienated subject internalized his own representation of this imaginary existence. He is a figure in a landscape. Here the function of film is to reproduce as accurately as possible the so-called natural conditions of human perception. Camera technology (as exemplified by deep focus in particular) and camera movements (determined by the action of the protagonist), combined with invisible editing (demanded by realism) all tend to blur the limits of screen space. The male protagonist is free to command the stage, a stage of spatial illusion in which he articulates the look and creates the action.

C.1   Sections III. A and B have set out a tension between a mode of representation of woman in film and conventions surrounding the diegesis. Each is associated with a look: that of the spectator in direct scopophilic contact with the female form displayed for his enjoyment (connoting male phantasy) and that of the spectator fascinated with the image of his like set in an illusion of natural space, and through him gaining control and possession of the woman within the diegesis. (This tension and the shift from one pole to the other can structure a single text. Thus both in *Only Angels Have Wings* and in *To Have and Have Not*, the film opens with the woman as object of the combined gaze of spectator and all the male protagonists in the film. She is isolated, glamorous, on display, sexualized. But as the narrative progresses she falls in love with the main male protagonist and becomes his property, losing her outward glamorous characteristics, her generalized sexuality, her showgirl connotations; her eroticism is subjected to the male star alone. By means of identification with him, through participation in his power, the spectator can indirectly possess her too.)

But in psychoanalytic terms, the female figure poses a deeper problem. She also connotes something that the look continually circles around but disavows: her lack of a penis, implying a threat of castration and hence unpleasure. Ultimately, the meaning of woman is sexual difference, the absence of the penis as visually ascertainable, the material evidence on which is based the castration complex essential for the organization of entrance to the Symbolic order and the Law of the Father. Thus the woman as icon, displayed for the gaze and enjoyment of men, the active controllers of the look, always threatens to evoke the anxiety it originally signified. The male unconscious has two avenues of escape from this castration anxiety: preoccupation with the re-enactment of the original trauma (investigating the woman, demystifying her mystery), counterbalanced by the devaluation, punishment or saving of the guilty object (an avenue typified by the concerns of the *film noir*); or else complete disavowal of castration by the substitution of a fetish object or turning the represented figure itself into a fetish so that it becomes reassuring rather than dangerous (hence overvaluation, the cult of the female star). This second avenue, fetishistic scopophilia, builds up the physical beauty of the object, transforming it into something satisfying in itself. The first avenue, voyeurism, on the contrary, has associations with sadism: pleasure lies in ascertaining guilt (immediately associated with castration), asserting control and subjecting the guilty person through punishment or forgiveness. This sadistic side fits in well with narrative. Sadism demands a story, depends on making something happen, forcing a change in another person, a battle of will and strength, victory/defeat, all occurring in a linear time with a beginning and an end. Fetishistic scopophilia, on the other hand, can exist outside linear time as the erotic instinct is focused on the look alone. These contradictions and ambiguities can be illustrated more simply by using works by Hitchcock and Sternberg, both of whom take the look almost as the content or subject matter of many of their films. Hitchcock is the more complex, as he uses both mechanisms. Sternberg's work, on the other hand, provides many pure examples of fetishistic scopophilia.

C.2   It is well known that Sternberg once said he would welcome his films being projected upside down so that story and character involvement would not interfere with the spectator's undiluted appreciation of the screen image. This statement is revealing but ingenuous. Ingenuous in that his films do demand that the figure of the woman (Dietrich, in the cycle of films with her, as the ultimate example) should be identifiable. But revealing in that it emphasizes the fact that for him the pictorial space enclosed by the frame is paramount rather than narrative or identification processes. While Hitchcock goes into the investigative side of voyeurism, Sternberg produces the ultimate fetish, taking it to the point where the powerful look of the male protagonist (characteristic of traditional narrative film) is broken in favour of the image in direct erotic rapport with the spectator. The beauty of the woman as object and the screen space coalesce; she is no longer the bearer of guilt but a perfect product, whose body, stylized and fragmented by close-ups, is the content of the film and the direct recipient of the spectator's look. Sternberg plays down the illusion of screen depth; his screen tends to be one-dimensional, as light and shade, lace, steam, foliage, net, streamers, etc. reduce the visual field. There is little or no mediation of the look through the eyes of the main male protagonist. On the contrary, shadowy presences like La Bessière in *Morocco* act as surrogates for the director, detached as they are from audience identification. Despite Sternberg's insistence that his stories are irrelevant, it is significant that they are concerned with situation, not suspense, and cyclical rather than linear time, while plot complications revolve around misunderstanding rather than conflict. The most important absence is that of the controlling male gaze within the screen scene. The high point of emotional drama in the most typical Dietrich films, her supreme moments of erotic meaning, take place in the absence of the man she loves in the fiction. There are other witnesses, other spectators watching her on the screen, their gaze is one with, not standing in for, that of the audience. At the end of *Morocco*, Tom Brown has already disappeared into the desert when Amy Jolly kicks off her gold sandals and walks after him. At the end of *Dishonoured*, Kranau is indifferent to the fate of Magda. In both cases, the erotic impact, sanctified by death, is displayed as a spectacle for the audience. The male hero misunderstands and, above all, does not see.

In Hitchcock, by contrast, the male hero does see precisely what the audience sees. However, in the films I shall discuss here, he takes fascination with an image through scopophilic eroticism as the subject of the film. Moreover, in these cases the hero portrays the contradictions and tensions experienced by the spectator. In *Vertigo* in particular, but also in *Marnie* and *Rear Window*, the look is central to the plot, oscillating between voyeurism and fetishistic fascination. As a twist, a further manipulation of the normal viewing process which in some sense reveals it, Hitchcock uses the process of identification normally associated with ideological correctness and the recognition of established morality and shows up its perverted side. Hitchcock has never concealed his interest in voyeurism, cinematic and non-cinematic. His heroes are exemplary of the symbolic order and the law – a policeman (*Vertigo*), a dominant male possessing money and power (*Marnie*) – but their erotic drives lead them into compromised situations. The power to subject another person to the will sadistically or to the gaze voyeuristically is turned on to the woman as the object of both. Power is backed by a certainty of legal right and the established guilt of the woman (evoking castration, psychoanalytically speaking). True perversion is barely concealed under a shallow mask of ideological correctness – the man is on the right side of the law, the woman on the wrong. Hitchcock's skilful use of identification processes and liberal use of subjective camera from the point-of-view of the male protagonist draw the spectators deeply into his position, making them share his uneasy gaze. The audience is absorbed into a voyeuristic situation within the screen scene and diegesis which parodies his own in the cinema. In his analysis of *Rear Window*, Douchet takes the film as a metaphor for the cinema. Jeffries is the audience, the events in the apartment block opposite correspond to the screen. As he watches, an erotic dimension is added to his look, a central image to the drama. His girlfriend Lisa had been of little sexual interest to him, more or less a drag, so long as she remained on the spectator side. When she crosses the barrier between his room and the block opposite, their relationship is reborn erotically. He does not merely watch her through his lens, as a distant meaningful image, he also sees her as a guilty intruder exposed by a dangerous man threatening her with punishment, and thus finally saves her. Lisa's exhibitionism has already been established by her obsessive interest in dress and style, in being a passive image of visual perfection; Jeffries's voyeurism and activity have also been established through his work as a photo-journalist, a maker of stories and captor of images. However, his enforced inactivity, binding him to his seat as a spectator, puts him squarely in the phantasy position of the cinema audience.

In *Vertigo*, subjective camera predominates. Apart from one flashback from Judy's point-of-view, the narrative is woven around what Scottie sees or fails to see. The audience follows the growth of his erotic obsession and subsequent despair precisely from his point-of-view. Scottie's voyeurism is blatant: he falls in love with a woman he follows and spies on without speaking to. Its sadistic side is equally blatant: he has chosen (and freely chosen, for he had been a successful lawyer) to be a policeman, with all the attendant possibilities of pursuit and investigation. As a result, he follows, watches and falls in love with a perfect image of female beauty and mystery. Once he actually confronts her, his erotic drive is to break her down and force her to tell by persistent cross-questioning. Then, in the second part of the film, he re-enacts his obsessive involvement with the image he loved to watch secretly. He reconstructs Judy as Madeleine, forces her to conform in every detail to the actual physical appearance of his fetish. Her exhibitionism, her masochism, make her an ideal passive counterpart to Scottie's active sadistic voyeurism. She knows her part is to perform, and only by playing it through and then replaying it can she keep Scottie's erotic interest. But in the repetition he does break her down and succeeds in exposing her guilt. His curiosity wins through and she is punished. In *Vertigo*, erotic involvement with the look is disorientating: the spectator's fascination is turned against him as the narrative carries him through and entwines him with the processes that he is himself exercising. The Hitchcock hero here is firmly placed within the symbolic order, in narrative terms. He has all the attributes of the patriarchal superego. Hence the spectator, lulled into a false sense of security by the apparent legality of his surrogate, sees through his look and finds himself exposed as complicit, caught in the moral ambiguity of looking. Far from being simply an aside on the perversion of the police, *Vertigo* focuses on the implications of the active/looking, passive/ looked-at split in terms of sexual difference and the power of the male Symbolic encapsulated in the hero. Marnie, too, performs for Mark Rutland's gaze and masquerades as the perfect to-be-looked-at image. He, too, is on the side of the law until, drawn in by obsession with her guilt, her secret, he longs to see her in the act of committing a crime, make her confess and thus save her. So he, too, becomes complicit as he acts out the implications of his power. He controls money and words, he can have his cake and eat it.

III SUMMARY

The psychoanalytic background that has been discussed in this article is relevant to the pleasure and unpleasure offered by traditional narrative film. The scopophilic instinct (pleasure in looking at another person as an erotic object), and, in contradistinction, ego libido (forming identification processes) act as formations, mechanisms, which this cinema has played on. The image of woman as (passive) raw material for the (active) gaze of man takes the argument a step further into the structure of representation, adding a further layer demanded by the ideology of the patriarchal order as it is worked out in its favourite cinematic form – illusionistic narrative film. The argument returns again to the psychoanalytic background in that woman as representation signifies castration, inducing voyeuristic or fetishistic mechanisms to circumvent her threat. None of these interacting layers is intrinsic to film, but it is only in the film form that they can reach a perfect and beautiful contradiction, thanks to the possibility in the cinema of shifting the emphasis of the look. It is the place of the look that defines cinema, the possibility of varying it and exposing it. This is what makes cinema quite different in its voyeuristic potential from, say, striptease, theatre, shows, etc. Going far beyond highlighting a woman's to-be-looked-at-ness, cinema builds the way she is to be looked at into the spectacle itself. Playing on the tension between film as controlling the dimension of time (editing, narrative) and film as controlling the dimension of space (changes in distance, editing), cinematic codes create a gaze, a world and an object, thereby producing an illusion cut to the measure of desire. It is these cinematic codes and their relationship to formative external structures that must be broken down before mainstream film and the pleasure it provides can be challenged.

To begin with (as an ending), the voyeuristic-scopophilic look that is a crucial part of traditional filmic pleasure can itself be broken down. There are three different looks associated with cinema: that of the camera as it records the profilmic event, that of the audience as it watches the final product, and that of the characters at each other within the screen illusion. The conventions of narrative film deny the first two and subordinate them to the third, the conscious aim being always to eliminate intrusive camera presence and prevent a distancing awareness in the audience. Without these two absences (the material existence of the recording process, the critical reading of the spectator), fictional drama cannot achieve reality, obviousness and truth. Nevertheless, as this article has argued, the structure of looking in narrative fiction film contains a contradiction in its own premises: the female image as a castration threat constantly endangers the unity of the diegesis and bursts through the world of illusion as an intrusive, static, one-dimensional fetish. Thus the two looks materially present in time and space are obsessively subordinated to the neurotic needs of the male ego. The camera becomes the mechanism for producing an illusion of Renaissance space, flowing movements compatible with the human eye, an ideology of representation that revolves around the perception of the subject; the camera's look is disavowed in order to create a convincing world in which the spectator's surrogate can perform with verisimilitude. Simultaneously, the look of the audience is denied an intrinsic force: as soon as fetishistic representation of the female image threatens to break the spell of illusion, and the erotic image on the screen appears directly (without mediation) to the spectator, the fact of fetishization, concealing as it does castration fear, freezes the look, fixates the spectator and prevents him from achieving any distance from the image in front of him.

This complex interaction of looks is specific to film. The first blow against the monolithic accumulation of traditional film conventions (already undertaken by radical filmmakers) is to free the look of the camera into its materiality in time and space and the look of the audience into dialectics, passionate detachment. There is no doubt that this destroys the satisfaction, pleasure and privilege of the 'invisible guest', and highlights how film has depended on voyeuristic active/passive mechanisms. Women, whose image has continually been stolen and used for this end, cannot view the decline of the traditional film form with anything much more than sentimental regret.

33

NOTE

A reworked version of a paper given in the French Department of the University of Wisconsin, Madison, in the spring of 1973, this chapter was originally published in *Screen*, Autumn 1975, vol. 16, no. 3, pp. 6–18.

1 There are films with a woman as main protagonist, of course. To analyse this phenomenon seriously here would take me too far afield. Pam Cook and Claire Johnston's study of *The Revolt of Mamie Stover* in Phil Hardy (ed.), *Raoul Walsh*, Edinburgh, Edinburgh Film Festival, 1974, shows in a striking case how the strength of this female protagonist is more apparent than real.

2

PSYCHOANALYSIS AND FILM

Edward Buscombe, Christine Gledhill,
Alan Lovell, Christopher Williams

Reference was made in the editorial in *Screen* (Summer 1975, vol. 16, no. 2) to reservations some members of the editorial board had about the recent use of psychoanalysis in *Screen* for understanding the cinema. We think it important to articulate these reservations because they are relevant not only to psychoanalysis but to the general task *Screen* has set itself over the past four years. Our reservations are in three main areas: the unproblematic acceptance of psychoanalysis implicit in the way it has been presented in *Screen*; the intelligibility of the various expositions and applications of it; and the validity of the attempts made to apply it directly to the cinema.

Like other members of the editorial board we accept that psychoanalysis is an intellectual discipline that may provide fruitful insights for film theory. However we feel that it has to be approached with a degree of critical caution since certain of its concepts and methods are undeveloped while others are matters of substantial debate both within psychoanalysis and outside it. There are two areas where these problems are of particular importance for the current use of psychoanalysis in film theory. The first is the account of women that is offered, the second, the interpretative method employed in the analysis of a patient's symptoms.

We will deal with these particular areas in relation to film theory later on. What we want to express first is our unease about the general lack of any critical distance from psychoanalysis in *Screen*. Without necessarily agreeing with all the criticisms Julia Lesage made of positions taken in the Brecht issue of *Screen*,[1] we welcomed it and asked for it to be reprinted because it did demand that a critical debate about psychoanalysis be set going.

The assumption that psychoanalysis is a science seems to underpin the lack of a critical distance from it. A particular notion of what constitutes a science is invoked in making this assumption. The notion is derived from Louis Althusser and broadly holds that a science is defined by three features. It defines its own object (it does not take as its object of study the empirically given world but discovers that object at another level – so psychoanalysis deals with the unconscious which is not something that can

35

be empirically observed but something constructed by psychoanalytic theory). The second feature of a science is internal coherence and consistency. The third is its development of its own methods of testing and proof.

The use of this notion of science can't justify any easy confidence about the status of psychoanalysis as an intellectual discipline since it is itself a controversial one. At present the philosophy of science is a confused and divided discipline with no general agreement about what constitutes a science or scientific method. It would be difficult to claim that Althusser's notion of science resolves the disagreements. On the key issue of what constitutes scientific proof (the popular notion that the 'truth' of scientific conclusions is guaranteed by experimental testing being no longer unquestioningly accepted) it effectively avoids the issue by claiming that a science develops its own methods of testing and proof and *in the last resort saying anything goes*.

The general position is further complicated by the particular version of psychoanalysis which is being drawn upon in *Screen*. This comes from Jacques Lacan's work, which attempts to develop psychoanalysis by drawing upon structural linguistics. Initially Lacan's work presents problems in that it is notoriously difficult to understand his writings – this inaccessibility is a matter of a conscious intellectual strategy on the part of Lacan. Even amongst those who feel they properly understand his position there is disagreement about its value. Both from within psychoanalysis itself and from within the general structuralist ambience, Lacan's position has been attacked. Claude Lévi-Strauss has, for example, criticized some of Lacan's central positions:

> We do not feel any indulgence towards this imposture which would substitute the left hand for the right to give to the worst philosophy under the table that which one claims to have taken from it over the top; which, simply replacing the self (*moi*) by the other and slipping a metaphysic of desire beneath the logic of the concept, takes away the foundation of the latter. For, in replacing the self on the one hand by an anonymous other and on the other by an individualised desire (no other is meaningful) one cannot succeed in hiding the fact that it is sufficient to stick them together and to turn the whole thing over to rediscover on the other side that self whose abolition one has proclaimed with a great show.[2]

We cite Lévi-Strauss not to side with him against Lacan but to show that substantial intellectual choices are being made in using Lacan's account of psychoanalysis, as they are about the philosophy of science and the general adequacy of psychoanalytic positions. A film theorist does not have any special competence in making such choices. In areas like psychoanalysis and philosophy of science she or he is likely to be at best a well-informed amateur. Crucially, in such a situation it is incumbent on a magazine like *Screen* to be as explicit as possible about its choices.

Screen seems to us to be deficient in this respect. Controversial intellectual choices are made to appear unproblematic. The appeal to science is central here. It is frequently made in the pages of *Screen*, not only in relation to psychoanalysis. The explicit appeal is always to the Althusserian notion of science but it would be impossible to learn from *Screen* that there are any problems about this. There is also an implicit appeal made to science that further confuses the situation and makes the choices being made harder to discern.

The implicit appeal is to the traditional notion of science as represented by disciplines like physics and chemistry. This appeal is made through the use of 'precise' terms, charts and diagrams which suggests a methodology that searches for abstraction and precision as the classical sciences are supposed to do. What these explicit and implicit appeals add up to is the attempt to bring the great prestige science has in our culture to support the use of disciplines like psychoanalysis. Inevitably this inhibits criticism.

Our second area of concern is the intelligibility of the various expositions and applications of psychoanalysis. Recurrently we find such expositions and applications are full of obscure passages so that the reading of *Screen* becomes a torment of endless rereadings in the effort to understand. We should say immediately that we don't think all ideas can be presented in simple terms but neither do we think that obscurity is a guarantee of profundity.

There are two different kinds of obscurity present in *Screen* that need to be separated out. The first kind is represented by the following passage:

Jacques Lacan, the French psychoanalyst, has read Freud as reformulating the Cartesian cogito and destroying the subject as source and foundation – Lacan rewrites the cogito, in the light of Freud's discoveries as: I think where I am not and I am where I do not think. We can understand this formulation as the indicating of the fundamental misunderstanding (*méconnaissance*) which is involved in the successful use of language (or any other area of the symbolic which is similarly structured) in which the subject is continually ignored as being caught up in a process of articulation to be taken as a fixed place founding the discourse. The unconscious is that effect of language which escapes the conscious subject in the distance between the act of signification in which the subject passes from signifier to signifier and what is signified in which the subject finds himself in place as, for example, the pronoun 'I'. The importance of phenomena like verbal slips is that they testify to the existence of the unconscious through the distance between what was said and what the conscious subject intended to say. They thus testify to the distance between the subject of the act of signification and the conscious subject (the ego). In this distance there is opened a gap which is the area of desire. What is essential to all of those psychic productions

37

which Freud uses in the analytic interpretation is that they bear witness to the lack of control of the conscious subject over his discourses.[3]

The whole passage is full of ambiguities and uncertainties. In the sentence beginning 'We can understand this formulation as . . .', who or what is doing the ignoring? And what should the phrase 'to be taken as a fixed place founding the discourse' be attached to: 'the process of articulation' or 'the subject'? In the next sentence what does 'the act of signification in which the subject passes from signifier to signifier' mean? How does the subject find himself in place in what is signified? Is 'what is signified' not part of 'the act of signification'? Later on in the passage another uncertainty is created when 'desire' is suddenly introduced without any explanation, a simple assertion being made that in the distance between the subject of the act of signification and the conscious subject there is opened a gap which is the area of desire.

The obscurity in this case is caused by the attempt to compress complicated ideas. Such a failure is likely to occur in any magazine. What concerns us about *Screen* is that the failure is so frequent. This frequency prevents us from explaining the failure as a local one on the part of editors or writers. It seems rather to come from a gap between editors/writers and (some?) readers. If you are familiar with the ideas of Lacan it is possible to fill in gaps and resolve ambiguities in a passage like the one we have quoted. If you're unfamiliar with the ideas it's impossible to do this. But since such a passage is clearly intended for those unfamiliar with Lacan's ideas, the failure is an important one for a magazine with the cultural aims of *Screen*.

The second kind of obscurity is more a matter of a particular strategy of writing. To cite a representative example of this strategy, we have no clear notion of what the following passage means:

> The problem is to understand the terms of construction of the subject and the modalities of the replacement of this construction but also, more difficultly, the supplacement – the overplacing: supplementation or, in certain circumstances, supplantation (critical interruption) of that construction in its place of repetition.[4]

This is an example of a strategy of writing derived from Roland Barthes in which the use of 'precise' terms from other intellectual disciplines is combined with an interest in the play of language (a play in this instance of the similar sounds in the words 'supplacement', 'overplacing', 'supplementation', 'supplantation'). The strategy seems to us a confusing one with the play of language undermining the attempt to be precise.

To give a concrete example of the kind of confusion produced (we need to move outside of the area of psychoanalysis for the most convenient one): when the term 'diegesis' was introduced into *Screen* we were assured it was a precise term not to be confused with terms like 'fiction' or 'story'. In the analysis of *Touch of Evil*[5] we find the following statement: 'the synopsis is a narrative outline, the statement of a kind of ideal entity – the narrative (the diegesis, the story) – that can be realized in a range of matters . . .' In this the habitual putting together of synonyms seems to make 'diegesis' assimilable to 'story' and possibly to 'narrative' – we're unclear what the function of the brackets is in this sentence. We don't believe that *Screen*'s efforts to present difficult and/or unfamiliar ideas is helped by such a strategy of writing.

When an appeal to science is combined with the use of scientific terms, it is possible to deal with the problem of obscurity through believing that science is necessarily obscure and that a failure to understand is therefore a failure on the part of the reader. We know from our own experience that *Screen* often demoralizes readers in this way.

Our criticisms would be less urgent if it could be demonstrated that the readership of *Screen* was likely to be generally familiar with the intellectual territory that is being explored and aware of choices that are being made. But we know this is not the case. From our own experience of reading *Screen* and through our contact with readers we have discovered immensely varying degrees of knowledge of areas like psychoanalysis, Marxism, semiotics, philosophy of science, etc.

Given such a readership we think the careful exposition of ideas and clear indications of the issues involved in taking particular positions must have a high priority. Unless it does there is likely to develop amongst readers a lack of understanding and puzzlement about positions expounded in *Screen* that will eventually lead to its abandonment. We know this process is occurring in some measure already (rather than stop buying *Screen* it tends to be put on one side to be read at an indefinite future date). And if *Screen* were to lose many of its present readers with their involvement in the education system, it would drift into a cultural void and become a conventional academic magazine with a 'leftist' colouring and no political situation in which it could specifically engage.

We don't see the careful exposition of ideas and the indicating of intellectual choices as only a 'popularizing' task – though we regard this as important. *Screen* is not simply in the position of having well worked out positions that it has to find the right way of presenting to its readers. Given the undeveloped state of film theory in this country many of the positions taken in *Screen* are bound to be inadequate or confused. The effort to articulate positions as clearly and fully as possible will help to bring out those inadequacies and confusions and create some of the conditions for the kind of intellectual discussion necessary for the development of film theory and education.

Apart from general questions about the intellectual status of psychoanalysis and the obscurity with which it is often presented, there is also the question of the usefulness of the attempts to apply it to the cinema. There are two distinct areas where it has been applied: critical interpretation and the spectator's relationship with what she or he sees on the screen.

The use of psychoanalysis as a model for the process of critical interpretation is best represented by the *Cahiers du Cinéma* analysis of *Young Mr Lincoln*.[6] This analysis treats the film in a way analogous to the psychoanalyst's relationship with a patient, examining it for gaps and contradictions as indicators of the substantial forces at work in the film. In so far as it suggests another goal for criticism than the perfect and/or coherent work and reveals the waywardness with which ideology operates in a film we regard the analysis as an advance in film criticism. But we feel that its unawareness of the problems of critical interpretation needs to be criticized.

These problems are bound up with the analogy made with psychoanalytic methods of interpretation. These methods are themselves open to substantial objection. In his article 'The Freudian Slip'[7] Sebastiano Timpanaro describes the problems surrounding Freud's methods of interpreting a patient's linguistic slips and argues that the methods are too unsystematic for one to have confidence in their validity. When this interpretative method is transferred to film criticism the objections become even stronger. The psychoanalyst at least has some definite idea of the structure of human psychology and the way that structure functions. She or he can then relate the gaps, slips and contradictions found in the patient's responses to something reasonably well defined. The analyst also has the patient's response (resistance) to his analytic conclusions as one kind of check on them. The critic has only the crudest notion of the structure of a film; some version of the form/content dichotomy – in the *Cahiers* analysis a distinction between ideology and writing. The way that even this crude structure functions is unclear. Does form determine content or vice versa? Or is the question a chicken and egg one, impossible to answer? And unlike the analyst the critic does not have the film's responses to his analysis as any kind of check on it.

In that its approach has a good deal in common with the analysis of *Young Mr Lincoln*, Stephen Heath's analysis of *Touch of Evil*[8] is open to similar objections. Indeed the problems of interpretative method are much more sharply raised. In the analysis, important interpretative points often rest on the loose metaphorical use of language. For example, in trying to establish a relationship that is key for his analysis, one between the two couples, Vargas/Susan, the Blonde/Linneker, Heath argues 'Vargas is to Susan as Linneker to the Blonde, therefore if Linneker is torn to bits in the explosion, Vargas must be torn from Susan by the force of contagion'.[9] A seeming similarity is set up by the use of the word 'torn' about both Linneker and Vargas/Susan and by the common associations of 'explosion' and 'force'. But 'torn' is Heath's choice of metaphor to describe what happens in the sequence. He nowhere demonstrates that the film encourages the critic to see what happens as a 'tearing' process. Why shouldn't we say that Linneker was 'blown' to bits except that we couldn't then go on to say that Susan was 'blown' from Vargas? The association of 'explosion' and 'force' is similarly loose. 'Explosion' might be agreed upon as a reasonably neutral way of describing what happens to the car with Linneker and the Blonde in it whereas 'force of contagion' is again a choice of metaphor which it is far from clear the film authorizes.

Apart from this loose metaphorical use of language, the interpretative method is made even more arbitrary by the willingness to use any detail, however insignificant, in support of the general thesis so that, for example, the fact that an actor has the same name as a fictional character (Vargas) can be used as evidence of the relation between two fictional characters. It seems that in this analysis one of the worst 'popular' effects of psychoanalysis is at work, the encouragement it is taken to give to ingenious interpretation where the ingenuity is thought to guarantee the interest of the exercise.

Effectively, it seems to us that for all its theoretical ambitions what one is confronted with in the analysis of *Touch of Evil* is a critical interpretation not substantially different from critical interpretations offered by critics who make no use of psychoanalysis and whose intellectual perspective is very different. The method is a familiar one: interpretation mainly depends on an examination of narrative situations with occasional references to camera movements, sound, etc. The interpretative conclusion, that the film effects a denial of sexuality which is thought of as socially disruptive, is not a particularly distinctive one. And overall there is the same sense of an arbitrary interpretative method at work.

Recently the most substantial and distinctive use of psychoanalysis in *Screen* has been the attempt to explain the relationship between the spectator and film. On the face of it the various attempts, 'Lessons from Brecht' by Stephen Heath,[10] the reply to Julia Lesage's criticism,[11] 'The Imaginary Signifier' by Christian Metz,[12] 'Visual Pleasure and Narrative Cinema' by Laura Mulvey[13] present a similar account of certain psychological processes at work in the cinema which make it a servant of the dominant ideology. This similarity is marked by the shared use in the articles of concepts like fetishism, voyeurism, the castration complex and the mirror phase.

When examined closely, it becomes clear that the appearance of similarity is in crucial respects deceptive. The psychoanalytic concepts are being used in different ways and for different purposes. Fetishism, for example, is central to Stephen Heath's account of how the cinema serves the dominant ideology and he sees it at work in all forms of representation. Christian Metz attaches fetishism more specifically to the cinema than Heath does. For Metz fetishism plays a more neutral ideological role. He uses it to deal with the problems of the suspension of disbelief and the general appeal the cinema has for its enthusiasts. For him the setting of the subject into position, which like Heath he sees as the central ideological role of the cinema, is explained by an appeal to the mirror phase. So the same conclusion about the ideological role of the cinema is backed by reference to two different psychological processes: fetishism and the mirror phase. Laura Mulvey provides a third account of the place of fetishism in the cinema, relating it to the way women, and the castration anxiety they are held to evoke, are treated.

The mirror phase is also used in different ways. Laura Mulvey makes a direct analogy between the cinema and the mirror phase, describing identification in terms of the spectator identifying with stars. Metz refuses such a direct analogy between the cinema and the mirror phase and produces a much more indirect analogy which leads him to describe identification in terms of the spectator's identifying with himself as 'pure act of perception'. In the reply to Julia Lesage there is a similar refusal of any direct analogy: 'there is a relation between mirror phase and cinematic institution that should be examined, yet the condition of such an examination is exactly the non-reduction of the relation: nothing is to be gained by describing cinema as the mirror phase.' But we're not clear about what kind of analogy the reply seeks to maintain: 'the crux is the relation, that is, the difference, the supplacement – refiguration of a subject-spectator who has already completed the mirror phase; it is the figure of the subject as turning point (circulation) between image and industry (poles of the cinematic institution) that demands study'.[14] (Trying to understand the kind of analogy being proposed in this passage brings us up against the problems of writing strategy that we have already commented on. We find it very difficult to understand what demands study – why is it the *figure* of the subject rather than the subject? Is 'turning point' a metaphor? What is the relationship between 'turning point' and 'circulation'? And if the subject spectator has completed the mirror phase what place does the mirror phase have in studying 'the figure of the subject as turning point between image and industry'?)

Ever since Freud first developed his ideas, psychoanalysis has been raided by other disciplines and some of its concepts appropriated. In the course of this appropriation, the concepts have usually become imprecise and devalued. We're concerned that the differing uses of psychoanalytic concepts in *Screen* may be a mark of this process occurring in film theory. One way the concepts might be prevented from becoming imprecise and valueless would be through the articulation and discussion of the differences in the various articles. This we see as an important part of the editorial work of *Screen* but one where it is again deficient. Neither in editorials nor in presentations are these differences pointed to.

In an area like the spectator's experience of the cinema it is particularly important to make this articulation because there is a view of the cinema that the accounts offered in *Screen* could easily slot into. Traditionally one view of the cinema has been a puritanical one where the spectator's experience is considered to be of a 'nasty' or 'perverted' kind. (Characteristically this puritanism has been class based and connected with a sense of the working class as barbarous.) It would be inaccurate to say that the articles in *Screen* simply support this puritanical view but it would be fair to say that there is enough ambiguity in the articles to create uncertainty about their position — they sometimes edge towards the reactionary view – Laura Mulvey, for example, does connect the cinema with the popular notion of perversion when in discussing the place of voyeurism in the cinema she writes 'At first glance, the cinema would seem to be remote from the *undercover world of the surreptitious observation of an unknowing and unwilling victim*' (our italics),[15] but then she goes on to suggest that the cinema is not so remote from that world.

We are also still concerned about the place women have in these psychoanalytic accounts. So far as we understand the reply to Julia Lesage's criticisms it appears to argue that women aren't allowed a place as spectators, they are 'a blind spot' for the cinema as it at present exists. Laura Mulvey's account also suggests that women are put into the position of being a blind spot since the audience implicit in her article is a male one. If patriarchal and/or bourgeois societies ignore women in this way in forms like the cinema, if there is not to be a tacit acceptance of this ignoring, it is urgent to examine the consequences of women being a blind spot. How do women relate to the films they see if the cinema is constructed for a male audience? Although it can be argued that women have been conditioned to accept the same way of seeing as men, they must be in a potentially anomalous and contradictory position within the viewing structures described here.

It is, of course, possible that the blind spot is not created by patriarchal or capitalist societies but by psychoanalytic theory. Freud's account of women is still controversial and we certainly don't feel ready to take final positions in that controversy. In this connection we're uneasy about the uncritical acceptance of Juliet Mitchell's defence of Freud in her book *Psychoanalysis and Feminism*. Whatever its undoubted merits *Psychoanalysis and Feminism* can hardly be thought to have resolved the problems in a decisive way. It would be hard to gather from the pages of *Screen* that the book has produced a substantial debate within both the socialist and feminist movements.[16]

One further point needs to be made about this particular attempt to apply psychoanalysis to the cinema. Too often abundant reference to psychoanalysis distracts attention from dubious arguments. The account of representation in terms of fetishism in 'Lessons from Brecht' is a case in point. Freud's description of a specific case of fetishism is summarized. The case turns on a play between the English word 'glance' and the German word *Glanz* which means 'gleam, brilliance, shine'. Fetishism in the cinema is then closely allied to this particular case because of the special appropriateness of words like 'glance, gleam, brilliance, shine' to the cinematic situation. 'The fetish is indeed a brilliance, something lit up, heightened, depicted as under an arc light, a point of (theatrical) representation; hence the glance: the subject is installed (as at the theatre or at the movies) for the representation.'[17]

But not all cases of fetishism depend on the play of words that are appropriate to the cinematic situation and it is therefore misleading to try and attach the concept of fetishism to the cinema on the basis of local coincidence.

Moreover the argument is basically irrelevant to the main argument about fetishism and representation. The main argument is put in the following way:

> The structure of representation is a structure of fetishism: the subject is produced in a position of separation from which he is confirmed in an imaginary coherence (the representation is the guarantee of his self-coherence) the condition of which is the ignorance of the structure of his production, of his setting in position.[18]

We take this argument to mean that two situations are being related to each other. The first is the fetishistic one described by Freud. The fetishist cannot come to terms with the woman's seeming lack of a penis because of its threat of castration. He finds a fetish for the missing penis in some other object (the fetish). This process allows him to operate on the illusory basis that he has come to terms with the initial situation. The second situation is that of a representation system (theatre, cinema, etc.). This system is thought to disguise the way it operates and therefore leaves the spectator unaware of the contradictions of her or his existence and allows her or him to maintain the illusion that she or he is a coherent being (a subject).

If we have followed the account of these two situations properly (and leaving aside whether they are true or meaningful) it seems illegitimate to claim that the structure of representation is a structure of fetishism. The two situations are very different; in the situation of the representation system there is no equivalent of the initial discovery of the woman's lack of a penis in the fetishist situation. All the two situations have in common is a structural similarity in that in both something is disguised from the people involved and that disguising process allows the people to continue to function but in ignorance of their real position. It is hard to see what useful conclusion can be drawn from this structural similarity. All the argument seems to achieve is the implication that representation systems are somehow perverse (in the popular sense of that word) – all the spectators in the cinema are fetishists.

We find the same elusiveness in Metz's account of the mirror phase in relation to the cinema. After convincingly showing that no direct analogy can be drawn between the mirror phase and the cinematic situation, Metz maintains the analogy by arguing that the spectator identifies with himself as 'a pure act of perception'. But what meaning can be given to such a notion? It suggests an extraordinary feat of psychological gymnastics.

Beyond the confines of a debate about psychoanalysis, we are finally concerned about the politico-cultural position psychoanalysis is being used to sustain. In broad outline it is the familiar high-bourgeois one that sadly has been all too prevalent in the Marxist tradition and helped to block the development of any adequate account of the role of art in mature capitalist societies. An ill-defined monolith (sometimes described as classic American cinema, sometimes as mainstream cinema) produces a passive audience, which is also conceived as a monolith and never investigated. The effective conclusion of this account is then the validation of avant-garde art (Godard, Oshima, Straub or more generally, the counter-cinema) as against any other.

If we try to translate this position into educational terms (and any positions developed in *Screen* ought to have some relevance to film education) we reach the position that educationalists have been uneasy about for a number of years where the education system deprives working-class children of their own cultural values and offers middle-class ones in their place. By saying this we are not arguing that working-class values are sacrosanct but suggesting the need to carefully scrutinize positions that seek to replace them. If the Society for Education in Film and Television is to contribute to the development of film education it is important that its commitments to film *and* education should be brought to bear on each other.

In relation to psychoanalysis our general conclusion is, to return to a point made at the beginning of this article, that a greater critical distance is needed. It is at this point it seems to us that there are the strongest divisions between our position and that of other members of the board. Much of the writing about psychoanalysis comes from a commitment that doesn't allow a critical distance to be taken. The presentation of Lacan's ideas provides a convenient example of how this commitment blocks criticism.[19] We believe that no socialist educationalist could be happy with Lacan's authoritarian account of the learning process,

> *The master breaks the silence with a sarcasm, a kick – anything at all.*
> It is thus in the quest for meaning that a Buddhist master proceeds according to Zen technique. For it is the pupils' business to seek the reply to their own questions. A master does not teach ex cathedra a completed science; *he brings forth the reply when his students are on the point of discovering it themselves.* (Our italics)

Yet this is enthusiastically presented as an example of Lacan's unorthodoxy.

Lacan's position as presented raises many of the problems that have become familiar in discussion of F.R. Leavis's critical position – the refusal of a metalanguage, the attempt to explicate concepts only by showing them at work. Indeed in confronting the use of Lacanian concepts in *Screen* we have come up against one of the special problems of Leavisite criticism: the use of terms whose repetition suggests they are important for the system of thought but whose meaning is hard to specify.

Screen has often been criticized as parasitic on ideas developed elsewhere. We reject this criticism in that we regard it as important to make available ideas which seem potentially fruitful wherever they are first developed. But the criticism has force if the ideas are presented and used uncritically without a sufficient awareness of the political situation they are likely to operate in. Which brings us back to *Screen*'s relationship with its readers – the fundamental issue underlying the particular discussion of psychoanalysis we have tried to open up.

NOTES

First published in *Screen*, Winter 1975–6, vol. 16, no. 4, pp. 119–30.

1 *Screen*, Summer 1974, vol. 15, no. 2; for Lesage's criticisms see *Screen*, Summer 1975, vol. 16, no. 2, pp. 77–83.
2 Jacques Lacan, *L'Homme nu*, Paris, Plon, n.d., pp. 562–3.
3 Colin McCabe, 'Realism and the Cinema', *Screen*, Summer 1974, vol. 15, no. 2, pp. 17–18.
4 Ben Brewster, Stephen Heath and Colin McCabe, 'Comment', *Screen*, Summer 1975, vol. 16, no. 2, p. 87.
5 Stephen Heath, 'Film and System: Terms of Analysis, Part I', *Screen*, Spring 1975, vol. 16, no. 1, pp. 7–77; quotation from p. 11. 'Part II' published *Screen*, Summer 1975, vol. 16, no. 2, pp. 91–113.
6 Translated in *Screen*, Autumn 1972, vol. 13, no. 3, pp. 5–44.
7 *New Left Review*, May–June 1975, no. 91, pp. 43–56.
8 *Screen*, Spring/Summer 1975, vol. 16, no. 1, pp. 7–77/vol. 16, no. 2, pp. 91–113.
9 *Screen*, Spring 1975, vol. 16, no. 1, p. 37.
10 *Screen*, Summer 1974, vol. 15, no. 2, pp. 103–28.
11 ibid., Summer 1975, vol. 16, no. 2, pp. 83–90.
12 ibid., pp. 14–76.
13 ibid., Autumn 1975, vol. 16, no. 3, pp. 6–8; reprinted as chapter 1 of this volume, pp. 22–34.
14 *Screen* editors' reply to Julia Lesage, Summer 1975, vol. 16, no. 2, p. 87.
15 Mulvey, p. 25 of this volume.
16 Juliet Mitchell, *Psychoanalysis and Feminism: Freud, Reich, Lang and Women*, New York, Vintage Books, 1974. For a lucid exposition and defence of the book see Christopher Lasch's review in the *New York Review of Books*, 3 October 1974. For criticisms of varying degrees of severity see Liz Long's review cited by Julia Lesage, op. cit.; Eli Zaretsky, 'Male Supremacy and the Unconscious', *Socialist Revolution*, 1973, nos. 21–2; Richard Wollheim, 'Psychoanalysis and Feminism, *New Left Review*, Sept.–Oct. 1975, no. 93, pp. 61–9; and Mark Poster's review in *Telos*, Fall 1974, no. 21.
17 Stephen Heath, 'Lessons from Brecht', *Screen*, Summer 1974, vol. 15, no. 2, pp. 103–28; quotation from p. 107.
18 ibid., p. 106.
19 *Screen*, Summer 1975, vol. 16, no. 2, p. 7.

3

DIFFERENCE

Stephen Heath

I

From *Encore*, Lacan's 1972/3 seminar devoted to 'what Freud expressly left aside, the *Was will das Weib?*, the *What does woman want?*' (*SXX*, p. 75),[1] this passage on female pleasure, enjoyment, *jouissance*:

> just as with Saint Teresa – you only have to go and look at the Bernini statue in Rome to understand immediately she's coming, no doubt about it. And what is she enjoying, coming from? It's clear that the essential testimony of the mystics is that of saying they experience it but know nothing about it. These mystical ejaculations are neither idle gossip nor mere verbiage, in fact they're the best thing you can read – note, right at the bottom of the page, *Add to them Jacques Lacan's Ecrits*, a work of the same order. Given which, naturally, you're all going to be convinced I believe in God. I believe in the *jouissance* of the woman in so far as it is *en plus*, something more, on condition you block out that *more* until I've thoroughly explained it.
>
> (*SXX*, p. 70)

Ignoring the habitual self-presentation (the famous style, which is indeed the insistence on the movement of psychoanalysis in its attention to the unconscious as against the simple determination of any concluded theorization but which is also, and thereby, the construction of a formidable persona, Lacan the embodiment of a word always elusively ahead, Lacan the term of an irresolvable transference), ignoring the assurance of the position of knowledge (they – Saint Teresa for example – feel, Lacan *knows*, in the conviction, carried by the theory, of a woman's incapacity to say anything of consequence regarding the reality of her experience: 'women do not know what they are saying, which is all the difference between them and me' (*SXX*, p. 68); even women analysts are disappointingly no better: 'since the time we've been begging them, begging them on our knees – I mentioned previously women analysts – to try to tell us, well, not a word! never been able to get anything out of them' (*SXX*, p. 69), ignoring all this, what is striking in the passage is the certainty in a representation and its vision (the cover of the book of the seminar is provided by a full-page photograph of the sculpture, see Figure 3:1). No doubt, not the

47

Figure 3:1 © Editions du Seuil, 1975

trace of any difficulty, to see the Bernini statue is to understand at once, is to have one's gaze filled with Saint Teresa's coming, with the *jouissance* of the woman; the statue is adequate, the image it gives enough.

Yet who exactly is Lacan addressing? Men? Women? Whose is the certainty he assumes so easily ('you only have to')? The passage is indifferent to such questions, as is Lacan's work generally in the forms of its enunciation: the topic is so often sexual difference but the treatment of that topic has no incidence as the possibility of a problem of sexual difference across the subject of the enunciation and the pattern of address of a discourse, of this discourse; the property of the discourse remains assured, assurance of the relation of Lacan to audience, the imaginary of the *evidence* of the statue. Thus any answer to the questions posed will be in terms of the identification of a discourse that is finally masculine, not because of some conception of theory as male but because in the last resort any discourse which fails to take account of the problem of sexual differ-

48

ence in its enunciation and address will be, within a patriarchal order, precisely indifferent, a reflection of male domination. It might be added, moreover, as a kind of working rule, that where a discourse appeals directly to an image, to an immediacy of seeing, as a point of its argument or demonstration, one can be sure that all difference is being elided, that the unity of some accepted vision is being reproduced.

The something more, the *en plus* that Lacan sees so readily in the statue as the *jouissance* of the woman, makes up for the something less, the absence, that the woman represents, represents in the first instance according to a scenario that is another certainty of seeing. Time and time again, Freud proposes the initiation of the castration complex in women, as it were, at sight: 'little girls . . . notice the penis of a brother or playmate, strikingly visible and of large proportions, at once recognise it as the superior counterpart of their own small and inconspicuous organ'; 'A little girl behaves differently. She makes her judgement and her decision in a flash. She has seen it and knows that she is without it and wants to have it'; 'the little girl discovers her own deficiency from seeing a male genital'; etc.[2] As in the Lacan passage, seeing is understanding, only here it is the under-standing of the lack, the condition of the more to which the woman will subsequently be returned by psychoanalysis; the woman sees and knows at once, in a flash, that she has nothing to see. The account effectively operates in a binding tourniquet in which the little girl resolves the hesi-tations of the little boy who 'when he first catches sight of a girl's genital region . . . begins by showing irresolution and lack of interest . . . he sees nothing or disavows what he has seen':[3] the girl is given in analytic theory to know at once the nothing she sees, confirming in that certainty – the certainty of the analytic scenario that premises the woman as the difference of the man, his term – the nothing to see that the boy is brought to know; the woman does represent the lack to see on her body, acknowledging, as little girl, visibility on the side of the man. Freud refers to the 'strikingly visible', Lacan to the phallus as 'something the symbolic use of which is possible because it can be seen, because it is erect; of what cannot be seen, of what is hidden, there is no possible symbolic use' (*SII*, p. 315).[4] Naturally, given the perspective of visibility established, it is the sex of the woman that is taken as the very instance of the unseeable, the hidden: Freud records his belief that 'probably no male human being is spared the fright of castration at the sight of a female genital',[5] Lacan talks of 'the pre-eminently original object, the abyss of the female organ from which all life comes forth' (*SII*, p. 196).

The function of castration as the articulation of the subject in difference is brought down to a matter of sight, the articulation of the symbolic to a vision. Where the conception of the symbolic as movement and production of difference, as chain of signifiers in which the subject is effected in division, should forbid the notion of some presence from which difference is then derived, Lacan instates the visible as the condition of symbolic functioning, with the phallus the standard of the visibility required: seeing is from the male organ. The problem, moreover, is maintained, not eased, by the distinction between penis and phallus customarily asserted. The golden rule of Lacanian theory is 'to *detach* the phallus from the organ by which it *consists*':[6] the phallus is a signifier, is not an object, not the penis, but the latter nevertheless is its consistence as symbol; the phallus is said to symbolize the penis which, strikingly visible, is the condition of that symbolization. Lacan is often no further than the limits of pure analogical rationalization in this respect:

> It can be said that this signifier [the phallus] is chosen because it is what stands out most in what can be grasped in the real of sexual copulation, and as being also the most symbolic in the literal (typographical) sense of the term, since it is equivalent there to the (logical) copula. It can also be said that, by virtue of its turgidity, it is the image of the vital flow as it is transmitted in generation.
>
> $(E, \text{p. } 692)$[7]

The penis/phallus distinction-oscillation-relation is symptomatic: on the one hand, psychoanalysis points to the production of subject, unconscious, desire in the symbolic; on the other, it derives that production from the fact of a perceived castration – the woman's lack – in a theory of infantile sexuality; the penis/phallus is the join of the two emphases, the 'privileged signifier of that mark in which the part of the logos comes together with the advent of desire' $(E, \text{p. } 692)$[8] where the privilege can only be founded from a difference in nature *to be seen*; a recognition of lack is given outside of any signifying process as a fact of each individual subject with a return in the symbolic – the phallic function – that ties process to vision. What is at stake and shut off in the logic of the penis/phallus is the history of the subject in as far as that history might include effects of social organization, and, for example, of patriarchal order. That such a logic may really describe the production of subjectivity in a relation of sexual difference in a patriarchal society is not necessarily in question; that production, however, cannot be inverted – except to reproduce and confirm its established terms – into the fixed point of an origin, the translation of a vision. The vision, any vision, is constructed, not given; appealing to its certainty, psychoanalysis can only repeat the ideological impasse of the natural, the mythical representation of things.

The woman who is there in psychoanalysis, whom it hears, is the hysteric. Hysteria, as is well enough known, has its importance as the very beginning of psychoanalysis: Freud attends Charcot's famous 'lessons' in the Salpêtrière, interests himself in Breuer's experience with Anna O and the 'talking cure', publishes with Breuer the *Studies on Hysteria* ('the starting point of psychoanalysis'), moves back, with the recognition of the importance of the sexual element, from the clinical definition of hysteria accomplished by Charcot to its understanding as a psychological disturbance now posed as an implication of the subject in specific unconscious mental processes; from compression of the ovaries to compression of the brain, the hand pressing on the patient's forehead, to the final analytic situation, only the contact of speech, association, interpretation. It is with the hysteric that psychoanalysis encounters symptom as meaning, the other scene that speaks across the body, a knowledge produced from the subject as effect: 'The hysteric produces knowledge. The hysteric is an effect, as every subject is an effect. The hysteric forces the "signifying matter" to confess, and thereby constitutes a discourse.'[9] The discourse of hysteria is not just a beginning of psychoanalysis, it is, in its forcing of the signifying matter, a fundamental condition. When Lacan identifies four basic positions of discourse, that of the analyst is a quarter of a turn away from that of the hysteric which is its constant impetus; analysis is said to be nothing other than the structural introduction of the discourse of the hysteric, the analyst is 'a perfect hysteric, that is, without symptoms'.[10] This function of hysteria, the appeal to the discourse of the hysteric, is not as such implicated in any division based on sexual difference and it should be remembered that Charcot and Freud after him insisted on a reappropriation of the disturbance hysteria outside of its limitation as a female condition (Freud described himself as ridiculed after a lecture to the Viennese Medical Society in 1886 in which he described cases of male hysteria: an old surgeon railed at such absurdity when everyone knew that hysteria was to do with the uterus). Yet, at the same time, hysteria constantly comes back to the woman: already in Freud (the *Studies on Hysteria* are all of women), today in psychoanalysis in the obligatory reference to hysteria in analytic writing concerned with questions of the female; the latter reference is so strong indeed that 'feminine' and 'hysterical' are taken as more or less interchangeable: 'so-called "hysterical" speech which ought rather to be called feminine'; after all, 'all women play on the uterus'[11] (stupefying, we are back with the Viennese Medical Society against Freud).

The success of Freud and psychoanalysis with female hysteria was an understanding of it as a problem of sexual identity in phallic terms: the hysteric is unsure as to being woman or man, 'the hysterical position – having or not having the phallus'.[12] Hers is a body in trouble with language, that forcing of the signifying matter, simultaneously resisting and accepting the given signs, the given order. Listening to the woman as hysteric, psychoanalysis opens and closes the other scene, with the point of closure exactly 'sexual identity', 'sexual difference'; hence, symptomatically, the curious lag of psychoanalysis felt by Freud with regard to femininity, women still the great enigma, the 'dark continent', which feeling gives rise in the 1920s and 1930s (after Freud's major work is accomplished) to the flurry of new interest and discussion (writings by Freud himself, De Groot, Deutsch, Horney, Jones, etc.) – curious just because of that beginning with hysteria, the cures with women, the attention focused there. When Dora, subject of a case which is published in development of the theses set out in the *Studies on Hysteria*,[13] politely disappears from Freud's sight on the last day of 1900, interrupts her treatment, she breaks with a Freud, with an analysis, caught up in a logic of sexual identity and difference, unable to envisage any other economy (thus unable, for example, to engage with what it could only anyway see as her 'homosexuality'). In every sense, psychoanalysis answered to the hysteria it realized as its initial and decisive object: what works is identity, the phallus, that difference, having or not, variations from there, with the woman as other, less and more, falling short and beyond. Start from the hysteric, the problem of identity, focus centrally the term of identity with the male as measure, as standard ('we have been in the habit of taking as the subject of our investigations the male child'),[14] come back to the woman as still, as always, unknown ('we need not feel ashamed')[15] – the lag is produced by the logic, the woman can only be 'the woman', *different from*. But for centuries, hysteria has named an incapacity to take that place, to be the difference, 'the woman'. To explain hysteria by the problem of sexual identity is to miss the struggle in female hysteria against *that* assumption of difference, against *that* identity, is to refind hysteria as a nature of women and not the site of a resistance – nothing to do with an essence – in culture.

In Charcot's clinical teaching practice at the Salpêtrière, the Tuesday lessons attended by Freud, attention was paid to the realization of a photographic record of the cases presented, a veritable iconography of hysteria: 'we saw,' write the compilers of the record, 'from M. Charcot's example how considerable were the benefits to be had from representations of this kind'.[16]

Charcot's cases included men and children, the photographs are of women, plates interspersed within the text of the clinical details; often a portrait of the particular woman as she is at rest, the 'normal physiognomy', much like any other late nineteenth-century portrait photograph; then the stages of the 'attack' so dear to Charcot in his endeavour to bring hysteria into the order of medicine, to define a clinical *picture*, the '*tableau clinique*'; very occasionally (as, for example, in volume I plate XVI), nurses intrude, by the side of the patient, fixing the camera, determinedly posing; now and again an effect of 'beauty', a young girl composed on her bed (volume I plate XVIII), something of Millais's *Ophelia*, 'terminal stage of the attack', no trace of disturbance, in her 'the delirium sometimes takes on a religious character' – the *aura* of hysteria, part of the picture. The interest for Charcot, and for the compilers, is in the stages, the step-by-step unfolding of the attack. Where others had seen only disorder, merely the random, Charcot saw order, a repeated pattern which the photographs must serve to give; hence the series of plates for a single patient, an attempt at duration, a movement in time. Plates XVII–XXV of volume II, for instance, are devoted to a sixteen-year-old girl in the throes of the period of delirium: the various 'passionate attitudes' are shown in sequence and named – attitudes of 'threat', 'appeal', 'amorous supplication', 'eroticism', 'ecstasy', 'hallucinations of hearing'. The effect is of a kind of cinema: the spacing of gestures in a succession of images, the holding of those same gestures to the clarity of a narrative meaning; one can imagine the Salpêtrière *Iconographie* as a catalogue of gestural signs for the use of performers in silent films – and such an imagination would not be too far from the spectacle of the lessons, which all the contemporary pictures and prints pick up: the excited audience, the master, the young woman in a series of pathetic scenes according to script (there is a certain controversy over the demonstrations and the repetitions of the stages of the attack: hypnotized by the master's zealous assistants, with pressure applied to their 'hysterogenic zones', was there any other part for these women?).

What is missing in the photographs is the voice, an absence signalled, as it were, in the naming of the 'hallucinations of hearing' plate; the absence of speech across the body in convulsion, delirious. The text restores a little of the voice, almost nothing: when a patient cries 'Mummy!', Charcot comments, 'You see how hysterics shout. Much ado about nothing. Epilepsy which is much more serious is much quieter'; when another is said by her mother to talk of 'someone with a beard, man or woman', the response is 'whether man or woman is not without importance, but let us slide over that mystery'. Charcot sees, Freud hears. All the cinema is banished, the spectacle gives way to the analytic situation (not quite all, something remains in the establishment of that situation, the couch, the analyst seated behind, which, says Freud, allowed him to see without being seen,[17] a perfect definition of the position of the cinema spectator). Psychoanalysis is the anti-visible; significant in this respect, moreover, are Freud's distrust of projects for rendering analysis on the screen and, conversely, the powerful social desire to bring that same analysis into sight, the fascination of so many films with psychoanalysis. Hence no certainty in seeing, which comes back round to the paradox of such certainty nevertheless in Freud, in Lacan, to the terms of the difference it assumes and sustains.

II

The spectacle of the woman then, the more and the less of *Encore* with its Freudian question as to what woman wants; in the first instance, the main theses of Lacan's answer, how the question works:

(a) *There is no sexual relation*, this being the very reality of psychoanalysis: 'the only basis of analytic discourse is the statement that there is no – that it is impossible to pose – sexual relation' (*SXX*, p. 14). No sexual relation does not mean no relation to a sex; on the contrary, this latter relation is precisely what is at stake in the function of castration which is in fact the point of the absence of the former. The division of the subject in the symbolic, in the desire of the Other, is the impossibility of any unity of relation: 'in so far as it is sexual, *jouissance* is phallic, which is to say that it does not relate to the Other as such' (*SXX*, p. 14); 'the *jouissance* of the Other taken as a body is always inadequate' (*SXX*, p. 131). Male or female, the subject is implicated from and in the phallus, phallic *jouissance*, but differently: there is a male and a female way of failing relation. In other words, the structure of a subject is a division in the symbolic and that division is not the fact of some immediately given sexual difference: men and women are not complementary to one another, two halves that could be joined in union, both are produced in division. The phallus is the term of that production in as much as it functions as the signifier in the articulation of castration; male and female differ in consequence of the phallic function in castration, are in the position of a different relation to phallus and castration; thus there can be no sexual relation, only a relation to phallic *jouissance*, in the woman as in the man.

(b) *The woman is not-all*: 'the woman is defined from a position that I've noted as not-all in respect of phallic *jouissance*' (*SXX*, p. 13). The woman cannot really sustain phallic *jouissance*, her relation to the phallus as term of symbolic castration is lacking: 'in her body' she is 'not-all as sexed being', 'the sexed being of these women not-all passes not via the body but via what results from a logical requirement of discourse' (*SXX*, p. 15); 'the woman is not-all, there is always something with her which eludes discourse' (*SXX*, p. 34). The gist of this is that in as far as the phallus marks the turn of the symbolic representation of the sexual, the woman is not all – not quite, not whole, not completely – in that representation: she misses out on the phallus and misses in the discourse which it organizes and which is the relay of her excess, her sexuality.

(c) *Everything revolves round phallic jouissance*. Sexual *jouissance* is phallic, *jouissance* – enjoyment, pleasure – of the organ; it is not a sexual relation, a relation to the Other as such. The order of the symbolic, the phallus being the privileged signifier of that order, causes and limits *jouissance*, the phallic being that limitation, and for both men and women: the woman is caught up in *phallic jouissance* but not-all, there is 'something more', 'a supplementary *jouissance*' (*SXX*, pp. 68–9); the man sustains phallic *jouissance* which is then the obstacle that prevents him from really enjoying the body of the woman, what he has is 'the enjoyment of the organ' (*SXX*, p. 13). Thus, 'the enjoyment of the Other . . . is something else again, namely the not-all' (*SXX*, p. 26).

(d) *There is a jouissance beyond the phallus which is the jouissance of the woman*. 'When I say that the woman is not-all and that it is for that reason that I cannot say *the* woman, it is precisely because I am raising the question of a *jouissance* which in regard of everything which serves in the phallic function is of the order of the infinite' (*SXX*, p. 94).

(e) *The woman is that which relates to the Other*. Woman *and* Other, 'locus of the signifying cause of the subject' (*E*, p. 841), are not-all, more and less than the order of the phallus, radically other: 'The Other is not simply that locus of the stammering of truth. . . . By her being in the sexual relation, in relation to what can be said of the unconscious, radically the Other, the woman is that which relates to the Other' (*SXX*, p. 75). Woman is equivalent to truth, 'at least for the man' (*SXX*, p. 108); the questions of the desire of the Other and the desire of the woman are one and the same, the question of the truth: '*What does woman want?* – woman being on the occasion the equivalent of the truth' (*SXX*, p. 115).

(f) *Thus (the jouissance of) the woman is (in the position of) God.* The Other is the only place left 'in which to put the term God' (*SXX*, p. 44). Since the Other 'must have some relation to what appears of the other sex' (*SXX*, p. 65), 'why not interpret a face of the Other, the God face, as supported by feminine *jouissance*?' (*SXX*, p. 71); 'it is in as much as her *jouissance* is radically other that the woman has more relation to God' (*SXX*, p. 77); in the *jouissance* of the woman one can mark that 'God has not yet made his exit' (*SXX*, p. 78).

'Nothing can be said of the woman' (*SXX*, p. 75), but Lacan in *Encore* does nothing but talk of the woman (concerned perhaps to give 'a real consistency to the Women's Movement' *SXX*, p. 69). True, at one level 'the woman' is emptied of any essence, produced in function of a symbolic order, but that function itself is universal, 'the woman part of speaking beings' (*SXX*, p. 74), and the woman everywhere returns in her common places – close to unconscious, Other, Truth, and God. To say that the 'the' of 'the woman', 'definite article designating the universal' (*SXX*, p. 68), is to be crossed out, barred through, is in no way to challenge the universalization; indeed, it is its very renewal, another turn of the screw, the same discourse of the essence continues: 'there is no woman but excluded by the nature of things which is the nature of words . . .' (*SXX*, p. 68).

When psychoanalysis produces woman, the woman, as not-all, it falls short, remains locked in a static assignation. It is not the woman who is not-all but psychoanalysis, which is what the latter has been so generally unwilling to grasp. Psychoanalysis discovers and ceaselessly fails – in its theory – the unconscious, and that failure is history, the social relations of production, classes, sexes. It is not by chance that Lacan devotes a year's seminar to 'What does woman want?' – a seminar dotted with little references to women's struggle (of the kind: 'I was in Italy, there was a person who was furious, a lady from the local women's movement, she was really . . . so I said "Come back tomorrow morning, I'll explain what it's all about" ' *SXX*, p. 54) – at the very time that 'the woman', as women, is intervening against the given relations, for social transformation, and with a political claim on psychoanalysis in the theoretical constructions and concepts it elaborates.

There is in Lacan's writing the presence of an unquestioned imaginary of the woman. When he expresses his enthusiastic liking for Benoît Jacquot's *L'Assassin musicien*, what strikes him, a bubbling fascination, is the little girl – a little girl is 'a virtual woman, hence a being much more engaged in the real than males' (*SI*, p. 187)[18] – and above all her spontaneity, her naturalness, a real little girl.[19] Somewhere, for Lacan, the woman is always the exact image of herself, contained such as she is, on the God face of the Other, infinitely unknowable, knowable only as the different, visibly, certainly that. Thus the image of Saint Teresa, the sureness of the religious representation, the woman held as the truth of that view. If that image fails, there is nothing left but the threat of castration, the abyss, the tearing vagina: 'Queen Victoria, there's a woman . . . when one encounters a toothed vagina of such exceptional size. . . .'[20]

III

Lacan's work is vastly more important that the positions he is led to develop, the worst stereotypes he grotesquely rejoins and repeats. That importance, the sense of the 'return to Freud', is the attention given to the constitution of the subject in the symbolic and the relation of the unconscious there, with questions of sexuality posed accordingly – Freud's discovery was not that of sexuality but of the unconscious as site of meaning. It is necessary now to try to take up something of that attention to the subject, under the theses of *Encore*, in connection with issues of sexual difference and with the problem of difference as division of sex.

For memory simply,[21] a passage from one of Freud's last pieces of writing in which he summarizes his thinking in a difficult area:

> We are faced here by the great enigma of the biological fact of the duality of the sexes: it is an ultimate fact for our knowledge, it defies every attempt to trace it back to something else. Psychoanalysis has contributed nothing to clearing up this problem, which clearly falls wholly within the province of biology. In mental life, we find only reflections of this great antithesis; and their interpretation is made more difficult by the fact, long suspected, that no individual is limited to the modes of reaction of a single sex . . . for distinguishing between male and female in mental life we make use of what is obviously an inadequate empirical and conventional equation: we call everything that is strong and active male, and everything that is weak and passive female.[22]

Biological fact and mental reflections are complicated in their relation on the individual, the psychical having an independence from the physical ('to a great extent independent'),[23] the biological development of sexuality accompanied by a psychological development which is the effective determination of an individual's sexuality. Both developments are concerned in the bisexual disposition of every individual; psychically, 'the reactions of human individuals of both sexes are of course made up of masculine and feminine traits'.[24] Thus, 'pure masculinity and femininity remain theoretical constructions of uncertain content';[25] which leaves the problem of definition intact, run back into an assumed necessity of the expression of the biological in the psychological, 'the morphological distinction is bound to find expression in differences of psychical development',[26] or resolved for better or worse by 'an inadequate empirical and conventional equation' that simply accepts a given representation of man and woman and, witness the reference to conventional *and* empirical, its given foundation-justification as nature.

Lacan comes back to the relation of sexuality in the symbolic constitution of the subject. Language is the condition of the unconscious,[27] which latter is a concept forged on the trace of what operates to constitute the subject. Caused in language, which is division and representation, the subject is taken up as such in an interminable movement of the signifier, the process of the symbolic, and in a structure of desire, the implication of the subject's experience of division, of lack, in language. Hence the importance of language for psychoanalysis as the site of its object, unconscious desire. To grasp language as the condition of the unconscious is to insist on desire in language and to make the subject the term of a constant construction and representation, outside of the expression of any unity, biological included. 'Analytic discourse allows us to glimpse that it is through language that man is separated, blocked from everything concerning the sexual relation, and that it is thereby that he enters the real, more precisely that he is lacking in this real.'[28] There is no sexual relation because there is no one, no two together, man and woman given complementarily; language is and recounts a division which constitutes the subject in relation to the Other not to any one, the Other as point of the distribution-circulation of signifiers within which the subject is produced in a structure of desire, 'the desire of man is the desire of the Other' (*E*, p. 693).[29] Desire passes through, is in relation to the Other, not through or to some 'partner', is a function of the subject in language in its implication of the unconscious: 'The function of desire is a last residuum of the effect of the signifier in the subject' (*SXI*, p. 141).[30]

In order to advance a little further in this context, the following passage may be quoted in which Lacan refers sexuality in the subject to lack and goes on to specify the overlap of two lacks:

> what must be done, as man or as woman, the human being has always to learn entirely from the Other . . .
>
> That it be the drive, the partial drive, that orientates the human being in the field of sexual fulfilment, that it be the partial drive alone

that is the representative in the psyche of the consequences of sexuality, there is the sign that sexuality is represented in the psyche by a relation of the subject that is deduced from something other than sexuality itself. Sexuality is established in the field of the subject by a path that is that of lack.

Two lacks overlap here. The first has to do with the central default around which turns the dialectic of the advent of the subject to its own being in the relation to the Other – by the fact that the subject depends on the signifier and that the signifier is first of all in the field of the Other. This lack takes up the other lack which is the real, initial lack, to be situated at the advent of the living being, that is, in the fact of sexed reproduction. The real lack is what the living being loses, of its portion of living, in reproducing itself through the way of sex. This lack is real because it relates to something real, namely, that the living being, by its being subject to sex, has fallen under the jurisdiction of individual death.

$$(SXI, \text{ p. } 186)[31]$$

Effectively, the passage reformulates the join of the biological and the psychological seen at issue in Freud. On the sexual hinge species, individual and subject, and the hinge is the overlap of the two lacks. The species exists through its individuals who are transitory in the function of its reproduction, the assurance of its continuation; hence 'the presence of sex in the living being is bound up with death' (SXI, p. 162).[32] The individual exists as subject in the relations of the symbolic – the human being is a speaking subject, which is the condition of unconscious and desire – the articulation of sexuality for the individual as subject. The biological apparatus is returned – parasited (Lacan talks of phallic *jouissance* as 'something which parasites the sexual organs')[33] – by the production of the signifier, its representation of the subject, its process of the body. When Lacan stresses the fundamental role of drive, it is exactly as the point of this return (Freud introduced the concept of drive as 'lying on the frontier between the mental and the physical'):[34] 'sexuality comes into play only in the form of partial drives; the drive is precisely that montage by which sexuality participates in the psychical life' (SXI p. 160);[35] 'with regard to the instance of sexuality, all subjects are equal, from the child to the adult: their dealings are solely with what of sexuality passes in the networks of the constitution of subjectivity, in the networks of the signifier; sexuality is realised only through the operation of the drives in so far as they are partial drives, partial with regard to the biological finality of sexuality' (SXI, p. 161).[36] Drives, then, are 'the echo on the body of the fact of language':[37] the frontier between 'the mental and the physical' across the individual is an overlap, joining and disjoining, the partiality of the return – the circuit – of drives out of line with the simple biological finality of sexuality, reproduction; in its subjectivity, caused by language, the individual is excessive with regard to that finality, with the terms of the excess being unconscious, desire, death. What is crucial, in other words, is not the relation between masculine and feminine but that between the living subject and its loss in the sexual cycle of reproduction; 'In this way I explain the essential affinity of every drive with the zone of death, and reconcile the two sides of drive – which at once gives the presence of sexuality in the unconscious and represents, in its essence, death' (*SXI*, p. 181).[38]

It is in this perspective that sexuality is to be understood as the reality of the unconscious: sexuality is not a 'content' of the unconscious but a process, the process of desire – 'in our experience, sexual desire has nothing objectified about it' (*SII*, p. 263). The desire of the subject from its division in the field of the Other, in the symbolic, is the relation of sexuality for the individual subject; desire is that 'nodal point by which the pulsation of the unconscious is linked to sexual reality' (*SXI*, p. 141).[39] Thus it becomes difficult to establish a difference expressible as male unconscious/ female unconscious (this is one aspect of Freud's conception of libido – the force of the presence of desire, the dynamic manifestation in mental life of sexual drive – as 'masculine': 'active' in both men and women): the unconscious is the fact of the division of the subject in the symbolic, not of the male from the female; the mechanisms of desire, the dialectic of subject and object, fully engage the bisexual disposition of the individual. Yet to indicate that difficulty is not to suggest a simple indifference, it is to stress only that difference must be specified in respect of the division in the symbolic, of the history of the subject. In psychoanalysis, such specification depends on the phallus, the privileged signifier; the variety of mental structures that overrun the anatomical difference of the sexes has nevertheless a fixed reference, phallic sexual difference.

The joining–disjoining overlap of the biological by the mental as the turn of the subject allows a quite radical conception of sexuality, allows the possibility of a quite other posing of difference. Sexuality is not given in nature but produced; the individual subject is not constructed from sexuality, sexuality is constructed in the history of the subject, with difference a function of that construction not its cause, a function which is not necessarily single (on the contrary) and which, *a fortiori*, is not necessarily the holding of that difference to anatomical difference (phallic singularity). Production, construction in the history of the subject, sexuality engages also from the beginning, *and thereby*, the social relations of production, classes, sexes – an engagement which cannot be, the lesson of psychoanalysis, a reduction but which equally, the lesson of the limiting certainties of psychoanalysis against the effective implications of its theory, cannot be left aside, for later, set beyond the enclosure of an analytically defined area.

An example in this context, fairly small but significant. Exploring the idea of the sexual reality of the unconscious, Lacan speculates, with a panoply of supporting references to the study of mitosis, the maturation of sexual cells, chromosomes, and so on, that 'it is through sexual reality that the signifier came into the world' (*SXI*, p. 138).[40] If that speculation is accepted, then the effect, contrary to the fundamental emphases of the psychoanalytic theory developed by Lacan, is to make sexual reality the condition of the symbolic, hence of the unconscious – of which it is thus, finally, as original sexual 'reality', the content. Lacan is close here to Freud's laying down of arms before the ultimate reality of the great enigma of the biological fact of the duality of the sexes (note in both Freud and Lacan the appeal beyond psychoanalysis, to science, the answer that must lie within the province of biology). In the theory, there is no place for sexual reality as foundation, as nature; the reality of sexuality is bound up with the reality of the symbolic construction of the subject – what returns is a history, unconscious desire, not the expression of an origin. That Lacan can nevertheless countenance the idea of the latter, can run analysis back into biology and myth, is symptomatic. The constant limit of the theory is the phallus, the phallic function, and the theorization of that limit is constantly eluded, held off, and, for example, by collapsing castration into a scenario of vision; to say that it is through sexual reality that the signifier comes into the world is not far from deriving the phallus as privileged signifier from an essence in nature and not from an order of the symbolic – but then the problem, the debate, is precisely there.

IV

It is that problem, that debate, that will now be of concern in connection with the production of sexuality and the question of difference. The body is worked over in the symbolic, is sexed from its passage there, articulation of castration, moment of lack, drama of the subject. The phallus is given as the signifier of lack and the measure of desire, the veritable function of the symbolic: 'the phallus . . . is the signifier of the very loss the subject suffers by the fragmentation of the signifier' (*E*, p. 715); 'the phallus . . . is the signifier destined to designate the whole set of effects of signified, in that the signifier conditions them by its presence as signifier' (*E*, p. 690);[41] the phallus, in fact, is thus what *makes exchange* (of subject, language, body). The site of castration is the body of the mother, with the father possessor and figure of the phallus, guarantor of the order of the symbolic; 'it is when the father is deficient in one way or another (dead, absent, blind even) that the most serious neuroses are produced'.[42] Mother and infant are two, that is, *one*, the imaginary possibility of a unity; the third, the father, makes *two*, assures the phallus as term of division in each individual subject; never the complementarity of two subjects, the division between them, but always the drama of the subject in the field of the Other, the experience of its lack-in-being, its being from lack, the lack of which the phallus is the signifier, inscribing its effects in the unconscious, in the gap between enunciation and enounced, a logic of the subject in the symbolic. That logic is then specified as a dialectic of being and having in which male and female positions can be distinguished: 'One can, simply by reference to the function of the phallus, indicate the structures that will govern the relations between the sexes. Let us say that these relations will turn around a being and a having . . . with regard to a signifier, the phallus' (*E*, p. 694).[43] Man and woman are not together in a sexual relation but each separate in the relation of phallic *jouissance*: the man invests the woman as being the phallus, giving what she does not have, denies the function of castration; the woman invests the man as having the phallus, wishing to be the phallus for him, desiring his castration. In short, the phallus as privileged signifier, the constant and final meaning of symbolic exchange, for men and for women.

For men and for women . . . On the side of the woman, the passage from being to having is none too strong; the difference, 'the other sex' (*SXX*, p. 65), woman must be distinguished *from* man in psychoanalytic theory. Distinguished in 'her specific function in the symbolic order' (*SII*, p. 305), a position 'with no issue' (*SII*, p. 304), 'a relation of second degree to the symbolic order' (*SII*, p. 305), which is why man is God incarnate for her, the second sex indeed, though of course there are conflicts, eternal conflicts – 'the feminine revolt doesn't date from yesterday' (*SII*, p. 305). No illusions are permitted when Lacan returns to the question in the *Encore* seminar:

> There is no woman but excluded by the nature of things which is the nature of words, and it has to be said that if there is one thing about which women themselves are complaining at the moment, it's well and truly that – it's just that they don't know what they are saying, which is all the difference between them and me.
>
> (*SXX*, p. 68)

This is the context of notions of woman's negative relation to the symbolic: the woman is lacking in respect of the phallus, of castration; in Cixous's formula, 'what analysis signals as marking woman is that she lacks lack'.[44] How then do these notions work in analytic theory, what does the latter make of the woman?

Take, as example, the account given by a member of Lacan's Ecole Freudienne, the analyst Eugénie Lemoine-Luccioni.[45] Both man and woman are subject to a regime of lack which produces between them a specific differentiation, locatable in the dialectic of being and having: 'they are distinguished immediately by the direction taken by lack of being in the man from having: the man sticks with having in consequence of his having a penis; the woman sticks with the lack in being, having or not having remaining for her in the realm of the imaginary.'[46] In other words, woman fails symbolic castration which catches up in her, problematically, an imaginary partition (in the sense of a dividing up, a separating out) that is specifically feminine. Woman's order is that of the double: duality of sexual organs (clitoris, vagina) duality of the relation to the mother (the woman is of the same sex as the parent who bears her), duality in her doubling-loss of herself as one (menstruation, childbirth). Divided up in this order of the double, the woman experiences the symbolic castration from a site elsewhere to the man: the penis has never been a part of her, the 'you are not the phallus' of castration with its process of being and having accords differently, difficultly for her; she passes from loss of an imaginary part of herself – the doubling, the partition – to loss of an organ that can only be a superimposition on that other loss which it then continues to figure (so, for instance, 'when she comes to make love, the detumescence and withdrawal of the penis quite naturally figure and summarise – pending the future act of giving birth – all these losses'):[47] hence, 'rather than castration anxiety the woman knows the anxiety of partition; she lives truly under the sign of abandonment: mother, father, children, husband, penis, everybody leaves her'.[48] The mechanism of the superimposition, the join of partition and castration, is identification, identification with the man (which is where the equation of woman and hysteric emerges, woman defined as a problem of identity):

> Through identification with the man, the woman imagines herself a lacking penis (whereas strictly speaking it is not lacking in the man) and symbolises in this way the lack of which all the phenomena of partition deprive her. Thus she moves from the imaginary loss of a half of herself to the imaginary loss of the male sexual organ, then to the symbolisable loss of a sexual organ, no matter which; provided, however, that 'penis envy' does not fix her to the real absence of the particular sexual organ, the penis. But whose penis? Is the consequent castration symbolic or only imaginary, as a result of the fact that the penis has never been there, on the woman? Her own sexual organ is not threatened. Another process of specifically feminine symbolisation necessarily intervenes here, in the course of which the woman takes herself as lost object and stake of the symbolisation. To lose the half of oneself is indeed to lose oneself in one's unity and thus in one's being. The symbol of the lost unity would be the body as whole, without fissure.[49]

The woman is caught up in the symbolic and the phallic function as its articulation – contaminated, 'the moment of the contamination via the man of the fear of losing the penis (which becomes in her the feeling of never having had it)'[50] – but one cannot say the woman is really achieved in symbolic castration, there is only 'superimposition', 'substitution', 'transplantation', 'only imaginary castration'. [51] Hence, coming back to being and having, the so-to-speak logical difference of man and woman:

> The man is one, by the grace of the signifier of his lack, the phallus, which happens to be the symbol of his sexual organ, the penis, which happens to be the organ through which passes and is manifested his desire for the woman, the instrument which organises his libido. His *jouissance* is to find in the woman the Other and also, a little, knowing and having. But this knowledge does not divide him. The man is and remains, as man, and assuming that he exists as a man who is not also a woman, one. The *jouissance* of the woman is the revelation of this one in the Other, which makes her one for the duration of love. But being one makes her Other and separates her from her 'mother body', like bark from a tree. [52]

Less than one and lost from one, failing castration, 'badly castrated', [53] the woman can only invoke the man as 'the very ideal of unity', [54] the ideal that she is not, namely one. If she becomes one, in love, in the relation of phallic *jouissance*, she is thereby alienated once again, alienated from her specificity, the Other for herself as she is for the man – which, given the fixed point of the relation of phallic *jouissance*, amounts to defining this alienation as her effective specificity: 'no sexual revolution will shift these lines of division'. [55]

It is true that no sexual revolution will shift dividing lines, the problem is one of social revolution. Privileging the sexual has nothing necessarily liberating about it; on the contrary, the sexual functions only too readily as an instance by development of and reference to which the social guarantees its order outside of any real process of transformation, produces exactly a containing ideology of 'liberation'. It is much the same story as with the inclusion in the theory of the possibility of the idea that 'it is through sexual reality that the signifier came into the world'. Hold to such an idea and difference will easily return as nature, not within the terms of a symbolic production; which is what patriarchy has always asserted, pinning women down to their sex, to a sex: the woman as the difference in nature. The political question is the avoidance of any collapse into that difference (which is to deny any difference, to accept the term of the given order, the interminable same of the phallus). A question, for example, of what from the perspective of that given order can appear as a radical desexualization, and which is nothing other than the reposing of sexuality in its symbolic and social production. Paradoxically perhaps at first view, this may well be one of the decisive aspects of the insistence on the extensiveness of women's sexuality: 'the woman has sexes all over'; [56] 'is not the "adult" woman one who reconstructs her sexuality in a field which goes beyond sex?' [57] Which is to say that in current ideological struggle it is not enough to assert in opposition women's relation to a non-genital, 'dispersed' sexuality, since such an emphasis (moreover close to Freud, who can talk of a feminine sexuality 'dispersed over the body from head to foot')[58] is a powerful representation of women from within, and as part of, the existing oppression, woman as a kind of total equivalent of sex, her identity as that; the need is precisely to come back on the production of sexuality, women and men (the reduction of sexuality to genitality in their representation), and to understand the history of the subject in difference from there, in the social relations of its symbolic order, in a possibility of transformation.

When Lemoine-Luccioni says that 'no sexual revolution will shift the lines of division', she is not there, but remains within the restricted field of psychoanalysis, a theory which so often assumes that restriction as end, as grasp of the universal ('the man will always . . . the woman will always . . .');[59] she remains in that context in which, as regards politics, Lacan simply declares that he does not believe in progress;[60] which, of course, can be provided with a positive gloss, heard as a criticism of evolutionist versions of history, but which functions finally as a fact of analysis: no progress, only the truth, the truth of the impossibility of progress, fundamental change, the conversion of history into that truth. With Lemoine-Luccioni's book, one is left with a strong theoretical construction which takes direct account of a problem of difference, which continually exceeds the logic of the sole phallus (the whole of the counterpointing development of the idea of partition works in this excess), but which never poses the problem of the very concept of difference and the conception of difference assumed, the phallus thus remaining the constant and universalizing reference, giving its form to that which is proposed as the different (partition as difference from the phallic constitution of the subject). This is the problematic of psychoanalysis, its problem, the problem of its history: the history it envisages in its account of the construction of the subject; the history of the situation of that account, the historical terms of its descriptions, descriptions which may adequately hold for the given social order without the adequacy necessarily implying the translation of their terms into absolute ones, adequate to every social historical realization of the construction of the subject, the specific and properly 'absolute' area of psychoanalysis. To follow through now one or two points in Lemoine-Luccioni's characterization of the woman in respect of the symbolic is to make evident something of that problematic – and is to find issues that are typical and important in current debate, issues that are important also, with resonances for, thinking about cinema.

If the woman is in some sort failing with regard to symbolic castration, then she fails equally with regard to the repression which accompanies the constitution of the unconscious. Taking up this common thesis, Lemoine-Luccioni refers to the powerful version of it given by Michèle Montrelay: 'the sexuality of the woman is capable of remaining apart from all repression';[61] female sexuality is censored rather than repressed, in as much as it 'lends itself less easily to a "losing itself" as the stake of unconscious representation',[62] in as much, that is, as castration is difficult, the phallus a 'superimposition' in Lemoine-Luccioni's term. We come back here to that closeness of woman and unconscious of which Lacan talks in the *Encore* seminar; the positions may vary, but within the limits of the shared notion of closeness which depends on the function of the phallus. Lacan stresses the proximity of the woman to the Other (and God): in the sexual relation she is 'in relation to what can be said of the unconscious, radically the Other' (*SXX*, p. 75). From this proximity, either she is the unconscious for the man, 'it is only from where the man sees her that the dear woman can have an unconscious' (*SXX*, p. 90), or, for herself, she is the term of an unconscious which is simply unspeakable, 'she has unconscious effects, but as for her unconscious . . . what can be said of it? – if not to hold with Freud that it is not to her advantage' (*SXX*, pp. 90–1). For Montrelay, the woman pulls towards the unrepresentable, towards the ruin of representation. Feminine sexuality is 'unexplorable',[63] a dark continent 'outside the circuit of the symbolic economy'[64] which the woman's *jouissance* contains and exceeds as an end of language: 'feminine *jouissance* of which nothing can be said, exceeding all meaning, contains by its very "madness" the symbolic order';[65] thus, 'to the extent that it does not know repression, femininity is the downfall of interpretation',[66] is as something of a time 'when the body and the world were confounded in one chaotic intimacy which was too present, too immediate'.[67] Lemoine-Luccioni is in general agreement but differs with regard to the consequent availability of women for analysis: femininity may be ruin and downfall of representation and interpretation yet 'the woman does hear voices, which speaks well, a tongue of gold, for psychoanalysis'.[68] Safouan finds himself able to accept Montrelay's thesis in as much as 'the woman's *jouissance* is obtained at a cheaper price, not requiring as exhaustive a liquidation of phallicism or the castration complex as in the case of the man' and indicates a 'relative ease of women in their relations to the unconscious'.[69]

The danger in all this is that it matches perfectly with the historical positions of patriarchal society in which 'woman' has been constantly identified as a locus of dis-order and women held to the forms of oppression constructed and justified in its terms (the oppression including, of course, the 'values' derived from that identification). Woman as sphinx, confronting Oedipus and the Oedipus, is never far away, the eternal feminine which menaces the subject, male and female, and to which women are constantly close. Montrelay, for example, introduces the sphinx into her inquiry as follows:

> To what does it refer, this reasoning and devouring hybrid being, which beats its wings as it talks? Why does this monster, a woman with the body of a beast, take up its place at the gates of Thebes?

> Does not the encounter with this enigmatic figure of femininity threaten every subject? Is it not she who is at the root of the ruin of representation?[70]

The line in the figure of the sphinx-woman between the posing of a question and the idea that women are the question is very thin;[71] female sexuality is dark and unexplorable, women, as Freud put it, are that half of the audience which is the enigma, the great enigma.[72] This is the problem and the difficulty – the area of debate and criticism – of Mulvey and Wollen's film *Riddles of the Sphinx*[73] where the sphinx is produced as a point of resistance that seems nevertheless to repeat, in its very terms, the relations of women made within patriarchy, their representation in the conjunction of such elements as motherhood as mystery, the unconscious, a voice that speaks far off from the past through dream or forgotten language. The film is as though poised on the edge of a politics of the unconscious, of the imagination of a politics of the unconscious ('what would the politics of the unconscious be like?')[74] with a simultaneous falling short, that politics and imagination not yet there, coming back with old definitions, the given images. It is not necessarily reactionary, finally reconfirming, to pose a connection between unconscious and women via a conception of a censored area of the feminine provided that, in so doing, the informing idea of the unconscious and its symbolic order is not a simple abstraction from the historical; to accept that unconscious, symbolic are constitutive in the determination of human subjects is not at all to regard those functions as outside of historical determinations. If a sexual reality is the condition of the symbolic, that through which the signifier comes into the world, then there is little to do, nature wins; if sexuality is always a symbolic production, then there is a place for a politics of the unconscious, for, that is, a grasp of the unconscious not as closed but as historically open, taken up in the historical process of its realizations, existing in transformation. The equation of woman and unconscious leads only to essence; the raising of questions as to the operation of an equation between the feminine and the unconscious as assignment of a place of woman and its complex effects with regard to resistance from that place within a history and economy of repression is a fully political task. It is the task engaged, for example, by the work of Irigaray (fashionably scorned *in toto* in certain analytic circles),[75] work again on that edge of *Riddles of the Sphinx*; its force the consideration of the links between current designations of the unconscious and the definition of the feminine, of the traces to be followed in those links of different logics, different economies. Of course, the edge, she risks thereby the commonplace, the return, echoingly, mirroringly, of the defined area of the feminine for the given order, of a simple inversion of values, negative to positive. But the force remains in the risk, more than the woman-and-unconscious equation for which Irigaray and *Riddles* are so often criticized and rejected, remains, for instance, in the position taken in a passage such as the following, and with importance again for the Mulvey and Wollen film:

> 'Can I sketch out something of the content of what this other uncon-scious, woman's unconscious, would be?' No, of course not, since that supposes detaching the feminine from the present economy of the unconscious. It would be to anticipate a certain historical process and check its interpretation and movement by prescribing, as from now, themes and contents to the feminine unconscious. I could say, however, that there is something that has been singularly ignored, scarcely broached, in the theory of the unconscious: *the relation of the woman to the mother and the relation of women amongst themselves.* But would this, for all that, be a sketch of the 'content' of the 'feminine' unconscious? No. It is merely a question addressed to the way in which the functioning of the unconscious is interpreted. Why are psychoanalytic theory and practice so far so poor and reductive as regards those matters? Can the latter find a better interpretation in a patriarchal-type economy and logic? In the Oedipal systematic their formulation supposes?'[76]

A further issue arising is that of a determination by the problematic situation in the symbolic of a specific relation of woman and imaginary. Irigaray herself, often effectively thematically substantializing her question of the unconscious and the feminine and indeed running the feminine back into an anatomically mimetic expression of the body, stresses the 'rejec-tion', the 'exclusion' of a feminine imaginary, a particular unfolding of woman's desire.[77] More generally, the idea of the woman's negative position in the symbolic order leads to emphasis on 'her privileged relation to the imaginary dyad, she is bound to the principle of reversibility which it contains',[78] where the imaginary is a site of reference to the pre-Oedipal bond of daughter–mother (remember Lemoine-Luccioni's focus on the doubling of woman as mother and child): 'the imaginary also contains the realm of pre-Oedipality to which the sexuality of the woman is bound . . . a repressed reference to the pre-Oedipal relation between the mother and the girl-child'.[79] In this form, the argument is in keeping with the view developed by Freud, the very term 'pre-Oedipus phase' being introduced in the context of his late considerations of female sexuality and hinging on the surprise at the importance and intensity of the original attachment of girl to mother ('our insight into this early, pre-Oedipus, phase in girls comes to us as a surprise, like the discovery in another field of the Minoan-Mycenaean civilisation behind the civilisation of Greece').[80] The modern argument takes up the differentiation of men and women in terms of the significance of the pre-Oedipal ('the phase of exclusive attachment to the mother, which may be called the pre-Oedipus phase, possesses a far greater importance in women than it can have in men; many phenomena of female sexual life which were not properly understood before can be fully explained by reference to this phase')[81] and values the latter as difference, a specificity of the woman (no value is attributed by Freud to the strength of the pre-Oedipus phase; on the contrary, a major factor in the length and circuitousness of the path to the feminine form of the Oedipus complex which is all too often not surmounted at all, it marks the woman out as in some sense unfinished, apt for regression, slightly archaic). Montrelay offers a powerful development of this argument through her conception of a feminine primary imaginary, the woman confronted always on her own body with the original enjoyment of the mother, doubled in that:

> For the woman enjoys her body as she would the body of another. Every occurrence of a sexual kind (puberty, erotic experiences, maternity, etc.) *happens* to *her* as if it came from a feminine other; every occurrence is the fascinating actualisation of *the* femininity of all women, but also and above all, of that of the mother. It is as if 'to become a woman', 'to be woman' gave access to a *jouissance* of the body as feminine *and/or* maternal. In the self-love she bears herself, the woman cannot differentiate her own body from that which was 'the first object'.[82]

What is then needed is the rediscovery, the revaluation, of that body of the imaginary:

> Can we not ask ourselves whether the imaginary, by giving 'consistency' (as Lacan puts it) to the symbolic which is a gap, is not just as operative, just as determining of the structure as are the real and the symbolic? Giving consistency, giving body to the symbolic dividing up: that operation precedes any possible grasp of the subject in its image and that of the other. A primary imaginary exists which is not without its relation with feminine *jouissance*.[83]

The movement that links feminine and imaginary and understands a specificity of and for women from there brings with it, again, problems of the foundation of difference. To define a difference on the basis of this imaginary, taken as specific value, with characteristic effects of stressed relations between woman and narcissism, regression, and so on, can seem very quickly to repeat a definition maintained in the existing order, whose own imaginary, and imagery, of the woman is heavily implicated in attributions of defining narcissism (woman and the mirror . . .). *Riddles of the Sphinx* has its difficulty here too. Mulvey indicates that she 'wanted to set up narcissism and a sense of the female as something quite strong in opposition to the Oedipus complex';[84] but then the place of the sense of the female is taken from within the terms of the given structure, a point of resistance that is also a point of oppression, and something of the accepted imaginary comes back, the old images, the room full of mirrors in which the women are shut in dreams, something of the habitual cinema returns.

The habitual cinema . . . Cinema itself is never far away, is there on the horizon. The aim is a new place, 'this side of the specular image'; but the evocation of 'her' femininity attracts all femininity 'into the brilliance of an image';[85] the order of the double is always close to an imagery, an imaging. Failing the symbolic, outside of representation, it is difficult then not to reproduce the woman as site of the specular, the enclosed reversibility of specularity, a cinema for the man and for herself; and it is not by chance that Montrelay can refer to the evidence of films: to Fellini's *Juliet of the Spirits*, for example, a film which 'brings out the presence of the "dark continent" so well'.[86] The woman stands once more in sight, in her fascinating and fascinated duality – 'I saw myself seeing myself . . . assuredly this statement has its rich and complex implications when what is in question is the theme developed in [Valéry's poem] "La Jeune Parque", the theme of femininity' (*SXI*, p. 76).[87]

Perhaps it could be added here, a little aside, that the imaginary and the specular are not, as is too commonly thought, a simple equivalence; the latter – reflections, mirrorings, imagings – is part of the former but does not exhaust it. The analytic account of the construction of the subject is not one of a simple progression from imaginary to symbolic. True, Lacan sets the imaginary very precisely in the biographical moment of the mirror stage, but that is not to make it in any sense original, primary: symbolic, real are always there; the subject is a representation of the signifier held in a structuration which is the shifting imbrication – the knotting – of real, symbolic and imaginary, the latter modelling desire in the subject's image of itself from the structure, not some separate area prior to the subject that it is given in some way to possess. If imaginary and specular are taken as equivalent, the conception of the imaginary slides easily towards such a priority, the area to be repossessed, a separate enclosure; where the need is much rather to avoid limiting the imaginary to a biographical evolution of the individual, to grasp that it is a necessary and permanent function of the history of the subject, and, simultaneously, of the subject in history. It can then no longer be a question of 'rediscovering' (nor, conversely, of 'abandoning'), but one of displacing, transforming. It might be said, to add to the addition, that the play on the equivalence/disextensiveness of specular and imaginary as regards the history of the subject is a major factor in the force of cinema's ideological effects.

The preceding addition is finally not so intrusive since the one thing that has been constantly stressed here is that if there is a way of thinking that works in the specular-imaginary, it is well and truly that of difference – the establishment of the difference of one and the other sides from the fact of the biological division of the sexes, with its consequent motion of reversal of images, from side to side, the same images. Difference in these terms is always treacherous, reactionary; a tourniquet operates in which the real necessity to claim difference binds back, and precisely from the difference claimed, into the renewal of the same, a reflection of the place assigned, assigned as difference. Patriarchy, men in its order, has never said anything but that women are – the woman is – different: they are *not men*, the difference maintained supports the status quo, the difference derived, derived ideologically, from nature, the appeal to the biological, 'undeniable'. The problem, for men as for women, is to pose specificity away from the specularity of difference; which means a critical attention to the certainties of difference, the certainty of the phallus, proposed in and from psychoanalysis itself.

V

'There is no woman but excluded by the nature of things which is the nature of words' (*SXX*, p. 68). A Howard Hawks film, *Ball of Fire*, shows a gathering of lexicographers, amongst them Gary Cooper as Bertram Potts, troubled by a night-club dancer, Barbara Stanwyck as Linda 'Sugarpuss' O'Shea: they have the words, the law of the word; she has the body, is less, falling short of their law, and more, the excess she brings. Lacan and Hawks share the same view; we are back with the analysis of the failing of woman's relation in the symbolic order.

That analysis can then suggest the possibility of a specifically feminine practice of language in writing, where writing is understood in a modern perspective as an activity of transgression, breaking with the fixed positions of language, opening out a moving tissue of meanings. The problem of difference and specificity is importantly posed here, in a way that directly engages meaning, representation and sexual division.

Some theses, arguments made:

1 The woman is more naturally a writer: since close to the mother tongue, close to creation, 'it is the woman who is more the writer, by the very fact that she creates an idiom; and the poet knows well that it is the mother tongue he speaks and no other';[88] since her excessive *jouissance* is at the expense of the phallus, the signifier, is itself writing: 'feminine *jouissance* can be understood as *writing* . . . this *jouissance* and the literary text (which is also written like an orgasm produced from within discourse) are the effect of the same murder of the signifier'.[89]

2 The woman is close to the body, the source of writing: 'it is obvious that a woman does not write like a man, because she speaks with the body; writing is of the body';[90] writing resembles the body and the sexual division of male and female is expressed in the difference of women's writing, 'a feminine textual body can be recognised by the fact that it is always without end, has no finish, which moreover is what makes the feminine text very often difficult to read'.[91]

3 The woman in language is there outside the law, the order of the

symbolic; a woman's writing thus 'jams the machinery of theory', has no place for 'the concept as such', is 'spoken, not meta-spoken', 'fluid' in style, moving towards a syntax of 'auto-affection' with 'neither subject nor object'.[92]

4 There is no specific identity of the feminine in writing: 'it is not man, woman, that one encounters, nor masculine, feminine, but difference itself, at work, in the midst of its agitations, and the changing experiences of identity: "I am no one! who are you?", asks Emily Dickinson'.[93] The notion of a feminine writing that would be the property of women poses a principle of sexual identity which the experience of writing precisely calls into question: 'It is becoming more and more difficult today, confronted by the experiments of modern art, not to question along with the identity of the subject the very principle of a sexual identity, which is nevertheless claimed by feminist movements. I do not find it easy to define a masculine or feminine specificity when I think of the great aesthetic experiences of the decentering of identity.'[94] What is at stake is a body that is radically strange, neither man nor woman.

Set out in this way, these theses lack the detail of their complex elaboration; they are sketched out simply as an indication of arguments that have been strongly developed and that raise issues of sexual differentiation in language and its practice. The first, second and third have clear links, run into one another at various points (the separation into theses here is no more than a convenience of presentation). The fourth too has its intersections with the others; the idea of writing as feminine *jouissance* indicated in the first, for example, is not necessarily mapped on to the sexual division of male and female individuals: Montrelay herself cites male-sex writers in this connection (Bataille, Jarry, Jabès), on the same grounds as those from which writing is with the woman, across men and women, not in the sense of a feminine specificity but in that of a work against existing orders:

> Faced with language, woman and writer (man or woman) are in one and the same situation. For their existence, they must force into reality a discourse that is already in submission to a functional irreality (officially called reality) . . . It remains to them to practice the forgetting of the hierarchical orders, the categories . . . Forgetting, it is exactly in that that any writer, man or woman, must become woman in order to operate.[95]

Writing is a practice of language and there is need for some consideration of the fact of the latter, consideration that comes before, must underlie, the question of specificity in the former.

The language given itself as object of study by the science of linguistics excludes the problem of sexual difference from its central systematic constructions; *langue* in Saussure, *competence* in Chomsky propose general

71

systems or logics of a language in which subject and subjectivity are not at issue. The problem of sexual difference, taken as one of variation in the language use of men and women, appears in particular branches of linguistics, most notably that of sociolinguistics. Examples of linguistic sex differentiation are noted and described that occur as systematic distinctions at the phonological, grammatical and semantic levels; distinctions, that is, are commonly to be found that are part of the language system (for example, man-*phom*, woman-*dichan* in Thai for the first person singular *I*). In other words, it is possible to distinguish within many languages male and female varieties, the 'variation' often involving central aspects of the language. It is generally considered in sociolinguistic accounts that *distinct* varieties will be found in 'technologically primitive food-gathering or nomadic communities where sex roles are much more clearly delineated';[96] a language such as English, on the contrary, will have differences that 'are generally of the smaller, less obvious and more subconscious type',[97] will have tendencies discernible in speech patterns rather than systematic differences in the language itself (for example, in London English men tend to use glottal stops in words like *butter* more than women).

It is this area in sociolinguistics that linguistic work from a feminist perspective has cut across, developed and recast, work such as that by Lakoff and Key in respect of English.[98] The notion of a relative absence of any clear sexual difference is rejected: sex roles are no less 'clearly delineated' and language is a part of that delineation and the oppression it supports, constantly making and remaking difference at the expense of women. It is thus possible, and politically necessary, to describe a 'women's language' that is the place of women's oppression, a linguistic masquerade of femininity. Note that this work is in no sense a laying claim to a specific language for women; on the contrary, the language it describes as women's language is to be fought against as a major site of sexism.

What is at stake is speech, language in discourse, a speech in which women are assigned, expected as woman, remarked as such, rather than a systematic constraint in the language: in Amazonian Cocama male and female speakers necessarily – a necessity of the language – use different pronoun series; in American English both male and female speakers can and do use modal constructions (with *could*, *might*, etc.) but the use of such constructions can also be seen, according to Lakoff and Key, as a defining tendency in the speech of women: 'females use more of these words which show indefiniteness, inconclusiveness, and uncertainty'.[99] Absent in Lakoff and Key is any idea that this difference in speech, in language use, is a positive value, that there is a difference which could provide an authentic realization of the feminine for women in the way suggested in the first three theses on writing listed above. Indeed, the characteristics given as value in those theses are echoed negatively in the descriptions of women's language proposed by Lakoff and Key, where they are grasped as the very terms of the identity of the woman defined within patriachy. It may be that 'the phallic is the seriousness of meaning'[100] (a position close to *Ball of Fire* – and to Lacan); Lakoff and Key, however, are concerned to reject not seriousness but, precisely, the discursive speci-fications of woman as inconsistent, unfinished, fluid; for them, the point is not to jam theory and refuse metalanguage but to combat the 'bilingual-ism', the additional women's language, that constrains women to being always also the woman, the difference, and thus always lacking, divided against themselves in language. From the other side, at it were, reversing the perspective, Lakoff and Key might be reproached with a certain indifference. Women's language is attacked, but towards what? Nothing is *fundamentally* changed, displaced, in the existing order. Lakoff talks of 'women's language' and 'neutral language', but that 'neutral' language can itself be regarded as an area of oppression, the alienation of difference in the order of the same of the phallus which, accepting that language, the woman then becomes: 'as soon as she speaks the discourse of the commu-nity, a woman becomes phallus';[101]

> one is born in a language and the language speaks us, dictates to us its law which is a law of death; it dictates its family model, its marital model; as soon as one is producing a sentence, as one is posing being, a question on being, ontology, one is already caught in a certain type of masculine desire that is the motor force of philosophical discourse; as soon as one asks the question 'what is it?', as soon as one asks a question, demands an answer, one is already taken up in masculine interpellation.[102]

Which comes back round to the arguments concerning a feminine speci-ficity in writing: for the woman, either silence, she silenced in the discur-sive reality, the reality of discourse, or writing as silence, her silencing – Forrester's 'forgetting' – of the orders of language, her practice of a language that is wild, on the body, unauthorized.

The woman is the ruin of representation, unrepresentable, but everywhere represented in language, speech and writing – from the theses on writing to the descriptions of Lakoff and Key, a spiral, an overlap with no join.

Caused in language, the subject, man or woman, is there divided, subject to the division, the symbolic order, in which, against which, it returns, fixing with signifiers and images its interrogation of desire, the desire of the Other; and the penis-phallus is such a fixing, such a point of return, not the foundation of the signifier, the symbolic itself. Language, symbolic, con-struction of the subject are not simply ideological (for example the signifier does not contain a meaning, be it the phallus) but neither are they simply not not simply ideological (for example, the phallus can be given to order the signifier to its meaning); there is a simultaneity of symbolic and ideology, one image for which could be that of the recto and verso of a piece of paper.[103] Like that of the man, the return of the woman, her separation from the alienation of the symbolic division, her replies to the desire of the Other, is a return according to the rules of the representations given, of the order gained over the movement of symbolic divisions, the chain of signifying elements. What is designated unrepresentable is what is finally the most strongly represented, an absence or lack named and figured as such, a real which comes back to the subject in its system, its suture of symbolic and imaginary. Lacan says something important when he stresses that 'images and symbols *in* the woman cannot be isolated from images and symbols *of* the woman . . . the representation of female sexuality conditions, repressed or not, its working . . .' (*E*, p. 728). It is not so easy to distinguish the represented and something else; what is repressed is not something unrepresentable, it is something structured, in representation (repression in the Freudian theory of the unconscious bears exactly on representations). In this sense the woman is not the ruin of representation but its veritable support in the partriarchal order, the assigned point at – on – which representation holds and makes up lack, the vanishing point on which the subject that representation represents fixes to close the division of which it is the effect; setting in place then, in the alienation–separation return, of a modelling of desire in which the woman takes the (imaginary) place of the Other, is procured as the truth of the man. What is always in question is a closure of the subject, of subjects, in a specific join – the suture – of symbolic and imaginary as field of the representation of the subject that ceaselessly holds in desire, puts it into a perspective, and the perspective above all of *man* and *woman*. Thus the massive functioning today of the eroticization of castration: the symbolic division, effect of the subject, is taken over on man and woman as difference around the penis-phallus as 'normal' fetish ('the normal proto-type of fetishes is a man's penis'),[104] which is the relation of men, women and desire in a particular economy of representation, that of disavowal, the recognition and refusal of lack; the difference of the woman is the visibility of the man, the assured perspective, the form of exchange; with woman's representing as *the* lack, *the* difference, her projection as image and screen, the point – the erotic return – of a *certain* mystery, the veil of truth ('this lack is only ever presented as reflection on a veil', *SII*, p. 261).

VI

In discussions of a specifically feminine writing, emphasis is often put on the voice: 'all the feminine texts that I have read are very close to the *voice*, are very close to the flesh of the language, much more than in masculine texts'.[105] A closeness to the voice as a trace of the intensity of the attachment to the mother: 'to write in the feminine is to put over what is cut off by the symbolic, the voice of the mother, it is to put over what is most archaic';[106] a closeness in the voice to words 'as in the first moments of life when they extended the body of the mother and simultaneously

74

circumscribed the place of suspension of her desire';[107] a voice imagined in the field of the Other as invocation of the mother, movement through words to the invocatory 'grain of the voice',[108] 'her' body in language – 'something of the circuit of drive of the voice erogenises the feminine'.[109]

The emphasis is on the voice as against the look; in women's texts, writes Montrelay, 'no contour is traced on which the eye could rest'.[110] The look is a distance, an absence of grain,[111] is 'theoretical' in Hegel's use of the term in the *Aesthetik* to privilege vision over the other senses: 'vision, on the contrary, finds itself in a purely theoretical relationship with objects, through the intermediary of light, that immaterial matter which truly leaves objects their freedom, lighting and illuminating without consuming them'.[112] Irigaray reverses the valuation in that description for women:

> Investment in the look is not privileged in women as in men. More than the other senses, the eye objectifies and masters. It sets at a distance, maintains the distance. In our culture, the predominance of the look over smell, taste, touch, hearing has brought an impoverishment of bodily relations. It has contributed to disembodying sexuality. The moment the look dominates, the body loses in materiality'.[113]

Cixous talks of 'looking with closed eyes'.[114]

> She looked very lovely under her black hair hung loose over her neck and bosom, sparkling with drops to imitate dew, and it seemed a pity that only ladies were to look at her.

> Gustave was made to kneel down on the ground in front of the sofa, and support a round mirror, before which the wilful little lady had elected to try on the silken hose and dainty boots.

These brief passages are from a work of nineteenth-century pornography (an example of the common whipping literature of the period), the author and narrator of which is given as being a woman.[115] This proposition of female author/narratorship is a convention that doubles over from and against itself in the spectacle of the book's discourse. The desire is the intimacy of the woman, the order of women, for the man, the intimacy existing only from the term of its intrusion, the male gaze; what is said is the intact beauty of the woman, all her flawless brilliance, and the absence of a look ('it seemed a pity . . .') which is thus simultaneously present, in the enunciation, the very point of the passage and the point from which it is written, the spectacle constructed. The book's scenes are, without surprise, those of the whole panoply of the male, a mixture of voyeurism and fetishism: the young Gustave, man allowed into the fiction as child in order to preserve the intimacy and the fetishistic moment, at the woman's feet, holding the mirror, the spectator and the spectacularity of the woman, the objects of disavowal and its erotic – hose, boots. No doubt that the writing is a representation-representing in which subjects are joined in the perspective of 'the man' and 'the woman' from the site – and from the sight – of the man as model of the elaboration-translation of desire; the woman author/narrator is a fiction – and had a woman been the book's writer, she would have been that fiction of the man, a term of its repeated order. All this, it might be added, is not too far from Lacan's writing of St Teresa: there is an intimacy of the woman, a certain aura, call it *jouissance*, the truth of which it is ceaselessly necessary to surprise, to catch in the veil of its images with a look that masters, preserving the certainty, 'you only have to go and look . . .'

A mixture of voyeurism and fetishism . . . the characterization of an area inevitably encountered in considering the look, in thinking of cinema.[116] Voyeurism and fetishism, clinically, are male perversions ('fetishism is found mostly in males, rarely in females', 'voyeurs, seemingly all males'),[117] and perversions that it is not too rare to find linked in the standard medical textbooks themselves with discussions of theatre and cinema, discussions which note, for example, the adverse effects of 'the exploitation of sex known as glamour'.[118]

Freud poses from early on a libidinal investment in looking to see, in seeing: 'A desire to see the organs peculiar to each sex exposed is one of the original components of our libido . . . . The libido for looking . . . is present in everyone in two forms, active and passive, male and female; and, according to the preponderance of the sexual character, one form or the other predominates.'[119] The pleasure in looking is in relation to knowledge which makes use of it, the looking to see, to know the other body. It was emphasized earlier how important to Freud is the appeal to the look to establish castration: boy and girl *see* the lack.

In this context, the following points may be noted:

1 Seeing for Freud is 'an activity that ultimately is derived from touching',[120] which it thus extends and displaces.
2 The eye as organ is the locus of at least two functions: 'the eyes perceive not only alterations in the external world which are important for the preservation of life, but also characteristics of objects which lead to their being chosen as objects of love – their charms'.[121] There are more or less serious disturbances if the two functions are not held together in unity and the sexual aspect begins to dominate; Freud notes in this connection 'pathological consequences if the two fundamental instincts are disunited and if the ego maintains a repression of the sexual component instinct concerned . . . the sexual component instinct which makes use of looking – sexual pleasure in looking – has drawn upon itself defensive action by the ego instincts in consequence of its excessive demands.'[122] The classic example of such psychogenic disturbance of vision is provided by the 'blindness' often found in hysterics but Freud is at pains to

stress equally the common experience of this 'blindness of the seeing eye'.[123]

3 The common experience is had by men and women. The fact of the importance of that experience, at its extreme, in hysteria, in the case of the women who alone furnish the material for the *Studies on Hysteria*, links it as much with the latter as with the former. Yet it is not by chance that Freud's major illustration for the disturbance caused by the conflict of sexual and ego in vision is the story of Peeping Tom, the active scopophilia (pleasure in seeing) of voyeurism:

> As regards the eye, we are in the habit of translating the obscure psychical processes concerned in the repression of sexual scopophilia and in the development of the psychogenic disturbance of vision as though a punishing voice was speaking from within the subject and saying: 'Because you sought to misuse your organ of sight for evil sensual pleasures, it is fitting that you should not see anything at all any more', and as though it was in this way approving the outcome of the process. The idea of talion punishment is involved in this, and in fact our explanation of psychogenic disturbance of vision coincides with what is suggested by myths and legends. The beautiful legend of Lady Godiva tells how all the town's inhabitants hid behind their shuttered windows, so as to make easier the lady's task of riding naked through the streets in broad daylight, and how the only man who peeped through the shutters at her revealed loveliness was punished by going blind.[124]

Not by chance, because Freud's constant emphasis elsewhere is on libidinal investment in the eye as phallus, which is what is at stake in the Lady Godiva/Peeping Tom legend: the scene of the woman, the violation, the blinding-castration. As Freud puts it in the essay on 'The Uncanny', which is perhaps the most important reference for this emphasis, 'the substitutive relation between the eye and the male organ . . . is seen to exist in dreams and myths and phantasies'.[125] One might cite, as a kind of condensation here, the recorded case of a male patient who identified his eye with a speculum and was then racked with the fear of his look becoming 'stuck' on things and his losing his sight.[126]

4 Lacan has it that the scopic drive is 'that which most completely eludes the term of castration', referring at the same time to Freud's paper on 'Instincts and Their Vicissitudes' (*SXI*, p. 4).[127] In that paper, written just after the one introducing narcissism,[128] Freud identifies an initial auto-erotic element in scopophilia, not formulated in the description quoted earlier from 'Jokes and Their Relation to the Unconscious', which distinguishes it from other drives: 'for the beginning of its activity the scopophilic instinct is auto-erotic: it has indeed an object, but that object is the subject's own body'.[129] This is the context of the imbrication of specular and imaginary and of the importance of the mirror stage; the

perceived image of the body gives the principle of unity, the one, identity – an identity that can never be other than that imaginary, in which, through the look, castration can be eluded, held off.

5 The imaginary can then be taken as 'before' sexual difference since, precisely, it identifies, is elusion, proposes the one for the subject. Yet the symbolic, division, is always there, and, for example, in the mirror stage in the surrounds of the child who sees, the person who holds, encourages, confirms, but also accompanies from the place of otherness. The scopic drive may elude the term of castration but the look returns the other, castration, the other – the evil – eye. Hence Lacan's long account of the dialectic of eye and look. The look presents itself to us in an uncanny contingence, symbolic of 'the lack that constitutes castration anxiety' (*SXI*, p. 70):[130] your look is never from where I see, my look is never what I want to see. In this dialectic, however, the look is constantly evanescent, elided in the self-turning power of the investment in the eye, in seeing, in the constitution of the imaginary, in 'that form of vision that is satisfied with itself in imagining itself as consciousness' (*SXI*, p. 71),[131] consciousness in its illusion 'of *seeing itself seeing itself*, in which the look is elided' (*SXI*, p. 79).[132] The world is given itself as spectacle by the subject, as vision, something like a pure consciousness, at rest, indifferent, all seeing (with the ambiguity there the catch of the subject in the imaginary): 'The world is omnivoyeur, not exhibitionistic – it does not provoke our look. When it does begin to provoke it, then begins too the feeling of strangeness' (*SXI*, pp. 71–2).[133] Note that Lacan compares this all-seeingness to 'the satisfaction of a woman who knows that she is being looked at, on condition that she is not shown it' (*SXI*, p. 71).[134]

The comparison is significant. Throughout the discussion of the eye/look dialectic, Lacan indicates no sexual differentiation as between male and female or masculine and feminine, yet such a differentiation is not absent, the comparison is its trace.

The eye/look dialectic functions as division, symbolizes lack, sets the subject in the field of the desire of the Other, with the imaginary of the eye, the evanescence of the look, then defined as the eluding of the term of castration. Which term is that of the articulation of symbolic and sexual difference. The imaginary is never 'before', it is always from, from the symbolic construction of the subject, is a join of the subject, its identifications of desire. The difficulty in the theory is that castration is the term both of the division of the subject in the movement of symbolic difference and of a sexual difference that differentiates individual subjects as between male and female; it crosses, in other words, from universal function to effective realization without doubt, with the latter thus becoming the constant form of the former and, in fact, its nature – we are back with

Freud's 'inadequate empirical and conventional equation', Lacan's 'through sexual reality that the signifier came into the world'.

The castration that is posed and eluded in the shifts of the eye/look dialectic is a relation of the symbolic in a specific production of sexual difference. The difference is specific in Lacan's account which pulls towards a voycurism that is its underlying order: the dialectic is also, immediately, the look of the man, the image of the woman, 'the satisfaction of a woman who knows she is being looked at'. Everything turns on the castration complex and the central phallus, its visibility and the spectacle of lack; the subject, as Lacan puts it at one point, 'looks at itself in its sexual member' (*SXI*, p. 177)[135] and delights in being seen from that look. What the voyeur seeks, poses, is not the phallus on the body of the other but its absence as the definition of the mastering presence, the security, of his position, his seeing, his phallus (Peeping Tom behind the shutters, penetrating the space of the other, holding its image . . .); the desire is for the Other to be spectacle not subject, or only the subject of that same desire, its exact echo – the echo that Lacan hears to *his* satisfaction when he talks of that 'satisfaction of a woman who knows she is being looked at'. Fetishism too, which often involves the scopophilic drive, has its scenario of the spectacle of castration; and where what is at stake is not to assert that the woman has the penis-phallus but to believe in the intact, to hold that the woman is not castrated, that nothing is lost, that his representation, and of him, works. Always, from voyeurism to fetishism, the eroticization of castration.

'*The* woman' is the support of this eroticization, the whole scene of the phallus, *is* representation. There is a painting by Magritte that is clear in this respect (clear not from any certainty to be seen but from the elements it assembles as a statement on that very certainty). Entitled *Representation* (*La représentation*, 1937, Penrose Collection, London), it shows the frame of a mirror in the form of a keyhole, with, on the surface of the mirror, filling its frame, the keyhole, the torso of a nude woman, with the line of the thighs in a perfect discretion of any sex. The woman is to be seen, completely, she is all seeing, satisfied in that, always there in the mirror, hidden and visible, behind the keyhole; which is to say that, omnivoyeur, spectacle of vision, she has no look, provokes only in image and not as subject in return; and, above all, no look of her sex. The discretion of the sex in the Magritte painting is an important element in its statement on representation. The history of the nude in western art from classical times is one of the omission of a sex for the woman (where the penis is figured readily on any statue of the nude man): what is thus presented in her representation is not any lack, not the lack, but nothing, the fully intact, the body smooth without break, the scopophilic defence of 'beauty'.[136] For beauty is exactly *the* woman as *all*, undivided in herself, the perfect image. 'Like a god, just as empty, beauty can say only: *I am as I am*',[137] and, within the *I am as I am*, the *I saw myself seeing myself* which Lacan regards as the 'theme' of 'femininity': the contained spectacle, for me, the man, and, as my desire, the support of my representation, for herself.

Here, a problem can be posed as follows:[138] agreed, the terms of representation classically are those of the production and representing of woman as all, beauty to see, the woman; it is nevertheless the case that the coming of the photograph changes something: something that can be grasped, for example, in developments in social pornography (pornography of wide and open distribution in society, for example *Penthouse*) where what are now given are directly vaginal images.[139] That there is change is certain; as to the transformation of the economy of representation, the question is more difficult.

By its weight of reality ('record', 'reproduction'), the photograph disturbs the established order of art and beauty; hence a kind of balance of tensions in its immediate practice and conception: the photograph is too real, obliterates beauty, is thus not fitted for the depiction of the body (Nadar, for instance, disapproves of the use of photography for the nude); the photograph because of that real is to be directly exploited as a commerce of the body seen, as the possession of its actuality in image (a police raid on just one specialist London photographer in 1874 allows the seizure of some 130,248 obscene photographs plus 5,000 stereoscopic slides).[140] Obviously, that commerce is not without its relations to the established representations of art: various sublimations of the photographic real of the body through strategies of focus, lighting, retouching, and so on; various 'reframings', realignments to the same attention, as with the massive speculation on the photograph of the nude girl-child, the female-not-a-sexed-woman, before 'stream and river meet'.[141] It remains, however, that the photograph is not the painting; it points to a real as an immediate – as an immediately visible – source of its image, says somewhere an actuality of a body, a once-present here-now. In the painting or sculpture, the sex of the woman is not 'hidden', there is nothing 'not seen'; the photograph, posing the woman discretely, reproduces perhaps the same figure as of the nude in art but brings with it a certain effect of the withheld, the out-of-sight. The completely satisfiable curiosity of the real that is the photograph's view, its ideological currency, is inevitably the compulsion to 'show everything', to 'really present' the sex of the woman, women's sexual organs (it then being, in a mirror reversal from classic representation in the history of art, the depiction of the male sex that is problematic, that lags behind, only very recently a possibility for social pornography – as though the penis-phallus hold might be threatened).

And yet . . . and yet the real of the photograph is a real that is always an image; the veil, the completion of representation, persists, a whole imaginary of the body's presence. The real of the body, the body now in its symbolic relation in the process of the individual as subject, is discordant, takes voice from the unconscious ('as though, precisely, it was not from the unconscious that the body had voice')[142] not from the photograph, which is always in a sense concordant, making an image. The photograph can only show and can never show the woman's sex, 'her' sexuality retained as exhibition. Something changes but the economy remains more or less stable, still of the order of phallic castration. One, the man, perhaps the woman in place in his perspective, is assured of the sex of the woman, as of his own thereby (the look as phallus); assured again and again, since the unit here is not the possible knowledge of a single photograph but the continual confirmation of the series, the exhaustion of all women, the guarantee of *the* woman, in this image. Pornography plays exactly the series: the resumption from scene to scene, film to film, from one photograph to the next, one magazine issue to another; according to a kind of metonymization of the imaginary, the finite number standing open for the total number of women which would make the final *one*. At any moment, moreover, the confirmation can never be sure, since its only basis is in the movement of the accountability for vision, an interminable summing; the photographer Henri Maccheroni takes 2,000 photographs of one woman's sex, envisages a further set. . . .[143] No truth is produced with the multiplication of such photographs other than that the woman is the difference of the man who is reassured in his place, compulsively reposing the fact of his certainty, his vision: sex and sexuality are brought back to the sex, woman is her sex, the phallic stakes are won over and over.

What then of the look for the woman, of woman subjects in seeing? The reply given by psychoanalysis is from the phallus. If the woman looks, the spectacle provokes, castration is in the air, the Medusa's head not far off; thus, she must not look, is absorbed herself on the side of the seen, seeing herself seeing herself, Lacan's femininity. By virtue of the doubling unity of her specular relation to the mother, parent of the same sex, the woman is specified as being in a particular, different relation to the scopic function, to pleasure in seeing:

> For the girl, the setting at a distance is a difficult experience. She prefers to tip over into the image guaranteed for her (as she believes) by the quite as captive look of the mother and, later, by the all powerful look of the father. So she prefers to believe in that image. She believes she is herself. She thus equates herself with the full and flawless figure, no crack, which preserves and is preserved by the parental authority. In so doing, she substitutes for the person of the mother crucial in the *fort/da* game her own person figured by her body in the specular image; an image that the mother's look brings out, 'causes'. It is an inverted *fort/da*, and it is the whole body which becomes the stake of symbolisation, with the consequent risks of fragmentation and hysterical paralyses. But in thus offering herself to

the look, in giving herself for sight, according to the sequence: see, see oneself, give oneself to be seen, be seen, the girl – unless she falls into the complete alienation of the hysteric – provokes the Other to an encounter and a reply which give her pleasure.[144]

VII

Cinema then, and, to start, the question of its seeing, its look. It is commonly said that cinema is voyeurist, a statement which can go from the simple idea that there is a pleasure of seeing involved in the experience of films to the argument made by Laura Mulvey to the effect that visual pleasure in narrative cinema is a structure of voyeurism which is oppressive in its relation of women and which must thus be challenged quite radically – what is needed is the destruction of the visual pleasure of the narrative fiction film, of film's dependence on voyeuristic active/passive mechanisms. Along the line of that statement can be found positions which, from a perspective of feminist film criticism and practice, nevertheless argue a use rather than a destruction of cinema's voyeurism; Claire Johnston, for example, writes that: 'voyeuristic pleasure itself cannot be eliminated from the cinema; indeed, it is vital for the cinema's survival and its development as a political weapon'.[145]

In several essays, Metz has attempted to characterize a specific regime of voyeurism that is a function of the cinema machine, the institution of cinema as signifier. Cinema's voyeurism is unilateral: what is seen does not know it is being seen, is present in its absence, the spectator is thus not constrained to any knowledge of he or she as voyeur, the experience is that of a 'surprise' of vision, figures and objects as though surprised by the spectator's look. The primary identification of the spectator, moreover, is with him or herself as a pure '*voyance*', a pure act of seeing, a conscious-ness set up – untroubled – for spectacle.[146]

The characterization seems to pose an instance of the spectator in the machine outside of any problem of sexual difference, a total *voyance*, and to relay that instance with regard to what is seen in terms that pull towards such a problem, the spectator as *voyeur*. It is, after all, difficult to intro-duce voyeurism into the discussion without engaging its definition of a look that is male and phallic. Metz is not far from the 'quasi obscenity of seeing' in cinema noted by Bazin, the keyhole aspect, the impression of a violation of space:[147] the spectator who looks from the comfort of the dark on to the illuminated scene of the bodies moving on screen – just like Peeping Tom in Freud's description, with the single and vital exception that here the seeing is allowed, the intrusion and its pleasure permitted, unpunished, no division only images, the spectator's images, images *for*.

In fact, Metz links cinematic scopophilia particularly to the primal scene: 'It is never my partner I see but a photograph of my partner. I am still a voyeur but according to a different regime: that of the primal scene and the keyhole';[148] 'the cinema retains something of the peculiar prohibited character of the vision of the primal scene – the latter is always surprised, never contemplated at leisure.'[149] Agreed, but then the 'surprise' here is evidently the term of a controlled repetition, cinema as something of the fabrication of a *wanted* primal scene, a constant presence for the subject at its leisure, seeing knowing, outside anguish, deferment, a definitive answer in the seen. Which is simply to stress again cinema as the establishment – the institution – of the security of the look: the image holds and the eye is smoothed over castration, images for me, my representations, mine; the privilege of the subject in that 'bipolar reflexive relation by which, as soon as I perceive, my representations belong to me' (*SXI*, p. 76).[150]

'The film is not exhibitionist. I look at it, but it does not look at me looking at it. It knows what I am doing, but it does not want to know.'[151] Thus the film, remember Lacan, is like the world, not exhibitionist but omnivoyeur, all seeing, a showing, a giving for sight, a kind of here-see (film as spectacle of the world, reproduction of life). Lacan talks of an 'appetite of the eye' (*SXI*, p. 105)[152] that the production of images – his specific example is painting – serves to feed, an appetite that is the force of the subject's desire in the dialectic of eye and look mentioned earlier. The subject seeing through the keyhole is the subject as 'hidden look entirely' (*SXI*, p. 166),[153] maintained in the totality of the seen scene, its mastery. For the eye of that seen scene, the look itself is an object for sight and a site of desire: of desire of the Other, something which substitutes for the Other in the form of the cause of desire, and desire in the Other, a look imagined as the desire of the Other in which the subject can identify against the strangeness, the castration, of the Other's look in the dialectic. From the desire of the Other to desire in the Other, a certain 'descent of desire' to the effect of a 'giving to be seen' (*SXI*, p. 105),[154] the subject is confirmed in its own eyes, produced as unity – as certainty – of vision; and that descent, that confirmation, is the function of picture or film, of the subject's representation in image: 'it is to this register of the eye as made desperate by the look that we must go if we are to grasp the calming, civilising and fascinating power of the function of the picture' (*SXI*, p. 106).[155]

The statement that the film is not exhibitionist, moreover, brings with it not just the echo of Lacan's similar description of the world for the subject but equally that of the comparison he then immediately makes with the satisfaction of the woman who knows she is being looked at while preserving the negation of the knowledge of the fact of that looking. And there is a rightness about this sudden echoing join of film and world and woman, the woman who is the omnipresent centre of film's world in the institution of cinema, who is the real spectacle, the place where the look – the desire of the Other – is to be finally held and elided. Elided not by denying difference but by containing difference in her image, the good image of the woman, the difference of the phallus (which is what is at stake for voyeur or fetishist). Once again Lacan's reference to the Bernini statue has its exemplariness: the certain vision of the woman, the certainty in the image, the spectator's gaze carried by the angelic figure looking down on the swooning Teresa, her eyes – the woman's – closing, her look – any return of difference against the difference – absent, foreclosed.

In an interview, Chantal Akerman talks of a non-voyeuristic camera in her film *Jeanne Dielman, 23 Quai du Commerce, 1080 Bruxelles* ('But the camera was not voyeuristic in the commercial way because you always knew where I was. You know, it wasn't shot through the keyhole')[156] and stresses at the same time the importance for her work of pleasure in seeing, '*la jouissance du voir*' ('When I saw *Hotel Monterey* again this morning, I really thought it was an erotic film. I felt that way – *la jouissance du voir.*')[157]

Pleasure in seeing, *la jouissance du voir*, Freud's *Schaulust*. The question is as to the possibility of a relation of that pleasure other than in terms of voyeurism (Lacan, while retaining the scopic drive as independent of its relation as the place of the subject in perversion, nevertheless states at once that *Schaulust* is manifested in the latter and moves immediately to discussion of voyeurism, *SXI*, pp. 165–7).[158] Mulvey's call for the destruction of visual pleasure leaves the question open inasmuch as it concerns the visual pleasure of 'narrative cinema', 'traditional film form', perhaps avoids it – but to pose it elsewhere in her and Wollen's films – inasmuch as the informing conception of an alternative practice is from the standpoint of that call, that destruction:

> The first blow against the monolithic accumulation of traditional film conventions (already undertaken by radical filmmakers) is to free the look of the camera into its materiality in time and space and the look of the audience into dialectics, passionate detachment. There is no doubt that this destroys the satisfaction, pleasure and privilege of the 'invisible guest', and highlights how film has depended on voyeuristic active/passive mechanisms.[159]

Akerman could argue her non-voyeuristic camera in line with this conception: the control, her implication, knowing where she was, is given precisely as a refusal to recreate the 'invisible guest', the privilege of a subject produced as undifferentiated unity of vision, in the security of its own sight. What becomes urgent is the dissociation of the bind of relaying looks (of spectator, camera, character) that is the force and the pleasure of cinema in its fundamental ideological and commercial development, the fiction film. That dissociation, however, is a very difficult problem of representation, of the differentiation of the discursive relations of the subject. The bind of looks is a specific representation, a position and an

84

image, but that specificity is not a simple choice; in a sense, indeed, 'specific' here should be taken as a limitation *from* representation, not *on* it, the bind is a construction of the difference that is the determining point of the very institution of the bind, the establishment of its whole machinery, its elements. The bind may be loosened, the terms of representation remain – and, for example, the look. Is it possible for a woman to take place in a film without representing a male desire?[160]

'Taking place' there refers both to position and image, producing a film as maker or spectator and produced in a film as instance of its scene. The fiction film has massively excluded women as makers, envisaged them as spectators through genre definitions (the woman's film, melodrama, etc.), and held them endlessly in its binding play of looks, its imaging and imaginary of the woman, the final purpose of the bind. Women return only as resistance to and from the place thus assigned, their image as sign of the difference and guarantee of its order; a resistance recognized, for example, and to cite three very different films, in the critique or bafflement of the voyeuristic situation in Dorothy Arzner's *Dance, Girl, Dance*, Stephanie Rothman's *The Working Girls*, Jackie Raynal's *Deux fois*.[161] Which resistance, however, can still itself be questioned at the point of its limits, those of the cinema within which it operates and is defined, the voyeurism it repeats as the grounds of its struggle; one implication of such a questioning then being that any image of a woman in a film, by the fact of its engagement in a process of representation that brings with it, as preconstruction, the significance of the showing of the woman as difference, her representing (a significance, a representing, to which cinema in its institution is historically committed), inevitably re-encloses women in a structure of cultural oppression that functions precisely by the currency of 'images of women'. The problem, as noted above, is always the difficult one of representation; a problem not of something outside representation to be added or substituted simply, but much rather of the constantly actual completeness of representation that grasps and redetermines in its lines of exchange, and from the outset, any alternative economy. The image is at once a position, and the effective work of resistance is first and foremost, the emphasis of Akerman and Mulvey, a matter of the transformation of the relations of subjectivity in the production of the enunciation, the movement against the single unity of the subject, the confirmation of the difference. Akerman in *News from Home* gives something of this: a visibility of control as a certain demonstration of the hazard of the personal ('where I was'); a join but apart of image and soundtracks and a constant margin of rhythm; a non-appropriation of looks in a relaying fiction; a question of a woman in the discourse of the Other that finds many of the places, the topics, important earlier here (Akerman's voice reading letters from her mother, the singular everyday of family romance); a question of an image in its impossibility (the reverse shot image of the looker missing in the film, Akerman as image, this the woman, nowhere represented, other than as the fantasy of the mother receiving a photograph on the soundtrack, 'so glad to see how you look now', the problem of 'you', of identity and identification, and for the spectator), the production of a woman in opposition to the position, the produced, of the image; another differencing regarded in the movement of maker and spectator in the film.

A recent article on 'The Avant-garde and its imaginary' was ended by its author, Constance Penley, as follows: 'If filmic practice, like the fetishistic ritual, is an inscription of the look on the body of the mother, we must now begin to consider the possibilities and consequences of the mother returning the look.'[162] To which Peter Gidal, whose writings towards definition of a 'structural/materialist' film practice had been a major focus of discussion, replied: 'The last words of your piece say it all. You search for the simple inversion, the *mother looking back*. I consider the possibilities of the not-mother, not-father (looking or not).'[163]

The exchange seems to crystallize much of what is most importantly at stake. To invert, the mother returning the look, is not radically to transform, is to return as well the same economy, the same dialectic of phallic castration, the same imaginary (and cinema in the fiction film has always and exactly been concerned to consider the possibilities and consequences within the fetishistic ritual, including the *constitutive* threat of its endangerment, the play of eye and look, vision and lack); the difference inverted is also the difference maintained. It might be said, moreover, that many of the films supported by the *Camera Obscura* collective in which Penley works themselves seem quite contrary to such notions of return and inversion; thus *News from Home*, shown and discussed by the collective in London,[164] is caught up in a problematic of a woman subject of desire divided in the symbolic, not of the mother looking back, which latter is indeed a very specific site of the film's struggle, of its struggle in representation. Here, however, crossing the sides of the exchange, is the limit of Gidal's reply. To point to the complicities of the simple inversion cannot be allowed to justify the argument of a wish for a practice somehow freed from any representing signifier – in the sense in which Lacan can say that 'men, women and children are only signifiers' (*SXX*, p. 34), in the sense in which in *News from Home* identity is posed immediately as a question of symbolic production, of discursive reality in the terms of which men and women have their existence as men and women, are represented as such, those terms including the specific history and practice and effects of cinema ('looking or not' then far from being a matter of indifference). There is no abstract managing without representation and its forms of representing, only a struggle in and across representation and representings as, every time, a specific historical demonstration and transformation of identity, difference, the process of their order, the given relations of subjectivity. In that struggle, returns, inversions *may* have their particular necessity in certain concrete instances of the demonstration-transformation; in respect, for example, of sexual differentiation which cannot be collapsed into a singularity of viewer and film, the event of their passage together, other than as avoidance of the issue – the reproduction, that is, of the existing status quo in so far as it can encompass the individual, the variation, a differentiation that is operated outside of direct challenge to the founding difference of the representation of subjects, men and women.

'We do not know the look of the woman.'[165] But could we ever in these terms? We find ourselves in a social representing of desire determined by and redetermining a structure of division – the social and economic distinction of male/female, man/woman – and oppression on the basis of that distinction – the difference assigned and confirmed in representation serving to justify and resolve the contradictions of the oppression. Specifically, the subject relations of vision are realized – realized and sustained in representation by institutions, machines, such as cinema – in function of the establishment of sexual differentiation as the difference and of difference as the differentiation of sexes, as a representing and placing of woman to man and vice versa according to the values of seeing/being seen, active/passive, 'male'/'female'. The humanist gesture is to appeal to an unknown 'look of the woman' to be given expression, the political – as in Mulvey – is to analyse the fact of 'look' and 'woman' in the structure of its definition and to appeal to the necessity to work to end that structure and the location of man/woman it operates. Yet it is clear, except in some realm of the theoretical abstracting of contradiction, conjuncture, historical multiplicity, that that necessity can coexist with and contain within it strategies implying the aim of constructing the look of the woman, the attempt to distinguish positively feminine elements in particular film practices, the posing of the question of visual pleasure from there. As in *Riddles of the Sphinx*, the risk of essence may have to be taken – certainly those not women have everything to learn from that process.

In his *Histoire de la révolution française*, Michelet describes the preparations for the Festival of Reason, the *Fête de la Raison*, held on 10 November 1793, the figure of Reason eventually to be played by a woman: 'The 7th still, the wish was for a statue. It was objected that a fixed image might recall the Virgin Mary and give rise to a new idolatry. A moving image was preferred, animated and living, which, changed from festival to festival, could not become an object of superstition.'[166]

Traditionally, the problem of cinema has been the reverse of that Festival of Reason, the project of its films the fixing of the image, the woman, a suspended scenario of phallic desire, at the same time that they move, shift, displace images. Hence the balancing act that is the perform-

87

ance of those films: the image, the images in movement, the narrative as the join of the one and the other, the join of the spectator to the film, the locus of difference and its regulation. The narrative is the film's superstition, the production of the film as object in its image.

A film is always, however, and this is the need for the balancing out, fully symbolic, is not given in the imaginary which, on the contrary, it must construct, including the imaginary of the cinematic institution that it has to reproduce. In this context, one can understand the imaginary of the woman as lost and found in a film: the imaginary is there, the film's point of reference, but lost, the film's desire, its symbolic process and recovery. The suspended scenario is so often *visibly* a moment of spectacle, the masquerade laid out, known as 'cinema' (the scenes of Lisa-Joan Fontaine modelling dresses in *Letter from an Unknown Woman*); a moment in that movement of the film in which the image is constantly caught up, disturbed in its fiction, its fixity, potentially troubled by the woman as a woman (for which she is punished: Susan-Janet Leigh in *Touch of Evil* is object of male spectacle and exchange but also resistance to be eliminated). It is as though the fiction film of the dominant cinema knows the imaginary of its image of the woman at the same time that it seeks to reconfirm it, with the narrative the arena of that knowledge and the tactic of its containment as coherently as possible. Not much has changed today: the woman's body is displayed, the 'obligatory' nudity, and the narrative allows a certain action of a woman in order to keep her in image, the same image (*Coma* is a striking recent example). Not much has changed but something nevertheless, the pressure on the image of the woman that has made the production of images of women in the interests of the restabilization of that image the major preoccupation of current dominant cinema (*Coma, Three Women, The Turning Point, Julia, The Goodbye Girl* – the list is extensive and continuing); something new, the impact of the Women's Movement ('impact' is exactly the term of the cultural reception), that must be assumed and put back in place (hence the strategies of a film like *Coma*: produce a strong woman's image in one emphasis of the narrative in order to weaken it and bring her back into line: she refuses to fix him a beer but to allow the film to fix her in the shower; she leaves but, alone, her hand stretches out too late to the ringing phone in a pathetically held shot; and so on, a constant admission and erasure; and anyway always a bind of images, the woman there, a whole cinema). It is not ideologically by chance, moreover, that the pressure on the image of the woman is simultaneous with the social spread of an available pornography. At all costs sexuality must be maintained between, as the separation of, men and women and the woman produced as the difference, the *other*, the other *sex*. The habitual claimed response of men to pornographic films, that they are 'boring', is absolutely correct (not just a defensive denial of personal involvement): their regime, as noted, is that of a perpetual repetition, once and once more and once more again, a ceaseless verification, the truth of the image – my sex exists

and the woman is different and is her sex, the difference, my representation. And that representation of the pornographic film is not far from the
ever renewed once-upon-a-time of Hollywood narrative from film to film,
the primal scene of the institution of cinema, the keyhole, the quasi-
obscenity of seeing, and so on. The machine must represent – a prime
factor of its ideological and commercial exploitation together – and the
variations of its representing are held to the effect of that imperative.

Which is why the struggle is there, in and on representation, a constant
attention to the contemporary *history* of the subject, why the radically new
is not elsewhere, absent, unknown, but is in that struggle itself, the
transformation of that contemporary history, of the relations of men and
women as subjects of the difference in which, exactly, they are represented
and from which, exactly again, representation works.

VIII

For my cinema . . . the most suitable word is *phenomenological*: it is
always a succession of events, of little actions which are described in a
precise manner. And what interests me is just this relation to the
immediate look, with the how you look at these little actions going
on. And it is also a relation to strangeness.[167]

I *do* think it's a feminist film because I give space to things which were
never, almost never, shown in that way, like the daily gestures of a
woman. They are the lowest in the hierarchy of film images . . . But
more than the content, it's because of the style. If you choose to show
a woman's gestures so precisely, it's because you love them. In some
way you recognise those gestures that have always been denied and
ignored.[168]

But I indeed believe (even if we are not there yet, it's important to
say it, to know it) that if we manage to become really decolonised,
there can be a language that is women's, which is not moreover the
same for all women. There are things that are quite stupid: for
example, I am often asked why I set my camera so low. It's probably
linked to my size, quite simply, at what level and from what point of
view I look at things.[169]

It's really a hard problem to try to say what differentiates a woman's
rhythm in film because a man can use these same forms of expression
. . . We speak of 'women's rhythm', but it isn't necessarily the same
for all women. I also think that Hollywood doesn't express a man's

rhythm either, but the rhythm of capitalism or fascism. Men are cheated by it too.[170]

Passages quoted from interviews on her work given by Chantal Akerman, brought together for the importance here of the simple complexity – the *fineness* – of their commitment.

IX

If hysterics suffer from reminiscences,[171] the fiction film suffers from its reminiscence of the woman, its problem of memory, the memory it seeks to control, again and again. Women in their representation to men, for men, are the support of an economy which at the same time they trouble in the very difference they must represent. Hence the need to remember the place of the woman; hence the resistance that women produce in this economy, even from there ('an element of female resistance, if only a passive one, has always contributed to artistic production').[172]

Another way of putting it: 'the psychoanalytic fact of the sexual difference of woman (the "lack", the fact of castration) is a nodal point in the structuration of classical narrative.'[173] Exactly, this is the problem of that narrative, the problem belonging to it, that is in its possession. The lack, the psychoanalytic fact of the sexual difference of woman, *works*, works for its representation. Which is not then to say that women are the unrepresentable – precisely the position of all this working, the assignment of the lack, the definition of the woman – but that the struggle is for another function and functioning of representation, that struggle being the resistance that women are in this order.

'Resistance is the current state of an interpretation of the subject' (*SII*, p. 266). The narrative film has tried always to *complete* an interpretation of the subject (the image, the identity, it proposes, the reading of the spectator it maintains), resisting resistance as best it can, its best being the constant image, and of the woman.

One way of understanding what can be grasped as 'of women', against the image, is in terms of a negativity, a not-that, a process of disinterpretation: 'a woman's practice can only be negative with respect to what exists, saying "it's not that" and "it's not yet" '.[174] (But then the negativity has in turn to be understood as struggle and transformation, not allowed to pull back towards condition and essence – 'negative'/'positive', always the terms of the difference.)

The sex of the 'author' of a film (book, painting, etc.) cannot be confused with that negativity, with its effective operation (which is not to fail to recognize that the question of the sex is fundamental economically, socially, that there is the constant need to fight for the opening of the cultural production of meanings to women); nor can it be confused with the sexuality a film inscribes, the resistances it provokes (which is not to fail to recognize that it is the productions of women that now most challenge the given inscriptions). What is at stake is never the immediacy of a meaning directly expressed from a sex but always the terrain of representation and representing in which meanings are formed and instituted, offered and possessed, in which 'man' and 'woman', 'male' and 'female', 'masculine' and 'feminine' are defined, implicated.

Nothing in a film's organization of sounds and images will allow it to be specified as *necessarily* having been made by a woman (by women) or by a man (by men); it is impossible, that is, to specify marks of cinematic enunciation that could *only* appear in films made by women or by men, that are *essentially* of a woman or of a man (this is the difficulty of the question that often occurs in debates: how can we know *from the film* that it is made by a woman or a man?). What one has is always a structure of representation in and from the terms of which positions, enunciations can be engaged, specified as 'masculine', 'feminine', with the possibility of reappropriating the latter as site of resistance to the domination, the definitions, the assignments of the former. (This is difficult, uneasy: when I see Carola Klein's *Mirror Phase*, for example, I do know from the film that it is made by a woman, the filmmaker's voice comments the film in the first person on the soundtrack, she is identified as present in some of the shots; but I cannot point to anything in the production of the sounds and images, in the film's discursive organization, that means it could not have been made by a man and the specification of the filmmaker as a woman in the film could be a fiction; but yet in some way I do know it to be by a woman; but yet that knowing might be my implication in a reactionary identification of women with certain contents, certain themes; but yet again . . . and so on.)

Films by women cannot be pushed together in a simple equivalence, nor can those by men. To do so seems finally to deny difference, to come back to the function of the difference. The assumption of 'feminist' by the dominant ideology as a term of equivalence and containment might be one indication of this: the political and ideological force of feminism is countered as far as possible by its reduction to a 'sphere of women' with, behind that, a return of the expression of the woman. The term 'sexist' can go the same way: given as the behaviour of men, thence of the man, it serves to assert an inevitable failing and to confuse, defensively, issues of the relations of individual and social and of their effective transformation ('all men are sexist' is men's perfect excuse).

The representation of sexuality – 'masculine', 'feminine' – is one of the most dangerous operations of equivalence (in which psychoanalysis has played and plays its part), and it is no surprise that such representation should be the great problem, the great affair, of dominant cinema today (with its 'new sexuality'). An urgent question for any alternative practice is thus how *not* to contribute to this representation, how not to valorize its terms of identity and identification.

91

A crucial question underlying the last, that of the modes of possession, of ownership, of appropriation of images and sounds – in short, of the political problems of representation.[175]

X

Cinema divides not in any immediate sense on men and women but on the positions and relations of meaning of 'man' and 'woman' in its representations and its production of those representations, the subjectivity – the history of the subject – it engages. From that emphasis, it is possible to take up in return something of the difficulties involved in developing an adequate understanding of the effective conjuncture of a film in cinema with the practice and experience of specific individuals and groups including groupings according to a primary distinction by sex as male or female.

Debate around particular films often stumbles over the issue of effectivity, 'the real effect of a film', deadlocks on notions of – on a choice between – either 'the text itself', its meanings 'in it', or else the text as nonexistent other than 'outside itself', in the various responses it derives from any individual or audience; the text 'closed' or 'open'. The terms are weak on both sides: to hold that a given text is 'different for everybody' is as much the end of any consequent political analysis and practice as to hold that it is 'the same for everybody'; the implication of the latter is the possibility of a definitive analysis able to determine the use-value of a film in abstraction from the actual historical situations of its use; that of the former is a malleable transparency of the particular film to the determinations of the particular individual or audience, thus removing in the end all real basis for supporting through political-cultural analysis any film or films against any other or others. The extreme version of this last position is provided by Jonas Mekas's 'own final statement' on the films of Leni Riefenstahl: 'if you are an idealist, you will see idealism; if you are a classicist, you will see classicism; if you are a Nazi, you will see Nazism'[176] – and if you are caught up in an established bourgeois view of art as the accomplishment of a transcending universality, you will be concerned to refuse analysis of the ideological constructions at stake in a film's discursive production and organization. The idea that films can be pulled into more or less any ideological space – significantly enough, Mekas's alternative spaces, idealism and classicism, are entirely compatible with and utilized by Nazism – is itself perfectly abstract in the conception of freedom it posits, its forgetting of the determining and defining domination at any moment of specific ideologies, specific institutions of meaning, within the spaces *of which* are given the grounds of contradiction, mobilization, reappropriation. More interesting and relevant in the present context is the question that can be elaborated from a comment by Agnès Varda expressing her reaction to the woman in Jean-Louis Comolli's *La Cecilia*, 'I liked the woman in *La Cecilia*',[177] setting against it the frequent criticism voiced in debates by women and men of just this central woman figure. Is there a way to deal with difference in relations to a film without falling either into indifference, the simple assertion of the same, or into some pure difference, an apolitical singularity, the effects only of individual (and) event?

The reading of a film is neither constrained absolutely nor free absolutely but historical, that history including the determinations of the institution cinema, the conditions of the production of meanings, of specific terms of address in films, a film. The property of a film is not yours or mine, whether makers or spectators, nor its; it is in a number of instances of relations across the film's preconstruction, passage and construction that engage the spectator-subject in a multiplicity of levels of reading, reception, response.

It is possible with regard to a film or group of films to analyse a discursive organization, a system of address, a placing – a construction – of the spectator (in its address, its placing, the film – to come back on Metz's formulation quoted earlier – does look to the spectator, does want to know his or her activity); the narrative fiction film of commercial cinema providing an example of address and placing at their most evidently regular and unifying. This is not to say, however, that any and every spectator – and for instance, man or woman, of this class or that – will be completely and equally in the given construction, completely and equally there in the film; and nor then is it to say that the discursive organization and its production can exhaust – be taken as equivalent to – the effectivity, the potential effects, of a film. No film can impose simply the spectator it poses (poses from its reproduction of cinematic apparatus and institution down to the slightest elements of signification that it particularly envisages), can impose an absolutely constraining place of places; such a place being only ever the imaginary of the constructed spectator, a consistence from the symbolic which latter is always there in return in its excess of any unity, any subject consistence, always a process – 'alienation' and 'separation' – of the subject in relation of and to the Other that is the opening of a constant sliding and difference of meaning for – across – the individual subject (the film invites *me* to come in its place but that place is never where *I* can be, only the projection-identification of *me*, an effect of identity). A corollary of this is that different discursive organizations cannot be merely accepted at the face value – the identification – of their addressed difference. Thus, for example, while a film may be specified as engaging Marxist and feminist issues, demonstrated indeed as constructing a Marxist and feminist position, and supported in these terms, as a 'Marxist film', a 'feminist film', there seems to be difficulty in finally labelling a film a 'Marxist film', or a 'feminist film', since in this sense no film *is* anything (hence the possibility of the quite radical disagreements so often encountered as to whether or not this or that film should be so described – witness the arguments around *Riddles of the Sphinx*). To designate a film in this way, that is, can quickly come close to suggesting an essential unity and a single effectivity, definitively accomplished 'in' the film, at the expense of consideration of the realizable multiplicity of effects and the problems of that multiplicity in any concrete situation of the film (in which concrete situation it may nevertheless be politically vital to hold to the designation and argue for and from it).

The spectator addressed by a film is distinct from, is not equivalent to, the spectating individual, the individual in the act of spectatorship, who may come into its invited place. It should be stressed, moreover, that the spectator addressed by a film is a multiple rather than a single instance, though the discursive organization of the film may accomplish a certain unification (for example, much recent work in film theory has been concerned to describe the effect of a spectator-subject of cinema – the apparatus, the institution – 'before' the spectator-subject of any particular film which reproduces that effect in – as part of – its own terms of address).

The spectating individual is always an individual subject, 'subject' designating not an achieved unity, once and for all, but a construction and a process, a heterogeneity, an intersection of histories – social and individual (the latter in the sense in which psychoanalysis can be taken as specifying and describing the area of the history of the construction of the individual as subjectivity in the division, relations of the symbolic, these relations themselves always – remember the image of the recto and verso of a piece of paper – a social implication).

Every individual is the site of a singularity, the fact of his or her individual history. The social implication, the social formation, of all discursive systems, symbolic relations, in no way prevents the production and inscription of singular events – which events, which individual history, will be caught up in the reception of a film for any spectator (watching *The Collector*, I think I recognize such and such a street in Hampstead, wonder which was the last Wyler film I saw, am struck by a shade of yellow in a dress worn by Samantha Eggar whose name, and the colour of the dress, runs into a certain pattern of personal obsession, remember that Nabokov was also interested in butterflies, dislike something in Terence Stamp's appearance, and so on, interminably). Varda's 'I liked the woman in *La Cecilia*', formulated in that way, can be understood at this level of singularity (note the ambiguity – the clumsiness – of the habitual question of liking a film: 'did you like it?'; the whole problem of the 'you' – the 'I' – assumed as the subject of the liking).

'Production not only creates an object for the subject, but also a subject for the object.'[178] Everyone is the possibility of a difference in reading, reception, response (with that difference a plurality of differences across the 'one'), but the film is the same, a certain organization, a certain address; the film, that is, offers something of a common terrain on which meanings are made and remade, assumed and displaced in any concrete situation of spectatorship, on which difference is represented, shifted, represented again in the difference of that shift for you and I.

Representation, with its senses of image, argumentation, deputation; the turn together – the bind of representing – of these various elements is important. The history of the individual as subject and as subject in and for a given social formation is never finished. Its constant termination, the stable relation of subject in constructed meaning, a specific subject-construction, is the effect of representation, and an ideological effect: any social formation depends for its existence not simply on the economic and political instances but also on a reasoning of the individual as subject, reproduced in images, identities of meaning, finding his or her delegation there. The term of this process is suture, suture as representing: the join of the subject as unity of the recognition of sense, point of intelligibility; the achievement in representation of the bind of the spectator as subject-construction, as in possession (the representation 'for me', as 'mine'). Cinema is an institution of representing, a machine for the fabrication-maintenance of representation; it is as such that it is a crucial ideological investment, as such that it is developed and exploited for a narration of the subject in a narrative that is its mapping – again and again, the constant termination – in representation, on the grounds of existing representations and their new accommodations.

What was stressed in immediately preceding paragraphs was that the unity of the 'one' – I, you, he, she, man or woman – is a complex mesh of instances: the accident of the individual; the subject history of the realization of the individual as subject in the division and relations of the symbolic, the production of the individual in structures of difference and desire; the subject-constructions of the discursive formations that are the representation-representing of the social, the individual in the social (a discourse is always a social relation, organizing a coherence of desire, a conversion of subjectivity to the position and image of that coherence, its representation). The bind of representation, the representing, is its completion of address, exactly the effecting and effect of the 'for me', the 'mine', position as possession. It is that mesh of instances and the problem of their representation that cinema finds and returns in its films and their reading, reception, response, that is the site of its operation. A film, that is, is the production of a past for the subject, the spectator bound in time with the film to the meanings it proposes, constructs to make sense of that time, occupying – entertaining – him or her, defining their possibilities; the regime of the narrative fiction film being simply that of the more or less *successful* past – hierarchization and continuity of discursive organization, imaginary of the 'one', assurance of the conversion of difference, desire, the slip of symbolic representation (the subject a process of the signifier, 'a signifier is what represents a subject for another signifier') into an order of sign and subject possession ('a sign represents something for someone') –

the film functioning as a mode of exchange of subjects, a universal representative, the standard of the 'one'; which universality, which standard for any subject, is its representing operation.

Alternative practices are then alternative in so far as they transform the relations of the symbolic in representation *against* representing, against the universalizing conditions of exchange: representation held to use (a definition of Brechtian distanciation); to another difference again, division, disunity, disturbance of the (social) contract (of cinema, film, the spectator). There is a politics of 'reality' and its struggle is in representation and its institutions, passes across the subject represented, the representing holds of meaning.

Nowhere perhaps is that struggle more important today than in the 'reality' of sexual difference and the stabilization of sexuality there, in the representation of difference and the representing of men and women as that, the hold of the difference. Men and women may be differentiated on the basis of biological sex but that differentiation is always a position in representation, a specification of the individual as subject in meaning (and from the very earliest of interpellations, the 'it's a boy'/'it's a girl', where 'boy' and 'girl' are the terms of a whole force of representation-representing); the individual is a sexed being in representation, always represented in his or her sexuality. Psychoanalysis demonstrates the body as tissue of signifiers, desire as a function of division in the symbolic difficult to sexualize as male or female, but the relations of tissue, desire, division are always immediately returning in representation, with, exactly, a structure of sexual division, a sexualized representation of desire, a specific order of difference.

The problem of representation for psychoanalysis, barely posed by it as such but there in occasional debates as to status, is the Oedipus complex. The radical weight of Lacan's work is that the law of castration passes through the symbolic not through the Oedipal structure as foundation of the unconscious. The latter is a concept forged on the trace of what operates to constitute a subject and the constitution of the subject is its division in the symbolic, the movement of desire from there, in that division-constitution. Man and woman, mother and child are signifiers, terms in particular representations, not contents, not even the contents of a founding Oedipus complex. What is important is the promotion of the function of castration in the constitution of the subject, not the form of that promotion which is culturally variable ('the Oedipus is finally only *one cultural form* amongst others, which are equally possible provided that they accomplish the same function, *the promotion of the function of castration in the psyche*').[179] But that formulation is itself still inadequate if it merely replaces one universalized structure by another, the Oedipus complex by castration, is inadequate inasmuch as it refuses to face the question of the representation in which it is implicated and which it implicates in the very moment of its attempt to specify the universal function. The unconscious is not anatomical, from a given division of the sexes, but symbolic, from a division of the individual as subject in language, meaning, difference; the production of the sexual reality of the unconscious ('the reality of the unconscious is sexual reality', *SXI*, p. 138)[180] then being precisely that, a *production*. The function of castration may stand as the term of that production, the articulation – 'integration' (*SXI*, p. 138)[181] – of symbolic and sexual division but at every stage of the appeal to that term its specific representation-representing of that articulation must be grasped and its own position within the existing order of representation understood accordingly.

Contemporary with cinema, rooted in the novel (the very form of so many case histories), psychoanalysis is itself, and powerfully, an institution of representation, another family machine. The family, indeed, is the historical site and difficulty of psychoanalysis, the area of its investigations of subjectivity and of the effective structures of sexuality for the individual subject, of the fit of the Oedipus complex, and the point of the limitation of the terms of its descriptions, the problem of its own representations and their permanent displacement by the activity of the unconscious which it both knows and constantly misses (it may be that those great and embarrassing anthropological and cultural works of Freud's later years are to be read, find their real force of sense, in this context). Not simply a reflection of the state, the family is a specific production of sexuality, of language, of ideology, the realization of the individual subject, locus of representation, his or her representing. Psychoanalysis discovers and understands the fundamental instability of production and realization – process, division, unconscious, desire, the interminability of the subject in meaning, the slip of representation – but the Oedipus becomes the representation of that discovery and understanding, a new machine that reassures the same identifications, the same novelistic in which cinema is invested, the same difference – that of the man and the woman in the order of the phallus with its symbolic presence, its certainty of vision, its image of the woman from castration, troubling, enigmatic, but fixed in his gaze, and as that enigma, like the statue of Teresa, the mystery of the woman to be seen, in all its evidence, for the man, for him.

* * *

In many ways this piece has come back over the last sections of the 'Notes on Suture' that accompanied the translations of articles by Miller and Oudart in a recent *Screen*.[182] At the close of those notes, I indicated a need to examine more carefully the concept of *the history of the subject*; the present piece can be regarded as a contribution to such an examination.

Thus it may be placed in a certain project of work, given something of a justification – an inevitability – in that place. And I am really concerned to stress that it does continue previous work, since the criticism it makes of Lacanian-Freudian psychoanalysis should be read and remembered in conjunction with the earlier attempts to define and use the radical aspects of psychoanalysis (in fact, the criticism is often made on the basis of that definition and use, in terms of those radical aspects). Places, however, are full of imaginary coherence and the writing of this piece for me has exceeded simple continuation, has been more difficult.

Difficult for me, for me not a woman. Throughout, the topic of difference involves quite centrally issues that are feminist issues; the piece, the idea of which has been pressing me for a year or so, crystallized indeed as an immediate commitment during a weekend conference in the area of film led by a feminist collective (*Camera Obscura*) and is situated directly in relation to feminist work in *Screen* (most notably and obviously Mulvey's 'Visual Pleasure and Narrative Cinema') and outside (for example, the discussion of *Riddles of the Sphinx* at the Other Cinema initiated by women connected with what at one stage had been known as the Lacan Study Group). The real pressure of the writing of the piece was in that context, or, to put it another way and more exactly, the continuation of previous work was under the pressure of that context, its problems and questions.

Which too is the context of the difficulty, what I experience as the impossibility of the position of writing of someone not a woman in direct discussion of those problems and questions. I can know the issues to be fundamental, politically and theoretically unavoidable for men as for women, can find them constantly in my work, feel it to be neither correct nor possible to ignore or somehow get round them or ease out with vague expressions of sympathy but, at the same time, to engage them is at once this difficulty of writing, of my return in discourse as a certain possession, the representing of me for the reader and to myself as a certain position, a confidence of knowledge or – probably and – a problematic appropriation of feminist criticisms, voices, yet another stratagem of oppression. For instance, a little example: in section VIII I bring together some quotations from interviews with Chantal Akerman; those quotations together at that point are very important – very real – for me; simple but complex, they summarize and extend much of what I have been trying to say, and in addition (or first and foremost) I like them, not least because they pay no attention to the currently received truths of intellectualism, also because of the space they create, because of the particular mix of the theoretical and the personal, and so on. The best word I have to describe the effect of these quotations, the word I want to use, is 'fineness'; for me they have just that effect, and I hope too for the reader. Yet as I write 'fineness', I cannot prevent the return from the enunciation of a representation in which it and I as subject are held as a position of domination, as in the difference from which women are placed from men, a representation that makes the word patronizing or containing or whatever (and I cannot deny this by advancing my contrary intention, discourse pays no heed to intentions which it anyway defines in its relations, and my contrary intention is anyway already suspect, itself discursively defined and produced and positioned within an order that I wish to be against).

'For in fact, we do not exactly know "masculine" language. As long as men claim to say everything and define everything, how could we know what the language of the male sex is?'[183] The notion of the language of a sex, difference as the difference there, has been critically at issue here but this piece has nevertheless followed something of the logic of Irigaray's question and its terms. What it has done, tried to do, is to pose the problem of sexual difference and representation and the functioning of the production of representation as the fixing of the difference, the relation of the woman as that, and then to come back from there on the indifference of the existing order, the sameness it asserts through that very fixing of difference, grounding and masking a male domination, at the expense of women and of other relations for men in meaning to sexual difference.

NOTES

First published in *Screen*, Autumn 1978, vol. 19, no. 3, pp. 51–112.

1 *SXX* – J. Lacan, *Le Séminaire livre XX: Encore (1972–1973)*, in *Le Champ freudien*, ed. J.-A. Miller, Paris, Editions du Seuil, 1975. Freud's question, *Was will das Weib?*, occurs in a letter to Marie Bonaparte: 'The great question that has never been answered and which I have not yet been able to answer, despite my thirty years of research into the feminine soul, is "What does a woman want?" ' cited in E. Jones, *Sigmund Freud: Life and Work*, vol. 2, London, Hogarth Press, 1955, p. 468. One or two remarks need to be made at the outset in connection with the discussion of psychoanalysis in what follows. The term 'psychoanalysis' will be used to refer to that area of investigation described and theorized as psychoanalysis in the – extensive – writings of Freud, Lacan and those close to the latter (as is well known, Lacan's work is intended as a 'return to Freud', as the effective elaboration of the implications of the 'science of unconscious mental processes' developed by Freud). Discussion and criticism are of aspects of that body of theoretical work, which is to say that the actual practice of psychoanalysis in its specific analytic situation is not here in question. A principle much stressed by Lacan is that 'the analyst is authorised from himself or herself', psychoanalysis exists and is learned, that is, in the analytic situation, cannot be contained, at best only approached, in theoretical constructions (the unconscious is *radically* another scene), cannot be authorized by master or institution (the analyst is not the possessor of a diploma but the site of a listening attention in which he or she is constantly surprised, reimplicated). The problem must then arise of the status of psychoanalytic theory and of the teaching – the transmission – of psychoanalysis: Lacan is after all the director of a school with grades, forms of authorization, and the purveyor of a teaching which is a complex theoretical production (even, apparently, available for transmission in quasi-mathematical formulae, 'mathemes'). That problem itself, currently under debate, is of less concern here than the importance and influence, the effect of

psychoanalytic theory today – including in thinking about film and cinema – far beyond the specific practice of psychoanalysis. To criticize psychoanalysis in aspects of that theory is not, of course, to reject or refuse psychoanalysis, it is merely to treat the theory, and psychoanalysis with it, as non-homogeneous; to recognize the fundamental significance of Lacan's work, often built upon in *Screen*, is not to accept all its developments, positions, presentations.

2 Sigmund Freud, 'Some Psychical Consequences of the Anatomical Distinction between the Sexes', in *The Standard Edition of the Complete Psychological Works*, trans. and ed. James Strachey, London, Hogarth Press, 1951–73, vol. XIX, p. 252, hereafter abbreviated as *Standard Edition*; 'Female Sexuality', *Standard Edition*, vol. XXI, p. 233.

3 Freud, 'Some Psychical Consequences of the Anatomical Distinction between the Sexes', *Standard Edition*, vol. XIX p. 252.

4 *SII* – J. Lacan, *Le Séminaire livre II*, Paris, Editions du Seuil, 1978.

5 Sigmund Freud, 'Fetishism', *Standard Edition*, vol. XXI, p. 154.

6 Irène Diamantis, Michel Silvestre, 'Annonce d'un enseignement sur "Recherche sur la fonction phallique" ', *Ornicar?*, 1976–7, no. 8, p. 106.

7 *E* – J. Lacan, *Ecrits*, Paris, Editions du Seuil, 1966; *Ecrits: A Selection*, trans. Alan Sheridan, London, Tavistock, 1977, p. 287 (where the English selection includes an essay quoted here from the *Ecrits*, reference will be given to the translation in an endnote, as in the present instance, though the wording of the translation may be modified). That Lacan then goes on to say that such statements still hide the fact that the phallus plays its role only when 'veiled', when 'the signifiable is raised to the function of signifier', changes nothing in the necessity nevertheless of the rationalization, the logic of its appearance in the argument, merely enacts the golden rule: exactly the detaching – the 'raising' – of the phallus *from the penis*.

8 Lacan, *Ecrits: A Selection*, p. 287.

9 J. Lacan, 'Conférence, Yale University 1975', *Scilicet*, nos. 6–7, p. 38.

10 J. Lacan, 'Seminar, 16 November 1976', *Ornicar?*, 1977, nos. 12–13, p. 12 ('without symptoms, except from time to time mistakes in gender . . .').

11 Michèle Montrelay, *L'ombre et le nom: sur la féminité*, Paris, Minuit, 1977, p. 28.

12 Irène Diamantis, 'Recherches sur la féminité', *Ornicar?-Analytica*, 1977, vol. 5, p. 27.

13 Sigmund Freud, 'Fragment of an Analysis of a Case of Hysteria', *Standard Edition*, vol VII, pp. 3–122.

14 Freud, 'Some Psychical Consequences of the Anatomical Distinction between the Sexes', *Standard Edition*, vol. XIX, p. 249.

15 Sigmund Freud, 'The Question of Lay Analysis', *Standard Edition*, vol. XX, p. 212.

16 P. Regnard, D.-M. Bourneville, *Iconographie photographique de la Salpêtrière (Service de M. Charcot)*, 2 vols, Paris, 1876 – 8 (the quotation is from the preface to volume I).

17 Sigmund Freud, 'An Autobiographical Study', *Standard Edition*, vol. XX, p. 28 ('seeing, but not seen myself').

18 *SI* – J. Lacan, *Le Séminaire livre I*, Paris, Editions du Seuil, 1975.

19 Cf. J. Lacan, 'Faire mouche', *Le Nouvel Observateur*, 29 March–4 April 1976, no. 594, p. 64.

20 J. Lacan, 'Seminar, 11 February 1975', *Ornicar?*, 1975, no. 4, p. 94.

21 Extended presentation of Freud's work as concerned here can be found in Juliet Mitchell, *Psychoanalysis and Feminism*, Harmondsworth, Penguin Books, 1974, and, extremely critically, in Luce Irigaray, *Speculum: de l'autre femme*, Paris, Minuit, 1974; a brief account, including discussion of Lacan, is

100

Rosalind Coward, 'Rereading Freud: the Making of the Feminine', *Spare Rib*, May 1978, pp. 43–6.

22 Sigmund Freud, 'An Outline of Psychoanalysis', *Standard Edition*, vol. XXIII, p. 188.

23 Sigmund Freud, 'The Psychogenesis of a Case of Homosexuality in a Woman', *Standard Edition*, vol. XVIII, p. 154.

24 Freud, 'Some Psychical Consequences of the Anatomical Distinction Between the Sexes', *Standard Edition*, vol. XIX, p. 255.

25 ibid., p. 258.

26 Sigmund Freud, 'The Dissolution of the Oedipus Complex', *Standard Edition*, vol. XIX, p. 178.

27 For a detailed exposition, see 'Notes on Suture', *Screen*, Winter 1977–8, vol. 18, no. 4, pp. 48–56.

28 J. Lacan, 'Sur l'expérience de la passe', *Ornicar?*, 1977, nos. 12–13, p. 120.

29 Lacan, *Ecrits: A Selection*, p. 288.

30 *SXI* – J. Lacan, *Le Séminaire livre XI*, Paris, Editions du Seuil, 1973; *The Four Fundamental Concepts of Psychoanalysis*, trans. Alan Sheridan, London, Hogarth Press, 1977, p. 154. (Reference to this English version will be given in an end-note as in the present instance, though the wording of the translation may be modified.)

31 Lacan, *The Four Fundamental Concepts of Psychoanalysis*, pp. 204–25.

32 ibid., p. 177.

33 Lacan, 'Conférence, Yale University 1975', p. 41.

34 Sigmund Freud, 'Three Essays on the Theory of Sexuality', *Standard Edition*, vol. VII, p. 168.

35 Lacan, *The Four Fundamental Concepts of Psychoanalysis*, p. 176.

36 ibid., pp. 176–7.

37 J. Lacan, 'Seminar, 18 November 1975', *Ornicar?*, 1976, no. 6, p. 8.

38 Lacan, *The Four Fundamental Concepts of Psychoanalysis*, p. 199.

39 ibid., p. 154.

40 ibid., p. 151.

41 Lacan, *Ecrits: A Selection*, p. 285.

42 J. Lacan in discussion at the Société Psychanalytique de Paris, *Revue Française de psychanalyse*, April–June 1949, p. 317.

43 Lacan, *Ecrits: A Selection*, p. 289. The dialectic of having and being is suggested in a late note by Freud: ' "Having" and "being" in children. Children like expressing an object-relation by an identification: "I am the object". "Having" is the later of the two; after loss of the object it relapses into "being" . . .': note, 12 July 1938, *Standard Edition*, vol. XXIII, p. 299.

44 Hélène Cixous, 'Le sexe ou la tête?', *Les Cahiers du GRIF*, October 1976, no. 13, p. 8.

45 Eugénie Lemoine-Luccioni, *Partage des femmes*, Paris, Editions du Seuil, 1976.

46 ibid., p. 9.

47 ibid., p. 82.

48 ibid., p. 71.

49 ibid., p. 84.

50 ibid., p. 100.

51 ibid.

52 ibid., p. 9.

53 ibid., p. 72.

54 ibid., p. 8.

55 ibid., p. 9. Cf. Moustapha Safouan (again an analyst-member of Lacan's School): 'finally the woman finds her being not as woman but as phallus, which

is the sense of the fundamental alienation of her being', *La Sexualité féminine*, Paris, Editions du Seuil, 1976, p. 137.

56 Luce Irigaray, *Ce Sexe qui n'en est pas un*, Paris, Minuit, 1977, p. 28.
57 Montrelay, op. cit., p. 72; the chapter of Montrelay's book from which this quotation comes has been translated in English as 'Inquiry into Femininity', *m/f*, 1978, no. 1, (quotation p. 94).
58 Sigmund Freud, 'Psychoanalytic Notes on an Autobiographical Account of a Case of Paranoia', *Standard Edition*, vol. XII, p. 33.
59 Lemoine-Luccioni, op. cit., p. 9.
60 Cf. e.g. 'Entretien avec des étudiants', Yale University, 24 November 1975, *Scilicet*, nos. 6–7, p. 37.
61 Montrelay, op. cit., p. 68; 'Inquiry into Femininity', p. 90 (translation modified); cf. Lemoine-Luccioni, op. cit., p. 58.
62 Montrelay, op. cit., p. 67; 'Inquiry into Femininity', p. 90.
63 ibid., p. 66; 'Inquiry into Femininity', p. 89.
64 ibid., p. 67; 'Inquiry into Femininity', p. 90.
65 ibid., pp. 143–4.
66 ibid., p. 66; 'Inquiry into Femininity', p. 89.
67 ibid., p. 64; 'Inquiry into Femininity', p. 88.
68 Lemoine-Luccioni, op. cit., p. 60.
69 Safouan, op. cit., p. 132.
70 Montrelay, op. cit., p. 66; 'Inquiry into Femininity', p. 89.
71 The formulation here is borrowed from an unpublished paper by Judith Williamson, 'Two or Three Things We Know About Ourselves', London, 1977.
72 Sigmund Freud, 'New Introductory Lectures on Psychoanalysis', *Standard Edition*, vol. XXII, p. 113 ('those of you who are women . . . you are yourselves the problem').
73 *Riddles of the Sphinx*, script published in *Screen*, Summer 1977, vol. 18, no. 2, pp. 61–77.
74 ibid., p. 69.
75 In 1974 Irigaray was suspended from her teaching in the Lacanian psychoanalysis department of the Université de Paris VIII (Vincennes).
76 Irigaray, *Ce Sexe*, pp. 123–4.
77 ibid., p. 29.
78 Jacqueline Rose, 'Paranoia and the Film system', *Screen*, Winter 1976–7, vol. 17, no. 4, p. 102.
79 ibid.
80 Sigmund Freud, 'Female Sexuality', *Standard Edition*, vol. XXI, p. 226.
81 ibid., p. 230.
82 Montrelay, op. cit., p. 69; 'Inquiry into Femininity', p. 91.
83 ibid., pp. 155–6.
84 'Women and Representation: a Discussion with Laura Mulvey', *Wedge*, Spring 1978, no. 2, p. 51.
85 Montrelay, op. cit., p. 163.
86 ibid, p. 71; 'Inquiry into Femininity', p. 99.
87 Lacan, *The Four Fundamental Concepts of Psychoanalysis*, p. 80.
88 E. Lemoine-Luccioni, 'Ecrire', *Sorcières*, no. 7, p. 14.
89 Montrelay, op. cit., pp. 80–1; 'Inquiry into Femininity', p. 99.
90 Hélène Cixous, 'Quelques questions à Hélène Cixous', *Les Cahiers du GRIF*, October 1976, no. 13, p. 20.
91 Cixous, 'Le sexe ou la tête?', p. 14.
92 Irigaray, *Ce Sexe*, pp. 75, 122, 141, 76, 130, 132.
93 Viviane Forrester, 'Féminin pluriel', *Tel Quel*, Winter 1977, no. 74, p. 77.
94 Julia Kristeva, 'L'autre du sexe', *Sorcières*, no. 10, p. 37.

95 Forrester, op. cit., p. 69.
96 Peter Trudgill, *Sociolinguistics: An Introduction*, Harmondsworth, Penguin Books, 1974, p. 95.
97 ibid., p. 90.
98 Robin Lakoff, *Language and Woman's Place*, New York, Harper Collins, 1975; Mary Ritchie Key, *Male/Female Language*, Metuchen, NJ: Scarecrow Press, 1975.
99 Key, op. cit., p. 76.
100 Irigaray, *Ce Sexe*, p. 157.
101 Julia Kristeva, 'Sujet dans le langage et pratique politique', in *Psychanalyse et politique*, Paris, Editions du Seuil, 1974, p. 61.
102 Cixous, 'Le sexe ou la tête?', p. 7.
103 'There is a material history of the construction of the individual as subject and that history is also the social construction of the subject; it is not, in other words, that there is first of all the construction of a subject for social/ideological formations and then the placing of that constructed subject-support in those formations, it is that the two processes are one, in a kind of necessary simultaneity – like the recto and verso of a piece of paper', Stephen Heath, '*Anata mo*', *Screen*, Winter 1976–7, vol. 17, no. 4, p. 62.
104 Freud, 'Fetishism', *Standard Edition*, vol. XXI, p. 157.
105 Cixous, 'Le sexe ou la tête?' p. 14; cf. *Sorcières*, no. 2, an issue devoted entirely to 'the voice'.
106 ibid., p. 14.
107 Montrelay, op. cit., p. 64; 'Inquiry into Femininity', p. 87.
108 'The "grain" is that: the materiality of the body speaking its mother tongue': Roland Barthes, 'The Grain of the Voice', *Image-Music-Text*, trans. S. Heath, London, Fontana, 1977, p. 182.
109 Diamantis, 'Recherches sur la féminité', p. 32.
110 Montrelay, op. cit., p. 153.
111 Unless, for instance, grain is to be sought somewhere with regard to colour – colour which finally disturbs perspective representation in the history of painting, colour which is a factor in 'the perversion of the sense of sight', in the 'blindness' often noted in hysteria, a shift in the balance of the intensities of the normal state of colour vision (cf. J. M. Charcot, *Leçons sur les maladies du système nerveux, Oeuvres complètes*, vol. I, Paris, 1886, pp. 427–34).
112 G. W. F. Hegel, *Vorlesungen über die Aesthetik, Sämtliche Werke*, vol. XIII, Stuttgart, 1927–8, p. 254. Hegel also admits hearing as a theoretical sense but only in so far as he can separate it from any of that intimacy with the body stressed as the reality of the voice in feminine writing.
113 Luce Irigaray, interview, in M.–F. Hans and G. Lapouge (eds), *Les femmes, la pornographie, l'érotisme*, Paris, Editions du Seuil, 1978, p. 50.
114 Hélène Cixous, 'Entretien avec Françoise van Rossum-Guyon', *Revue des sciences humaines*, 1977, no. 168, p. 487.
115 Margaret Anson, *The Merry Order of St Bridget: Personal Recollections of the Use of the Rod*, York, 1857 (place and date of publication as on title page but, as often with works of this kind, certainly deliberately erroneous).
116 Cf. Laura Mulvey, 'Visual Pleasure and Narrative Cinema', *Screen*, Autumn 1975, vol. 16, no. 3, pp. 6–18, reprinted as chapter 1 in this volume, pp. 22–34; much of what follows is indebted to Mulvey's influential study.
117 'Sexual Deviations', in *Encyclopaedia Britannica* (Macropaedia), 15th edn, vol. XVI, Chicago, 1974, pp. 607–8.
118 Clifford Allen, *The Sexual Perversions and Abnormalities*, London, Oxford University Press, 1949, p. 281.
119 Sigmund Freud, 'Jokes and Their Relation to the Unconscious', *Standard Edition*, vol. VIII, p. 98.

120 Freud, 'Three Essays on the Theory of Sexuality', *Standard Edition*, vol. VII, p. 156.
121 Sigmund Freud, 'The Psychoanalytic View of Psychogenic Disturbance of Vision', *Standard Edition*, vol. XI, p. 216.
122 ibid.
123 Sigmund Freud, 'Studies on Hysteria', *Standard Edition*, vol. II, p. 117.
124 Freud, 'The Psychoanalytic View of Psychogenic Disturbance of Vision', *Standard Edition*, vol. XI, p. 217.
125 Sigmund Freud, 'The Uncanny', *Standard Edition*, vol. XVII, p. 231.
126 Jacques Chazaud, *Les Perversions sexuelles*, Toulouse, Privat, 1973, p. 119.
127 Lacan, *The Four Fundamental Concepts of Psychoanalysis*, p. 78.
128 Sigmund Freud, 'On Narcissism: an Introduction', *Standard Edition*, vol. XIV, pp. 69–102; 'Instincts and Their Vicissitudes', *Standard Edition*, vol. XIV, pp. 111–40.
129 Freud, 'Instincts and Their Vicissitudes', *Standard Edition*, vol. XIV, p. 130.
130 Lacan, *The Four Fundamental Concepts of Psychoanalysis*, p. 73.
131 ibid., p. 74.
132 ibid., p. 82.
133 ibid., p. 75.
134 ibid.
135 ibid., p. 194.
136 Cf. Robert Fliess, *Erogeneity and Libido*, New York, International Universities Press, 1956, pp. 171–2.
137 Roland Barthes, *S/Z*, Paris, Editions du Seuil; 1970, p. 40; trans. Richard Miller, *S/Z*, London, Cape, 1975, pp. 135-45.
138 The problem is suggested by Griselda Pollock, 'What's Wrong with Images of Women?', chapter 5 in this volume, pp. 135–45; originally published in *Screen Education*, Autumn 1977, no. 24, pp. 25–33.
139 'A directness that radically questions the psychoanalytically based analyses of images of women undertaken by Claire Johnston and Laura Mulvey and the notions of castration fears and the phallic woman', ibid., pp. 141–2 in this volume.
140 Report in the London *Times*, 20 April 1874, p. 14.
141 'About nine out of ten, I think, of my child friendships get shipwrecked at the critical point "where the stream and river meet", and the child friends, once so affectionate, become uninteresting acquaintances whom I have no wish to set eyes on again.' C. L. Dodgson, in H. Gernsheim (ed.), *Lewis Carroll, Photographer*, New York, Dover Publications, 1969, p. 18.
142 J. Lacan, 'L'étourdit', *Scilicet*, 1973, no. 4, p. 20.
143 A sample of Maccheroni's work can be found in 'Trente-deux photographies du sexe d'une femme', *Obliques*, 1977, nos. 12–13, pp. 313–28.
144 Lemoine-Luccioni, *Partage des femmes*, p. 85.
145 Claire Johnston, 'Towards a Feminist Film Practice: Some Theses', *Edinburgh 76 Magazine*, 1976, p. 50.
146 Cf. Christian Metz, *Le Signifiant imaginaire*, Paris, Union générale d'éditions, 1977, pp. 82–91, 113–20; trans. as 'The Imaginary Signifier', *Screen*, Summer 1975, vol. 16, no. 2, pp. 61–6; 'History/Discourse: Note on Two Voyeurisms', *Edinburgh 76 Magazine*, 1976, pp. 21–5.
147 A. Bazin, 'Théâtre et cinéma', in *Qu'est-ce que le cinéma?*, vol. II, Paris, Cerf, 1959, p. 86.
148 Metz, *Le Signifiant imaginaire*, pp. 117–18; 'History/Discourse: Note on Two Voyeurisms', p. 23.
149 ibid., p. 91; 'The Imaginary Signifier', p. 65.
150 Lacan, *The Four Fundamental Concepts of Psychoanalysis*, p. 81.
151 Metz, *Le Signifiant imaginaire*, p. 117; 'History/Discourse: Note on Two

Voyeurisms', p. 23.
152 Lacan, *The Four Fundamental Concepts of Psychoanalysis*, p. 115.
153 ibid., p. 182.
154 ibid., p. 115.
155 ibid., p. 116.
156 Akerman, 'Chantal Akerman on *Jeanne Dielman*', *Camera Obscura*, 1978, no. 2, p. 119.
157 ibid., p. 121.
158 Lacan, *The Four Fundamental Concepts of Psychoanalysis*, pp. 181–4.
159 Laura Mulvey, 'Visual Pleasure and Narrative Cinema'; see p. 33 of this volume.
160 Cf. Cixous: 'one is always in representation, and when a woman is asked to take place in this representation, she is, of course, asked to represent a man's desire': 'Entretien avec Françoise van Rossum-Guyon', p. 487.
161 For the recognition, see Karyn Kay and Gerald Peary, 'Dorothy Arzner's *Dance, Girl, Dance*', in K. Kay and G. Peary (eds), *Women and the Cinema: A Critical Anthology*, New York, Dutton, 1977, pp. 9–25; Dannis Peary, 'Stephanie Rothman: R-Rated Feminist', ibid., pp. 179–92; Collective, 'An Interrogation of the Cinematic Sign: Woman as Sexual Signifer in Jackie Raynal's *Deux Fois*', and 'Shot Commentary', *Camera Obscura*, 1976, no. 1, pp. 11–38.
162 Constance Penley, 'The Avant-garde and its Imaginary', *Camera Obscura*, 1978, no. 2, p. 26.
163 Peter Gidal, unpublished open letter to Constance Penley, London, January 1978, para. 19.
164 'Feminism, Fiction, and the Avant-garde' conference, Filmmakers Co-operative, London 6–7 May 1978. (The present article was written prior to receiving Janet Bergstrom's comments on *News from Home* included in her piece in this issue of *Screen*.) [Constance Penley and Janet Bergstrom, 'The avant-garde: histories and theories', *Screen*, Autumn 1978, vol. 19, no. 3, pp. 113–27.]
165 Viviane Forrester, 'Le regard des femmes', in Musidora, *Paroles . . . elles tournent!*, Paris, Des Femmes, 1976, p. 12.
166 J. Michelet, *Histoire de la révolution française*, vol. XI, Paris, Pléiade, 1952, p. 645.
167 Chantal Akerman, 'Entretien', *Cahiers du Cinéma*, July 1977, no. 278, p. 41.
168 Akerman, 'Chantal Akerman on *Jeanne Dielman*', p. 118.
169 Akerman, 'Entretien', p. 37.
170 Akerman, 'Chantal Akerman on *Jeanne Dielman*', p. 121.
171 Sigmund Freud, 'Hysterics suffer mainly from reminiscences', *Studies on Hysteria*, in *Standard Edition*, vol. II, p. 7.
172 Silvia Bovenschen, 'Is There a Feminine Aesthetic?', *New German Critique*, Winter 1977, no. 10, p. 125.
173 *Camera Obscura* Collective, 'An Interrogation of the Cinematic Sign: Woman as Sexual Signifier in Jackie Raynal's *Deux Fois*', p. 13. (*Camera Obscura* here refer to work done by Pam Cook and Claire Johnston, notably 'The Place of Women in the Cinema of Raoul Walsh', in Phil Hardy (ed.), *Raoul Walsh*, Edinburgh, Edinburgh Film Festival, 1974, pp. 93–109.)
174 Julia Kristeva, 'La femme, ce n'est jamais ça', *Tel Quel*, Autumn 1974, no. 59, p. 21.
175 Initial approach in Stephen Heath, 'Questions of Property', *Ciné-tracts*, 1978, no. 4, pp. 2–11.
176 Jonas Mekas, citing Susan Sontag, 'Fascinating Fascism', in Kay and Peary, *Women and the Cinema*, p. 362.
177 A. Varda, 'Entretien', *Cahiers du Cinéma*, May 1977, no. 276, p. 25.
178 K. Marx, *Grundrisse: Foundations of the Critique of Political Economy*, trans.

David McLellan, London, Paladin, 1973, p. 92 (Marx is here discussing art).
179 Moustafa Safouan, *Etudes sur l'Oedipe*, Paris, Editions du Seuil, 1974, p. 124.
180 Lacan, *The Four Fundamental Concepts of Psychoanalysis*, p. 150.
181 ibid.
182 'Notes on Suture', *Screen*, Winter 1977–8, vol. 18, no. 4, pp. 48–76; see also Heath, '*Anata mo*'.
183 Irigaray, *Ce Sexe,* p. 127.

4

LANGUAGE AND SEXUAL DIFFERENCE

Dugald Williamson

The theoretical work of Lacan has been instrumental in linking structural linguistics with psychoanalysis to give an account of the formation of the human subject, including its construction in relations of sexual difference. Readers of *Screen* will be familiar with the influence which Lacanian theory has exercised in the attempts within film theory to provide a materialist view of subjectivity, which would solve problems associated with the formalism of semiotics and the functionalism of Marxist cultural analysis. They will recognize, too, its role in feminist theory concerned with the conditions of sexual representation, including pornography. The aim of this article is to demonstrate the problems of certain 'discursive figures', repeatable forms of reasoning, which organize the Lacanian theory and the objects it constructs, especially its version of 'the formation of the subject in language' and 'sexual difference'. It is these discursive figures or schemata which ground recent debates over biologism and phallocentrism in Lacan's work. This description of the co-ordinates of a theoretical field allows us to call into question the idea that, in the conjunction of psychoanalysis and linguistics, Lacanian theory 'discovers' an essential inter-relation of subjectivity, sexuality and language.

'THE FORMATION OF THE SUBJECT IN LANGUAGE'

In Lacanian theory, the subject is seen not as the origin of thought and language that it is for an idealist tradition, but as an effect created of language. Further, the means of signification themselves are sexualized, the positions of male and female identity are associated with the constitutive processes of enunciation. To show the instability of the key metaphors of Lacanian discourse, we shall look first at the more specifically linguistic terms, then at those concerned more extensively with sexual difference.

Lacan's speculation on the nature of the sign is well known:

> To pinpoint the emergence of linguistic science we may say that . . . it is contained in the constitutive moment of an algorithm that is its foundation. This algorithm is the following:

107

$$\frac{S}{s}$$

which is read as: the signifier over the signified, 'over' corresponding to the bar separating the two stages.[1]

Elaborating the model of Saussure in which elements are defined through their rule-governed relations within the language system, Lacan says that the signifier and signified are 'distant orders separated initially by a barrier resisting signification' (this barrier being symbolized, of course, by the bar in the algorithm).[2] He argues that the signifier has its own principle of articulation, that is, it belongs to a realm of differential elements (phonemes) which combine according to 'the laws of a closed order' and thus form a signifying chain, 'rings of a necklace that is a ring in another necklace made of rings'.[3] This articulation can be identified not only at the level of the phoneme but also at higher levels such as the sentence, where the signifier always anticipates meaning by spreading its own dimension before it, as when we wait all the more expectantly for the meaning of a sentence interrupted before a significant term: 'I shall never . . .'.[4]

This argument helps to debunk any assumption that the signifier exists just to represent the signified or to serve a meaning that somehow exists outside language in an ideal world of intention or spirit. The manner in which the signifier is capable of signification is located in 'an incessant sliding of the signified under the signifier' where 'anchoring points' are possible.[5] So for Lacan, it is in the chain of the signifier that meaning *insists*, but none of that chain's elements *consists* in the signification of which it is capable at any moment.[6] Subject and signified tug at the sleeve of the signifier, as it were, but they remain effects of its dominion.[7]

Lacan connects the signifier and the types of figuration to which it lends itself, of course, with the theme of the unconscious.[8] So, for instance, he links the categories of metaphor and metonymy to the principles of condensation and displacement used by Freud to describe the dreamwork and primary processes. Freud's more restricted view of the unconscious processes becomes generalized by Lacan as that unconsciousness, occurring for a subject, of the very process by which its own being is formed or changed in the defiles of the signifier. For instance, by linking the principle of metaphor to the Freudian idea of repression, Lacan argues that as the signifier of the sexual trauma is substituted by another term in the signifying chain there passes between them a spark whose significance is inaccessible at least initially to the conscious subject.[9] Similarly, the principle of significance of dreams as interpreted by Freud (the royal road to the unconscious) is said to be the linguistic structure in which the signifier is articulated.[10] And, more generally than these instances, the unconscious is structured like a language, since the signifier marks the 'other scene', constituting the subject in a process which eludes awareness.

Such an argument is committed to relegating the Cartesian ego by decentring the consciousness in relation to the unconscious. It is also meant to rescue the idea of the unconscious from the net of various empiricisms. In opposing both biological ideas of the body and 'its' needs as natural givens, and psychologistic ideas of the mind as the ego's authentic experience of itself, Lacan returns such categories as instinct, need and ego to the condition of language and its structuring of experience.[11]

However, a problem may be registered here in terms which in no way reinstate empiricist methodology. The link between language and the unconscious in Lacanian theory is secured by an epistemological ploy, characteristic of structuralism more generally, whereby the structure is defined as an ideal form existing in a dialectical relation to the subject, who must realize the potential effects of the structure at the level of experience. An empiricist view of knowledge as guaranteed by the subject's immediate experience is retained, even though it is now relegated as a moment within a dialectic of structure and experience such that the subject is deprived of its constitutive status. The unconscious referred to by Lacan is simply the notion that the subject cannot *know* the conditions of its own historical act of speech, existing as they are supposed to beneath the limits of consciousness. The subject cannot know the pre-existing structure of language in the instance of speech since that structure is, by definition, what makes it possible for the subject to speak or know anything, including its imaginary identifications of itself as subject. We thus come to Lacan's reliance on the figure of misrecognition, the alleged failure of the subject to see the conditions which govern recognition and identity. In order to deal with this problem, it is necessary to discuss the Imaginary/Symbolic dialectic found in Lacan.

THE IMAGINARY AND THE SYMBOLIC

The Imaginary/Symbolic relation involves two interdependent features: an illusory identity of the subject, and a splitting of that identity through a recognition of difference which places the subject within linguistic and cultural patterning. This dialectic is closely associated with Lacan's account of the mirror phase.[12] In this account, the infant between the ages of six and eighteen months, still sunk in its motor incapacity and without language, recognizes its reflected image which symbolizes a possible unity of the body and a mental permanence of the *I*. However, ambiguity already sets in, for this first sense of coherent identity is provided by an image which is detached from the child, an exterior counterpart: one might understand this as a split between the perceiving subject and the perceived image. Moreover, the unity is said to be usually experienced in the context of the mother's directing look, that is in relation to otherness. None the less, this initial recognition is said to have a 'fictional' integrity which strikes deep, even while providing a model for all subsequent identifications across the exchanges of language.[13] Jacqueline Rose points out that, for Lacan, 'the subject is constituted through language – the mirror image represents the moment when the subject is located in an order outside itself to which it will henceforth refer'.[14] It is language, more decisively than the image, which provides the possibility of an identity yet fractures the subject. This is the fact of life in the Symbolic, that the subject represents itself in language, but can do so only through the signifier which divisively passes it by in the avenues of speech.

In general, then, the terms Imaginary and Symbolic are understood not as standing alone, but as presupposing one another. Central to their relation is the idea of misrecognition, in which the imaginary recognition of identity is made possible only within a network of relations which subsume the subject and constitute its 'unconscious'. The extent to which these Lacanian terms have been taken up in film theory and some areas of feminism hardly needs to be underscored here. Instead of referring in detail to particular texts in these fields at this point, it might be useful to make three general comments about the Imaginary/Symbolic relation, together with the idea of subject-formation which it helps to generate and upon which such widespread reliance has been placed.[15]

First, the theory of the Imaginary/Symbolic dialectic has the form of a narrative and might have attracted more suspicion on this count than it has, given the teleological problems associated with that form. The story of a subject predestined to assume an identity through misrecognition in 'an ontological structure of the human world'[16] glosses over a number of discontinuities, which will be analysed below.[17]

Second, it is worth noting that two incompatible ideas of lack and difference are often confused for the sake of the dialectic. One is the realist notion that the word could be experienced as a loss of the presence of the object named: the other is the idea that signifying elements necessarily enter relations of difference within a system. It is said that:

> Symbolisation starts . . . when the child gets its first sense that something could be missing; words stand for objects, because they have to be spoken at the moment when the first object is lost. For Lacan, the subject can only operate within language by constantly repeating that moment of fundamental and irreducible division. The subject is therefore constituted in language *as* this division or splitting (Freud's *Ichspaltung*, or splitting of the ego).[18]

The cinematic image has been treated in similar fashion to the word, as the absence of the object experienced in the presence of the sign, most strikingly perhaps in Christian Metz's 'The Imaginary Signifier'.[19] Metz argues: 'in order to understand the film (at all), I must perceive the photographed object as absent, its photograph as present, and the presence of this absence as signifying.'[20] That the image is made present in a mode of absence is ostensibly a structural fact about how cinema signifies. This fact supposedly sets up the desire to see and (according to a similar principle in relation to auditory mechanisms) the desire to hear, both of which depend on a 'lack' that is made intensely present or 'concrete' in the cinematic signifier as it is given to consciousness. This lack links cinema to the pursuit of the absent object, in an Imaginary which must be retheorized from the side of the Symbolic.[21]

One should note that the argument depends here on setting the signifier in relation to the referent (shades of the conflation of signified and referent in early cine-semiotics, but now in order to point up the imaginary and conditional nature of realism). And it is a little surprising, perhaps, that the relation of object and image or object and word can be used to adduce evidence for, on the one hand, the subject's anticipation of signifying difference and, on the other, the subject's belief in the Imaginary. This is explicable by the fact that such arguments retain the problematic concept of language as representation and hence the variants which it is possible to play upon it. Once that concept is preserved, it can be used to argue either that the word (or image) represents the object in a unifying relation, as in the imaginary identity of self, word and world; or that it creates a loss experienced in the gap across which it makes absent an object which is presumed once to have been immediately present to consciousness. To argue that the subject actually experiences language as a formative loss suffered in the strait between words and things allows a pun on the Freudian notion of the lost object and its drama of desire and repetition. Yet this argument begs the question, since it succeeds only as long as one takes for granted the realist idea of language as representation or as failed representation. The problem with retaining this concept is, of course, that signs are assumed to have the single, essential function of reflecting the object to the subject; while no criteria are provided for how either the object or its representation are rendered intelligible, other than an idealist assumption of cognitive powers natural to consciousness. In which case, the empiricist concept of representation can have nothing to do with the definition of the sign in structural linguistics (its own realist moments aside), and should not be used to designate some supposed anticipation of the symbolic order.

This realist idea is incompatible with the idea of language as a system of phonematic and grammatical differences since the latter does not require the signifier to be thought of as a representation of the referent, nor as an empirical element whose relation to an object could be the content of an independent perception in the mind. In this linguistic framework, the signifier is defined by the action of the rules or codes governing the relations of elements in a system, and this definition can work perfectly well without setting the system in any relation to 'consciousness'. Lacanian theory has, however, allowed the different definitions of language to

111

run together, in order to support its ideas of subject-formation, as for example when it is assumed that the experience of the word/object relation provides either the anticipation of a signifying loss or an experience of difference that is analogous to, and even acts as the motor of, linguistic signification:

> given that each word in a language gains its value (its meaning) from the set of differences in which it is caught, it follows that for language to be set in motion there are a necessary set of absences at its heart – a necessary tearing of the word from the world so that the object can only appear there where its identify has been transformed into differ-ence – where it can find a name. Similarly, for the speaking subject there is an absence there where he speaks.[22]

The conflation of two incompatible ideas of difference – the linguistic definition of relations between elements in a system, and the realist notion of the referential loss in language – thus marks one of the conditions under which the peculiar figure of the formation of the subject in language is produced.

Third, even when the old empiricist chestnut of representation is not reintroduced into the definition of language, Lacan will not allow his view of language-as-system to stand simply as the work of a particular theoreti-cal model, whose own techniques and rules (of combination, substitution, etc.) determine what *counts* as linguistic organization for certain purposes (these techniques and purposes being different from those found in other linguistic models such as Chomsky's generative grammar). On the con-trary, it is assumed that the theoretical model embodies a structure which operates in relation to consciousness and which thus provides a necessary drama of misrecognition in the subject's entry into language. This point can be taken further by discussing the psychoanalytic metaphors relating specifically to sexual difference.

'THE RECOGNITION OF DIFFERENCE'

Like the Freudian castration complex, Lacan's use of the term 'phallus' to describe the ordering of sexual difference has been a contentious issue in psychoanalysis and feminism. Some writers have seen Lacan's theory as continuing a phallocratic tradition in which 'woman' does not have her own positive definition, but is seen negatively from the male position as that which is different from it: she is assumed to exist in the singular, to lack something, as in the Freudian idea of penis envy, and to be important primarily in the way she poses a threat to male sexuality that must in turn be disavowed. Luce Irigaray, for example, has proposed an alternative to the Lacanian idea of signification, an idea of the feminine as plural, fluid and impossible to define as an effect of the phallic order.[23] In general, the main contention has occurred over whether Lacan allows the system of signification to appear under the limits set by a term which is ultimately the definition of the male.[24]

In defence of Lacan, it is said that in his return to Freud he shows that sexuality and sexual difference are never natural givens, but are effects constructed in signification and cultural relations. So, for example, it is argued that 'need' is mediated through 'desire' which links the subject to the Other, the serialized absence and presence of signifying processes.[25] This idea applies not only to the infant but to love and sexual relations more generally: as Stephen Heath remarks, in relation to the unconscious there is no sexual relation as such, one subject complementing another, but rather a movement of desire through the signifier.[26]

Along similar lines, Rose states that the phallus is privileged only because it is the mark of a symbolic ordering of sexual difference which is never the realization of a biological or psychological essence.[27] For Lacan, 'there is nothing in the unconscious which accords with the body'.[28] Hence it is important not to confuse the phallus with the penis: the former marks the fact of symbolic differentiation through which the subject is constructed, and which undercuts even the most secure recognitions of male or female identity. Rose adds that Lacan is questioning exactly that consistency of difference whereby the feminine is catalogued as other, with reference to difference in the body as something given in nature.[29]

Heath, too, accepts these claims but argues that Lacan does in fact lapse into biologism, and that consequently he naturalizes a phallic or patriarchal bias in the process of signification itself, and hence in sexual representations at the very level of form. Heath argues that the notion of the phallus as mark of the symbolic construction of subjectivity is allowed to coincide with a vision of sexual difference as given, apparently, in nature, thus reducing sexuality to genitality.[30] A circle thus develops: to see sexual difference is to know its meaning, which confirms the phallus as that which the male has and the female lacks: in turn, a whole ideological representation of difference can thus be guaranteed by 'the way things are'. Belief in some natural reality of sexuality thus threatens to undermine the idea that subjectivity is symbolically organized. 'Woman', although supposedly equal with 'man', is defined again as mere alterity, missing out on the phallus and missing in the discourse it organizes.[31] It is only in this way that the phallus can appear as 'the logical copula',[32] as the self-evident symbol for sexual difference. This fixation is measured, by Heath, against the historically open transformations in the unconscious.[33] For Heath, it is necessary to return constantly to the Symbolic, the unconscious, as a process of *producing* differences, and so resist the danger of accepting that difference which is already *produced*, accepted, which closes the signifier on the signified, and is justified by mythic reference to the phallic norm as natural.[34]

Now, while it is true that Lacan has recourse to an idea of seeing and knowing difference in the body, this problem is not solved by referring to the Symbolic as the site of a genuine articulation of subjectivity and difference, that is irreducible to phallic bias. Within the framework which we are analysing, to force the subject to retreat to the mediations of the symbolic structure is already a means of inviting it to return yet again, as that which experiences the effects of that structure in the Imaginary. The problem which Heath identifies in Lacan's biologism is only an element in a much wider deployment of discursive figures, including the Symbolic, where the idea of consciousness is retained in order to argue that the subject is formed in division. It is a different kind of criticism from those just summarized, therefore, to say that, as an instance of this retention, the Lacanian theory *has* to refer to the phallus as both signifier and object (organ), and that what is problematic is the configuration into which these two kinds of reference are moulded. To elucidate this point, we return to Lacan's text, 'The Signification of the Phallus'.[35]

Here we find that the phallus does, indeed, have the function of a signifier, so that from this point of view it is not the penis: the meaning of the latter could only ever be articulated through the principle of symbolization like any other signified. The phallus marks the two interrelated kinds of symbolic regulation: the linguistic structure of the unconscious, and the Oedipal complex understood as the structuring of subjectivity. So, for example, the imaginary unity of the mother/child dyad is broken by the father, who functions not as a referent but as a signifier, relating to the law of the formation of the subject in difference, so that the male definition of sexualities is not natural, merely normative.[36] But in relation to both kinds of regulation, a major problem arises. How does the subject, defined initially in the Imaginary, 'recognize' difference? (Without such recognition, the subject cannot enter the Symbolic, which in turn has no historical realization or effect.) Arguably, the phallus (difference) is not something which a subject can 'see' or 'recognize' at all, and this applies not only to Lacan's speculation about 'vision' but also to the category of the Symbolic which Lacan's critics continue to employ as the key to subjectivity.

As already seen, recognition of the phallus is not something which can be given in a pure experience of the body, the whole attempt being to resist ideas of nature, instinct, need, as points of origin and to see them as signifieds organized through the signifier.[37] However, the Lacanian theory only works by assuming that the systemic difference which effects the subject is acceded to by an empirical perception of difference: no structural consequence of language or of the castration complex can take effect unless there occurs in the subject a 'moment of experience' of difference.[38]

The recognition of difference is actually quite difficult to pin down in Lacan's account. On the one hand, the phallus as signifier is what governs the field of the signified, articulating desire and subjectivity at the level of language. Lacan can detach himself from any notion that the phallus is empirically knowable as 'the most tangible element in the real of sexual copulation', or as a natural equivalent to the already mentioned 'logical copula' of difference, since such locutions conceal the fact that the role of the phallus is 'veiled'. On the other hand, in order to argue that the function of the signifier is hidden from the subject of the Imaginary, Lacan must retain the idea of the subject of consciousness. His claim that the role of the phallus is veiled is thus merely a variant on the structuralist theme of misrecognition which we are analysing. Now, the experience of difference can be identified with the subject's perception of anatomical difference, even if this perception is not constitutive of the subject. But there is no overriding reason for Lacan to define the experience of difference in this particular way. So, for instance, he can define it as the point at which the subject recognizes that its own imaginary investment in the mother as having the phallus must fail, since the phallus as signifier in the field of the Other inevitably brings division to any subject and relation.[39]

The key point to make here is that effects of difference in the signifier must be registered as an empirical event in the consciousness. The figure of subject-formation thus operates strategically by keeping the idea of consciousness as the site of immediate recognition of difference, allegedly in a form coinciding with difference in the signifier. At the same time, the latter, since it is also construed as a purely logical relation, can be said to evade the grasp of consciousness and so comprise its unconscious. The conflation of two discontinuous ideas of difference is thus found at the heart of the figure of subject-constitution in the Symbolic.

'Difference' at the level of the signifier in fact can be treated as a quite limited effect of a particular linguistic model. It can be identified with methods of establishing differential couplings (for example, making the distinction between voiced and unvoiced phonemes), or more generally with the processes of identifying paradigmatic relations between elements that can be drawn into syntagmatic articulations according to certain codes, such as rules of word-order in a language (or analogously for cinema, rules of editing). The phallus, in the sense of the system of the signifier, is not something one can happen to 'see' or fail to see, because it is simply the name rather imaginatively given to what ought to be treated as the action of a limited set of rules or conventions, by means of which one defines elements in oppositive relations such that they can be articulated. That is, the signifier is something which one 'recognizes' only when one activates the discursive rules or techniques of the linguistic model in which it is constituted, and it ought not to be thought of as given to (or withheld from) consciousness independently of the circulation and use of those rules. The signifying chain is 'interminable' only in the sense that one continues to repeat particular procedures of linguistic patterning.

115

Moreover, in Lacan's account of the Imaginary and Symbolic, if a subject is said to *experience* difference (for example, the presence or absence of an object, its identity with or separateness from the subject), then it is still situated in the Imaginary, precisely because the *form* of difference here is an event of meaning given to consciousness. And at that point, the only criterion offered for the recognition of presence and absence, identity and difference, is the sensationalist one of experience and its mysterious intelligibility in the mind. The idea of an interplay of Imaginary and Symbolic can thus be seen to break down.[40]

The Oedipal and cultural inflection of the Symbolic is similarly predicated on this *play on the word* 'difference'. The phallus recognized cannot be the system of differential relations, since this is taken as the principle which *organizes* subject-positions and the ideas of identity which it is possible to have. Such a principle is not something one could see as present or absent in the body: it is a condition of perception rather than the content of an individual perception. To say that the subject in the Imaginary recognizes the phallus must therefore mean that he or she *perceives* the possibility that the body could be different, in a way that somehow allows the passage into the Symbolic. But merely to see genital difference tells one nothing about those conditions of symbolic ordering which construct representations of the body. Either the subject is already in the symbolic, cultural ordering, or it must be assumed that such ordering coincides with a pre-discursive capacity to experience difference in a form which is appropriate to all subsequent codings. Again, in the latter case, the empiricist appeal to experience means the subject is still construed as being in the Imaginary.

These remarks indicate that the Lacanian schema of subject-formation is ultimately incoherent. It may also be noted that the use of this schema does not solve the types of problem which Paul Hirst has identified in an adjacent area, namely Althusser's theory of subjectivity and ideology.[41] Hirst has demonstrated the contradictions involved in the idea that the individual, who is not yet a subject, is formed as a subject for a social structure through a process of hailing and recognition. It will be remembered that, for Althusser, this process is a dual mirror relation in which the individual sees and identifies with that image of itself as subject which the structure provides. But how can it identify with that image unless it already has the capacity for recognition appropriate to its existence as subject? This capacity is simply assumed, independently of any determinate means of recognition which are supposed to constitute subjectivity. The idea of interpellation retains an empiricist conception of recognition as the universally given capacity of the subject to know self-evident objects through experience. This assumed process of recognition is now treated, however, as one in which the subject fails to see that the obviousness of its knowledge of the world has been made possible by its interpellation within the structure. The subject thus imagines itself to be the origin of its own modes

116

of action and speech, and is blind to the fact that it has already been constituted for this apparently constitutive role. Through this imaginary relation to its real conditions of existence, that is, through ideology, the subject thus comes to support the structure in which it is interpellated. The idea of misrecognition thus requires Althusser to posit the subject of consciousness whose formation is supposedly being explained. The Lacanian theory of the Imaginary/Symbolic relation, although problematizing the unity of the ego which Althusser appears to accept, only compounds these problems: it continues to posit the subject of consciousness who is caught up in a relation of misrecognition, a relation now located in a continuous play of the signifier and necessary lack in being, or desire.

A SUMMARY OF STRATEGIES IN LACANIAN THEORY

Misrecognition is that assumed process in which knowledge of the conditions of representation is withheld from consciousness.[42] In relation to this problem in Lacan, it may be useful to expand on our comments about his conflation of two distinct concepts of language.

On the one hand, as indicated above, the hypothesis is retained, in a kind of theoretical chess-move, that language could transparently show the world to the mind. The definition of the Imaginary depends on the idea of representation to evoke a provisional unity of the world and word, and on the idea of expression to suggest an apparent unity of self and word. On the other hand, language is defined in terms of a grammar, or set of codes which determine the formation of utterances. The system of language here can be treated as a material ensemble of techniques and conventions which *produce* particular effects of meaning and recognition, and which need not be construed as existing in relation to a subject who somehow experiences meaning autonomously, or realizes the effects of an ideal structure in an indeterminate moment of experience.

Only within the first-mentioned of these conceptions is it possible to think of language as expressing consciousness and representing the world to the subject, or as failing to do these things. In the second (systemic) conception, what counts as linguistic organization is determined by a set of grammatical and conventional relations. It is only by continually blurring these opposed concepts of language, and consequently treating the systemic relations as a point where subject and language fail to have an integrally expressive relation, and where the subject fails to know what it is that organizes its experience, that one can conjure up the figure of the subject's formation in language through misrecognition. Given this strategy of argument, it then appears that, in the real, something called the subject undergoes a constant experience of division and formation, Lacan's 'essential vacillation'[43] between a wanting-to-be in language and a loss experienced because the subject can only ever come into being through the system of the signifier which already divides it. This view shows the wishful

117

thinking of a rationalism, which assumes that the theoretical model it builds comprises an ontological structure which must find its realization in history. What should be displaced by a materialist view of language as a set of techniques which produces effects of meaning, is not consciousness (giving way to a logic of desire based on lack), but the *concept* of consciousness, in which case there would be no question of the capacity or failure of the subject to know the structure of the signifier.

The psychoanalytic theory discussed here draws support from a form of reasoning that is associated more generally with phenomenological interventions in linguistics, such as those made by Benveniste and Ricoeur. Very broadly, the interest of such phenomenological writings is in how to understand the dynamics of subjectivity in relation to linguistics, which seems to construct language as the self-contained object of a science. In the work of the writers just referred to[44] a reality of language is defined in terms which go beyond either an idealism of the subject or a formalism of linguistic structures. Subject and structure are seen not as independently existing categories to be set in a dualistic exchange, but as mutually constitutive terms, whose genuinely dialectical relation gives rise to a sense of language and subjectivity as process. The linguistic system is realized, its abstract signifying potential is moved towards meaning and reference, through the act in which a subject draws upon it to speak. At the same time, however, this subject who realizes the possibilities held in the system is not a predefined entity for whom language would merely be an instrument of communication. On the contrary, the subject is formed by bringing into play the co-ordinates of the sign; it is to be understood precisely as a speaking subject.

To illustrate this, we may cite Benveniste's contrast between 'language' as the formal system whose terms await realization, and 'discourse' as an instance in which the subject is constituted by using language:

> Language is . . . the possibility of subjectivity because it always contains the linguistic forms appropriate to the expression of subjectivity, and discourse provokes the emergence of subjectivity because it consists of discrete instances. In some way language puts forth 'empty' forms which each speaker, in the exercise of discourse, appropriates to himself and which he relates to his 'person', at the same time defining himself as *I* and a partner as *you*. The instance of discourse is thus constitutive of all the coordinates that define the subject.[45]

The subject thus fills the empty forms of language, but its relations *as* subject arise within the forms of speaking which are mobilised. ' "Ego" is he who says "ego" '.[46] For Benveniste, enunciation is the process of making a statement, which is irreducible to the grammatical form of the statement made. To take the important case of the first person: the *I* who speaks is not the same as the subject referred to in the utterance (as seen in the famous paradox, 'I am lying'). The value of the pronoun is not given by the system alone, but nor does the individuality of *I* stem from some prior being ('How could the same term refer indifferently to any individual whatsoever and still at the same time identify him in his individuality?').[47] The first person, because it is without a fixed signified, is suited to use by different individuals: through its function we see that language comes to signify, but on the condition that the speaker refer each time to the instance of discourse in which he or she is constructed by saying *I*. This exemplifies the way that the subject is constituted by performing the possibilities contained in the structure of language which, through that performance, finds its reason to be.[48]

Lacan's writings repeat the theme that structure and subject can be understood only through an interplay which constitutes a further dialectical term, the formation of the subject in language, now treating the latter not as a positive guarantee of being (as it may appear for a Benveniste), but as an experience of division and lack. So, for example, the relation of enunciation and enounced is experienced as a splitting: I can become a subject only by saying *I*, but this very term is not 'mine', since it belongs to the signifying chain and refers to its articulation of differential elements, including the *you*, *he* or *she*, in structuring relations of which the one who speaks is but a passing effect. Thus, instead of the plenitude and unity of Benveniste's 'instance of discourse', there is disunity, a lacuna in the very process of coming into being, referred to as desire, and through which the structural Other is itself realized in history without ever being reduced to particular instances of experience. Once again, this kind of account relies on our supposing that the linguistic terms, in this case pronouns, are not simply conventional signs of identity, but that (as with Benveniste) they must come into an existential relation with consciousness and be invested with the real presence of the subject in time and space, or (as with Lacan) that they mark the displacement of the consciousness which hypothetically might have appeared in its own right there where it cannot, in the structure which founds it.

In either of its variants, this kind of argument reproduces what Foucault has referred to as the transcendental/empirical couple by means of which the modern figure of the subject ('man') is constructed. This is the figure in which subjectivity and knowledge are formed within certain empirical mechanisms (life, labour and language), whose perceived historical limits give rise to an attempt in the human sciences to make them stand also for the transcendental conditions of subjectivity. 'Man' can no longer 'posit himself in the immediate and sovereign transparency of a *cogito*': instead, the image of transcendental subjectivity is recovered by bringing out the value of the empirical determinations at the level of experience which in turn makes their functioning possible.[49]

119

To make the connection here, let us pursue Benveniste's idea of 'address'. According to his account, I posit myself as subject only by saying *I* in relation to a *you*, who in turn may become an *I* to my *you*. To become a subject is to be inducted into the purely empirical, pronominal play of differences. This situation of address marks the emergence of a fundamental property of language in being, and language provides the very definition of subjectivity.[50] This subjectivity is not defined by a feeling one experiences of being oneself, which is subsequently expressed in language.[51] On the other hand, this grammatical precondition relies on the subject's experience of identity in and through language. In this sense, linguistics, while describing language as an empirical mechanism, begins to recover a knowledge of language as a transcendental staging of the possibility and forms of subjectivity. The basis of subjectivity may be 'determined by the linguistic status of person', yet 'language is possible because each speaker sets himself up as a *subject* by referring to himself as *I* in his discourse'.[52] Even though the relations of 'person' are linguistically founded, the *I* 'must be established in the individual's own consciousness in order to become accessible to that of the fellow human being'.[53] Hence, grammatical person is itself defined in relation to the individual, who experiences itself as a distinct entity through relations of difference from others, in the forms of exchange which are already appropriate to that experience. As seen in the quotation already given, language is, for Benveniste, 'the possibility of subjectivity' because it contains the forms already geared 'to the *expression* of subjectivity' (my emphasis).[54] Such a definition thus assumes that the individual already has the capacity to experience that identity to which language will come to refer.

Our earlier discussion should indicate that for Lacan, too, language is a transcendental *mise-en-scène*. The system of the signifier is that which makes possible the emergence of the subject. At the same time, as we have seen, the idea of the experiencing subject is retained in order to give the point of realization of possibilities held in the system, with which the subject must always remain in a relation of misrecognition, marking (in contrast to Benveniste) the non-being in existence.[55] The interplay of the transcendental and empirical subject is a figure inscribed firmly in the Lacanian metaphors of subject-formation which we have discussed.

CONCLUSION

Some problems in using Lacanian theory to analyse cinema and other cultural practices may be noted briefly. This model tends to reduce diverse representational practices to the single mechanism of psychoanalytic subject-formation through misrecognition. Different kinds of mental and bodily capacities (for instance, in relation to reading and acting), which individuals may acquire within particular cultural relations, organizations of knowledge, uses of representational techniques and technologies, tend to be seen as manifestations of this essential structure of subjectivity.[56] The focus on the relation of subject and signifier also arguably assigns too narrow a logic, on the basis of linguistic ordering, to the various styles of discursive and institutional practice which are encountered in a medium like film (with its uses of textual and cultural modes of constructing character, narrative, trainings in editing or acting, relations of dissemination etc.). Moreover, the teleological view of subject-formation makes it appear (in a very unBrechtian way) that the effects produced by some particular use of representational techniques, such as point-of-view editing, are necessary outcomes, since they are what is required to secure the subject's misrecognition, in its imaginary relation to the signifying order.

A corollary of the semiotic-psychoanalytic account has been a critique of realism in the cinema, as the concealment of the process by which sense is constructed: a critique which tends to lead into a utopian vote for the return of the repressed, another 'space', the irruption of the signifying chain whose infinite possibilities of *écriture* have been suppressed for the safety of some dominant signified.[57] This principle of excess may be brought to coincide with the oppositions of male and female. One finds this in a wide range of texts: from the kind of account represented in Laura Mulvey's 'Visual Pleasure and Narrative Cinema'[58] according to which cinematic representation embodies mechanisms of male voyeurism and fetishism, which seek to deny the threat of difference and potential excess posed by the woman as other; through familiar notions of feminine writing as closer than masculine writing to the body, as fluid and transgressive; to a style of argument found in Heath's *The Sexual Fix*,[59] in favour of transcending the normative 'fixing' of identities in representation, a possibility to be achieved by means of a continual, progressive movement *between* polarities, for a truth of subjectivity which it is still the privilege of supposedly repressed sexuality to promise.

The general aim here has not been to dismiss Lacanian and related theoretical work as total error, but to indicate a number of problems within it which have not been adequately acknowledged, and which might give reason to change some of its terms into less global and more flexible currency. So, for example, one might detach the idea of the effectivity of representational, discursive means in organizing particular forms of recognition, from the epistemological theory of subject-formation which it is made to underpin. Similarly, the totalizing categories of subject and linguistic structure used in the particular mode of analysis which we have discussed can clearly be disaggregated into various historical constructions of the person (including the sexual person and definitions of gender), techniques of individualization, organizations of conduct, modes of language training and so on.

Some criticisms of psychoanalytic theory imply that it could be explained away as the mere 'reflection' of immediate, sociological determinations and interests. Without accepting such reductivism, or implying that historical and psychoanalytic modes of analysis are mutually exclusive, it might be possible to reflect further on the paradigms of sexuality which are used in the account of subject-formation which we have considered. Arguably, in its use of the castration complex and the idea of the phallus as the mark of signification, this account essentializes certain elements of a sexual characterology formed in a particular nexus of sexual medicine and sexology (including the late nineteenth-century character types which Foucault describes in *The History of Sexuality*: the impotent male, the nervous female identified with a sexuality that might be dangerous, and so on).[60]

From one point of view, it seems curious that the idea of difference in the *signifier* should be associated with possibilities of sexual difference, whose recognition marks the division endlessly played out within the subject's own being. This has not always seemed a self-evident connection to make between linguistics and knowledges of sexuality. It is as if the current epistemological figure of the subject/language relation were simply able to fall in with character types and sexualizations of the body which circulated in earlier discourses, and rework them for a radical ontology of the subject. An example might be the conception of bisexuality used by Freud to indicate a stage in the genesis of the subject through polymorphous perverse possibilities towards 'normal' adult sexuality. In some current writing, a notion of bisexuality has been invested with a new (or greatly altered) potential, where it can give sexual content to a residually Romantic notion that true subjectivity is to be found in the incompletion of the self, the active tension between thought and feeling, mental consciousness and pulsional experience, and indeed, between the masculine closure of representation and the feminine possibility of excess. In this case, it becomes possible to speak in the same breath of a plethora of unrealized differences for the subject positioned in the signifying process, and an oscillation between sexual polarities, not bisexuality in any fixated form, but a continual, androgynous deferral of identity, the intermediate space of desire: these two terms coming together to create a sense of the radical possibilities of the subject's realization in history.[61] However, historical speculations concerning the relations between subjectivity, discourse and regulations of sexuality obviously go well beyond the scope of this article.[62] The main purpose here has been to counsel a divorce for the Lacanian marriage of psychoanalysis and linguistics which, despite the blessings of Saint Teresa,[63] was not made in heaven.

NOTES

This article is based on a section of my Ph.D. thesis, 'Reconsidering Film Theory', Griffith University, Brisbane, 1983. I would like to thank Ian Hunter, Jeffrey Minson, David Saunders and Beverley Brown for many discussions and for extensive comments on drafts. Responsibility for any problems in the article is, of course, my own. First published in *Screen*, Winter 1987, vol. 28, no. 1, pp. 10–25.

1 Jacques Lacan, 'The Agency of the Letter in the Unconscious or Reason since Freud', in *Ecrits: A Selection*, trans. Alan Sheridan, London, Tavistock, 1977, p. 149.
2 ibid.
3 ibid., pp. 152–3.
4 ibid., p. 153.
5 ibid., p. 154.
6 ibid., p. 153.
7 Cf. Jacques Lacan, *Le Séminaire livre XX: Encore*, Paris, Seuil, 1975, p. 48, where the subject is defined as the intermediate effect of the movement between signifiers.
8 See especially part II of Jacques Lacan, 'The Agency of the Letter . . .', op. cit.
9 ibid., p. 166.
10 ibid., p. 159.
11 Cf. Colin MacCabe, 'Presentation of "The Imaginary Signifier" ', *Screen*, Summer 1975, vol. 16, no. 2, p. 7.
12 Jacques Lacan, 'The Mirror Stage as Formative of the Function of the I', in *Ecrits: A Selection*, op. cit., pp. 1–7.
13 As Rosalind Coward and John Ellis point out in *Language and Materialism*, London, Routledge & Kegan Paul, 1977, pp. 110–11, this initial image of the ego's unity can take on new investments after entering the world of social difference and critical judgement.
14 Juliet Mitchell and Jacqueline Rose (eds), *Feminine Sexuality: Jacques Lacan and the Ecole Freudienne*, London, Macmillan, 1982, p. 31.
15 To mention just a few of the texts in which Lacanian theory plays a significant role: Christian Metz, *Psychoanalysis and Cinema*, London, Macmillan, 1982; Stephen Heath, *Questions of Cinema*, London, Macmillan, 1981; Coward and Ellis, op. cit.; Annette Kuhn, *Women's Pictures: Feminism and Cinema*, London, Routledge & Kegan Paul, 1982; together with many of the articles which have appeared in *Screen, Camera Obscura*, etc.
16 Lacan, *Ecrits: A Selection*, op. cit., pp. 1–2.
17 It is sometimes observed that the Imaginary/Symbolic dialectic is a diachronic fable used to describe a synchronic relation, which is not completed once and for all, but persists as a continuous process of forming the subject. However, this qualification does not settle the issue of misrecognition. See, for example, Colin MacCabe, 'On Discourse', *Economy and Society*, 1979, vol. 8, no. 4, p. 284.
18 Jacqueline Rose, 'Introduction – II', in Mitchell and Rose, op. cit., p. 31.
19 Christian Metz, 'The Imaginary Signifier', *Screen*, Summer 1975, vol. 16, no. 2, pp. 14–76.
20 ibid., p. 58.
21 ibid., pp. 59–61 and 14–18.
22 MacCabe, 'Presentation of "The Imaginary Signifier" ', op. cit., p. 10. In relation to the general issue at stake here, Foucault argues that structuralism depends on a particular conception of the subject of consciousness. The subject retreats behind the linguistic mechanism of which it is the limited construct, only to return in the form of an experience necessary to set the machine of language in motion (cf. the theme of misrecognition and the Imaginary). See Michel Foucault, *The Order of Things*, New York, Vintage Books, 1973, especially chapters 8 and 9.

23 For example, Luce Irigaray, *This Sex Which is Not One*, trans. Catherine Porter with Carolyn Burke, Ithaca, Cornell University Press, 1985.

24 For discussion of this, see Mitchell and Rose, op. cit.; Jane Gallop, *The Daughter's Seduction*, Ithaca, Cornell University Press, 1982; Stephen Heath, 'Difference', Chapter 3, pp. 47–106 in this volume; originally published in *Screen*, Autumn 1978, vol. 19, no. 3, pp. 51–112. Page numbers cited in the following notes refer to the present book.

25 Lacan, *Ecrits: A Selection*, op. cit. pp. 286–7.

26 Heath, 'Difference', op. cit., p. 57.

27 Jacqueline Rose, 'Introduction – II', in Mitchell and Rose, op. cit., pp. 27–57.

28 Jacques Lacan, 'Seminar of 21 January 1975', in Mitchell and Rose, op. cit., p. 165.

29 ibid., p. 56: 'For Lacan, to say that difference is "phallic" difference is to expose the symbolic and arbitrary nature of its division as such.'

30 Heath, 'Difference', op. cit. On this point see especially part 1, including the reference (p. 49) to Freud's assumption that the girl's 'deficiency' is discovered by seeing the penis.

31 ibid., p. 54.

32 Lacan, *Ecrits: A Selection*, op. cit., p. 287.

33 Heath, 'Difference', op. cit., p. 64 and elsewhere.

34 ibid., p. 96.

35 Lacan, *Ecrits: A Selection*, op. cit., pp. 281–91.

36 Cf. Mitchell and Rose, op. cit., pp. 39 and 69.

37 Cf. Lacan, *Ecrits: A Selection*, op. cit., pp. 285–6.

38 For this and the phrases quoted in the next paragraph, see ibid., pp. 287–9.

39 ibid., pp. 288–9.

40 A further example of the conflation of experiential and linguistic difference is provided by Lacan's reference to the *fort/da* game described by Freud. See Jacques Lacan, *Speech and Language in Psychoanalysis*, Baltimore, Johns Hopkins University Press, 1981, p. 39, and cf. Coward and Ellis, op. cit., pp. 104–5.

41 Louis Althusser, 'Ideology and Ideological State Apparatuses', in *Lenin and Philosophy*, New York, Monthly Review Press, 1971; Paul Q. Hirst, *On Law and Ideology*, London, Macmillan, 1979, chapter 3. For a different view on the relation of Lacan to Althusser, see Stephen Heath, 'The Turn of the Subject', *Ciné-Tracts*, 1979, vol. 2, nos. 3–4, pp. 32–48.

42 Cf. MacCabe, 'Presentation of "The Imaginary Signifier" ', op. cit., p. 11: 'The introduction of the symbolic allows language to function as the grasping of opposition and difference. But this recognition can never exist at the moment of speaking (else how could we say anything?).'

43 Jacques Lacan, *The Four Fundamental Concepts of Psychoanalysis*, London, Hogarth Press, 1977, p. 83.

44 See, for example, 'Structure, Word, Event', in C. Reagan and D. Stewart (eds), *The Philosophy of Paul Ricoeur*, Boston, Beacon Press, 1978, pp. 109–19; and Emile Benveniste, *Problems in General Linguistics*, Coral Gables, Florida, University of Miami Press, 1971, especially chapters 18–22, although not all Benveniste's work is reducible to the philosophical argument identified here.

45 Benveniste, op. cit., p. 227.

46 ibid., p. 224.

47 ibid., p. 226.

48 Of course, not all language use is referred to as 'discourse' by Benveniste, since some statements (in the mode of *histoire* or story) allegedly fail to show their own enunciation, but this does not affect the main argument here.

49 Michel Foucault, *The Order of Things: An Archaeology of the Human Sciences*, London, Tavistock, 1974, chapter 9: these citations are from pp. 320–2.
50 Benveniste, op. cit., pp. 224–5.
51 ibid., p. 224.
52 ibid., p. 225.
53 ibid.
54 ibid., p. 227.
55 Cf. Lacan, *Le Séminaire livre XX*, op. cit., p. 35.
56 The topic of differential social formations of human attributes is explored in Paul Hirst and Penny Woolley, *Social Relations and Human Attributes*, London, Tavistock, 1982; see, for example, chapter 2.
57 See, for example, Stephen Heath, 'Narrative Space', *Screen*, Autumn 1976, vol. 17, no. 3, pp. 68–112.
58 Laura Mulvey, 'Visual Pleasure and Narrative Cinema', chapter 1, pp. 22–34 in this volume; originally published in *Screen*, Autumn 1975, vol. 16, no. 3, pp. 6–18.
59 Stephen Heath, *The Sexual Fix*, London, Macmillan, 1982.
60 Cf. Michel Foucault, *The History of Sexuality, Volume 1*, New York, Vintage Books, 1980, especially part 4, chapters 3 and 4.
61 See, for example, arguments mounted in Heath, 'Difference', op. cit. and *The Sexual Fix*, op. cit.
62 One area of historical relations, the encounter between literature, sexuality and obscenity law, is the subject of a forthcoming book, co-authored by Ian Hunter, David Saunders and Dugald Williamson, entitled *On Pornography: Literature, Sexuality and Obscenity Law*, London, Macmillan.
63 Lacan's *Séminaire XX* discusses Bernini's *The Ecstasy of Saint Teresa* as a representation of 'the *jouissance* of the woman' and it is illustrated on the cover.

Part II
PORNOGRAPHY

INTRODUCTION

Why treat pornography seriously? When *Screen* published its first articles on pornography in 1980, pornography had already become the focus for a great deal of feminist writing, activity and debate. Initially, the feminist attack on pornography targetted obvious forms of pornography: gradually, however, the definition of pornography was extended by some groups to include all images of women designed to perpetuate what was seen as a male, sexist, patriarchal perspective. Images of women in advertising and glossy magazines were considered just as offensive as those in porno-graphic films, *Playboy* and *Penthouse*. This all-embracing definition of pornography was evident in the slogans that proclaimed that pornography not only *caused* violence against women, it *was* violence against women. Not all feminists adopted such a dogmatic position; those who criticized this view did so on the grounds that it not only ignored the question of woman's sexual fantasies and desires, it also assumed that the images of women displayed in pornography were 'real'; that is, that the images presented a simple and unconstructed 'reflection' of events in the real world.

Screen's contribution to this highly controversial issue was to provide a forum for a discussion of pornography as a form of representation. Emphasis was also placed on pornography as a regime of representation which exploited a network of relations between sexuality, gender and power. All of the chapters in part II at some point discuss pornography as representation and stress the importance of studying the various visual codes, narrative structures and forms of identification which characterize pornography. Most of the articles draw on theories of the classic realist text, that is of the non-pornographic mainstream film, as a basis from which to hypothesize about the nature of pornography. On the one hand, notions of spectatorship in Laura Mulvey's highly influential 'Visual Pleasure' (chapter 1) provided a means of understanding pornography, while on the other hand pornography provided a means of questioning some of the assumptions in the Mulvey article. In particular pornography, with its blatant display of the female genitalia, raised problems for the notion of fetishism which was central to her theory of fetishism and the male gaze.

One of the most important and interesting developments arising from the pornography debate in *Screen* was the inclusion of fantasy as a crucial issue in debates involving identification and spectatorship. This opened the way for a preliminary discussion of the multiple, fluid, mobile nature of identification. Feminists were asked to consider the relationship between sexuality and aggression in the human psyche – not just the male psyche. In other words, what kind of pleasure might the female spectator derive from watching pornography designed with a male spectator in mind? The following chapters trace the development of the pornography debate, its key issues and concerns. Two areas which were not taken up until later, and are not explored here, relate to the nature of female desire. If women were to construct their own pornography – or erotica – what would it be like? Would lesbian pornography, aimed at the lesbian spectator, differ from a pornography for heterosexual women? Another aspect of pornography relates to the issue of masculinity. What do we make of those films which depict man as the victim of the dominating, cruel woman? To what extent does pornography position the male spectator as a masochist? In general, it is assumed that pornography represents men as powerful and in control and women as objects of their sexual pleasure. A comprehensive study of the range of sexualities and subjectivities presented in pornography makes it clear that pornography is a complex and unpredictable regime of representation.

Griselda Pollock's 'What's Wrong with "Images of Women"?' raises a number of issues about the representation of women in patriarchal society which are crucial to an understanding of pornography. Her analysis continues to have relevance to contemporary debates of the 1980s despite the advances made in the general level of understanding about the nature of representation and the role ideology plays in that process. Pollock sees an 'unbridged gap' between feminists who are highly critical of the way women are portrayed in the media but lack an understanding of the role ideology plays in that process, and a smaller group of feminists, many of whom are involved professionally in the area and who have developed a sophisticated theoretical analysis of representation. The views of the latter are only circulated in publications of small study groups. In Pollock's opinion it is crucial that feminists develop a full understanding of the way visual codes work, as well as of the role ideology plays in representation, if they are to make successful political interventions concerning the portrayal of women in the media. To illustrate her point she draws attention to the misleading term 'images of women', which is increasingly used to describe workshops and courses of study.

The problem with a term such as 'images of women' is that it assumes that the 'image' presents an accurate reflection of the real world, that the relationship between the image and its referent is in no way mediated or constructed. A 'good' image is one which presents a 'truthful' reflection of women's real lives and is found in realist photographs; a bad image is one which presents women from an 'untruthful' or sexist perspective and is found in glossy magazines, advertisements, and so on. This view fails to consider that all 'images of women', regardless of their context, are constructions. Pollock argues that in order to undertake a radical critique of visual imagery, women need to understand how meanings are constructed and attached to different representations of women in all forms of visual discourse, including those produced by women. A failure to understand how meanings are constructed can lead women to create images which they believe are subversive of patriarchal forms of representations, but which in reality serve to reinforce these forms. She provides a number of extremely helpful analyses of various images drawn from advertising, popular culture, pornography, art and feminism.

Pollock's analysis of these issues is relevant to all discussions of the representation of women in different media forms – particularly pornography. As a genre form, pornography constructs representations of women according to a number of highly formalized codes and conventions. In order to combat pornography, it is first essential to understand how pornography constructs its imagery and the relationship of these to the dominant ideology. Pollock totally rejects the view that women can create an alternative set of images, for instance vaginal images, which would exist completely outside of prevailing modes of pornographic representation. She also points out that a study of pornography, particularly its confronting display of images of the female genitalia, questions the approach developed by Mulvey and Johnston in which they emphasize the crucial role of male castration anxiety. In her view a psychoanalytic approach to representation is inadequate. Pollock stresses that a proper study of representation must include an understanding not only of the workings of patriarchal ideology and psychoanalysis but also of bourgeois ideology and capitalism. Her article is of particular use to anyone contemplating a study of representation. It also provides an excellent introduction to the subject of pornography.

In publishing 'On Pornography' by John Ellis, *Screen* presented for the first time a sustained discussion of the nature of pornography. His article sparked a heated debate in later editions of *Screen*. He isolates three main positions regarding pornography in Britain in the early 1980s: the right-wing view represented by the Festival of Light; the liberal position represented by the Williams Report; and a number of feminist positions extending to either end of the Left–Right spectrum. Ellis considers the different approach of each group to issues surrounding pornography – its meaning, social function, legitimacy and future. In discussing the various feminist approaches to pornography, he raises an issue also explored by Pollock. This concerns the problems which arise when the pornographic image is seen as a simple and unmediated reflection of the 'real' world.

131

Ellis examines in detail one aspect of pornographic representation, that of the female genitals, in order to show that pornographic representation is not a coherent but a contradictory form. He begins with Pollock's observation that the representation of vaginal images in pornography challenges Mulvey's argument that mainstream narrative cinema attempts to deny the true nature of the female genitalia through the processes of fetishization. Unlike popular narrative cinema, pornography presents explicit images of the female genitalia; it does not fetishize woman's genitalia. Yet pornography adopts other structures associated with fetishism: the repetition of events, emphasis on woman's body, a direct and erotic presentation of woman's image. Rather than reject Mulvey's thesis, Ellis re-examines Freud's original argument about fetishism and concludes that fetishism involves a process of substitution of signifiers and is not necessarily dependent upon a 'primal look'. His suggestion that different structures of the gaze are brought into play in relation to the viewing of pornography held important implications for later debates about spectatorship.

An interesting point, argues Ellis, is that woman's orgasm, a central focus of pornography, is given the status of a fetish. Because of its obsession not with male but with female pleasure, Ellis argues, pornography is a profoundly unstable form of representation. Its instability is manifest in the kinds of attendant issues raised by pornography: What is the nature of male pleasure? What is sexuality? However, not all writers would agree with Ellis that pornography fails to raise questions about male desire. For instance, pornographic texts which depict scenes of male bondage, in which the male is victimized by an aggressive phallic woman, raise interesting questions about the possibility of a masochistic male spectator.

In 'Letter to John', Paul Willemen wonders why pornography should be asked at all to deal with questions such as 'what is sexuality'? Unlike Ellis, Willemen does not regard pornography as a particularly unstable form of representation. He takes issue with Ellis's article on several fronts, but his major criticism is that Ellis does not ask the most relevant questions. In Willemen's view the important issues are those which deal not with the more abstract areas of textual instability, sexuality and spectatorship, but with questions of economics and exhibition and the way in which social factors affect the reading of texts. Willemen argues that the direct-address images of pornography, particularly those of the genitalia, are more usefully understood in terms of 'the fourth look'. This is the look of the other which the viewer *imagines* might catch him/her in the act of looking at images which should not be looked at. In other words, the fourth look is the one which catches Peeping Tom peeping. One wonders how the fourth look might operate for a female spectator. Does she need to imagine that she might be caught in the act?

Willemen disagrees with Ellis that the proliferation of vaginal images suggests an improvement on previous forms of representation in that it brings the dreaded vagina into the open and consequently has an educative influence on the viewer. Willemen argues that the increasing availability of pornographic imagery points rather to a growing need to reassure the male of his continuing dominance. In this context, the imagined look of the other – the fourth look – is the look of woman. The power of the male spectatorial position is enhanced by imagining that it is woman who catches him looking at images which guarantee her submission to the power of the phallus. In contrast to Ellis, Willemen appears to see porno-graphy as more firmly under the sway of patriarchal ideology and thereby the less likely to exhibit instabilities which might be exploited by the theorist/filmmaker.

In 'The Heterosexual Presumption', Claire Pajaczkowska presents a strongly worded critique of the way in which the debate on pornography has either misappropriated or excluded crucial areas related to sexual difference: woman's pleasure; bisexuality; pre-oedipal sexuality. She argues that important issues, such as woman's pleasure, are often not addressed properly, particularly when used as pawns in a game of intellec-tual rivalry between men. Pajaczkowska takes issue with a number of the positions advanced in John Ellis's article, and criticizes him for using areas of psychoanalytic theory without thinking through the political ramifi-cations of these. She argues that the Freudian theory of fetishism which he uses is problematic, and questions the view that images of the female genitals always give rise to castration anxiety – a position which is central to Ellis's argument. Fear of castration alone does not explain the full nature of the threat: what is really at stake is the subject's fear of separation which has its roots in the pre-oedipal relationship with the mother – it is the fear which lies behind and augments the boy's later fear of castration. She also sees the infant's relationship with the maternal body as crucial to an understanding of other areas associated with pornography, such as sadism.

In particular, Pajaczkowska stresses that individuals are not simply gendered as male or female; gender identity is something laboured after but never finally achieved. She supports the poststructuralist view that masculinity and femininity should be conceptualized as 'positions' articu-lated within the text and offering a complex network of identifications. In view of this, we cannot presume that the pornographic text simply addresses the heterosexual male. All analyses should include a consider-ation of the bisexuality of the pre-Oedipal subject. Rather than bracketing off a discussion of homosexual pornography, it would be more honest to acknowledge the presence of a repressed homosexual desire at work within all texts, including pornography. Pajaczkowska, however, does not appear to include the question of lesbian desire in this context. Her article is particularly interesting in that it anticipated a number of debates which were to become central to feminist theory in the late 1980s, particularly the interest in the pre-oedipal and the maternal body.

133

Lesley Stern's 'The Body as Evidence' presents a comprehensive discussion of a number of areas not covered in the previous articles. First Stern traces the development of the feminist concern with pornography. Pornography was taken up as an issue by the Women's Movement at a time when its power had been seriously undermined by a number of successful attacks organized by right-wing forces whose aim was to get women out of the workforce and back into the home. Pornography provided an effective rallying point for the Women's Movement, particularly because it provided a clear, tangible, visible target. Stern, however, is critical, on a number of fronts, of the way in which pornography became a privileged feminist issue. One problem arose from a tendency to conflate the explicit *sex* of pornography with explicit *sexism*. Stern sees this as a retrograde step for feminism. Similarly, there is a tendency to conflate the representation of sex in pornography with violence, so that in some feminist quarters all representations of women signify a form of violence against women. Stern presents a thoughtful and much-needed critique of both the sex/sexism and sex/violence conflation in some feminist approaches to the subject.

Stern opens up a new area for consideration in theoretical discussions of pornography – the notion of 'fiction'. In her view, one reason why the subject of fiction has been ignored has to do with the relationship of fiction to phantasy and the confusing way in which the latter has been used. She draws a distinction between 'phantasy' and 'fantasy' and presents an interesting discussion of the various meanings of these terms in relation to fiction. What is most interesting is her discussion of the way in which theories of the classic realist text have dominated theoretical debates and in so doing have tended to preclude a discussion of the role of fiction in both mainstream film and pornography. Fiction is not specifically concerned with the real, nor does it offer pleasure through the processes of suture in the mode of the classic realist text. Her discussion of fiction – its characteristics and pleasures – opens up new ways of viewing both pornographic and non-pornographic texts. Like Pajaczkowska, Stern also stresses the importance of viewing sexuality as something which is not fixed. The view that sexuality is somehow pre-ordained invokes the problematic notion that there are 'natural', innate, forms of sexuality as well as ideologically 'correct' female fantasies. It is this notion which has led to ideological and theoretical splits between different feminist groups on the controversial subject of pornography.

5

WHAT'S WRONG WITH 'IMAGES OF WOMEN'?*

Griselda Pollock

I want to address myself within this article to what I consider to be an unbridged gap within the Women's Movement between an awareness of the role of ideology in visual representations of women in our oppression and the level of critical and theoretical analysis developed by a small number of largely professionally involved women. The political interest in images is evidenced by the frequency with which courses are set up under the misleading title 'Images of Women' in a variety of educational establishments and at women's studies conferences. The theoretical analysis is more specialized and therefore only appears in small distribution journals of small study groups. I have found myself working within both camps and I would like here both to examine the practical problems of bridging this gap without failing to incorporate the important theoretical issues and also to explore some of those issues without losing sight of their practical exercise in teaching. Many of the points I shall raise were originally developed by the collective work of a group of women over a long period, collecting images and experimenting in different teaching situations. Limitations of space do not allow for a full elaboration of issues, which are both complex and part of a much wider study of women and representations. For instance I cannot acknowledge properly within this article the full implications of the differences of media and qualities of photographs to be used as illustrations to the argument. Instead I shall try to outline the main points of our analysis and show certain images which we have found useful in teaching in this area.

* This title should be read as having a double meaning. It starts from the point of critique of images of women and moves on towards a critique of that formulation. At the time of publication I received a very useful commentary and critical response to the article from Jennifer Craig, of the Department of Cultural Studies at Griffith University, Brisbane, which indicated that some readers had not recognized the secondary implied title, which could be indicated thus: 'What's wrong with "Images of Women"?'. Two further articles return to the problem posed by this very early essay on the theme: G. Pollock, 'Missing Women: Rethinking Early Thoughts on Images of Women', in Carol Squiers (ed.), *The Critical Image*, Brighton, Harvester Press, 1990, and G. Pollock, 'Degas/Images/Women: Women/Degas/Images', in G. Pollock and R. Kendall (eds), *Dealing with Degas: Representations of Women and the Politics of Vision*, London, Pandora Books, 1992.

In 1972 a group of women involved in art and media practice, art history and feminist criticism formed the Women's Art History Collective in order to attempt some analysis of women's position in, and in relation to, the history of art and representations. Our starting point was first, an identification with the direct relevance of the issue to ourselves and our work as part of a political movement of women and second, a response to the still limited literature on the subject, for instance John Berger's *Ways of Seeing* and American publications which included the work of feminist academics like Hess and Baker, *Art and Sexual Politics* (Collier, 1971), and Hess and Nochlin, *Woman as Sex Object* (Allen Lane, 1973)[1], as well as documentary material in art magazines, notably the *Feminist Art Journal*. The literature highlighted many important problems but was not on the whole theoretically very rigorous or helpful. A third influence was the attempt made by certain feminist artists to provide what they termed an alternative and positive imagery of women which, though important in terms of the political solidarity it encouraged, in fact foregrounded the impossibility of challenging existing imagery without an adequate theory of ideology and representation.

Of all the areas to which the Women's Art History Collective addressed itself, that of 'Images of Women' has consistently proved itself the most difficult and resistant to satisfactory theory or practice. The problem can, I think, be analysed on four major fronts: the confusion and mystification of the issue created by the title 'Images of Women'; the problematic and as yet undefined relation between so called 'high culture' and the 'media' or 'popular culture'; the lack of theoretical definitions of what terms like sexist, patriarchal or bourgeois mean when applied to images; and finally what practice can be suggested in order to rupture dominant ideology and undertake a radical critique and transformation of visual imagery.

The first difficulty arises out of labelling the area of study as 'Images of Women'. The term implies a juxtaposition of two separable elements – women as a gender or social group versus representations of women, or a real entity, women, opposed to falsified, distorted or male views of women. It is a common misconception to see images as merely a reflection, good or bad, and compare 'bad' images of women (glossy magazine photographs, fashion advertisements etc.) to 'good' images of women ('realist' photographs, of women working, housewives, older women etc.). This conception represented by the title 'Images of Women' needs to be challenged and replaced by the notion of woman as a signifier in an ideological discourse in which one can identify the meanings that are attached to woman in different images and how the meanings are constructed in relation to other signifiers in that discourse. Thus rather than compare different kinds of images of women one needs to study the meanings signified by woman in images with reference, for instance, to man in images. A useful device for initiating this kind of work is the use of male/female reversals.

136

Figure 5:1   Figure 5:2

In 1973 *Women's Report* [2] published a reversal of the then current Bayer advertisement on the Seven Ages of Man (Figures 5:1 and 5:2) posing a young man in exactly the same position as the ad had placed an adolescent girl and changing the gender of the pronouns in the accompanying copy, which then read:

> Adolescence – a time of misgiving. Doubts about the site offered by parents to build a life on. Both head and heart subject to the tyranny of hormones. Youth under stress in search of an identity.
>
> B . . . is there to help *him* through this period of self-seeking. With textile fibres and dyestuffs for the fashionable clothes *he* needs to wear. . . . With raw ingredients for the cosmetics *he* uses to *create his own personality*. And simple remedies too. Like Aspirin . . . for the pain *he* will experience. (my italics)

The advertisement was one of a series of seven, but it was both the only female image and the only nude. The reversal serves initially to make strange the original image in which femaleness and nudity are completely elided. The contrast between the actual photographs themselves also opens up space between the model and the nudity in so far as the original is soft-focused, with smudged edges, thus binding the image into the material of the photograph while the reversal is shot in sharper focus and the hard-edged lighting emphasizes the nakedness of the male model. The notion of woman as body which is thus made explicit is supported in the advertisement by the accompanying copy. By changing the original 'she' to 'he' the meanings become less automatic, denaturalized and a space is created between the signifier and the signified exposing the notion of the female as both subject to bodily processes and also the field of action for various products which will act on the body to complete the flowering of this bud-like creature.

Figure 5:3

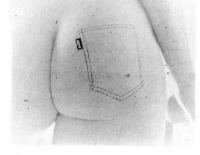

Figure 5:4

The density of meanings signified by the female nude can be further shown by a comparison of two other advertisements taken at random from the thousands that assault us daily (Figures 5:3 and 5:4). What is remarkable in this juxtaposition is the relative complexity of the advertisement for Lee Jeans and the startling economy of Levi's. To make its meaning clear, the Lee advertisement has to resort to a location on the wild pampas and the additional attributes in order to specify that which the Lee jeans will make of a man. Grotesque as this image is, it shows the necessary lengths to which one has to go to make a clear image of the desirability of purchasing the jeans when using a male model. The Levi's advertisement is of a completely different order – it simply offers its product for sale, but that it can do so merely by attaching the label to a nude portion of the female body depends on the identification of the female body and sale. A common critique of such an image simply condemns the exploitation of the female body in selling commodities. However, the use of the female nude is not arbitrary or exploitative, for a study of the transformation of the female nude in the history of representations does show how the body has come to signify 'sale'. It is not possible to adduce here all the illustrative material necessary to elaborate this point but at the risk of sounding too speculative I would contend that what recuperates a bottle of sherry or a car in advertisements from being read as still life, with its traditional associations, and indicates their status as purchasable commodities, is the presence of woman by virtue of what the woman introduces into an image.[3]

In suggesting this I am laying stress on the active relationship between the visual vocabulary, or what art historians prefer to call the iconographic traditions of high art and the media, which is the second point raised above. John Berger has already made some observations on the way in which contemporary advertisements 'borrow' their images from Old Master paintings by showing examples of advertisements that quote directly from an oil painting. The implications of this practice go beyond quotation, as Berger states,

> The continuity, however, between oil painting and publicity goes far deeper than the 'quoting' of specific paintings. Publicity relies to a very large extent on the language of oil painting. It speaks in the same voice about the same things. Sometimes the visual correspondences are so close that it is possible to play a game of 'Snap'. . . . It is not however on the level of exact pictorial correspondence that the continuity is important: it is at the level of the sets of signs used.[4]

The main thrust of Berger's argument is to show up the ideological meanings usually disclaimed for pure 'High Art'. But his final statement can be taken further and his argument, in a sense, reversed. Returning once again to reversals, one can cite an example from the misconceived attempts by certain magazines to offer to women erotic images of men, for instance the photograph of a nude man running through the woods which appeared in the magazine *Viva* (Figure 5:5).

The photograph bears comparison with the advertisement for Lee Jeans (Figure 5:3) in so far as the male figure does not stand alone or in a slight setting but is placed in an elaborate woody glade and is posed in conjunction with an animal, in this case the horse's head, whose position and shape is not only suggestively phallic but recalls the longstanding association of a horse and virility in earlier iconographic traditions. In attempting to construct an erotic image of man this picture foregrounds the difficulties of reversing erotic imagery and furthermore reveals a significant reliance on the images in European art, for this photograph is a fine paraphrase of the Hellenistic statue, the *Apollo Belvedere*.

One can read this image a number of ways in which it cannot be an equivalent of photographs of women in magazines for men. The figure is active, self-contained, does not engage with the gaze of the spectator whose hypothetical position can only be as some wood nymph catching a fleeting glimpse of this sylvan god through the blurred bushes of the foreground. What is absolutely lacking is any conceivable position of ownership or possession offered to the spectator. But in addition, the

Figure 5:5

image inscribes into itself the contradiction inherent in the use of the Apollonian prototype which occurs in the severe disjunction between head and body and the bizarre relation of the almost phallic horse's head with the man's genitals virtually barred off by the reins. That which can be signified by the male figure is therefore curtailed by the historical speci-ficity of the sign 'man' within patriarchal ideology whose synchronicity on the level of pre-presentations is ensured by the expansion of the art publishing industry and the production of so-called popular art books as well as television serials like the now famous *Civilisation*.

But a further and more dangerous aspect of this process appeared recently again in the pages of a sex magazine. The appropriation of woman as body in all forms of representation has spawned within the Women's Movement a consistent attempt to decolonize the female body, a tendency which walks a tightrope between subversion and reappropriation, and often serves rather to consolidate the potency of the signification rather than actually to rupture it. Much of this attempt has focused on a kind of body imagery and an affirmative exposure of female sexuality through celebratory imagery of the female genitals.

The threatening implications of this undertaking are witnessed by a recent episode when the work of Suzanne Santoro (Figure 5:6), who produced a small booklet of vaginal imagery, was censored by the Arts Council who, after some complaints, removed it from a travelling exhi-bition of art books on the grounds of indecency and obscenity. However, that the radical potential of this kind of feminist imagery can easily be reappropriated can be seen if one looks beyond the *petit bourgeois* ideo-

Figure 5:6

Figure 5:7

logy of the art establishment to the major conveyors of bourgeois patriarchal imagery in the big-selling sex magazines where a profoundly disturbing development has taken place.

In the pages of a recent *Penthouse* (Figure 5:7)[5] vaginal imagery appears in all its force and decorative glamour, liberated from the traditional coyness of such magazines' sexual invitations by a directness that radically

141

questions the psychoanalytically based analyses of images of women under-taken by Claire Johnston and Laura Mulvey and the notions of castration fears and the phallic woman. In some senses there is a similarity to the images of men illustrated above, with the lack of engagement between model and spectator and the sense of self-sufficiency which in the pages of *Penthouse* are underlined by the fact that these women are frequently engaged in private masturbation. The relation between spectator-buyer of these images and the picture of woman created in these photographs, is that of forceful intrusion or indeed possessive voyeurism inviting rape. While I can only remark at the present on the insufficiency of present theory in the analysis of this development, I want here to hypothesize on the direct relations between levels of representations from the high art undertakings of feminists to the mass market sex magazines. I would argue the absolute insufficiency of the notion current in the Women's Movement, which suggests that women artists can create an alternative imagery outside existing ideological forms; for not only is vaginal imagery recuperable but in that process the more sinister implications of sexual difference in ideological representations are exposed. Yet it must be acknowledged that certain feminist critics have been aware of these dangers, as for instance Lucy Lippard who comments in her essay on 'Body Art' in her book *From the Centre*: 'It is a subtle abyss that separates men's use of women for sexual titillation from women's use of women to expose that insult.'[6]

Even so, such a comment reveals a certain lack of focus on that which determines this process (this not-so-subtle abyss) and serves to illustrate my third introductory point concerning the lack of clear definitions of the precise ideological system within which the signification of woman is created and maintained. Notions of patriarchal ideology engendered by a recourse to psychoanalysis are on their own inadequate and insufficiently historical and the issue must be located in terms of capitalism and bourgeois ideology for, as I have briefly indicated above, one of the dominant significations of woman is that of sale and commodity. The transformation apparent in the pages of *Penthouse* is the replacement of willing transaction by what amounts to theft.

By way of conclusion and summary I would like to offer one final set of reversals which have proved useful in the exposition of such points by the Women's Art History Collective. In her essay, 'Eroticism and Female Imagery in Nineteenth Century Art'[7] Linda Nochlin published a nineteenth-century soft porn print entitled *Achetez des Pommes* (Figure 5:8) and juxtaposed it with a photograph of a man she had posed carrying instead a tray of bananas (Figure 5:9).

The usual reaction to this comparison is laughter, an embarrassed reac-tion to the recognition of that which we take for granted in the nineteenth-century print. This does, of course, invite some comment on its 'sexist' nature but it is none the less so naturalized that it is hard to isolate the precise ideological implications of such an image. On an obvious level, as

 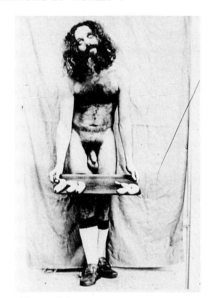

Figure 5:8   *Figure 5:9*

Nochlin points out, while there exists a long tradition of association between female breasts and genitals with fruit, which renders the sight of breast nestling amongst a tray of apples and the implied saleability of both unsurprising, no such precedents exist for a similar juxtaposition of a penis and its fruity analogue, the banana. However, what is more significant in this comparison is precisely the failure of the reversal.[8] It is clear that a bearded man with a silly expression, woolly socks and moccasins does not suggest the same things as the sickly smile of the booted and black-stockinged woman, not simply because there is no comparable tradition of erotic imagery addressed to women but rather because of the particular signification of woman as body and as sexual. There is a basic asymmetry, inscribed into the language of visual representation which such reversals serve to expose. The impossibility of effective reversal also exposes the mystification brought about by the attempt to isolate 'Images of Women' outside the total discourse whereby the meanings carried by male and female are predicated on difference and asymmetry.

Nochlin also adduces a painting contemporary with the print culled from the realms of high art: Gauguin's *Tahitian Women with Mango Blossoms* of 1899 (New York Metropolitan Museum of Art – Figure 5:10), in which a similar configuration of breasts and fruiting flowers is created within the idyllic setting of non-industrialized, pre-capitalist Oceania where all is natural and free. The comparison not only indicates the interconnections in terms of ideology of high art and popular prints but demands a reintegration in cultural studies which does not falsely privilege mass forms over what is often their source material in the more elite manifestations of dominant ideology in high culture and finally necessitates the rescue of the discourse of art history from its recent practices that are untouched by a radical critique or theoretical analysis.

Figure 5:10   *Figure 5:11*

A final example related to these works can be used to address the fourth point made above, which concerns the nature of the practice through which the ideological nature of the representations can be exposed and the ideology ruptured. Paula Modersohn Becker's *Self Portrait* (Figure 5:11) painted under the influence of Gauguin's Tahitian paintings at the turn of the century, and the combination of such a source with the attempt at self-portraiture, foregrounds the contradictions under which women attempt to represent themselves. The tension lies between the naturalness of the image of woman as nude and the unnaturalness of the portrait of the artist as a young woman. Two separate traditions collide, resulting in an image which neither works as a nude, for there is too much self-possession, nor as a statement of an artist, since the associations are those of nature, not culture. The painting must be considered as a failure not simply because an alternative iconographic tradition did not yet exist (for that presumes the possibility of simply creating one) but rather, I would maintain, because of the inseparability of the signifier and the signified. It is that false separation which the notion 'Images of Women' precisely attempts to make which renders the term so inescapably mystifying, and the study engendered by it, so difficult, and which cannot be maintained if we are to expose the roles of the signifier woman within ideological representations. Nor can a separation be maintained between various manifestations of these signifying practices for, in order to make any intervention in theory or practice, we require a soundly based historical analysis of the workings of ideology and codes of representation in their historical specificity and through the interrelated systems by which ideology is maintained and reproduced. It is precisely here that the gap I mentioned in the opening sentences of this article opens up between the direct relevance of this undertaking to women as we live out that ideology, seek to challenge it and the kind of analysis necessary to expose and rupture it. This article has outlined only some of the processes and examples which can be helpful in introducing this subject to students.

NOTES

Although this piece has been written entirely by me, the ideas and work contained within it are the result of the collective work of the Women's Art History Collective. The article was first published in *Screen Education*, Autumn 1977, no. 24, pp. 25–33.

1 John Berger, *Ways of Seeing*, Harmondsworth, Penguin Books, 1972; Thomas B. Hess and Elizabeth C. Baker, *Art and Sexual Politics*, New York, Collier, 1971; Thomas B. Hess and Linda Nochlin, *Woman as Sex Object*, London, Allen Lane, 1973.
2 *Women's Report*, 1973, vol. 1, no. 6.
3 This notion has to be carefully argued from the precise historical developments of bourgeois art and most importantly by a careful study of the transformations of the representations themselves. Verbal or purely theoretical argument without numerous illustrations would be disturbing. However, since the point is important I make it here and can only suggest that anyone interested awaits the publication of a book co-authored by myself and Roszika Parker, *Old Mistresses: Women, Art and Ideology*, London, Routledge & Kegan Paul, 1981.
4 Berger, op. cit., pp. 135–8.
5 *Penthouse*, 1977, vol. 12, no. 3.
6 Lucy Lippard, 'Body Art', in *From the Center: Feminist Essays on Women's Art*, New York, Dutton, 1976, p. 125.
7 Hess and Nochlin, op. cit., pp. 9–15.
8 Nochlin does not acknowledge its failure nor did she attempt to produce comparable images in terms of the photographic methods used.

6

ON PORNOGRAPHY

John Ellis

PREFACE

'Pornography' seems to me to be one of the urgent and unanswered questions that our culture presents to itself. The sense of urgency is provided by the constant activity in this area: police seizure of material; attacks by feminists on representations and those who market them; and the pornography industry's own attempts to get increased public acceptance. Now, the Williams Committee[1] has produced a series of recommendations for replacing the existing unworkable legislation in this area. My sense that the question remains unanswered is perhaps more contentious: several definitions of pornography do exist which are perfectly adequate for their protagonists. Yet they are purely moral definitions, concerned with recruiting for particular ideas of 'what should be done' about pornography. They all assume that 'pornography' is an inherent attribute of certain representations. This is an untenable assumption: 'pornography' is rather a designation given to a class of representations which is defined by particular ideological currents active in our society. These ideological currents are crystallized into particular political groupings which produce their own definitions of 'pornography' and propagate them through various kinds of actions against particular representations. Different criteria are used, so that the definition of 'pornography', its supposed effects, and methods of limiting them, are areas of struggle between differing positions.

The combination of vagueness and moralism in existing definitions of pornography has several effects. First, 'pornography' as a label always threatens to engulf any sexual representation that achieves a certain level of explicitness. There is no way that any representation – especially if it involves photography – can insure itself against such labelling. Second, it produces a real blockage in the analysis and the production of representations alike. A reticence about the portrayal of sexuality hovers over much British independent film production. I have felt a similar reticence in writing this article. Not only do definitions of pornography have an inhibiting moral force to them, but as a result of their blanket definitions,

146

adequate means of writing and portrayal of sexuality have not been developed. Pornography is difficult to discuss because there is no discourse which is analytic yet nevertheless engages the subjectivity of the individual uttering that discourse. We are caught between personal confessions and general theoretical systematizations; mutually exclusive modes, each inadequate to the problems addressed.

I have written this article to break through some of the problems of 'pornography' by displacing the category itself. This involves a double approach. There is a preliminary investigation of how 'pornography' is defined for us now, how a particular area of signification is separated out across a wide range of media. Then, I have used a particular approach which seems to be able to differentiate between kinds of representations that are usually lumped together as 'pornographic', and thus can offer a perspective for progressive work in this central and neglected area.

PORNOGRAPHIC DEFINITIONS

Sexuality is never left unspoken in our culture: it is massively present, but always subject to limitations. It is exhaustively defined across a series of specialist discourses (medicine, psychiatry, criminology etc.) but its more public manifestation is through allusion rather than description. Forms of humour, representations of women, clothing and other diverse practices all invoke sexuality. But they cannot be said to describe or to define sexual practices: they indicate obsessively, pointing towards sexuality, but they never differentiate, never show, never speak directly. Prohibitions exist not upon speaking about sexuality, but on explicit descriptions of sexual activities. Prohibitions exist upon representations which refer to sexual activity or display the human body in an overtly sexualized manner; on the public representation of sexual activity and the circulation of such representations. The conjunction of sexual activity and representation, where the representation specifies sexual activity rather than referring to it by inference or allusion, is the area of particular taboos and is the traditional area of pornography.

An industry has developed to produce and market such proscribed representations, ensuring their circulation outside the normal channels. This pornography industry is a reaction to the historically specific definitions of pornography, it is called into existence as a separate sector by campaigns and laws against pornography. Essentialist approaches to pornography as a particular kind of representation begin from the nature of the contemporary pornography industry and produce a definition of all that industry's products. Such an approach ignores the conditions of production of pornography as a proscribed area of signification. The various strong and specific definitions of pornography themselves produce this area, and it is with them that investigation of the constitution of 'pornography' must

147

begin if it is to be examined in its specific existence at a particular historical moment.

There will be no one unitary definition of 'pornography' but rather a struggle for predominance between several definitions. These definitions will work within a context defined by several forces, the current form of the pornography industry and its particular attempts at legitimization; the particular form of the laws relating to obscenity and censorship; and the general mobilization of various moral and philosophical positions and themes that characterize a particular social moment. It is beyond the scope of this article to examine the articulation of such general moral and philosophical currents with the specific question of pornography in the particular contemporary British attempts at definition of the area. More immediate is the complex question of the legal forms which are currently in use in Britain. These are by no means easy to describe (the Williams Report concludes that, here, in England and Wales at least, 'The law, in short, is in a mess' 2.29), yet their effects across various media are quite marked. In addition, censorship is often undertaken by bodies of no formal legal standing like the British Board of Film Censors, which exists as a convenient delegate and centralizer of local authority film censorship powers. At every point, however, whether in pre-censorship as with cinema, or prosecution after publication as with printed material, both the law and its individual implementations rely on contemporary morality and definitions of what might constitute permissible representations of sexual activity. The mid-nineteenth-century test of whether a particular representation has a tendency to 'deprave or corrupt' is used in most existing legislation. This requires jurors to have a definite image of what corruption and depravity might consist in their contemporaries: a definition which cannot but rely upon prevailing definitions of 'pornography', its supposed effects and its presumed social role.

Legal action against representations of a sexual nature depends upon the current prevailing definition of pornography. Legal action, or the possibility of it, in turn defines the nature of the pornography industry or institution. Representations become clandestine because they are threatened with prosecution; equally they confine themselves to particular ghettos to avoid the 'public concern' which can be produced by vocal interest groups espousing definitions of pornography that entail censorship. At every point 'pornography' appears to be an area of representations whose limits and nature are the subject of a struggle between differing definitions. Definitions with such powers as these are the product of wider and institutionalized political positions. In contemporary Britain there seem to be three main positions which have emerged in relation to pornography: the right-wing 'Nationwide Festival of Light'; the feminist concern with representation of women; and the liberal attitude exemplified by the Williams Report. Each has a distinctive power base. The Festival of

Light relies on traditional Christian notions which are conceived as in decline and under threat. It incorporates Mary Whitehouse's highly successful campaign to deliberalize television output, as well as many other such pressure groups, and has powerful support in the right-wing sections of the police force, for example the Chief Constable of Greater Manchester (see Williams, 4.23). The feminist campaigns against pornography have come particularly from those sections of the Women's Movement that see society as constituted by an antagonism between the sexes. This position finds its power base in a series of concerted campaigns, demonstrations, pickets of retailers of 'pornography', sloganizing of sexist advertising material, and so on. It is not primarily directed towards exploitation or change of existing legislation; it aims rather for a wholesale change in public attitudes by a redefinition of what constitutes an offensive representation. The final major position put forward in Britain is a liberal position, seeing society as pluralistic, containing many points of view in uneasy coexistence. This has recently been articulated by the Williams Committee, which was convened to produce a report proposing and justifying rationalization of English laws relating to obscenity. It regards the law as 'holding the ring', ensuring public safety and well-being, rather than as an interventationist instrument enforcing particular points of view. Thus the Williams Committee represents a particular and successful tactic by a liberal lobby: commissioned by a Labour Home Secretary, it has been delivered to a Conservative one. The choice which now faces the Home Secretary is one of maintaining the existing legal confusion or implementing something approximating to the Williams Report's recommendations.

Each of these positions defines 'pornography' as a different object. They produce definitions which class certain forms of representation as 'pornographic'; they produce arguments about the social place, function and influence of these representations; and they advocate different forms of action towards these representations by judiciary and public alike. All have a definite basis within particular organizations and institutions, and are therefore able to make political interventions of a public and influential nature. These interventions and the struggle for general public acceptability between these definitions together bring about the current form of the pornography industry.

Festival of Light

An exposition of the Nationwide Festival of Light's position can be found in the Longford Report.[2] This is a curious publication, taking the form of a report from a commission set up by Lord Longford to collect evidence about the pornography phenomenon. It was published as a mass-sale paperback amid a blaze of publicity, aiming to capture the definition of pornography for a semi-religious right-wing position. The report has the overall style of a government report, with a panel commissioning research and receiving submissions from anyone who cared to make them, yet it has none of the scrupulousness about its statements and their veracity that usually characterizes a government report. The Longford Report takes pornography as an object which exists incontrovertibly in the world beyond its writings: its main aim is to define its influences. Pornography, it argues, is a representation which isolates one physical activity – sex or violence – from the social context which would justify it as an activity or portray its consequences.

> Dr Claxton describes both 'hard' and 'soft' pornography as 'a symptom of preoccupation with sex which is unrelated to its purpose' – which he sees, of course, not exclusively in terms of the physical orgasm, but a relationship which transcends the merely physical. (p. 205)

Pornography has as its aim the excitation of the viewer rather than, as Lord Clark argues, one of provoking thought and contemplation:

> To my mind art exists in the realm of contemplation and is bound by some sort of imaginative transposition. The moment art becomes an incentive to action it loses its true character. This is my objection to painting with a communist programme, and it would also apply to pornography. (p. 100)

Pornography, it is argued, 'stimulates in the audience the kind of behaviour that may lead to violence' (p. 45). Many of its representations cause 'extreme offence to the great majority of people' (p. 193). It is a type of representation that is at once a symptom of a general decline of societal values (the 'permissive society'), and a cause of particular undesirable activities: perversions, rape, masturbation, dissatisfaction within marriages and so on. The metaphor of 'health' hovers over the report: healthy sexuality is a sexuality which is functional within a relationship; a healthy attitude towards representations is one of contemplation and uplift; a healthy society is one that contains no disruption of its tranquillity. Health defines the presumably normal: the report appeals to this sense of the average in order to promote it as the only acceptable form of behaviour. It then defines as pornography any representation that is capable of producing or suggesting behaviour outside this norm.

Pornography for the Festival of Light is a class of representations which are concerned with sex or violence without their social or moral context. The representations aim to excite the viewer and have a concentration upon violence. They stimulate anti-social behaviour where it might not have existed before, and are a symptom as well as a cause of a wholesale decline in social value. Pornography should be banned wherever possible, and should certainly be kept away from children. Rigorously enforced legislation is seen to be the means to achieve this aim.

One Feminist Approach

The most dominant feminist position finds itself confused with the Festival of Light's position at certain points, despite its different constituency and forms of campaigning. It produces a very similar definition of the object 'pornography', but traces its roots back to very different causes. Such a feminist definition of pornography points to violence, lack of social context of sexuality, and the symptomatic social role of pornography in the same way as the Longford Report. Pornography is seen as 'violent and mysogynistic, and nothing to do with the free expression of "healthy" sex, but rather the truly "perverted" desire to trample on another human being'.[3] Pornography is also described as a depiction of sexual activity deprived of its social significance and offered to excite the viewer:

> Pornography's principal and most humanly significant function is that of arousing sexual excitement. . . . It usually describes the sexual act not in explicit . . . but in purely inviting terms. The function of plot in a pornographic narrative is always the same. It exists to provide as many opportunities as possible for the sexual act to take place. . . . Characterisation is necessarily limited to the formal necessity for the actors to fuck as frequently and as ingeniously as possible.[4]

Pornography is even seen as the symptom of wider social trends, and as having a potential link with forms of violence perpetrated by men on women:

> There is no evidence that porn causes rape directly, and there may be no *causal* link. But they are linked in spirit. Both are manifestations of the same attitude towards women and sex – of a desire to avoid interaction with a woman as another human being.[5]

However, a feminist position would not base its notion of pornography on any notion of a 'healthy' society and its attitude to sex. Instead, many feminists perceive pornography as the product of a general antagonism between the sexes. Men are the subjects of pornography, it is produced for their gratification and pleasure; women are the objects of pornography, reduced to being sexual objects, degraded and humiliated. Sexuality and its representation in our society are both profoundly marked by the interpellation of men as aggressors, women as their victims. This argument is capable of designating a whole series of representations as 'pornographic', representations which do not feature in more conventional or right-wing definitions. A feminist definition based on the notion of an antagonism between the sexes sets up a continuum of representations of women classified according to their sexuality. This continuum stretches from many forms of public advertisement displays to hard-core pornography in the usual sense. Each representation is designated pornographic because it defines women as sexual objects offered for male pleasure. The terms of

151

this contention are not found entirely in written arguments: it appears equally and publicly in propagandist activities such as writing or putting stickers on posters, particularly in the Underground in London. One such sticker is 'KEEP MY BODY OFF YOUR ADS', which condenses many of the problems with this position. It (polemically) confuses the real with representation, but in doing so it reduces the representation to being that of 'a body', and the aim of the campaign to that of repression, the banning of representations of bodies. Interestingly, it also has a central confusion about address. 'I' refers to the collectivity of women; 'you' is either the collectivity of men who in an undifferentiated way 'portray women', or (as is more probable given the address of most posters) the power elite of marketing personnel. In the first case, it is only to those who already have access to such feminist arguments that such a reading is possible: the sticker has no effect as propaganda towards those who do not. In the second case, the (male) viewer is left in the same relationship to the poster plus sticker as he was to the poster alone: he is the voyeur to women speaking to the advertisers as he was voyeur to the woman performing in the poster.[6]

Attacking posters for their assumptions is one example of the distinctive forms of campaigning adopted by many feminists against all the manifestations that they perceive 'pornography' to have. This campaign is one to change public attitude, to render unacceptable many things that are currently taken for granted, like advertising, forms of sexual humour, 'beauty queens' and so on. The campaign includes a variety of signifying practices in an overall definition of 'pornography', and relies on 'popular opinion' to ensure that such forms fall into disuse. It is a campaign to change attitudes to sexuality and to women:

> I believe we should not agitate for more laws against pornography, but should rather stand up and say what we feel about it, and what we feel about our own sexuality, and force men to re-examine their own attitudes to sex and women explicit in their consumption of porn . . . We should make it clear that porn is a symptom of our sexist society, a reflection of its assumptions.[7]

As a polemical and urgent task of redefinition, this feminist notion of pornography cannot rely on legislation nor on traditional moral ideas. Its characteristic modes of operation are those of polemical writing, and forms of direct action such as those against advertising or the 'Reclaim the Night' marches through many cities in November 1977. This widespread position is the only conception of 'pornography' that is aware of itself as an active intervention, shifting and producing definitions. Such a self-awareness means that this basic position can give rise to a sophisticated debate which escapes sterile arguments about whether specific representations 'should be banned or not', and traces the complex links that exist between representations of sexuality and the practical attitudes of individuals to their sexuality. Within the dominant forms of representation in our society, women are posed as the objects of men's activity, and particularly as objects of men's sexual activity. Women's sexuality is produced in representations as a commodity for men's pleasure. Feminist definitions therefore intervene within representational practices to displace this exploitative definition of sexuality. It is a measure of the distinctiveness of this position that it is incompatible with most of the basic assumptions of the Williams Report; it is a measure of its effectiveness that the Williams Committee took special pains to gain evidence from the Women's Movement (1.2).

The Williams Report

The Williams Report is a major achievement for the liberal lobby for reform of the current laws relating to obscenity and censorship. Costing £99,692 and two years' work, it is able to summarize such positions as that of the Festival of Light rather more elegantly than that lobby itself can, and then to refute both its internal logic and the empirical 'proofs' that it calls upon. Its recommendations are for an overall rationalization and liberalization of laws in this area, artfully calculated to appeal to a wide range of legislative sensibilities. Liberalization entails 'one step to the left' in each medium, within an overall context of removing material that could 'cause offence to reasonable people' from public view.

The report classifies representations as pornographic according to their function and content:

> We take it that, as almost everyone understands the term, a pornographic representation is one that combines two features: it has a certain function or intention, to arouse its audience sexually, and also has a certain content, explicit representations of sexual material (organs, postures, activity, etc). A work has to have both this function and this content to be a piece of pornography. (8.2)

It reserves an aesthetic distance from the majority of such representations 'certainly most pornography is also trash: ugly, shallow and obvious' (7.2). It differs from both the feminist and the Festival of Light characterization of pornography because it makes a rigid separation between the realms of the public and the private. Both feminist and right-wing characterizations are based on the assumption that the public and the private are inseparable: they see attitudes as existing in a continuum between the two realms. The Williams Report maintains that the two are different because they entail different conceptions of freedom, and impose different duties upon the legislature. The private is seen as the area of the purely personal, the area of freedom of choice and individual predilection, into which others (whether individuals, groups or state) should make the least possible intervention. There should be no imposed morality, no attempt to legislate a prescriptive conception of the normal. The public is seen as the area of the uneasy coexistence of these plural private preferences. It is where individuals encounter each other and have effects upon each other, where individual activities have to be curbed for the safety and continued well-being of others. So the report provides as its first principle that there should be as little limitation upon the individual as possible, and that such limitation should be for the protection of the generality of other individuals. Pornography, however objectionable it might appear, should therefore be available for individuals unless it can be proved that its presence within society affronts other individuals going about their daily business, or indeed produces forms of anti-social behaviour such as aggression towards particular individuals. Therefore if it can be ensured that adult individuals can come across pornography only by their own conscious choice, and if no proof or strong evidence exists of a causal link between pornographic representations and particular, anti-social acts, then pornography should be given a legal existence in society. For this reason the report devotes much space to refuting the Festival of Light's empirical proofs of links between pornography and particular acts of violence. Once this direct evidence is demolished, then more general assertions of indirect harmful effects upon society as a whole can be refused by asserting pornography's relative insignificance compared to 'the many other problems that face our society today' (6.80), and the difficulty of distinguishing whether a particular phenomenon is a cause or a symptom of a particular social change (6.76).

The law is then framed to prevent the exposure of 'reasonable people' who might find certain material 'offensive'. The 'offensive to reasonable people' test then becomes the criterion for deciding what forms of representation should be restricted to particular designated sales points. If harm to individuals can be proved or strongly supposed to be involved in the production or dissemination of a representation, then it can be banned completely. So printed pornographic material is exempt from censorship except where its production has involved cruelty to those posing for it, or the exploitation of children. Written matter is exempt from any censorship. However, potentially 'offensive' material is only to be made available in separate premises which carry a standard designation and no other form of advertising. Most of the magazines currently available in ordinary newsagents' would then be restricted to these premises. Live entertainment would be prevented from staging actual sex acts as this 'carried some dangers of public order problems' (11.9), which is why they are no longer permitted in Denmark. Videotapes and their proliferation receive no attention in the report, for which it has been criticized. Film remains the only medium to be subject to prior censorship, and the report envisages that certain films could still be banned altogether. The report's considered assessments tend to collapse here, under a belief in a realist aesthetic:

> Film, in our view, is a uniquely powerful instrument: the close-up, fast cutting, the sophistication of modern make-up and special effects

techniques, the heightening effect of sound effects and music, all combine on the large screen to produce an impact which no other medium can create. . . . We are more impressed by the consideration that the extreme vividness and immediacy of film may make it harder rather than easier for some who are attracted to sadistic material to tell the difference between fantasy and reality. (12.10)

The argument is framed in terms of the possible consequences of violent material: it is conceived as possible that it could lead to violent acts in some way. Film censorship would be retained, able to ban certain films on the grounds of excessive cruelty, and allocating various certificates which would ban children under a series of specific ages from seeing particular films. An appeal against banning could be lodged on the grounds of the 'artistic merit' of a particular film. The present self-financing and advisory British Board of Film Censors would be abolished and replaced by an official state body allocating mandatory certificates. A new category of restricted film would be set up in addition to the current 'X' certificate banning children under 18. Such films could only be shown in halls licensed for the purpose by local authorities, who would thus retain their censorship powers only in so far as they could refuse to license any cinema in their area for the showing of restricted films. A cinema so designated would continue to be able to show '*Bambi* in the school holidays if it wishes to do so' (12.39).

> In practice [there will be] two sorts of designated cinemas. One will be a blue movie house, which rarely if ever shows anything else. The other will be, to some degree, an 'art' house, which shows a variety of films with various certificates, usually of minority appeal. (12.39)

The overall effect of the Williams Committee recommendations, if they become law, will be to heighten the conflict over the term 'pornography'. Its explicit effect is to make the legal definition of pornography one that is variable with shifts in public opinion. It does so by defining pornography as a private matter, as existing in an area where the law 'holds the ring' rather than intervenes with particular definitions. The effect then is to shift arguments about the legal definition of pornography into the public arena where a struggle takes place to define the public consensus. But this shift can only take place within a liberal notion of pornography as a private matter, a definition that neither feminists nor the right wing would accept. It is perhaps the kind of fiction that only liberals can believe. The Williams Report therefore embodies a particular liberal definition of 'pornography', distinct from other positions, whose power lies in its possible influence on legal definitions, enabling a wider range of material to become available in more restricted marketing channels.

The Institution of Pornography

The right wing, liberals and feminists have three distinct definitions of pornography that conflict in attempting to define what pornography might be. The articulation of these three major positions with the present, confused, legal definitions of 'obscenity' produces a particular industry, the institution of pornography. This is an agglomeration resulting from a series of *ad hoc* distinctions between classes of representation across a number of media, which are recognized to have a common existence. Specialized marketing and production methods have been evolved within this institution, which exists rather separately from the conventional business operations in particular media.

The current general rules in Britain are that the following will be designated 'pornographic': any representation of male or female genitals (not breasts); any form of enactment of sex whether simulated or actual that is of any duration and level of explicitness; and any sustained reference to 'perversions', particularly a use of sexually-charged violence. Even representations whose general purpose is other than the excitement of the viewer for sexual purposes is liable to inclusion in this category. The boundaries are fluid and shifting, but a large-scale change has taken place during the last decade through which the 'pin-up' (the female body deprived of any genitals by artful posing or photographic processes) has become non-pornographic. It is now available daily in popular newspapers. Similarly, it can be argued that much advertising makes use of themes and poses derived from pornography, without receiving many objections other than from feminists. Within the boundaries, another distinction takes place between classes of representation, depending upon an assessment of the likelihood of judicial seizure, and their acceptability to the potential advertisers of a wide range of consumer products. This distinction is usually designated 'hard-core'/ 'soft core', terms which originate in an American distinction as to whether real sex or simulated sex have been involved in the production of a representation, but it no longer has such a particular meaning. Soft-core pornography, available currently in public cinemas, in magazines on open sale in newsagents, attracts advertisements; hard-core pornography does not. Along with these advertisements comes a whole series of journalistic practices, from circulation audits to particular modes of address within written texts.

Pornography can designate itself by various simple mechanisms. An institution that is defined largely from outside by the suspicion of many vocal pressure groups is able to signify itself by exploiting the connotations associated with that suspicion. Thus 'Swedish', 'X', 'Emmanuelle', 'Sins' are precise generic indicators; as are a certain size of magazine with a near-naked female body portrayed on the cover, even before the list of contents develops the connotation. Similarly 'Books and Magazines', 'Adult' and 'Private' indicate 'hard-core' emporia. This activity of self-definition continues within the texts themselves, with the intrusive 'we' ('aren't we daring?') of editorial matter; the recurrence of models; and the habit in films of using the institution of pornography itself (e.g. photo sessions) as circumstances for sex. This process means that areas of representation constructed from outside as 'pornographic' never have to use that term to define themselves. The ground is never explicitly conceded.

Pornography in Britain occurs across a diversity of practices, each with its own means of marketing and dissemination, nevertheless unified by processes of self-designation into an institution of signification. Each practice has its own particular emphases and potentialities, both for marketing and for signification. Cinema is sharply divided into the kinds of soft-core films available in public cinemas, and the grades of sexually specific material to be found in 'clubs' of various sorts. The British Board of Film Censors ensures that public films are extensively cut from the form they take in other countries, reducing them to a traditional kind of 'teasing'; Tatler Cinema Clubs (associated with the Classic Cinema chain) show uncut American soft-core films; other clubs in city centres show film of actual sex acts of various kinds. Videotapes for home consumption are a fast developing industry, providing both material developed for the format (e.g. the video magazine *Electric Blue*, developed on an analogy with soft-core magazines), and full recordings of films sometimes banned or censor-cut for cinema. Magazines comprise a large and diversified market, with the half-dozen upmarket soft-core monthlies (e.g. *Mayfair*, *Club International*) having sales of between 150,000 and 250,000 each, and the downmarket publications (*Fiesta*, *Knave*) possibly around 150,000 each.[8] Readership of each copy is conventionally calculated at something like four times the number sold.

> Their editorial contents, both fictional and allegedly 'factual', extensively describe varieties of sexual experience but their illustrations, majoring on high-definition female nudity, will not generally cover scenes of intercourse. The magazines . . . would treat auto-eroticism fully, touch on bondage, but shun more extreme perversions.[9]

Magazines available only in specialized shops, for which no figures are available, provide what the generally circulated ones do not. Live performance in Britain takes advantage of the lack of censorship of theatre to present revues of various kinds in both 'legit' theatres and cabarets, which stop short of actual sex on stage. Writing and the fine arts are virtually freed from the emphasis that they used to have as major channels for pornography because they lack the immediacy of the 'photograph effect'. Prosecutions occur occasionally, however, but for some years have not involved pleas for the material made on the grounds of its 'artistic merit'.

The institution of pornography has been called into existence by the articulation of legal restraint and particular, conflicting, definitions of pornography. It produces no real justification of itself, no major articulation of 'pornography' as a class of representation no better and no worse than any other. To this extent, it accepts its own status as the pariah of representational practices. Practitioners in the industry tend to prefer silence to developing any kind of public definition of their activities. When forced into pleading their case, their definitions tend to weave through the interstices of other definitions, speaking of 'social function', 'liberation', 'sublimation' and other such gleanings from vulgar Freudianism or sociology. When a case is made for the ending of censorship on the grounds of intellectual freedom, it is not the pornography industry which makes it, but groups of liberal intellectuals who, like the Williams Committee, regard pornography as unappealing, but better permitted than banned.

The institution of pornography is a reaction to the designation of certain classes of representation as in some way objectionable. This designation is nowhere fixed, not even in law, but is the subject of a constant activity of redefinition as a result of struggles between definitions, particular initiatives on behalf of or against specific representations, and wider changes in moral attitudes.

INTERFACE

The next step for this analysis is to find a way of characterizing the representations designated as 'pornography' so that they can be seen as contradictory and open to change, even as undergoing change at the moment. This is the necessary other half of answering the inevitable (correct yet vexing) question: 'What position should be taken up in relation to the struggle between definitions?' In doing this I have employed a metalinguistic approach like that used in the previous passage. This approach is necessary as an initial gesture that seeks to define a terrain in which further work (and not solely analytic work) can take place. As writing, it describes and delimits other forms of utterance, and is content to do so from a position of surveying those utterances from the outside. As an expression of an author-figure, it tends to evacuate the question of subjective response which pornography brings to the fore through its compelling implication of a sexed observer. Such a metalinguistic approach tends towards the impersonal, even the magisterial. It is not particularly able to produce accounts of textual activity, of the process of *enunciation*; it tends towards characterization of the facts of the *enounced*. A metalinguistic approach has to be used before it can be displaced by more complex and supple forms of analysis which can sense the openness of specific texts, or by forms of filmmaking that develop along the lines of contradiction that metalanguage can delineate.

The passage that follows therefore uses a typology of regimes of visual representations to examine one particular manifestation of representations called 'pornography'. This is the startling appearance of female genitals in easily available photographs and films, even in magazines sold in news-agents and films that are widely shown. This phenomenon does not account for everything that appears in pornography. I have chosen to concentrate on one public fact of pornography that has particularly caught my atten-tion, because I think it can be made to reveal a particular shift within the area of representations that is designated 'pornography'. It is therefore a question that may be able to reveal 'pornography' as a contradictory area of signification, rather than as a regime of signification with a strong internal coherence.

FEMALE PLEASURE

The closest that a general typology of visual representations has come to a perception of a particular regime of representation involving particular audience positioning which is open to change is probably Laura Mulvey's highly influential article 'Visual Pleasure and Narrative Cinema'.[10] This has been central to the examination of the regimes of visual representation exploited in 'mainstream cinema', and particularly the centrality of women to that cinema. Through an examination of the forms of looking and their pleasures (informed by psychoanalytic theory), Mulvey is able to give an adequate characterization of such diverse phenomena as the star system, striptease and the narrative function of women in 'dominant cinema'. This characterization indicates directions for filmmaking practice which try to undermine these forms. However, it seems to be unable to account for and analyse the ways in which current visual pornography is obsessed with women's genitals: 'The directness [of vaginal imagery] radically questions the psychoanalytically based analyses of images of women undertaken by Claire Johnston and Laura Mulvey and the notions of castration fear and the phallic woman.'[11]

Mulvey's typology includes a notion of fetishism that is based on the letter of Freud's text,[12] taking fetishism as necessarily involving the dis-avowal of woman's lack of a penis. Hence current pornography would seem to contradict Mulvey's analysis, although in other areas it has proved to be crucial.

Mulvey describes cinema as an activity of looking[13] in which three looks are involved: that of the spectator to the screen; that of the camera to the event; and that of the actors within the event between each other. In classic cinema these are carefully arranged so that they never coincide: the camera never looks at the space that the audience 'occupies' (the 180° rule); the actors never look down the axis of the camera. This regime allows the full exploitation of all the 'pre-existing patterns of fascination already at work within the individual subject and the social formations that have moulded him' (p. 22 of this volume).[14] The first is the pleasure in looking itself, the scopophilic drive directed towards submitting others to a controlling and curious gaze. This drive is partly developed into a narcissistic form through which the viewer identifies him/her self with figures perceived as existing outside the self of the viewer. These two structures of looking exist in tension with each other, and are crossed by a further pair of contradictory structures produced within the castration complex: voyeurism and fetishism. Voyeurism is an active, mobile form, associated with change and narrativization. It 'demands a story, depends on making something happen, forcing a change in another person, a battle of will and strength, victory/defeat, all occurring in a linear time with a beginning and an end'.[15]

Fetishism, according to Mulvey, is in contradiction with voyeurism: it involves a fixation which impedes narrative, centres on repetition of situations, the display of a star. Fetishism is a form of looking which disavows castration and hence sexual difference, whereas voyeurism involves an acknowledgement of sexual difference in its attempts to demystify or punish woman as object of the look. In both forms

> ultimately, the meaning of woman is sexual difference, the absence of a penis as visually ascertainable, the material evidence on which is based the castration complex essential for the organisation of entrance into the symbolic order and the law of the father.[16]

Fetishism in Mulvey's account is a disavowal of woman's lack of a penis, and therefore should always involve avoiding the direct sight of the female genitals and finding a substitute penis in particular fetish objects, or in the whole figure of the woman-made-phallic. Current pornography would seem to refute this characterization. Yet in every other respect, current visual pornography maintains the kind of textual structure that Mulvey associates with fetishism. It presents the repetition of events rather than narrative development towards the resolution of an enigma; it relies upon a concentration on the figure of the woman which tends to oust any other considerations; and 'the image [is] in direct erotic rapport with the spectator'.[17]

The fetishistic representation attempts to abolish the distance between spectator and representation. Voyeurism installs a separation of seer and seen as the very principle of its operation, allowing the seer a secure position over and against a representation that permits the seen to change without threatening the position of the seer. This permits the development of editing, scene dissection and narrative in the cinema. Fetishism constantly attempts to reduce or annul this distance and separation. Hence it is only capable of producing an attenuated narration, a constant repetition of scenarios of desire, where the repetition around certain neuralgic points outweighs any resolution of a narrative enigma, any discovery or reordering of facts. At its most extreme, fetishism involves a concentration upon performance, explicitly posed for the viewer (sometimes involving the performer looking directly 'at' the audience), or even upon the frame-edge, or the two-dimensional reality of the realist photograph. A fetishist regime attempts to annul the separation of image and spectator, to reinstall an immediate relation that promises (in vain) to provide satisfaction to desire itself.

Thus Mulvey's use of the concepts of voyeurism and fetishism contains much that is vital to a metapsychological characterization of the various modes of cinematic and photographic representation. It cannot be discarded simply because it is unable in its current formulation to deal with the single (fairly ubiquitous) fact of direct depiction of female genitals. Rather, its Freudian basis should be re-examined.

Fetish: Penis or Phallus?

According to the text of Freud's essay 'Fetishism', the construction of a fetish represents a disavowal of the *physical* fact of sexual difference, occasioned by an actual glimpse of female genitals. The structure that Freud describes is one in which the knowledge of the woman's lack of a penis is retained, but the infant is saved from acknowledgement of it by the substitution of what is seen in the moment before the sight of the genitals for that sight itself. The desire that the woman should after all have a penis is transferred to a particular part of the body, or to an object (e.g. shoes, fur, stockings) or to other sensations. This substitute object maintains the belief that the woman has a penis whilst the knowledge of this physical lack is also maintained: in clinical fetishists 'the two facts persist side by side throughout their lives without influencing each other'.[18] The structure of disavowal is this: 'I know (woman has no penis), nevertheless (she has, through this fetish)'. In clinical fetishism the sight of the fetish is a necessary aid to sexual arousal, and Freud states that he has only encountered this state in males. Fetishism as a structure of (usually visual) perception however, can also be found in women: it is a matter of the fascination resulting from hesitation of the knowledge of sexual difference by a structure of disavowal, 'I know, but nevertheless'. For Freud's account of fetishism then, the penis, its presence or absence on the human body, is central.

Yet the presence or absence of a penis on a human body is only important in so far as it signifies, in so far as it already has meaning within a particular cultural formation of sexual difference. The penis, or its lack, operates as the inadequate physical stand-in for that signifier which institutes the play of signification and difference: the phallus. In effect Freud's essay is aware of this distinction, only formulated clearly thirty years later. The child is already aware of sexual difference in Freud's account: what he seeks is confirmation that this suspicion might not be true after all. The desire that the woman should have a phallus in spite of everything is what gives the strength to the fetish, and allows the promotion of the moment before the physical confirmation as a substitute. Fetishism as a disavowal of sexual difference is thus a disavowal of the phallus by promoting in its place something else that the woman does possess. As a disavowal, it nevertheless maintains the phallus and thus the possibility of difference and language.[19] The structure is therefore one of 'I know that woman does not have the phallus, nevertheless she does have the phallus in this fetish'.

The fetish is a signifier which stands in for the phallus. Freud's example of the 'shine on the nose' can demonstrate how this substitution of signifiers takes place through a process of metaphor or metonymy. His patient could become sexually aroused only through the sight (real or supposed) of a shine on the nose of his partner. Freud's analysis of this fetish has two components: a story and a sliding of signifiers. The 'little story' is that of the child seeing female genitals, and looking up at the woman's face to gain a reassuring 'nevertheless' from the nose. Hence the story which lies hidden in the fetish is one of a glance that traverses the woman's body. The notion of the 'shine' comes from the condensation of this 'glance' and its story into the German *Glanz* or 'shine'. Yet the condensation holds another possibility within itself, that the 'shine' could stand for a realization of being looked at:[20] the 'shine' is that of the gaze of the woman returned to the inquiring child. It then becomes the woman's *look* in which the fetish is located, rather than the 'shine upon the nose' that Freud indicates did not necessarily have to exist to other observers. The woman's gaze is where her phallus is located. If this is so, then the story of the child's gaze may well itself be a substitute for this complex (nose/glance/*Glanz*) around the phallic gaze of the woman. It would then be a substitute that is provided in analysis in the form of a narrative; and narrative is always a suspicious or inadequate form for satisfactory analysis because of its insistence upon the serial nature of events (narrative can be said to lie behind the notorious 'stages' interpretation of Freud's explanations), and its tendency to invite us into a literal scenario (narrative fiction's constant lure).

Such an interpretation of Freud's celebrated example questions the centrality of the child's active gaze to the account. The 'little story' of the child's horror at the woman's lack of a penis can legitimately be seen as a substitute for the central and powerful gaze which constructs the fetish. The way is then open to examine fetishism as a particular kind of substitution of signifiers which does not necessarily depend upon a 'primal look'. Indeed fetishism does not necessarily involve looking: a fetish can equally be something that is felt, heard or smelt. Fetishism can be concerned with any or all of the invocatory drives and not just with a particular one: scopophilia.

What seems to be necessary for a particular object to become a fetish is that it should be constituted as a sexual signification by its articulation in a discourse of sexuality. The parts of the body, the objects and the sensations that usually become fetishes are those which are already delimited and sexualized by a whole culture.[21] Hence those objects prone to fetishization are those which are already sexualized: underwear, visible parts of the body, the sound of clothes rustling, the smell of sweat.

This account of fetishism is able to avoid the problems that are inherent in Mulvey's account, and equally in Freud's, where he is forced by his insistence upon the woman's literal physical lack of a penis and the child's actual understanding sight of this lack to stress the horror that would be involved in such a realization: 'probably no male human being is spared the fright of castration at the sight of a female genital'.[22]

This horror cannot be involved in the massive dissemination of images of female genitals that characterizes particularly still photography in the pornographic sector. It is rather one result (and not the necessary result) of the quasi-identity that is produced between the phallus and the penis, between signifier and physical stand-in. It also produces the confusion between physical sexual difference and the distinction masculine/feminine that Freud took such pains to avoid.[23]

Fetish: The Woman's Sexual Pleasure

Mulvey's account of fetishistic modes of representation shows much that can be found in current pornography: cyclic narrative forms which re-enact scenarios of desire; particular stress upon performances addressed to the spectator of the representation and having only tenuous relation to any notion of verisimilitude within the representation; the reduction of diegetic space to the two-dimensional surface of the screen; the woman posed as phallus rather than as lack. In addition, the usual voyeuristic distance of spectator to representation is compromised such that the image poses itself as pure presence (as fulfilment of desire) rather than as present absence (as something photographed in another place, at another time). Such structures of fetishism appear in current visual pornography, but other phenomena also occur that cannot be readily accounted for in Mulvey's terms as they stand.

Besides the massive diffusion of vaginal imagery already remarked upon (imagery often described as 'explicit' or 'aggressive'), there also appears a concentration on lesbian activities in both film and photography, and upon female masturbation, particularly in still photography where it is often implied strongly by various poses. Feminist critics usually condemn the representation of masturbation as reinforcing the 'solipsism' of pornography,[24] but are much more equivocal about the representation of lesbianism. These diverse shifts in pornographic representations have appeared, particularly in the fairly public pornography of magazines available in local newsagents' shops, and in films available in public cinemas.

The fetish offered by these representations is no longer a fragment of clothing, or even the deceptively smooth body of the phallic woman, it is now the woman's sexual pleasure. The woman nevertheless has the phallus in sexual pleasure; the woman's lack of a phallus is disavowed in her orgasm. Hence physical sexual difference is no longer unmentionable within public representations of women that are designated 'pornographic'. Physical sexual difference can be promoted within these representations because the fetish has been shifted from compensating for woman's lack of a penis to the finding of the woman's phallus in her sexual pleasure.

In orgasm woman no longer is the phallus, she has the phallus. Films currently produced within the pornographic sector gain their impulsion from the repetition of instances of female sexual pleasure, and male pleasure is perfunctory in most cases. The films (and photographs) are concerned with the *mise-en-scène* of the female orgasm, they constantly circle around it, trying to find it, to abolish the spectator's separation from it.

Female sexual pleasure has been promoted to the status of a fetish in order to provide representations of sexuality which are more 'explicit' for an audience conceived of as male. The pornography industry has regarded the process as one of the legitimate expansion of the very restricted and clandestine 'hard-core' representations into the more public arena of 'soft-core'. Thus the progressive revelation of pubic hair in photographs, and of (limp) penises in cinema have been regarded as the stealthy emergence of 'pieces' of the body into the daylight of soft-core representations. Yet the industry's own characterization of the process, though to some extent a determinant of it, is very far from being the whole truth. Female sexual pleasure has become perhaps the dominant fetish within current public pornographic representation as a result of this 'stealthy extension' of the industry, but the consequences are many and difficult to assess.

First, not every form of female sexual pleasure has an equal emphasis. Lesbian activity and female masturbation, when contained within a narrative, are always shown as subsidiary forms of pleasure, as surrogates for sex with a male, or as a form of experience that the heroine gains on her odyssey towards sexual satisfaction. Even within these passages, the emphasis on dildos and other substitute penises is quite marked: a male presence is maintained even within scenes of masturbation or lesbianism. Sexual pleasure for women, then, is posited as being dependent upon a male. This provides a certain security to the inquiry into female sexual pleasure: it is a fetish because it is in the orgasm that the woman's phallus is refound. Woman finds her phallus in the orgasm; woman is given that orgasm and hence that phallus by men. Both security and abolition of separation from the representation are provided for the spectator by this arrangement. The male's phallus is the condition for female sexual pleasure, the condition for the always-expected, never-found fulfilment of desire. The phallus for the woman in the representation is provided by the male in the audience: it is a 'gift' from a man or men that provides woman's orgasm.

Angela Carter calls this process 'a gap left in the text of just the right size for the reader to insert his prick into':[25] the representation of female pleasure is addressed to an audience constructed as masculine, as possessing a phallus (usually but not exclusively a biological male), because it erects the phallus of the individual in the audience as the condition of female pleasure. Female pleasure is the result, ultimately, of the gift of the phallus from members of the audience. Hence the current regime of pornographic representation retains its security for a (male) audience: it completes the fetishistic regime by providing the viewer with a direct relation to the representation through the gift of the phallus as the ultimate condition of female pleasure.

This regime is unquestionably an advance upon previous modes of representation of women in association with sexuality: the pin-up, the star system, much advertising rhetoric. It is equally an advance upon many forms of construction of 'woman' within other regimes of representation. The question of female sexual pleasure has remained unasked within public discourses for many decades in our culture: in pornography it is now receiving attention on a massive scale. The availability of vaginal imagery can be said to have a directly educative effect for both men and women, as well as tending to dispel the aura of strangeness produced by the centuries of concealment of the vagina in western representations.

It is therefore an important shift in the representation of the female, a shift that is still the subject of a series of hard-fought battles, whether in legislation or in the streets. For it is a profoundly equivocal shift: all is not sweetness and light in this field, the shift cannot be counted as a simple advance, let alone a victory for feminism. The educative effects, the effects of dispelling a particular and deep-rooted form of disgust at part of another's body, these are little more than side-effects, especially given the current and probable future institutional connotations given to the forms of circulation of these images. For the fetishistic regime is maintained by the reassertion of the phallus as the possession of the male, and the female as dependent upon the phallus as access to pleasure. The male spectator is sutured into the representation as the possessor of this prerequisite; and thus confirmed in a particular psychosocial construction of self.

However, this regime of representation is profoundly unstable. It has asked the question 'what is female pleasure?', a question that cannot find its answer in representations. The tawdry British sex comedies (still produced by the likes of George Harrison Marks) at least were based upon a question which could receive an answer: 'What does a nude woman look like?' Current pornographic films have gone further and asked the question that lies behind that of nudity; the question of the nature of pleasure. But all that can be shown in a film or a photograph is the conditions of pleasure, its circumstances and outward manifestations. These are never enough: all that the viewer finds as the reply to the question are the outward displays, what is *expected*. What *happens*, 'the fading of the subject', eludes the representation if the representation seeks to discover the elusive nature of the experience of sexual pleasure. The pornographic film text responds by multiplying instances of possible pleasure by multiplying its little stories of sexual incidents. Either that, or, in its more hard-core manifestations, it turns upon the object of the inquiry, the woman, and vents its (and the audience's) frustrations at the impossibility of gaining an answer to the question by degrading and humiliating woman, by attacking her for her obstinate refusal to yield this impossible secret. This aggression reaffirms the power of the phallus in response to a terror at the possibilities of the woman's escape from that power.

The formulation of this question in terms of a fetishistic regime has one further consequence: it leaves the question of male pleasure unasked. Attention is directed towards women and through them, to woman; male figures are attenuated in the sense that their sexuality is never really in question. The closest that questioning comes is in the often portrayed incidence of impotence or timidity, always cured. Male pleasure is assumed rather than investigated; this provides the security of the male viewer. Yet in the very perfunctory treatment that it receives, the question begins to haunt the representation: a disparity between the pressure of desire and the inadequacy of its satisfaction begins to open the complementary question, 'what is male pleasure?' A question which, itself, has no real answer apart from the tautology of 'I know because I know it'.

All this points to an instability in the current regime of pornographic representation of sexuality, especially in the cinema. It is in cinema that the most hysterical responses to this instability occur. Two disparate manifestations of this hysteria: the extremes of brutality practised upon women within representations, and the proposal from the Williams Committee that cinema should be the sole medium in which active censorship is retained. The particular instability in this medium results from the cinema's ability to narrativize a response to the question of female pleasure, however inadequate the response might be. For the process of narrativization produces significations, 'moves' the spectator, and definitively introduces a voyeuristic form of viewing which threatens the whole security of the fetishist regime of representation. This perpetual displacement/replacement of signification and spectator is beyond the scope of conventional photographic layouts usually employed in magazines. Such layouts serve to enact the placement of the phallus as the condition of female pleasure, but do no more than that. In cinema, the fetishistic regime only operates on the condition that it is established across a variation of image, a perturbation of any stability. A form of voyeurism is always present. In cinematic representations there appears most acutely the instability of the current regime of pornographic representation oriented around the ques-

166

tion of female pleasure, initially posed as a fetish. The possibility exists, then, for some film work to begin to displace this fetishistic regime by foregrounding and promoting as the organizing principle of the text those questions which begin to raise themselves behind the fetishistic posing of the question of female pleasure. It is possible to throw into question the nature of male pleasure by examining and frustrating what construction of the feminine it demands in particular circumstances. This to some extent is the effect of Nelly Kaplan's *Néa* (1976) which appeared briefly in Britain within the institution of soft-core pornography as *A Young Emmanuelle* (in early 1978).[26] It is possible also to use the questioning of pleasure, both male and female, to promote the notion of desire as the structuring principle of the text: desire which is constantly pursued but always elusive. Such is the enterprise of *Ai No Corrida* (*Empire of the Senses*) sufficiently threatening to be liable to Customs seizure, and sufficiently enlightening for the Williams Committee to mention it as a film unjustly treated under the current regulation of film censorship. Stephen Heath has traced the film's concern with the impossibility of seeing, its hesitation of narration.[27] What is important here is the way the film demonstrates the possibilities that pornography offers for representations of sexuality and of women (and men). The instability of the current fetishistic regime, based on the question of female pleasure which is only partially answerable by the 'gift' of the phallus, provides opportunities for film-making practice. This would aim at a displacement of existing represen-tations through foregrounding the aspects of the question which trouble the regime of representation that asks it. The institution of pornography would then begin to ask the questions whose space it occupies without being aware of it: 'What is sexuality? What is desire?'

POSTFACE

This metapsychological approach has tried to characterize 'pornography' as a shifting arena of representation in which particular kinds of aesthetic struggle may be possible. The boundaries of this arena are defined by the major positions over 'pornography', the way that they articulate together, and the ways that they cross other definitions of morality, sexuality, representation and so on. If, because of its conception of representation as a process, this metapsychological approach has managed to move away from such definitions, then it should also have a rather different notion of politics in relation to the pornography question. In particular, to regard pornography as an area of struggle within representations necessarily involves a different conception of the role of legislation.

The major definitions of pornography all look to the law as a crucial power which can be recruited to enforce one conception of representation, one permissible 'pornography', or another. When the pornographic arena is regarded as the site of a particular struggle over representations, the law can be regarded only as providing or securing certain conditions for that struggle. This by no means coincides with the recommendations of the Williams Report. In some ways this report does not tackle the real problems faced by those attempting to change representations, their uses and their potential in our society; in other ways it actively blocks certain directions of work. The law as it stands provides certain obstacles for those trying to intervene actively (through stickers or graffiti for instance) in the area of public advertising. Recent cases have resulted in punitive fines for feminists undertaking such activity.[28] The Williams Report is unable to formulate any recommendations in this area, though recognizing that 'many people, as is clear from submissions to us, dislike [sexualized advertisements]' (9.9). Currently advertisements are regarded legally as private property (hence fines for defacing them), rather than as being in the public domain, on the grounds that their entire function is one of addressing all and sundry whether they choose to be so addressed or not. The implications of such an argument for legal reform are not considered by the Williams Report, and so in this sense it can be seen as not having tackled the problems for those attempting to change and challenge existing representations.

Other recommendations of the report may provide new obstacles. Its recommendations are based on a public disavowal of a representational activity that is designated 'pornography' by general opinion. This will mean that the production of such representations will be confirmed as a separate industry, difficult to move into, closely linked with organized crime. The construction of pornography as 'I know it exists, nevertheless I choose to ignore it' will deprive many practitioners of the flexibility to move in and out of particular forms of signification which is implied by the notion of 'struggle within representations'. Some work will be public, some will be in plain wrappers, behind discreet doors. Such designations will provide institutional determinants of the meanings that are being produced which will create severe problems. It may suit the industry to exchange relaxation of controls on representations for tighter controls on their dissemination; but this is bound to create further problems for disruptive representational work in the area of pornography.

The area of cinema is the only medium in which the Williams Report advocates specific censorship mechanisms. It allows that the defence of 'artistic merit' may be applied to films against the activities of the censor. If there is to be censorship of films by a government body, then this should be a *public* process, similar to that used in Weimar Germany. The censorship body would have to publish arguments for specific alterations to films or bans upon films, which would then be argued out with the producers/distributors in public, if challenged. The potential would then be provided for censorship itself to become an area of struggle, rather than a secretive and unargued process as it is now.

It is too simple to support the Williams recommendations as they stand merely because they offer a possible liberalization. Similarly, it is too simple to reject direct attacks upon public representations because the form of the attack is often open to accusations of puritanism. A politics in relation to pornography must develop from a conception of 'pornography' as a particular arena of representation in which certain displacements, refigurations, are or can be possible.

NOTES

An earlier version of this article was given as a paper at the Communist University of London in July 1979. My thanks to all those present for the suggestions which have been incorporated here, as well as to Maria Black, Ben Brewster and Film Studies graduate students at the University of Kent. First published in *Screen*, Spring, 1980, vol. 21, no. 1, pp. 81–108.

1 *Report of the Committee on Obscenity and Film Censorship* [Williams Report], November 1979, HMSO Cmnd 7772 (references are to the numbered sections of the report). The report does not consider Scottish law.
2 *Pornography* [The Longford Report], London, Coronet, 1972.
3 Ruth Wallsgrove, 'Pornography: Between the Devil and the True Blue Whitehouse', *Spare Rib*, December 1977, no. 65.
4 Angela Carter, *The Sadeian Woman*, London, Virago, 1979, pp. 12–13.
5 Wallsgrove, op. cit.
6 In this respect, the sticker 'Who does this poster think you are?' would be a more effective way of confronting the attitude that advertising promotes.
7 Wallsgrove, op. cit.
8 Michael Brown, Appendix 6 to Williams Report.
9 ibid., p. 250.
10 Laura Mulvey, 'Visual Pleasure and Narrative Cinema', originally published in *Screen*, Autumn 1975, vol. 16, no. 3, pp. 6–18; reprinted as chapter 1 of this volume, pp. 22–34.
11 Griselda Pollock, 'What's Wrong with "Images of Women"?', originally published in *Screen Education*, Autumn 1977, no. 24, pp. 25–33; reprinted as chapter 5, pp. 135–45 in this volume. Sebsequent references are to this volume.
12 Sigmund Freud, 'Fetishism', in *The Standard Edition of the Complete Psychological Works*, trans. and ed. James Strachey, London, Hogarth Press, 1951–73, vol. XXI.
13 Although addressed to cinema, much of Mulvey's analysis is relevant to still images.
14 Mulvey, op. cit., p. 22.
15 ibid., p. 29.
16 ibid.
17 ibid., p. 30.
18 Sigmund Freud, 'Outline of Psychoanalysis', *Standard Edition*, vol. XXIII, p. 203. 'Fetishism' is in vol. XXI.
19 Freud presents his clinical fetishists as in no real way discommoded: 'usually they are quite satisfied with it, or even praise the way in which it eases their erotic life', *Standard Edition*, vol. XXI, p. 152.
20 A bright point of light concentrated on the eyes of an actor is a standard indicator of an intense gaze in a film.
21 For an examination of this process see Rosalind Coward, 'Sexual Liberation

and the Family', *m/f*, 1978, no. 1, especially pp. 14–17.

22 Freud, 'Fetishism', *Standard Edition*, vol. XXI, p. 155.

23 For a similar discussion of fetishism, see Metz's 'The Imaginary Signifier', *Screen*, Summer 1975, vol. 16, no. 2, especially pp. 67–75. Metz, however, is only concerned with the fetishism of the cinematic apparatus.

24 A humanist notion dependent on conceiving sexuality as permissible *only* when involving more than one person.

25 Carter, op. cit., p. 16.

26 See *Monthly Film Bulletin*, December 1977, p. 263.

27 Stephen Heath, 'The Question Oshima', in Paul Willemen (ed.), *Ophuls*, London, British Film Institute, 1978.

28 Fines of £100 and over have been exacted for 'creative' writing on London Underground posters.

7

LETTER TO JOHN

Paul Willemen

Dear John,

Reading your article 'On Pornography' in the last issue of *Screen*[1] my initial admiration for the clarity and accuracy of your analysis gradually turned to a sort of irritation. This disturbance of the equilibrium in my libidinal economy sparked off an intense process of inner speech urging me to clarify my disagreements and to put my own reflections on the subject into a semblance of order.

I found our positions to be very similar – and in some cases where that was not so, your arguments convinced me that they should be – but that there were also passages which I thought skidded off the track. In the end, you arrived at a perfectly respectable destination although it is also a dead end. What does it mean to require porn to address the questions: 'What is sexuality? What is desire?' Either it is the case that porn has solved those questions in its daily and durable practice because it trades on the exploitation of their answer, or these are questions only psychoanalysis can deal with at all adequately. To ask porn to deal with them strikes me as an evasion of the very issues you raised. By bracketing questions of specific social-historical signifying regimes defined as porn and by redirecting attention to philosophical and psychoanalytical issues posed in such a general and abstract manner, the specific institution of porn, that is the terms on which it functions and changes, has been lost from sight. Of course I agree that we must try to go beyond the currently available positions and your essay provides some of the signposts for such a trajectory. All I hope to do in this letter is to pick up on those signposts and perhaps add a few more.

The focus of my irritation with the essay centred on your footnote number twelve [note 20, p. 169 of this volume] where you assert that 'A bright point of light concentrated on the eyes of an actor is a standard indicator of an intense gaze in a film.' That is a mistake. Such a bright light, whether a point or a beam of light on the eyes of an actor/character, if shown in close-up (a necessary extra specification) does not indicate an intense gaze in a film. True enough, it is the indicator of a look, that is to say, it functions as the signifier of a gaze, but not necessarily of a gaze *in* the film nor necessarily of an intense gaze anywhere. It may indicate that the actor/character is gazing intently at something or somebody, or that she or he is being gazed at intently, but it also may mean – and quite often does, as I pointed out in an analysis of *Pursued*[2] – that something is going on behind the eyes of the character, in which case it functions as the signifier in a metonymic process substituting the container for the content. This metonymy is particularly common in *noir* films where a horizontal band of light across the eyes, leaving the rest of the image in relative obscurity but still plainly visible, tells us that the character is a psycho or/and has been traumatized. As often as not, such an image can have the character gazing at nothing in particular, signifying madness, blindness, or initiating a memory sequence. In other words, what is being shown as going on behind the eyes is not at all what is being gazed at. The look inscribed into such an image is by no means always a gaze contained within the diegesis between characters or from a character to an object.

On the contrary, I would argue that the primary function of such an image is to mark the look *at* the image, that is the look of the viewer as distinct from that of the camera, two looks which in most films are mapped on to each other. While the look of the camera constitutes the frame, the beam of light on the eyes pinpoints a look which, although from the same position as the camera, is not coextensive with it, introducing negativity into the image, a mark of difference. A different look is being interpellated. If we can say that in classic cinema the frame is absented (it functions as a masking of a continuous, homogeneous plenitude: the diegetic world in which the characters continue to exist even when they are out of frame) and that the image as seen by the camera is thus naturalized, the beam or the point of light inscribes a different look which denaturalizes the image by presenting it in its 'to-be-looked-at-ness'.

Of course, that presentation can be and often is reintegrated into the diegesis by articulating it to a diegetically motivated look or assigning it to a diegetic light source, suturing the momentary fissure and binding the viewer's position back into the network of looks that sustains the narrative movement of the text. But such a recovery manoeuvre does not eradicate the moment of oscillation, the moment of risk. To put it somewhat crudely, and therefore perhaps misleadingly, the type of image you specify signifies (as opposed to 'implies') that it is one pole of an axis the other end of which is the viewer's eye. The look of the viewer is the signifier of that axis including its three constituent terms: viewer, image and the specular relation between the two. In that sense, its explicit inscription into the image functions as a mark of what in literature would be described as direct address. The mischaracterization of that type of image in the context of your discussion of fetishism (which is where the note occurs) is as significant as your selection of that particular example is revealing.

172

I think a comparison between the light-on-the-eyes image and other images which stress their perspectival or compositional features will clarify my point. Both looks are present in both types of image (the look of the camera at the profilmic event and the look of the viewer at the image), but whereas the 'eyes-image' distinguishes the two, the others don't and thus correspond much more directly to the structure of fetishism and its regime of split belief: the emphatically composed image both indicates and denies simultaneously its 'to-be-looked-at-ness', while the eyes-image designates the difference and thus goes against the grain of the fetishistic position, dislocating its regime of split belief to some extent. And I added that qualification only because there are more effective ways of designating the image as there 'for my look', as Buñuel showed with a razor blade. It is interesting to note that the more fetishized image, the one that both draws attention to its to-be-looked-at-ness and effaces, naturalized it by covering it with the camera's look, is usually regarded as the more aesthetically satisfying one. Freud's textbook example of fetishism, which you quote (the glance at the nose), is also an example of two looks being mapped on to each other: the look at the vagina and the look at the nose, the latter cancelling out the anxiety generated by the former. In that sense, it is the frame which constitutes the cinematic equivalent of the 'shine on the nose' and not the 'light on the eyes' type of image which works in the opposite direction by dissociating the two looks. The two processes are radically different.

I want to return to the 'to-be-looked-at-ness' of the image which goes together with the inscription of the look of the viewer, with the donation of the image to the looking eye/I. As I suggested earlier, the kinds of image that foreground compositional features such as strong perspectival arrangements or a double *mise en cadre* by having frames within frames, tend to play around, timidly, with the mapping of the camera's look on to that of the viewer and achieve an increased aesthetic effect. Such effects have come to be regarded as evidence of a strong authorial presence, as marks of the process of enunciation. But the fact that the eye-images you mention are in close-up separates them from the conventional forms of arty composition. Whereas images in classic narrative cinema (e.g. Budd Boetticher or Capra) use the frame as a mask, arty compositions (using that phrase as a slightly pejorative shorthand, although I am by no means prepared to dismiss all such images at all times) emphasize the frame and, in so doing, also stress that the look of the viewer is coextensive with that of the camera, that the two looks are one. In that way, they achieve an increase in their to-be-looked-at-ness in terms of an increase in aesthetic effectiveness while at the same time retaining the naturalization of frame as mask for a continuous and homogeneous diegetic world.

Such images, directly analogous to fetishes, stress the presence of an organizing 'I' which uses – directs – the camera's look to circumscribe and organize the viewer's field of vision, thus denying the autonomy while acknowledging the presence of the viewer's look, making it present yet absent at the same time. However, the type of close-up you refer to puts no such stress on the addresser of the enunciation: it opens up a space for the emergence of the addressee's position. Obviously, when one of these two protagonists emerges, the other one tags along in its shadow. But what I am arguing is that the two different types of image, one extremely common and liable to fill an entire film, the other more of a punctuation image, both stress a different side of the process of enunciation.

It is interesting that you should have evoked the light-in-the-eyes image because, although it cannot do what you ask of it, it nevertheless provides a useful way of engaging with the process of enunciation characteristic of pornographic imagery, that is, direct address: 'This is for you to look at.' What is at stake here is the fourth look:[3] that is to say, any articulation of images and looks which brings into play the position and activity of the viewer as a distinctly separate factor also destabilizes that position and puts it at risk. All drives have active and passive facets and the scopic drive is no exception. When the scopic drive is brought into focus, the viewer also runs the risk of becoming the object of the look, of being overlooked in the act of looking. The fourth look is the possibility of that overlooking-look and is always present in the wings, so to speak. The fourth look is not of the same order as the other three (intra-diegetic looks, the camera's look at the profilmic event and the viewer's look at the image), but a look imagined by me in the field of the other which surprises me in the act of voyeurism and causes a feeling of shame, as Jacques Lacan put it.[4]

When the look of the viewer is separated off from the look of the camera, the fourth look emerges particularly strongly when the viewer's scopic drive is being gratified in relation to an object or scene which heightens the sense of censorship inherent in any form of gratification. In simpler terms: the fourth look gains in force when the viewer is looking at something she or he is not supposed to look at, either according to an internalized censorship (superego) or an external, legal one (as in clandestine viewings) or, as in most cases, according to both censorships combined. In this way, that fourth look problematizes the social dimension, the field of the other of the system of looking at work in the cinematic institution as well as in the photographic and televisual ones.

Direct address imagery is offered explicitly 'for me to look at', stressing the addressee's look as opposed to the addresser's intervention, and is particularly liable to bring that fourth look into play in full force. When you suggest that the 'shine on the nose' image of Freud's example is produced as an avoidance of the woman's gaze back at the child, you correctly but perhaps inadvertently stress the presence of the fourth look in Freud's scenario. The child avoids the eyes of the woman whose nose allows him to disavow what he has (not) seen lower down, because to encounter that look would threaten the pleasurable and reassuring structure of fetishism he has just managed to install to avoid that very threat. Whether the woman was or was not actually looking back at the child is beside the point in this context.

Much has been written about the political importance of the activation of the viewer in relation to an imaged discourse and people such as Stephen Heath have commented on the importance of the look in that process.[5] But what has rarely been addressed (it has often been affirmed or denied but rarely addressed) is the question: how exactly, through which hybrid processes and in which mechanisms can the interweaving, the articulation of the textual and the social be traced in relation to the viewer. To my knowledge, only two credible processes partaking simultaneously of the textual and of the social situation within which it arises (as production or as reading) present themselves: inner speech and the fourth look. Inner speech is a complex problem I approached a couple of years ago.[6] The fourth look and its direct implication in both the social and the psychic aspects of censorship, of the law, introduces the social into the very act of looking while remaining an integral part of the textual relations.

The look at, say, a Wim Wenders film or an Altman film does not pose many problems. Firstly because the viewer's look is caught in the fetishistic process of disavowal through the play on framing and composition that simultaneously highlights and denies the incision effected by the frame. The looks of the camera and of the viewer are both inscribed, but as a unity, thus dimming the focus on the viewer's position and illuminating the marks of enunciation to be credited to the absent organizer of the discourse, that is to say, to the author who thus signals his desire to be recognized as artist.

Second, because the mapping of these looks binds the viewer into the spectacle, the fourth look is diverted and left dormant. Third, the problems inherent in the exercise of one's voyeurism having been contained (indeed, having been covered by the mantle of art), the decrease in the overtness of the look's sexual grounding facilitates displacement, sublimation and a reversal of affect: instead of the risk of being caught looking, a positive valuation has now been bestowed upon the voyeur's activity. Some would even go so far as to want to be seen looking at an Altman film. This process of reversal forms the basis of the arguments around so-called artistic merit as distinct from the 'free speech' arguments that are made in defence of a genre such as porn cinema.

The weakness of the artistic merit argument has to do with the need to identify marks of enunciation so that they can then be credited to or projected upon a mythic 'source' of the discourse: the artist. No matter that discourses such as porn cinema are riddled with emphases on the marks of enunciation, the argument is displaced from the text on to the 'quality',

175

which invariably means the journalistic reputation of that mythic source, the artist.

The circularity of that trajectory is evident: if the text bears the hallmarks of an expressive subjectivity, it must have been done by an artist, and if it emanates from an artist, it must be art, and art can be distinguished by its emphatic marks of enunciation, and so on. This is the circle the liberal position on porn tries to break by extending the right of free speech to (some) non-artists.

Your reference to the 'eyes-image' occurs when you are constructing a transition within a passage which is itself a transition. The example signals the shift from an account of Laura Mulvey's discussion of visual pleasure[7] to the proposition that female pleasure itself has become a fetish in porn representations. This passage is itself embedded in the shift from a partial but pertinent consideration of the institution of porn on the basis of the Williams Report[8] to an attempt 'to find a way of characterizing the representations designated as porn so that they can be seen as contradictory and open to change', in the words of the essay.

This is perhaps not the place to argue that representations do not have to be contradictory to be open to change: no representation is so univocal and homogeneous that it must remain outside history. Being caught up in contradictions is not quite the same as being contradictory. However, this second transition eventually allows you to arrive at the conclusion that the questions at stake in porn are: What is sexuality? What is desire?

Interesting and important as these questions are, I would suggest that more relevant, less all-encompassing questions might be: What are the terms of the social circulation of representations of sex? What are the terms of their economic exploitation? Perhaps my two questions can be subsumed in the formulation you propose, again in a note: Who do porn representations think you are?

I have no answers to these questions, but the issues they raise allow the discussion initiated in your essay to be put into a more productive framework. The mode of address of porn imagery is characterized by a strange anonymity, a kind of emphatic anonymity. Porn films and photographs mostly are unsigned or signed with pseudonyms. This is not really to avoid prosecution since publishers, exhibitors and retailers tend to carry the risk anyway. Besides, even where porn is legal, pseudonyms are still the rule.

At the same time, when compared to the smoothly flowing regime of mainstream cinema, porn is heavily marked by the process of enunciation. But there is no author to whom these marks could be credited and to whom can thus be delegated the responsibility for the fantasy articulated in and by the discourse. Moreover, the traditional strategies deployed by mainstream cinema to achieve an impersonal mode of narration, which nevertheless binds the viewer into the diegesis, are not open to the porn film.

The specificity of the genre requires a maximum number of sexually explicit images, which necessarily fragment the narrative, produce constant repetitions and render suspense or an elementary sense of verisimilitude virtually impossible. The images must bear the marks of realist verisimilitude, the narrative cannot.

Strategies to elicit identification with a character are necessarily rudimentary because there is virtually no time and no context within which to construct such a figure. Hence the massive use of stereotypes and stock situations. Narrative is reduced to a minimum and becomes a barely (sic) motivated procedure for the juxtaposition of fantasy scenes whose combinatory logic is more that of the catalogue than that of narration.

In addition, the very arrangement of the figures in the image reinforces their status as specifically designed for 'my' look. Their to-be-looked-at-ness is stressed by the absence of the taboo on the look into the lens, by the disposition of the body or bodies in the diegesis so as to grant direct access to the genital areas even if this means that the protagonists have to engage in most uncomfortable contortions, by the relentless use of punctuating close-ups of genitalia and their interactions, and so on. In porn there is no way the viewer can fade into the diegesis or, alternatively, shove responsibility for the discourse on to the author. The viewer is left squarely facing the image without even the semblance of an excuse justifying her or his presence at the other end of the look. Porn imagery may well be the most blatant and uncompromising form of direct address short of physical contact.

Besides, the substitution of the look for physical contact is precisely the essential precondition for porn and the specific difference which distinguishes it from other scopophilic regimes such as looking at family snapshots or at Hollywood movies. Porn involves a direct form of address in which the look substitutes for physical (sexual) contact in a structure determined by conditions of production along with the emphatic presence of the fourth look. It is via that look, imagined by me in the field of the other, that porn imagery affects and is affected by the competing discourses and institutions that assign it its changing place within the register of signifying practices.

Crudely speaking, when mention is made of changes in the public presence and acceptability of porn, it is the institutionalization of the fourth look within a social formation we are talking about. Within that structure, there are different modes of looking. The dominant one is no doubt the fetishistic look because images themselves, as objects, sustain the belief in a presence in the face of our knowledge of absence. This founding fetishism can be overlaid, doubled by a second order and more specific fetishism when the depicted figure relaunches the need for some further disavowal. Obviously, the depiction of genitalia is a prime candidate for such a second-order disavowal. Hence the fact that in many,

177

perhaps even in most, porn imagery the bodies depicted are shown as somehow contained, sheathed in paraphernalia such as boots, stockings, garter belts or leather gear, making these bodies into representatives of the phallus according to the mechanisms lucidly described by Laura Mulvey in her article on the work of Allen Jones.[9] The disavowal operates by making the body into a phallus or by inscribing elsewhere in the image, often in multiplied form, what is looked for and seen to be missing.

However, porn also often plays on a second, more reassuring type of looking which can quite easily coexist with the fetishistic look, although it is in some sense its inverse. It is less a disavowal of 'her' castration than a confirmation of the viewer's phallic power. This specular relation is dependent on the emphatic direct address interpellating the viewer as possessor and donor of the phallus, the one who is required to complete the picture, as it were.

The representation of women experiencing pleasure is one variant on this theme. In most porn, women are the space on to (into) which male pleasure and phallic power is inscribed. This can take different forms: through the disposition of the body so as to grant maximum access to the look; through the imprinting on women of the traces of male pleasure (the come-shot or money shot, as it's called in the trade, usually disperses its seminal signifiers on to the body of the woman, while her orgasm either precedes it, is triggered by it or is left out of the picture altogether). Even when a woman is shown to be deriving pleasure from masturbation, her body is always arranged in 'display' poses maximizing access of the look to her genital area, suggesting that the pleasure depicted is a narcissistic mirror for the viewer. Rare are the occasions when in such a scene the distinction between the look of the viewer and that of the camera are brought into play. The price the viewer pays for this guarantee of her/his phallic power is the price of porn itself: the radical separation from the object of desire required for the look to be able to function at all (as signifier of desire). The viewer's security depends on that separation: it is separation which guarantees (mostly) him phallic power. If it is true, as you suggest, that there is a proliferation of vaginal imagery and of women-in-pleasure images, then this is the very opposite of 'an advance upon previous modes of representation of women', as you write. On the contrary, such a development constitutes an emphatic insistence on the centrality of phallic, male pleasure and suggests that the male population in western societies now requires to be reassured more often, more directly and more publicly than before. The increase in public visibility and availability of such imagery does address women: it tells them to stop threatening that centrality. The terms on which representations of sexuality appear to circulate at present seem to point to a severe crisis of male self-confidence. It would even be possible to confirm this by way of analyses of analogous developments in mainstream cinema: the proliferation of disaster movies about burning and collapsing skyscrapers, crashing planes, suffocating and exploding ships, toppled presidents, and so on.

This address of women through the public display of porn operates indirectly through the fourth look: public visibility here means that the look imagined by me in the field of the Other is that of a woman who sees the images which guarantee that female pleasure depends on a phallus. The more women object to this, the more effective the operation of the images is for men. Of course, to actually be caught looking, to be found out as needing reassurance, is quite a different matter. Nevertheless, that the proliferation of such images coincides with the growth of the Women's Movement as well as with vocal demands for censorship is not a coincidence.

I would also like to make a few points about the social inscription of porn images in relation to fantasy. Fantasy images, framed image-objects and what we see around us are three different things existing in different spaces. Each involves different relations between subject and look. The actualization of fantasy scenarios into framed image-objects (still or moving) necessarily passes through 'the defiles of the signifier', as Lacan would say, as well as through the distortion processes unconscious signifiers are subjected to when passing into consciousness.

In relation to the imaged discourse, secondary elaboration and considerations of representability are extremely important. Figurative images, which is what porn images needs must be, require a social setting and an individuation which fantasy can do without. On the one hand, the surfeit of specific details due to the need for a frame to be filled produces an excess of signification. But this excess is also a loss: the lack of fit between the represented scenario and the fantasy transmuted into concrete images.

In porn, this inevitable mismatch plays a particularly important role because it is more acutely experienced. When a western such as *Pursued* evokes the primal scene as a structuring fantasy, it does so in oblique and distorted ways.

Porn imagery directly addresses the viewer with the fantasy itself. The fantasy no longer needs to be reconstructed. But now it is the very incarnation of the fantasy that cannot but produce a mismatch: the actors' bodies (pimples and all), the lighting, the sets, the noises on the soundtrack, everything is excessively concrete and never quite coincides with the selective vagueness of a fantasy image. A sexual fantasy can proceed very satisfactorily without having to specify the pattern on the wallpaper. A filmic fantasy cannot. In porn, and perhaps in all films, it is the loss generated by the friction between the fantasy looked for and the fantasy displayed which sustains the desire for ever-promised and never-found gratification.

Porn, as an institution, thrives on this repetition of loss, of the double separation between viewer and representation and between the fantasy looked for and the one on offer. It is in the tension between approximation and separation in relation to the representation of sex that perhaps the explanation can be found for the compensatory activity associated with porn: masturbation. And that pleasure in return relaunches the desire for the tensions provoked by porn in the first place. The close connection between porn and masturbation tends to generate defensiveness . . . and further compensatory action. It is difficult to talk about porn without becoming too aggressive, too puritanical, too jokey, too excessive in one way or another. (Hence also the slightly excessive and scandalous aspects of a direct address in the form of a letter intended to be overlooked by *Screen*'s readers.)

The most common defensive strategy in relation to porn is the mobiliz-ation of *double entendres*, sustained double meanings, witticisms, jokes, and so on. The verbal language that accompanies porn stresses this jokey aspect, insisting that it is not to be taken seriously. However, it is more than just a distancing device. Neither is the joke aspect of porn just a self-reflexive comment on the endlessly stereotyped and repetitive nature of the porn discourse itself. The way porn actualizes unconscious significa-tions is analogous to the way jokes do.

Allowing for the differences between Freud's verbal jokes and cinematic porn, there is at least one striking similarity between their discursive mechanisms. It is a similarity relating not so much to the place of the fourth look in the process but to its function as a space. Perhaps even the only space, as far as the viewer is concerned, where the social and the textual mesh. Tzvetan Todorov, in his book *Théories du symbole*,[10] schematizes the process of enunciation involved in rude jokes: A (the man) addresses B (the woman) seeking to satisfy his sexual desire; the intervention of C (the rival) makes the satisfaction of desire impossible. Hence, a second situ-ation develops: frustrated in his desire, A addresses aggressive remarks to B and appeals to C as an ally. A new transformation occurs, provoked by the absence of the woman or by the need to observe a social code: instead of addressing B, A addresses C by telling him a rude joke; B may well be absent, but instead of being the addressee she has become (implicitly) the object of what is said: C derives pleasure from A's joke.

The only modification I would want to make to this scenario is that C, the rival addressed by the joke and the one who becomes the subject of its pleasure, does not have to be another person. Any censorship mechanism, whether internal or external to A, is equally effective in setting in motion the series of substitutions and displacements described.

Taking into account that the mode of address in visualized discourse operates through the organization of a network of looks, the structure of address underpinning the joke process is very similar to that in play in porn: a man ends up showing a rude image of a woman (usually) to another man who becomes the subject of its pleasure. The male addressee arrives in that place because the woman has been expelled from it. But as Poe demonstrated in his story of the purloined letter, messages always reach their destination. The initial demand of the man addressed to the woman was a demand for his gratification, that is to say, it was a demand for self-gratification through the detour of the woman. The rival is in fact this narcissistic double whose gratification is at stake. It is the addresser in another place of the discursive process. His pleasure stands in for mine. In that process, the woman has been eliminated and relegated to the field of the other whence she, the repressed, returns as the subject of the fourth look. This allows the men to function as subjects and objects at the same time: one is the object of a look, the other is the subject of an enunciation. The representation of sexuality men circulate substitutes for an address of a woman who is thus relegated to a space below the barrier of repression, whence her look returns as the one that overlooks the male in his reassuringly defensive games of substitution.

This mechanism offers a way of understanding how a feminist politics can have effects within porn as a signifying practice. The historically changing content of porn imagery provides figurations of the contours, the imprint of women's struggles on the representations of male desire and its objects. The distance between the woman imagined as the subject of the fourth look and the woman (not) addressed in the first place measures the extent to which feminisms have impinged on male sexuality.

The porn industry addresses itself to women by representing back to them those changes – the crisis provoked in male sexuality – but it does so obliquely: the images are not for women to look at, they are for women to overlook. To get annoyed by that mirror may be understandable, but it is a little beside the point. Which is not to say that one shouldn't oppose aspects of the porn industry: that business institutionalizes and exploits both the crisis in male sexuality and the real women who are required to model for the images and the films. On the other hand, to oppose the representation of (sexual) fantasy merely modifies the regime of representation, not the fantasy.

POSTSCRIPT

Talking about changing the representation, not the fantasy, in Fleming's anaemic version of *Dr Jekyll and Mr Hyde* (1941) there is a strange sequence that appears to have been caused by such censorship. But it is the way the fantasy circumvented the censorship that is rather interesting in the context of a discussion about pornography. The passage occurs when Spencer Tracy/Hyde comes to visit Ingrid Bergman/Ivy in the secret apartment where Hyde keeps her to gratify his beastly desires. She is seen in a fairly distressed state when he enters. He starts by teasing her: 'What shall

I ask you to do tonight, dear?' (or words to that effect). He then proceeds to build up the tension, suggesting a series of innocent-sounding activities which are immediately rejected. He gets more and more excited as he gets closer to enouncing the awful, beastly thing he will require from her. Gradually, the full horror of what he is about to ask her to do dawns on her and she starts to whimper and moan in helpless despair: 'No, no . . . not *that*!' Tracy replies: 'Yes . . . Yes, my dear . . . you shall . . . *Sing* to me.' And then we are treated at length to the anguished, tearful face of Bergman as she is forced to submit to this filthy perversion.

I think there are few scenes in the cinema which avoid showing sex in so blatant and graphic a manner. (Perhaps in *Susan Slept Here*, the middle-aged Dick Powell/Mr Christopher and the 17-year-old Debbie Reynolds/Susan dancing throughout their wedding night, with dialogue lines about being able to keep it up all night, qualifies as another such sex scene.) This substitution of singing (and dancing) for sex may give a clue to the popularity of musicals.

Musicals do have a marked structural similarity with porn films. In both cases the importance of the generically obligatory sequences makes for a weak narrative as the story is simply there to link the graphic sex/musical numbers with fairly predictably coded transitions from the narrative to its interruptions, with the interruptions functioning as self-contained pieces. Moreover, the need to include such relatively autonomous segments arranged as spectacles 'arresting' the look and thus, at least to a significant extent, suspending the narrative flow, makes for films that proceed with a halting rhythm. Also in both genres, such a structure makes it easier to add or to cut scenes without substantially altering the plot development. Finally, in both genres the interrupting segments consist of bodies displaying their physicality either in isolation or in rhythmical unison.

All this makes the precise point where the narrative tends to give way to a musical number rather interesting. It cannot be a mere coincidence that moments of 'discovery' (when the lovers discover they are in love) or of 'union' tend to be the obvious points where the rhythmical interactions are be inserted. Other key moments are when one of the lead characters displays her/his body for seduction, for the look of the other: there too the narrative tends to swell into a musical number. Perhaps there is material here for a comparative study between Egyptian, Hindi and US musicals? One pertinent difference might be that in Hollywood the display of the male body is at least as significant as that of the female body, perhaps even more so (for example Astaire, Kelly).

NOTES

First published in *Screen*, Summer 1980, vol. 21, no. 2, pp. 53–65.

1 See chapter 6, pp. 146–70 of this volume.
2 Paul Willemen, 'Pursued – The Fugitive Subject', in Phil Hardy (ed.), *Raoul Walsh*, Edinburgh, Edinburgh Film Festival, 1974.
3 Paul Willemen, 'Voyeurism, the Look and Dwoskin', *Afterimage*, 1976, no. 6.
4 Jacques Lacan, *Le Séminaire*, XI, Paris, Editions du Seuil, 1973.
5 Stephen Heath, 'Anata mo', *Screen*, Winter 1976–7, vol. 17 no. 4, pp. 49–66.
6 Paul Willemen, 'Cinematic Discourse: The Problem of Inner Speech' in T. de Lauretis and S. Heath (eds), *Cinema and Language*, Maryland, University Publications of America, 1981.
7 Laura Mulvey, 'Visual Pleasure and Narrative Cinema', chapter 1, pp. 22–34, in this volume; originally published in *Screen*, Autumn 1975, vol. 16, no. 3, pp. 6–18.
8 *Report of the Committee on Obscenity and Film Censorship* [The Williams Report], HMSO Cmnd 7772, November 1979.
9 Laura Mulvey, 'You Don't Know What You're Doing, Do You Mr Jones?', *Spare Rib*, 1973, no. 8.
10 Tzvetan Todorov, *Théories du symbole*, Paris, Editions du Seuil, 1978.

8

THE HETEROSEXUAL PRESUMPTION

Claire Pajaczkowska

INTRODUCTION

I am writing this article because of the anger I feel at the way that 'woman's pleasure' has been used as a concept in some current discussions of pornography. The purpose of this piece is threefold; first, to look at the terms of the discussion, initially formalized in the conference on pornography at the ICA[1] and continued in John Ellis's article,[2] Paul Willemen's reply[3] and in Beverley Brown's recent article.[4] Second, I want to question the way in which psychoanalytic theory has been taken up by film theory and to show how this has led to the misplacement of 'sexual difference' in the analysis of signifying practice. In order to do these two things I have had to take two apparently disparate textual objects, the conference and the John Ellis text, and to treat them as if they were similar. What I am writing is neither a review of the conference nor an answer to John Ellis's theoretical text, and so is bound to fall clumsily in between these two categories.

My only justification for the methodological crime of treating two quite distinct textual productions as if they were the same is that by doing so, that is by seeing them as parts of the same discursive practice, I am able to subject them to the same question about the politics of their theory. My assumption is that there are, in each, *forms of thinking*, epistemological structures, of the same order. These structures or forms of thinking are both linguistic, for example the slippage allowed in language between a discursive and a historical enunciation, and extra-linguistic, which I won't attempt to define but which are to be found in the effects of contradictions in language that stem from affective levels that have yet to be adequately theorized by linguistics – the instance of the pre-Oedipal, for example. The punishment for this transgression of the rules of writing, the sentence to which I am subject, is that I am forced into circuitous syntax and uneconomical logic that come closer to being examples of 'deviant sentences' than to the logical coherence of the theoretical text. This, however, is part of the third point I want to raise for discussion, the state and status of theory itself, and specifically how theoretical practice at the conference was constructed as different from political practice.

The two distinguishing features of the weekend seminar on pornography were, first, that the people assembled to watch porn films were doing so in order to gather material for analysis rather than to be turned on by them, and second that an intervention by a group of homosexual men 'Gaze',[5] despite being debated at lunchtime, was never incorporated into the body of the conference and remained a marginal intervention from 'outside'. At the time the presence of the first and the absence of the second did not strike me as being necessarily related, but I now want to suggest that the politics of these two different features, or rather their respective functions in the process of the conference, are not as arbitrary as it would seem, and that the presence of the first, the theoretical and sociological inquiry we were making into 'pornography', necessitated the exclusion of the second.

The intervention of the 'Gaze' group, who were pointing out that the conference did not address the crucial question of homosexual pornography and the representation of homosexuality in pornography, caused a disturbance during the first morning of the two-day event, but after debating their views with participants and organizers at lunchtime on Saturday the three men went away and the conference continued as planned. It was not until the final plenary session that their intervention was reconsidered in order to take 'political' action on it: there was a formal proposal that the mimeographed broadsheet handed out by these men be presented to the editorial board of *Screen* and/or *Screen Education* who could then decide whether or not to publish it; a *vote* to do this was taken and it appeared to many that satisfactory action had been taken. Although this democratic liberalism met the ostensible demands of the interventionist group it was nevertheless an unsatisfactory conclusion because it did not begin to address the question raised by their appearance at, and subsequent exclusion from, the conference itself.

However, as planned, Beverley Brown and Elizabeth Cowie presented a critique of the Williams Committee's inquiry into pornography,[6] showing how it is impossible to think coherently in the terms that it sets up: the dual axis according to which the representation of sexuality in public places is legally differentiated from the use of such representations in 'private' which is the concern of 'individuals', and therefore not a social issue. They showed that this differentiation between public and private, essential to liberal legislation, is the attendant corollary of certain ideological misconceptions, which means that legal change is insufficient to affect anything but the most superficial aspects of pornography. This was augmented by Pam Cook's analysis of a Stephanie Rothman film, *Student Nurses* (1970), an intensive textual analysis of the multiplicity of forms of fetishism at work in the film, and of the dependence of the intelligibility of the narrative on these forms of fetishistic spectatorship in the viewing subject.

In their different ways both of these projects worked on the problematization of the idea of an autonomous subject, be it a legal subject or spectator, to whom it would be possible to attribute any position of exteriority in relation to pornographic texts.

The problem of the status of the subject was present in all of the papers given at the conference, from being the central concern of *m/f*'s work, through Richard Dyer's presentation, to John Ellis's autobiographical reference that prefaced his presentation, informing us that his work was that of a heterosexual man, and that he had chosen to work on the pornography targeted at this social group.

Richard Dyer's method of re-introjecting the problem of the subject in analysing image structures consisted of asking us as spectators to consider our 'subjective' feelings about the nature of the sexual practices represented, in order that we might be more 'objective' about analysing their meaning. This double-edged notion of analysis comprising 'feelings' and 'thinking' cannot wholly replace the more complex psychoanalytic and semiological methodology which has been developed precisely because of the need to understand 'the subject' in terms other than 'the individual', that is to replace the idea that feelings and thoughts are owned by us privately and as individuals by an account of how feelings, fantasies and thinking are articulated with other, more readily theorized, structures in what could be thought of as a general structure of subjectivity.

In the performance of Richard Dyer's slide show (which has mostly been used within the context of Campaign for Homosexual Equality workshops) Dyer moves between the audience and the slide image talking about his tastes in erotic imagery and about how all imagery works on us in a way that is most clearly manifested in the 'before & after' shots found in both pornography and advertising. In this to and fro between spectator and spectacle the physical presence of the speaker becomes overdetermined as significant. Dyer works within the tradition of performance whilst constantly subverting the place of the spectacle, refusing to let either himself or pornography be simply the object of our predatory gaze, thus suggesting that we understand pornography as a text–reader system rather than setting it up as a textual or sociological object.

John Ellis's presentation of his paper began, as I have said, with the prefatory remark on his own 'subjectivity', and then left aside the question of the subject in order to describe his object (which remains an object even if it is one that is heterogeneous and multiple) as it has been posited by some feminists, the Festival of Light and the Williams Committee, although these three groups are characterized by their opposition to pornography and John Ellis defines himself in opposition to them, so constructing his object by a negation of a negation. Having identified, or topographically located the territory thus designated as the pornographic oppositionally but nevertheless in terms of these groups, John Ellis moved on to the second half of his analysis. In this, the metapsychological, we already have our object 'pornography' which has been given us in the first place by the sociological definitions noted above, and second, by the methodological structure of the metapsychology, which is, precisely, a metalanguage. Any metalanguage must construct its object in order to theorize it, although this is usually thought of as 'finding' or 'discovering' it. Although the problem of the status of this metapsychology is obviously of primary importance I want to leave it aside until we have confronted the numerous problems *within* its epistemological territory, although it soon becomes evident that these are profoundly imbricated in the former.

John Ellis's metapsychological methodology is culled from disparate theories of fetishism, from Freud's metapsychology, through Lacan's work on the signification of the phallus, to Laura Mulvey's work in film theory and from positivist semiology (the search for the smallest discrete unit of signification/fetishism) through to Angela Carter's literary criticism. As the theory is such a composite one it is difficult to identify from where its epistemological fault-lines issue. The theory of fetishism is one of the elementary explanatory concepts of film theory, but its use in psycho-analytic theory is far from simple. The status of the explanatory structure of symbolic castration, of which the mechanism of fetishism is a corollary, is itself problematic, and constitutes the area in which many feminist analysts are working, because of the tenuous relation of the female child to the threat of deprivation of an organ which has never been hers to begin with. As is stands, the theory of fetishism does not account for female fetishists. Fetishism is thought to be specific to the boy's phallic stage, existing only in relation to the Oedipus complex, from which it is thought to be derived, and it is assumed that women's negative entry into the Oedipus complex precludes the possibility of their becoming fetishists.[7] If, however, we assume that fetishism is a process peculiar to men, why is it that films work for us women? The question is of course absurd, it is a problem of pre-Lacanian psycho-analytic theory, for although analysts such as Gillespie wrote on the issue at the same time as, or even after, Lacan their thinking remains pre-structuralist. Underlying their theory is the humanist tenet of ego psychology in which the ego is thought of as an organ 'belonging' to the human agent rather than being understood as a metaphor for psychic activity, and in their theory fetishism is seem to be a 'man's' problem in the way that psycho-analysis is seen to be case histories.[8] Within a post-Lacanian understanding fetishism is thought as a structural relation of the gaze, as partial drive bound to an economy of representation. It is not enough to characterize the fetish object (or the image). What we need is the description of a textual circuit articulating 'positions' of masculinity and femininity through processes of identification, the maintenance of these positions being the work effected by us as subjects each time we understand the meaning of a sentence, each time we 'get' the joke, each time we 'make' the film make sense.

Given that the problem is no longer one of a gendered individual with appropriate characteristics, but one of a textual circuit or economy within which we labour to achieve identity, the question of the inscription of sexual difference within this economy nevertheless remains the central problem, Lacan, for instance, is not a feminist, and his formulation of the place of sexual difference requires a suspension of disbelief in order to make sense. Yet it is neither necessary nor sufficient to 'disbelieve' the universality of the castration complex in order to use psychoanalytic theory. Feminist work in psychoanalysis, as Kristeva, Mitchell, Irigaray and others have demonstrated, consists of investigating those structures of *belief* necessary to the idealism of 'scientific' theory and of working through the contradictions of those phantasies that have been formalized into the mathematical proofs of Euclidean geometry, according them the interest they deserve as the products of the Imaginary. When, for example, we are given a universal such as symbolic castration, we listen to its *histoire* and recognize its discursive origins, which, within the discourse of psycho-analytic theory, is to locate it in its own history – the 'time' of the pre-Oedipal. Silvia Payne says 'A study of what the fetish *means* reveals that it is possible to demonstrate that every component of the infantile sexual instinct has some connection with the fetish object so that this object is associated with all the repressed infantile sexual experiences.'[9] The formu-lation of the theory of voyeurism and fetishism that is now common currency in film theory must be returned to the pre-oedipal, repeatedly and with its every component, in an attempt to trace the genesis of this 'universal'.

THE INSTANCE OF SIGHT

What makes the theory of fetishism of particular interest to film theorists is that it is centrally concerned with the look and visual symbolization. Freud states that it is at the sight of the female genitals that the search for the maternal penis results in the discovery of and disavowal of sexual differ-ence. But, as the story goes, before the glance up the maternal skirts, there was the imagined looking at the parents fucking, and it was whilst gazing at this 'primal scene' that the issue of penises and mothers began to be a problem for the child. Importantly, when the same elements are once again being juggled with (always in excess of logic, too much to get a firm grasp of), the child's look is directed toward the mother and these come to be articulated in the ubiquitous phantasy of the phallic mother, it is a halluci-nation of mummy plus penis, where the penis is the father's.[10] If Freud insisted that the fetish 'is not a substitute for any chance penis, but for a particular and quite special penis . . . is a substitute for the woman's (mother's) penis'[11] it is because he was waiting for science to carry out something he thought of as analogous to the archaeological excavation of Minoan-Mycenaean relics. It was the wrong analogy, because the pre-

Oedipal, far from lying quietly waiting to be discovered, unearthed, is all the more active for being unrecognized – and we shall see later of what use analogy is to us.

When we use Freud to inform film theory or any analysis of signifying practice we must not do this uncritically. What I want to suggest is that the premiss that cunt imagery must necessarily invoke castration anxiety in spectator-subjects is a mistaken consequence of the misappropriation of a metapsychology that conflates the instance of the *visual* with the instance of *threat*. Freud's speculation that 'probably no man is spared the fright of castration at the sight of a female genital' is hardly a theoretical statement. Jones is closer when he suggests

> It is not hard to see that these two fears – of the female genital and of castration – stand in a specially close relationship to each other (that is they are not the same thing) . . . [This relationship is established through] a repressed wish to play the feminine part in copulation, evidently with the father. Otherwise castration and copulation would not be equated.[12]

The logic being that it is in the boy's identification with the mother as the only known form of sexual access to the father that the question of the superfluity of the boy's genital arises for him. Pre-Oedipally, the aetiology and topography of sight and threat are quite different. If the visual instance is understood as the maternal body presenting the question of *sameness* and *difference* to the child and if it is understood that difference comes to mean having or lacking the phallus only through the secondary instance of the paternal threat we can begin to understand the senselessness of those theories that posit the primacy of the phallus as signifier.

But Lacan can be useful to feminists. Commenting on Jones's text and its context, the debate in 1928–32 on the status of the phallic stage, Lacan counters Jones's theorizing of the phallic stage as the effect of a repression, and the phallic object as symptom, correctly pointing out that in order to maintain this Jones has to locate the Oedipus complex at the early age of around nine months.[13] Lacan's criticism is useful; when the entire enterprise of feminist psychoanalysis is to open up the space of the 'pre'-Oedipal, we cannot follow Jones's attempt to make it disappear into nine months, we have to instead change the theoretical presupposition of the Oedipal itself. If we question the structuralism of Lacan's thinking, it is not in order to revert to Jones's empirical logic.

Laura Mulvey demonstrates how this is possible; her polemical use of an 'either punished or fetishized' schema for investigating the representation of women in the classic realist Hollywood text is crucial. But the original complexity of her question 'How can we appropriate psychoanalytic theory as a political weapon for the deconstruction of the monolithic accumulation of traditional film conventions?' has never really been taken up. Instead it has been transformed into an injunction to use Freud's metapsychology and Lacan to build a new monolith of conventions in theory. And this has led to an oversimplification in thinking the intricate and multiple forms of representations of women, and the place of sexual difference. The women I look at in films are not simply either castrated men or fetishes, they are necessarily multiple, because the maternal imagos in infantile subjectivity are multiple; they are also the mother of the oral stage and the mother of the anal stage. Thus the sadism that is articulated in the voyeuristic syndrome of spectatorship is firstly an oral sadism, which can come to be the sadism of the spectator's pleasure in a film's 'punishment' of a woman, a castrated other, or in her fetishization only through a specific psychic trajectory. How is it that the mother's (woman's) body can come to represent the paternal threat, if it is not through an inversion of the pleasure it once provided – a pleasure subsequently forbidden as incestuous by the paternal law?[14]

THE INSTANCE OF THREAT

We have yet to understand what it is that constitutes the threat. Many analysts (for example Lemoine-Luccionni, Weissman) suggest that the castration threat gets its impetus and meaning from separation anxiety, from the *danger* of separation, which is a pre-Oedipal danger. Just as Lacan traces back the post-Hegelian philosophical notion of a presupposed fear of death to its primary determination, the narcisistic *fear* of damage to one's own body, so we can trace this castration threat still further back to the danger of the infant's vulnerability in auto-eroticism: when what is experienced is a castration threat, what is being felt is a separation anxiety, which is to say that the threat, structurally, is the externalization or projection of anxiety. The infant responds to real danger with anxiety, which subsequently comes to be represented by a third term, the threat. Jones describes the threat of castration at the time of entry into the Oedipus structure, for both male and female children, as a real censorship by adults of any form of the child's sexual activity, 'for the child an indefinite postponement is the same thing as a permanent refusal'; thus, he says, the castration threat is ultimately the threat of the extinction of sexuality altogether, that of aphanisis.[15]

The representation of death, according to Lacan, derives its meaning from the experience of symbolic castration, and a feminist account takes this back still further and examines the meaning of symbolic castration as a representation of feelings of anxiety. In the oedipal structure the threat of castration, or the father's prohibition on rivalry towards the mother, comes to be conflated with the visual instance of the gaze at the female body, a repetition that recalls the earlier moments of sight and their unconscious symbolization as imagos, all of which make the Law of the Father have meaning. But in order for psychoanalysis to serve as theory, the explana-tory method cannot do what the infant does, conflate both parents to a 'phallic mother', nor can it do what the Oedipal boy does in conflating them once again in another hallucination, that of the woman's body as the representation of the castration threat. It is less a question of 'proving' that the castration complex is not universal, be it empirically, clinically or theoretically, for proof is in the service of belief; but of displacing the problem into the terms of a historical inquiry into the ontogenesis of subjectivity (or maybe even its phylogenesis), of inquiring into the status of the phallus as signifier in pre-phallic subjectivity, and of the supposed primacy of signification when the very meanings of symbolic structures are established in infancy (pre-speech), in order to show how the paternal metaphor can come to represent these processes of repression, without simply reconstructing the metaphor itself.

THE POLITICS OF THEORY

It is within this epistemological space opened up by the theoretical practice of analysts that it is possible to reconsider first, the question of the organization of the drives or instincts and 'desire' in the bisexual pre-Oedipal child and its ensuing transformation into a genital heterosexual subject; and second, the theory of the primacy of the phallus as signifier in visual signification. Christian Metz[16] distinguished three kinds of theoreti-cal failure in relation to the inadequacies of various psychoanalytic approaches to film studies: the 'nosographic', the 'typological or character-ological' and the 'study of film scripts'. We should add a fourth category to these failures which could be called 'psychoanalytic studies that forget to question the political ramifications of psychoanalytic theory itself'. What such a study does, like the theory it misappropriates, is to give 'sexual difference' the place that is really occupied by relation between father and son, it uses 'woman' once again as an adjectival function through which men avoid their homosexuality or conflict.

Nowhere is this fourth category clearer than in John Ellis's text, in which the structures of 'fetishistic viewing' are taken as given, and the problem of rethinking the pornographic text as a circuit of substitutions and exchanges articulated in a process of identification is unacknowledged, whilst the simpler quest for the fetish object is taken up. Rereading the Ellis text in the light of this displacement of psychoanalytic theory we can understand its use of the concept of fetishism in a different way; in his argument the process of *signification* is construed as an object, pornographic film. The film is slowed down, freeze framed, and within a single frame the new fetish is found – 'woman's pleasure'. Importantly, it is at this point in his argument that he must quote Angela Carter's metaphor (from *The Sadeian Woman*) '[there is] a gap left in the text of just the right size for the reader to insert his prick into', because it is only *metaphorically* that he can account for the operation of the text–reader circuit, the process of subjectivity. The citation of a metaphor at this point in the argument is what enables John Ellis to reach his conclusion; it is also a moment of textual excess and simultaneously an epistemological gap, a hole in his thinking. His conclusion, that in orgasm woman has the phallus, because somehow the reader/viewer is penetrating her:

> Woman is given that orgasm and hence that phallus by men . . . The male's phallus is the condition for female sexual pleasure . . . female pleasure is the result ultimately of the gift of the phallus from members of the audience[17]

is one that assumes that we can engage in some direct access to the text, that there is a moment of 'closeness' to the text unimpeded by the processes of identification – recognition, projection and incorporation of signification – which constitute film spectatorship.

The penises I see in porn films are introjected as visual signification; the incorporation of signification does not give me a penis, it changes me on the symbolic level, that of meaning. The condition for the meaningful incorporation of signification is fundamentally the logic of inside/outside, characteristic of the language of the oral phase. But it is important not to metaphorize this identificatory process of introjection. I neither swallow signification nor am I penetrated by signification, neither do men penetrate signification. That signification revolves around the phallus is nowhere clearer than in porn films, but in the analysis of these films it is silly to think of the process of introjection fundamental to cinematic identification as analogous to penetration, because in the final analysis the benefits derived from the analogy, however neat, do not outweigh its problems.

This fantasy of a closeness, of gaining direct access to the text, a fantasy which occupies the space of the hole in his theory, the epistemological gap into which he inserts his metaphor, is the same fantasy of the absence of separation which the fetishist is acting out. This short-circuiting, besides being itself a fetishism, presumes, on the symbolic level, that woman's orgasm is the result of men's penetration. A common fantasy amongst heterosexual men, but a fantasy none the less. When this was put to John Ellis at the conference he replied that this was indeed the assumption of such pornography, as it is inevitably part of patriarchal ideology.

But the question now arises of the status of this supposedly *meta*psychological inquiry, because as it stands the explanation is a simple description of that ideology, a manifestation of its fantasies; and it cannot account for the production of that ideological misrecognition, as theory should do, if it is to be of any use to us. John Ellis's theory of heterosexuality is simply heterosexist, just as his theory of fetishism is fetishistic (stopping the film to identify, to *find* the one thing that would constitute the fetish). These

192

theoretical 'mistakes' derive from the same structural fault, one that ultimately resides in the inability to accord the problem of sexual difference its true place. What I want to show is *how* this problem of sexual difference, in its articulation in the fetishistic defence, comes to be given the place that belongs to the problem of homosexuality. The mechanism of fetishism, we know, is that which provides a defence against symbolic castration and in so doing makes 'woman' adequate as a sexual object; it is that which enables the heterosexual manoeuvre to be successfully and completely enacted, thus providing a partial defence against homosexuality. This is the sense in which John Ellis's metapsychological manoeuvre is successfully enacted, that is, precisely because it is a fetishistic text. What then of its heterosexism and the sequence of the displacements of homosexual desire?

It is because the positions of masculinity and femininity are never unequivocally resolved or completely achieved, because gender identity must always be laboured towards in order for its crisis to be transcended, that it is always necessary to consider the problems raised, for theory, by the fact of the bisexuality of pre-Oedipal subjectivity. We must always account for the vicissitudes of the drives across the trajectory of symbolic castration and through the paternal metaphor, the representation of their repression. If this is not done then we can be sure of finding another kind of 'work' in the theory, the work of maintaining gender identity as unproblematic. In forgetting to do this John Ellis produces what Freud calls a 'paranoic' text.

In order to explain why the introduction of the concept of paranoia is necessary at this point I must make another two-sided excursion from what is strictly 'film theory' and refer first to the conference and second to psychoanalytic theory. Back then to the conference, from where we set out, and to the terms of the exclusion of the 'Gaze' group. The demands of the group, that the conference agenda should have included an analysis of homosexual pornography, do not answer their needs. It is not a question of whether we take homosexuality into account or not, but of how we produce homosexuality in our account. That is to say that instead of setting up a parallel analysis of the representation of homosexuality, the interest of gays would be better served by asking that existing analyses of the sexual processes at work in representation acknowledge the psychoanalytic premises of primary bisexuality and account for the presence, generally repressed, of the processes of homosexuality in the psychic structures of signifying practice. If this premiss is not acknowledged, then the positions of 'man' and 'woman' will be taken as given and the work of the production or maintenance of those positions will remain invisible, thus confirming the heterosexual presumption. This is the condition for the imaginary 'I' that misrecognizes itself as the 'heterosexual man' of the prefatory remark, to be believed, by us, to be talking sense.

In his main writing on paranoia, the Schreber case history (which is also the only case history to be made exclusively through a textual analysis, of

Schreber's writings), Freud differentiates between the paranoic text and the hysterical text. The former, he says, *decomposes*,[18] the other *condenses* (the article you are now reading being a good example of the latter). John Ellis, in his analysis of pornography first through the three social groups whose practices he takes to constitute it and then through the further division of pornography into its psychic components, gives us a good example of the former. However, the unintentional production of a paranoic text is simply the verso of its heterosexist conclusion, it is the return of the homosexuality that has been necessarily repressed. More importantly Freud goes on to say that the most striking characteristic of symptom-formation in paranoia is the process which deserves the name of *projection*.

The mechanism of projection is a 'normal' part of psychic subjectivity and belongs initially to the language of the oral instinct, working in terms of ingesting and expelling:

> In so far as the objects which are presented to it are sources of pleasure, it [the ego] takes them into itself, 'introjects' them (to use Ferenczi's term) and, on the other hand, expels whatever within itself becomes a cause of unpleasure.[19]

The distinction between projection as an omnipresent psychic process, as it is comprised in identification for example, and the mechanism of projection as privileged or excessive as it is constitutive of paranoia, is drawn by Freud in an earlier study, and he notes that in paranoia 'It is a misuse of the mechanism of projection for the purposes of defence'.[20] In order for the projection to allow an instinct or affect such as homosexual desire to be truly expelled, it is necessary for it to become embodied in an object, and what Freud shows us in the Schreber case is the process of cathexis to language, to 'knowledge'; the way in which a word can be a sexual object. (It may be that the recent invention of woman's pleasure as a plausible theoretical object is simply the result of a cathexis to the word-object *jouissance*.) Once again there is conflict amongst psychoanalysts, over the question of whether projection *presupposes* the differentiation between a subject and an object, or whether it is this process that *constitutes* the differentiation. Anna Freud suggests the first, and Melanie Klein suggests the latter, also relating this construction of the object knowledge to the maternal body: 'I pointed out that the object of sadism at its height, and of the desire for knowledge arising simultaneously with sadism, is the mother's body with its phantasised contents.'[21] It is nevertheless generally understood that in the mechanism of paranoia this use of projection in the construction of an object is overdetermined in that it takes on the work of returning the subject's repressed. The result, or benefits to be derived from paranoia, its effect, is 'permanent defence without gain'[22] and Paul Willemen echoes this when he says 'In the end, you arrived at a perfectly respectable destination although it is also a dead end'.[23]

Having suspended my disbelief, and taken as transparent the metalanguage of the metapsychology until some of the problems within it were brought up, I now want to return to the problem of the object, both integral and concrete, of the positivist methodology. 'What specifies a science is having an object,'[24] and yet it is psychoanalysis that demonstrates the impossibility of metalanguage, of speaking without desire: this is the contradiction we are faced with. If we believe in this object knowledge whilst simultaneously acknowledging the function that the projection of objects holds in the construction of paranoic subjectivity, we have to ask how and why it is that science or theory uses that mechanism of projection in the construction of knowledge. To return to the structure of the conference, to the institution of the production of knowledge, we are left with the question of whether the construction of 'pornography' was not itself occupying the psychic space of (repressed) homosexuality, which was thus already present in the institutional organization of knowledge. It was not the agenda nor the organizers that made it impossible for the presence of the gays to be incorporated, but the epistemological structure of the conference, and consequently the 'political' action needed is not a vote but the reappraisal of that epistemology.

If John Ellis thinks that the place for subjectivity is in a prefatory remark, where it will not clutter the field of vision of his object, or hamper the logic of the theory, it may simply be a miscalculation of the demands of theory. What is demanded of theory is changing: if it is impossible to believe in the truth of metalanguage, except as one might 'believe' a dream, it is because theory, like psychoanalysis, must in the first instance be a *practice* whether clinical, analytical, textual or political. And as feminism has shown, the success or failure of that theory is judged, not in terms of its scientific credibility (which leads only to producing 'permanent defence without gain') but according to whether it effects transformation, that is, whether it moves.

I am tired of men arguing amongst themselves as to who is the most feminist, frustrated by an object feminism becoming the stakes in a displaced rivalry between men because of a refusal by men to examine the structure of the relations between themselves. John Ellis's object of desire, woman's pleasure, is simply that which he can never know, that which can only be other. Maybe my own fascination with paranoia and male homosexuality is this desire for that which, ultimately, is other, the desire to know the link in that side of the triangle which is furthest from me, the desire of the Other. But in so far as this homosexuality is not merely a signifier in the infinite metonymy of my desire, but is also and primarily a history, or more precisely that consistently unspoken process by which the production of history is displaced from its discursive contradictions, it remains the issue that men must now address – that of men's sexualities, the problem of their own desire, the problem of their theory.

NOTES

I would like to thank Ivan Ward for discussions and generous help. First published in *Screen*, Spring 1981, vol. 22, no. 1, pp. 79–92.

1 Institute of Contemporary Arts/Society for Education in Film and Television weekend seminar on pornography in cinema and the visual arts, 17 and 18 May 1980.

2 John Ellis, 'On Pornography', chapter 6, pp. 146–70 in this volume; originally published in *Screen*, Spring 1980, vol. 21, no. 1, pp. 81–108.

3 Paul Willemen, 'Letter to John', chapter 7, pp. 171–83 in this volume; originally published in *Screen*, Summer 1980, vol. 21, no. 2.

4 Beverley Brown 'A feminist interest in pornography: some modest proposals', *m/f*, 1981, nos. 5–6, pp. 5–18.

5 A group of teachers, filmmakers and others.

6 *Report of the Committee on Obscenity and Film Censorship* [The Williams Report] November 1979, HMSO, Cmnd 7772.

7 W. H. Gillespie 'A Contribution to the Study of Fetishism', *International Journal of Psychoanalysis*, 1940, vol. 21, pp. 401–15.

8 P. Weissman, 'Some Aspects of Sexual Activity in a Fetishist', *Psychoanalytic Quarterly*, 1949, no. 26, pp. 494–507.

9 Silvia Payne, 'Some Observations on Ego Development of the Fetishist', *International Journal of Psychoanalysis*, 1939, no. 2, pp. 161–70.

10 Gillespie, op. cit.

11 Sigmund Freud, 'Fetishism', *The Standard Edition of the Complete Psychological Works*, trans. and ed. James Strachey, London, Hogarth Press, 1951–73, vol. XXI, p. 152.

12 Ernest Jones, 'The Phallic Phase', in *Papers on Psychoanalysis*, 5th edn, London, Baillière, Tindall, 1948, p. 456.

13 Jacques Lacan, 'On the Signification of the Phallus', in *Ecrits*, trans. Alan Sheridan, London and New York, Tavistock, 1977, p. 283.

14 'In fetishism, the penis is imagined in a part of the body where it does not exist. We have therefore to look for an infantile situation of universal occurrence in which a penis-like part of the body is taken from another person, given to the child as his own (a situation in which are associated pleasurable sensations) and then taken away from the child causing pain. This situation can be none other than the child at the breast' (A. Stärck, 'The Castration Complex', *International Journal of Psychoanalysis*, 1921, no. 2, pp. 179–201).

15 Ernest Jones, 'Early Female Sexuality', in *Papers*, p. 485.

16 Christian Metz, 'The Imaginary Signifier', *Screen*, Summer 1975, vol. 16, no. 2, pp. 14–76.

17 Ellis, op. cit., pp. 164–5.

18 Sigmund Freud, 'The Case of Schreber', *Standard Edition*, vol. XII, p. 49.

19 Sigmund Freud, 'Instincts and Their Vicissitudes', *Standard Edition*, vol. XIV, p. 136.

20 M. Bonaparte, A. Freud and E. Kriss (eds), *The Origins of Psychoanalysis, Letters to Fleiss*, New York, Basic Books, 1954, p. 112.

21 Melanie Klein, *Love, Guilt and Reparation: And Other Works, 1921–1945*, London, Hogarth Press, 1975, p. 112.

22 Bonaparte *et al.*, op. cit., p. 114.

23 Willemen, op. cit., p. 171.

24 Jacques Lacan, *The Four Fundamental Concepts of Psychoanalysis*, New York, Norton, 1976, p. 8.

9

THE BODY AS EVIDENCE

Lesley Stern

Pornography is currently a hot feminist issue. In the United States the anti-porn movement is one of the best organised and best funded campaigns in movement history. In Britain and Australia pornography has focused activity and lively debate in a way unparalleled by other issues in recent years. It might be argued that pornography oppresses women, but it has also ironically served to save feminism from falling apart by providing a target, a rallying point. The proliferation of activity, speech and writing about pornography is perhaps more revealing than pornography itself.

Before examining what pornography itself reveals, I want to question why it has been given such priority and to consider the implications of this for the future of feminism. This means charting the development of the feminist interest in pornography, but also situating the Women's Movement within a broader political spectrum. The relation of feminist film criticism to pornography will be located within this framework. How we might look at pornography, like the question of what pornography reveals, will be held in suspense. This might mean that, after much preamble, pornography changes its look so that the questions to do with looking and revealing may be inflected differently. But that remains to be seen.

THE EXPLICIT AND THE ILLICIT

One explanation often given for opposing pornography is that it has recently flourished as a counterattack on feminism:

> The increase of porn in mass media is also part of the backlash against feminism – along with the assault on abortion rights, the trashing of feminist presses, the packaging of the 'Total Woman'. Laura Lederer, coordinator of Women Against Violence in Pornography and Media (WAVPM), explained, 'Enough women have been reject-ing the traditional role of subordination to men to cause a crisis in the collective male ego.' The women's movement, following the civil

197

rights campaign, proved a devastating blow to the status quo. Also, feminism has surfaced at a time of declining economic and political stature. In the last decade, American men have lost job security, self-esteem, and have been confronted with massive guilt. They feel angry, threatened, impotent. Women are accessible targets.[1]

Conversely, I would argue that no backlash has simply erupted as a kind of pathological outburst against the power of the Women's Movement. Rather, the power of the movement has been gradually reduced, in part by fairly systematic economic, political and legal manoeuvres, and in part because feminism has not had the tools to develop a systematic counter-strategy. Along with lack of centralization there has existed the principle of an autonomous Women's Movement which has had paradoxical effects, particularly where it has meant autonomy from 'male politics', meaning divisions between the Left and Right, and where the enemy has been taken as patriarchy approximating to something like 'the collective male ego'. At a time when it is imperative for feminism to analyse its own location within a broader political spectrum, and for its own survival to scrutinize the logic of the Right, to take pornography as the prime target seems short-sighted and strategically inappropriate. This is mainly because in so far as pornography is taken as 'evidence' (of a backlash, of patriarchy flexing its muscles) the power that the campaign seems to have conferred on the movement is based on circumstantial evidence, on the power of showing, and actually deflects from an analysis of the workings of power at a state and bureaucratic level.

It seems to me that the proliferation of writings, speech and political organization against pornography is not a simple response to an actual increase in visibility but to that very visibility itself. It is a response to something that *is* evident, that is noticeable, and it arrived at precisely the time when the Women's Movement was losing energy and coherent organization. Because pornography is there, can be pointed to, shown, because it appears to be explicit in a way that sexism is usually not, it has been seized upon as a target. It is a short step from saying pornography shows explicit sex to saying that it is explicitly sexist, but it is a sidestep that involves many ramifications.

The appeal of pornography – its appeal as an object to focus on, a subject to write and agitate about – would seem to have to do with its visibility, its being-thereness, its explicitness. There is a certain paradox in this, for one of the conditions of porn, one of the things that establishes it as a category, is that it be illicit. However, the illicit can go together with the explicit. And in pornography the conjunction is important – not so much for the purposes of definition but for an understanding of its appeal, both for consumers and critics. Most writings on the subject begin by saying that pornography is difficult to define, but here are some attempts:

We take it that, as almost everyone understands the term, a pornographic representation is one that combines two features: it has a certain function or intention, to arouse its audience sexually, and also has a certain content, explicit representations of sexual material (organs, postures, activity, etc.).[2]

Pornography is the representation of sexual images, often including ridicule and violence, which degrades human beings for the purpose of entertaining or selling products.

To which is added an important corollary:

Pornography is more about the exercise of power than about the expression of sex.[3]

Pornography is a regime of representations of sex. By this I mean that pornography is not generally an act but representations – writings, films, photos, videos. These show bodies (usually naked) in a sexualised way, or people involved in the sex act, according to certain conventions that mean they are interpreted as pornographic by society.[4]

Material that explicitly represents or describes degrading and abusive sexual behaviour so as to endorse and/or recommend the behaviour.[5]

There are obvious (and important) differences between these understandings of what pornography is *about*. But there appears to be general agreement that pornography is representation, and that it *shows* sexual activity in an explicit way. I draw attention to this common ground, to the most neutral and commonsensical notion, not to neutralize either pornography itself, or the different attitudes towards it, but as a reminder of the provocation that pornography proffers. It is because it is both so visible and so invisible – explicit and illicit – that it has become at once something to hit out at and something to be uncovered. The hitting out may take the form of throwing bricks through sex shop windows or it may be manifested in a call for censorship. The uncovering may take the form of feminist tours through 42nd Street in New York or it may involve a more theoretical exercise that uncovers pornography not as a singular entity but as a ubiquitous phenomenon. One way or another, the target can be rendered *visible*. In pornography sex is made explicit. In those societies, including our own, where pornography is such a hot feminist issue, sexism is more often than not not explicit. Two nots make for a double negative and a double knot. I think there's a real danger of feminism tying itself up in that knot and delivering itself up as a package to be dispatched to a destination unknown – not by some omniscient patriarchy but by the body politic.

The knot involves reducing sexism to sex. Sex and sexism are not two distinct, mutually exclusive, categories. Sexism refers to oppression on the grounds of sex, but here 'sex' means gender, more specifically, female

199

gender. What feminist struggles have provoked is an awareness that resistance to sexism must involve an understanding of the relation between sex and sexism which goes beyond merely harnessing the two terms together; the complexities of the relation are understood by problematizing the two terms. Thus it has been necessary first to understand 'sex' not just as sexual activity, not just as gender, but also as sexuality, sexual identity, learned through, and constructed by, institutions like the family, eduction, the workplace; and second, to understand 'sexism' not just as an attitude manifest in individual behaviour, but as produced and sustained within material conditions. If sexuality is shaped, constructed by the social, it is also shaped differently for women and men, structured in terms of power, and sustained through policies, legislation and practices which serve to oppress women. However, it is not just woman as body that is oppressed, and neither is the body politic unified and monolithic – there is a diversity of practices which produce a number of notions of woman. Power is articulated, it is not an immutable force, and where there is power there is resistance. An understanding of the relation between sex and sexism has been developed not just on the level of the conceptual, but through struggle – for in order to effect any transformation it has been necessary to demonstrate how and why sexism operates, how and why it is oppressive. For sexism is not self-evident, certainly not to those who stand to gain, and frequently not to those who stand to lose (consciousness-raising is testimony to this).

A BODY OF EVIDENCE

To illustrate this I will sketch a hypothetical scenario which, as a story, bears no relation to pornography, but in so far as it has to do with methodology bears upon the pornography issue. A feminist group attacks a company because there are no women mechanics employed, arguing that this constitutes sexism, sustains the oppression of women. The management demands evidence, asking how can we be accused of sexism towards women who aren't even here? How can we be oppressing women when no one here is female? The management's argument rests with there being no body, no body of evidence. The first stage in the feminist campaign would be to refuse this mode of arguing, this resort to the phenomenological. It is not woman as oppressed body that needs to be produced; what needs to be demonstrated is that the sexism is constituted by ideas *about* woman. Furthermore, the struggle is likely to incorporate material practices such as retraining, equal opportunity legislation, childcare, and maternity leave.

I have used this example to suggest that the relation between sex and sexism pivots upon the construction of sexual difference and the articulation of power and resistance across a range of practices. Any reduction of sexism to sex, to either sexual activity or gender, seems to me a retrogressive step for feminism. The privileging of pornography as a site of oppression seems to me retrogressive precisely because it operates upon such a reduction. In using explicit sex to demonstrate explicit sexism the anti-porn movement locates itself within the discursive framework of pornography itself. Where pornography is posed as an embodiment of sexism, pornography itself comes to represent a body of evidence. The body is reinstated. Attacking, or even getting rid of the evidence, even assuming this evidence to be male power, does not deal with the way power is articulated not just between a class of men and a class of women but through and across a variety of social practices. The reduction of sexism to sex also involves a displacement. The gaze at porn involves turning a blind eye to the way in which various notions of woman, various sexualities, are constructed and promoted in areas such as the family, within the workplace, through health, education, legal practices and other regimes of representation.

So far I have suggested that the feminist interest in porn is new and relatively unitary. Nevertheless, it proceeds from distinct analytic perspectives which demand scrutiny. The feminist interest in pornography can be given a history, but I want to question that history as an automatic progression, the logical outcome of some original insight. By tracing various connections and disjunctions it may be possible to indicate where the porn trail may be leading, and in the process to examine how power has been articulated within the Women's Movement itself.

'Why was "violence against women" (campaigns against rape, battering and incest) superseded by "women against pornography" (campaigns against pornographic visual representation)?' The question is asked in *Diary of a Conference*, a documentation of the discussion and planning for the conference, 'Toward a Politics of Sexuality' held at Barnard College, New York, in April 1982. It both suggests the way in which links have been made in feminist campaigns between male violence and pornography, and also shows a shifting focus, an historical change.

The early work on rape was extremely important to the Women's Movement for a number of reasons. The campaigns established significant feminist support structures such as rape crisis centres, at the same time as agitating for legislative reform. Yet the struggle was not just about challenging the law but also, importantly, about challenging institutional procedures – judicial, police, medical, welfare, psychiatric. Media campaigns were also extended beyond agitation for 'equal rights' to question, very publicly, any idea of a natural balance between men and women which could be achieved and maintained through legislating for equality. And this question raised further implications leading to alternative theoretical formulations and practices. It could be assumed that if there is not a natural balance then there is a *natural imbalance* – men naturally have power, women are powerless; men are by nature sexually violent, women are destined to be victims – or that there is an *unnatural imbalance* – power relations are socially constructed and can be socially transformed.

Either way, the campaigns against rape raised important questions about how woman is understood, how sexual difference is organized and maintained, and thus asked: what are the conditions for rape, how is the climate created for sexual violence against women? Both assumptions remove rape from the area of criminal aberration and locate it within a much broader framework – a framework which examines the workings of ideology and locates rape as an instance (though not necessarily the exemplary instance) of sexist ideology. The difference between the two is not clear cut, not grounded in the absolute incompatibility of theoretical principles – and I stress this because it is the only way of understanding an historical shift in feminist focus (rather than an immutable opposition), a shifting alignment between theory and practice.

BALANCING ACTS

The proposal of an unnatural imbalance focuses on the structuring of power and the work of ideology: how is rape as a practice maintained not only by individual men but by institutions – the law, medicine, education, the media? What became a problem was how to conceptualize the ideological politically. While an overall critique of patriarchal ideology was developed, this was manifested primarily through work on the media. Different campaigns attempted to expose the ideology which sustained rape, for instance, or the opposition to abortion, or discrimination against women in work. But these issues were not linked through an analysis of the material conditions which sustain ideology. So, for instance, agitation for changing laws relating to, and institutions surrounding, rape and abortion were pursued more or less independently. Although there are good reasons for this – these areas do have a specificity, do require particular tactics – there are also good reasons to link the campaigns strategically, to show how female sexualities are constructed, how sexual difference is inscribed across social institutions and legal practices. Thus each campaign, while retaining a certain autonomy, would be located within a broader framework, providing a critique which situates sexism not just as an amorphous moving target, but in relation to the material.

The disparateness of the campaigns had a particularly adverse effect on organisation around rape. Two apparently contradictory developments occurred: first, an exclusive focus on rape, arising out of the isolation of the campaign, tended to foreground the notion of woman as victim; and second, rape became the obverse of specific, it became generalized so that its function as a metaphor (for the oppression of all women by all men) assumed more importance than the instance of rape itself. The development of rape as a generalized metaphor was partly the product of a failure to co-ordinate a programme (to politicize the ideological) but was markedly exacerbated as Conservative governments in the US, Britain and Australia began to erode feminist gains and embark on an ideological programme to get women back into the family and home. The Women's

Movement began to lose power. Quite literally weakened in its effectivity, it also lacked the tools for analysing and responding to what was going on on a larger political scene (the backlash against feminism being part of a broader and systematic programme). With the loss of power came a misrecognition of the function of power. The erosion of feminist gains was seen as evidence of irredeemable sexism, rather than analysed in terms of a right-wing political programme. The loose ends of feminism began to be pulled together on a new project, a project focusing on the ideological, but the ideological focused in a particular way.

Tendencies within the movement looked for something that would concretize this irredeemable sexism. What had now become established as a weighted metaphor – rape as the oppression of all women by all men – offered a key. But this metaphor proved to be somewhat empty in that it could not easily be concretized and therefore attacked. As a focus for organization the power that it offered was that of negativity. It's hard to take up arms against a metaphor. You can use raped and battered women as evidence, but you can't make them the target of attack. A reframing took place: the earlier questions – what are the conditions for rape, how is the climate for sexual violence created – were inflected to investigate causation, and the logic of inquiry produced an answer. The media, in particular pornography, usurped rape as the prime metaphor.

As a focus for organization pornography seemed to offer a positive power, for it could be concretized and attacked, precisely because it is representational. I stress this because many of the critiques of the feminist anti-pornography movement reiterate the importance of understanding porn as a mode of representation and not confusing this mode (a regime of significations) with reality. While I believe that there are crucial political issues at stake around representation, it is a mistake to accuse groups like Women Against Pornography of neglecting it, of confusing the real and the representational. What has happened is that ideology has been extrapolated from its material structures and reduced to the visible, the explicit, the explanatory. A precarious balancing act is being performed by trying to reconcile transformation (of relations between men and women) with some notion of their natural imbalance. Transformation seems possible, the argument goes, because although you can't stop violence against women through band-aid measures (like rape crisis centres) you can stop it by going to the roots, eliminating the cause. If rape is the grand metaphor of oppression, then porn is the original sin. And the case for the prosecution rests in part on preserving the evidence of original sin.

DISSENT: FRAMING PORNOGRAPHY

In becoming a privileged feminist issue, pornography has also become a site for relating sex and violence. But it is difficult to discern the status of this relationship. In tracing the proliferation of writings and activities, what emerges with the greatest clarity is a confusion about the connections. Sometimes the issues are conflated, sometimes sharply separated, but invariably they turn upon a reduction of sexism to sex.

In the mid-1970s a spate of books, pamphlets and articles on rape appeared, most prominently Susan Brownmiller's *Against Our Will: Men, Women and Rape*,[6] *Rape: The First Sourcebook for Women*[7] and *Sexual Assault: Confronting Rape in America* by Nancy Gager and Cathleen Schurr.[8] In Australia a number of articles emerged out of anti-rape campaigns which used a psychoanalytic and Marxist perspective.[9] Subsequently the British journal *m/f* has pursued work examining the strategies of anti-rape campaigns and the question of defining it as a crime of sex or violence.[10]

Against Our Will deals primarily with rape – pornography is not posed as its cause, but rather as a symptom of anti-woman sentiment and as evidence of the way in which male sexuality is exercised through violence against women. However, Brownmiller does define pornography as 'the undiluted essence of anti-female propaganda' and equates its philosophy with rape, going so far as to call for government censorship of pornography. Andrea Dworkin's *Woman Hating*[11] focuses on misogyny, but gives particular attention to pornography. An influential later work focusing on misogyny and tracing a history of violence against women is Mary Daly's *Gyn/Ecology: The Metaethics of Radical Feminism*.[12]

Around 1977 or 1978 pornography campaigns emerged and issues of sex and violence were foregrounded in writings addressed to the pornography issue. Two articles by Robin Morgan indicate a general direction: 'Theory and Practice: Pornography and Rape'[13] argues a causal relation between pornography and rape, and 'How to Run the Pornographers out of Town (And Preserve the First Amendment)[14] urges feminists to protest actively against pornography by boycotting businesses, condemning the use of pornographic imagery in advertising, and pushing legislators to take action. Two articles by Gloria Steinem, in their very titles, indicate the way in which sex and violence are being construed: 'Erotica and Pornography: a Clear and Present Difference'[15] and 'Pornography: Not Sex but the Obscene Use of Power'[16] in which it is argued that 'erotica is about sexuality, but pornography is about power and sex-as-weapon – in the same way that we have come to understand that rape is about violence, and not really about sexuality at all'. Angela Carter's *The Sadeian Woman*[17] extends her discussion of pornography to popular culture. In 1978 the San Francisco-based group Women Against Violence in Pornography and the Media (WAVPM) organized a large Take Back the Night March, and produced a literature packet. In 1979 Women Against Pornography (WAP), a New York Group which grew out of WAVPM, sponsored a conference to 'claim pornography as a feminist issue of national proportions'. There have since been many well attended conferences and marches on the issue throughout America, Britain and Australia.

In 1980 *Take Back the Night: Women on Pornography*[18] was published in the United States. A number of campaign groups were also formed, most prolifically in America – Women Against Violence Against Women (WAVAW), originally from Los Angeles, but now a national group (there is an active group of the same name in Britain), Women for the Abolition of Pornography, Men Against Sexist Violence. The US National Organization for Women (NOW), not specifically concerned with pornography, took up the issue and in 1980 passed a resolution which reaffirms support for lesbian rights, but specifically declares public sex, pederasty, sado-masochism and pornography to be issues of violence, not sexual preference. Political tactics range from picketing, boycotting and vandalism against porn shops to lobbying for censorship, and WAP organizes feminist tours of 42nd Street and Times Square as well as conducting extensive slide lecture tours using visual material to expose/shock as a form of feminist education.

Last year [1981] saw the publication of two feminist books on pornography – Andrea Dworkin's *Pornography: Men Possessing Women* and Susan Griffin's *Pornography and Silence: Culture's Revenge Against Nature*. In Britain both were published by the Women's Press, indicating the priority given to the porn issue. Both are concerned with pornography and sado-masochism as the linchpin of a misogynist culture, although Griffin's is more mystical – resting on the notion of a natural culture pertaining to women which has been systematically abused by men – and Dworkin's more polemical – insisting on the antagonism between a class of men and a class of women and stressing heterosexuality, symbolized as penetration, as intrinsically violence against women. Shortly before these publications *Women, Sex and Pornography: A Controversial and Unique Study*[19] emerged from Australia. Although strongly criticized by feminists of various persuasions for its failure to politicize pornography and for relying on biological categories to explain why men and women react differently to porn, it was promoted as a feminist work and became a bestseller.

The anti-porn movement has grown in momentum and impact. However, after the initial euphoria of massed demonstrations, the reaffirmation of solidarity reminiscent of earlier days, voices began to be raised against the swelling tide. Discussion began tentatively about tactics as well as modes of framing pornography through a feminist lens. In 'Pornography and Pleasure', Paula Webster prefaces her argument thus:

> A vast sea of feminist solidarity swelled around the issue of pornography. To move against the wave felt truly threatening. Although a few voices addressed contradictions in the anti-porn analysis, no dissenting movement developed. Criticism was kept to a minimum.[20]

By now there is considerable dissension within feminism; but it is dissension framed by porn. And thus pornography acquires a certain

205

power, so that confusions over sex and violence are written into the various discourses which insist on the insistence of porn. The dissenting voices follow various lines which inevitably intersect, but there seem to me five trajectories which can be distinguished. First there is a criticism of the anti-porn movement for its moralism. This line argues that defining pornography as a matter of violence rather than of sex comes dangerously close to assuming that sex, especially impersonal sex, *is* by nature violent, an assumption that leads to an over-idealization of romance, love and committed relationships. Second, the call for censorship has been criticized on the grounds both that it involves an alignment with the Right and can thus only rebound on feminist and gay interests, and that it is based on a questionable cause–effect relationship between imagery and violence. Third, there is a call for shift of focus from a patriarchal imaging of women to an examination of fantasy and a development of feminist erotica or pornography. Fourth, monolithic conceptions of pornography have been challenged and attempts made to theorize it as a variety of practices operating across various institutions, subject to change in place and time, and therefore open to interventions other than wholesale opposition. Fifth, beginnings have been made on the theorization of the codes and conventions which characterize pornographic representations, which construct sexual difference and order ways of seeing.

SEX AND VIOLENCE

We are not carving out any new exceptions to the First Amendment. The Supreme Court has traditionally held that 'obscenity' is not protected speech . . . We want to change the definition of obscenity so that it focuses on violence, not on sex.

This statement is from the Women Against Pornography position paper, 'Where We Stand on the First Amendment'.[21] A question presents itself: why choose pornography, an area specified by explicit sex, in order to make an argument about violence and in the name of violence deny the relevance of sex? Surely what is crucial to the argument is the connections between sex and violence in this area, connections which are not fixed and therefore require different levels of analysis. An initial step is to distinguish the kinds of connection between sex and violence that have been or might be established (a) within the legal sphere; (b) within pornographic representations; and (c) between pornography and 'everyday life' (which intersects with the other two categories).

There has been feminist agitation for change in laws regarding both rape and pornography, but the slogan 'pornography is the theory, rape the practice' has informed the campaigns with a reductive perspective that has served to suppress the discontinuous way in which the ideological is mediated by the law. While this slogan might seem to offer an account of patriarchy,˙ it certainly offers no theoretical perspective on the way in which different sexualities are constructed by the law, and provides no basis for a political practice that might intervene in the legal in a discontinuous manner to ensure *for feminism* different sexualities. Posing violence as the prime problem, as the expression of patriarchy, has led to certain feminist pressures for legal reclassification of rape – to remove the sexual element, and to situate it within the area of assault. In this case the separation of sex and violence has severe and debilitating repercussions for reform of rape legislation, for it completely diffuses the specificity of rape and undercuts the particularity of the feminist approach.

To insist, on the other hand, that the relation between sex and violence be maintained in the instance of rape, inscribed in legislation, is also an acknowledgement that sexualities are actively constructed through the law rather than simply rewarded or punished by it. And to insist on a connection on the legal level, to maintain the specificity of rape here, is not to generalize out to an all-embracing equation between sex and violence. It is still possible to ask what are the conditions for rape, how is the climate for rape created, to examine sexist ideology in various manifestations without conflating connection and causality. Once generalizations are instituted as prescriptive metaphors, when a picture of a woman being raped becomes more important than the rape of an actual woman, then feminist political practice suffers on several levels – not just because the concrete as some measure of the real is being usurped by the unreality of the image or the Imaginary, but because the ideological is being reduced to a very literal level, to the level of the explicit, of evidence.

The call for legal intervention in pornography via censorship has the same origin as the call for reclassification of rape as assault. The commonality lies in designating violence (male violence) not sex (female sexuality) as the problem. However, where it is imperative to inscribe the relation between sex and violence in legislation on rape, the problem posed by pornography is quite different. Any resort to censorship in the area of sexuality is informed by an assumption of an autonomous legal system operating upon already existing and complete sexualities. The Women Against Pornography position assumes that in the current state of affairs male sexuality is rewarded and female sexuality is punished, and suggests that legislation would redress this imbalance. What is more likely is that different kinds of sexualities would be constructed, not necessarily to the benefit of women.

The feminist lobby is not the only group fighting pornography. Other groups, such as Moral Majority and Festival of Light, are opposed to feminism as well as to pornography; and they have a far less confused position on sex and violence and the law, as well as a more coherent programme, of which pornography is only one part. That feminism is likely to lose out by censorship 'gains' has been pointed out[22] and most succinctly expressed in parallels drawn between the treatment of abortion on the Right and pornography among feminists: 'A fascinating workshop or audio-visual event: simultaneous showing of WAP and Right-to-Life slide shows. Actually, the ultimate meeting of these two groups is in the recently heard analysis that "abortion is violence against women".'[23]

The dangers, in legal terms, of conflating sex and violence can be seen here. But the flip side of the feminist coin is an attempt to legislate against any connection and this also, in the long term, is likely to be detrimental to the movement, although for different reasons to those encountered in the rape issue:

> The new feminist definition of true or healthy sexuality now receives its clearest and most explicit articulation in discussions of the issue feminist theory perceives to be deeply related to rape: the production, consumption, and underlying assumptions of pornography. It has been another short but significant step from divorcing rape and sex to divorcing pornography and sex . . . Feminists should increase the pressure toward changing rape legislation; but changing law and changing love are not the same thing. In the wish to 'untangle' sex and violence, we have entangled ourselves in a new myth, one that considers it both possible and desirable to clean up love to correspond to an ideal that utterly dualizes tenderness and aggression . . . Getting porn off 42nd Street will do nearly nothing about getting 'this stuff' out of the bedroom, because it does nothing about acknowledging the connections between sexuality and aggression in the human psyche, connections exploited rather than created by the pornographers.[24]

The relation between sex and violence within pornographic representations has been construed in a variety of ways. Where pornography is posed as an issue of violence, not sex, it is claimed that the representations are in themselves violent and assaulting and thus oppressive to women. There are connections here with the argument that rape is a question of assault, not sex. However, the separation of sex and violence, though common to arguments on both rape and pornography, has different implications for each. In the case of pornography the separation rests on casuistry – explicit sex is what informs the 'power' of the image, a power measured as violence. Like the law, pornography constructs sexed subjects, but viewing or reading, rather than legal ones. The casuistry involved in posing pornography as violent in itself denies the activity of reading and renders women totally powerless, oppressed by the representational in an identical way to the oppression experienced in rape.

The alternative is not to inscribe a connection between violence and sex in legislation on pornography. But since pornography, like any mode of representation, produces meanings, promotes certain kinds of reading, it is strategically necessary to examine the ways it articulates the connections between violence and sexuality (rather than to repress sex in the name of violence). Many feminist positions adopt this perspective, but the stress should be on articulation, that is on the work of representation, not on explicit content (be it sex or violence). The emphasis thus shifts from using pornography as evidence of explicit sexism to an examination of *how* sexism operates within the regime of pornographic representations. Any examination of this nature is likely to show that pornography produces a range of meanings about female sexuality, not all of them to do with violence. The axiomatic conjunction of sex and violence reduces our readings, and serves consequently to limit interventions within the representational arena itself – interventions which might elaborate diverse sexualities *for* feminism.

In the relation between the pornographic and everyday life the connection between sex and violence is frequently posed as causal. One line of reasoning says that pornography directly affects everyday life: the 'intention to arouse' which characterizes porn is interpreted as sexual arousal, which is then translated into acts of violence in the bedroom, in the streets. Here the claim that pornography is an issue of violence and not sex is spurious, because the argument for provocation rests on a content which is explicitly sexual. In this case there are layerings of conflation, but it is important tactically to disentangle the sex/violence connection. To say that there are connections between porn and everyday life (and few feminists would deny this) is not the same as saying that pornography causes violence in everyday life. The problem lies with the conflating of two positions: one, the posing of violence as an effect of pornography; and two, the posing of pornography as in itself violent, an embodiment of sexism. Violence is both cause and effect. Certainly pornography constructs meanings, works on an ideological level, but where the effect argument becomes circular, where it turns upon violence, it leads in on itself to political impasse. It converges with the position of the Right, in that violence and sex are apparently bad *per se*.

Another line of reasoning says that much of everyday life is pornographic. Here 'everyday life' can mean either all relations between men and women, but particularly those expressed in a certain kind of behaviour – heterosexuality; or modes of representation which are not 'illicit' in the way that porn is, such as advertising, movies, television. Within the framework of the Dworkin argument these are all manifestations of misogyny, of woman-hatred, and a continuum is posited with porn as simply one extreme of a much broader tendency. For many feminists it is these everyday manifestations that more crucially deserve attention. But to collapse everything under the metaphor of pornography is to seriously weaken feminist interventions across the whole range of representations, precisely because of the reduction of sexism to sex (and violence).

In both lines of reasoning on the relation between porn and everyday life, on the intersection of sex and violence, what is remarkable is that violence is not theorized in any way – it is either demonstrated (as in slides of bondage) or used as a metaphor for misogyny or male power. What we have here is a serious conflation of power and violence, and it seems to me that it is this, along with the reduction of sexism to sex, that really positions the anti-porn movement as reactionary. The Right similarly appears to lack a theorization of sex and violence, seems to pose both as bad *per se*, but in fact there is a logic to what the Right deems good and bad. There is good sex, which unites and reproduces the family, and there is also legitimate violence, as exercised by the state through the military and the police forces, which unites the nation.

Yet much of the coercion exercised by the Right is not manifested in acts of violence, but through resort to legislation which ensures, among other things, the construction of sexualities (acts around homosexuality, age of consent, parental rights, access to birth control and abortion, adultery, marriage and divorce, child custody), and the construction of 'peace' through, for instance, industrial legislation limiting trade union activism and delimiting what may be interpreted as subversive activities. The feminist campaign against pornography is very useful to the Right, not just because it chooses to misinterpret the feminist position, but because that position is confused. Both power and violence are neutralized in the campaign because the two terms are abstracted from the political sphere and used to mirror each other in a metaphoric way. Instead of scrutinizing pornography for a revelation of male power, feminism would do well to scrutinize the Right, to see how power is being articulated not just as a backlash but in order actively to structure positions for feminism.

It is necessary for feminism to see the way in which the Right's opposition to working mothers and wives, abortion and pornography, to take three obvious issues, are not unrelated to each other or to an overall political strategy. In the United States the Family Protection Act offers a good example of the formulation of a coherent programme. It was first proposed in 1979 by Senator Laxalt, who significantly plays a double role as Reagan's campaign manager and Moral Majority spokesman in Congress. The bill was rejected as a package deal but is being systematically introduced and passed piecemeal. Those of its provisions so far enacted include stipulations that textbooks belittling the traditional role of women in society not be purchased with federal money, that federally funded legal services be denied for abortions, school desegregation, divorce or homosexual rights litigation, and that parents of people under eighteen seeking birth control devices and drugs from government-funded clinics must be informed.[25]

TAKING OFFENCE/TAKING THE OFFENSIVE

WARNING: If you are offended by graphic subject matter, We urge you not to see this film.

This warning, in large type, accompanied a half-page advertisement for *Not a Love Story* in New York. The text describes the film as 'a motion picture about Pornography'. The word 'Pornography', in heavy type, is arranged to balance symmetrically with 'Not a Love Story'. The advertisement also carries three review quotations which situate the film as a feminist 'look' at porn. But the hook which catches the reader is the warning – at once a repellant and an enticement. The selling technique is familiar, but its familiarity relates less to the promotion of porn than to horror films. The warning about 'graphic subject matter' refers, of course, to explicit sex. The film is being sold on its pornographic content. It could be argued that this is a skilful expedient for luring an audience which, once captive, can be converted. I am sceptical about this – not because of some notion of dishonesty in advertising, nor because of some belief in the overriding power of pornographic imagery, but because of the resort to the graphic, to the explicit. The problem is not that the feminist critique uses porn images but that it 'shows' pornography in order to show how pornography illustrates sexism.

I have argued that the appeal of pornography as a target lies in its visibility, and that this involves a misrecognition – both of the problems facing feminism, and of the status of the visible. The appeal of the cinema also lies in its visibility, its being-there-to-be-looked-at quality. The pleasure of looking has been much discussed in film theory, and in the process the 'innocence' of pleasure has been put under scrutiny. Attention has been focused not on what we see (content) but on how we see, how pleasure is structured by the filmic text. From a feminist perspective this has involved an exploration of the way in which sexual difference is constructed in the cinema, of the way in which the gaze is split between active/male and passive/female, and the representation of female pleasure. Representation here extends beyond depiction to questions of viewing; how can feminine desire be inscribed within viewing practices? These developments have turned upon the axis of recognition/misrecognition. The status of the visible has been interrogated with ruthless persistence.

Feminist film theory and the feminist interest in pornography could well be travelling towards a convergence or a collision. If the dominant anti-pornography tendency misrecognizes the status of the visible, feminist film theory is well equipped to 'correct' this vision by problematizing the visible, by posing representation as a mediation rather than as transparent illustration. The question of effects is thus disengaged from causality and reformulated in terms of effectivity. Here it is not a question of what kind of behaviour is caused by pornographic representations, but rather how are meanings effected through the work of the text? Another potential mode of 'correction' is to refuse complicity with the victim syndrome which reduces pleasure to male pleasure and equates this with male power (so that pleasure is not simply not innocent, but positively guilty) – to focus instead on female pleasure, either 'uncovering' this in what is established as pornography, or generating its presence in a feminist visual erotica.

A further possibility is a refined attention to the relation between desire and representation. Pornography becomes a site of exploration, a sighting, where explicitness is posed not as an embodiment of sexism, but as an embodiment of desire. Or rather, as an *attempt* to embody desire. If desire is somewhat literally put in the picture, what of desire that is left out of the picture? What is the status of the Imaginary and the Real in this cinema? One of the paradoxes of pornography lies in a simultaneous compulsion to fetishize (to fragment the body) and a compulsion to 'reveal all'. It's possible to envisage this paradox providing a new entrée to the essence of the cinema. Here the marginal illuminates the mainstream, the body of the text (classical cinema) is reanimated as a textualized body feeding the vampirish appetites of that endlessly desiring machine – film theory.

I am not at all sure that any of these developments would be of benefit to feminism at the present time. A feminist 'correction' to the WAP or WAVAW position is not likely to lead very far if it is based upon arguments about representation (such as 'no image is intrinsically pornographic') because its questions are still addressed to the 'body of evidence' presented by the agenda-setters. This is not to say that we should disregard pornography as a feminist issue or close our eyes and hope it will go away. Although it seems crucial to challenge the explanation of pornography that rests on explicitness (of sex, and of sexism) it also seems important to acknowledge that pornography is an industry – one that organizes not just images, but ways of selling its product for primarily male consumption. Thus, the pornographic maintains some specificity, is not simply collapsed into everyday sexism, nor is its power measured purely in terms of visual impact. This project of specification is a difficult one, as demonstrated by Kathy Myers, who argues that we should 'shift the debate on representation away from the image' and pay more attention to 'the conditions of its production and consumption', and yet still concentrates on 'reading' images.[26] I shall avoid the difficulties here, but there are a number of attempts to specify the 'conditions of its production and consumption', to outline the parameters of the 'institution' or 'regime' or 'apparatus' of pornography.[27]

EDEN AND AFTER

To return to an earlier question – what are the possibilities for a feminist oppositional practice? Developing an alternative look either through a critique as in *Not a Love Story*, or through an oppositional female erotica, will not dislodge the pornography industry; but it is surely desirable to shift the grounds of attack from a logic which begins by taking offence and proceeds to taking the offensive, to shift the critique from a power nurtured by negativity to a critique which incorporates a politics of pleasure.

Important work done in feminist film theory and practice, informed by broader feminist developments, can provide the basis for new directions.

One of the more positive by-products of the pornography controversy has been a recent opening up, within the Women's Movement, of discussions about sexuality, an emerging critique of the way in which the movement itself has constructed (through prohibition and advocacy) certain sexualities and repressed others, a process which has been referred to as 'the missionary position of the women's movement'.[28] The critique of this process has involved some spectacularly staged entrances from a variety of concealed closets, as well as testimonials about 'secret gardens' of sexual phantasies that do not always show up as a bed of roses.[29] This kind of coming out (which dislocates the lesbian/heterosexual opposition) could lead either to a war of contesting identities or to a liberal pluralism which tolerates all differences. However, the insertion of phantasy as a question provides a challenge to the notion of sexuality as fixed by identity. In fact it is precisely the gap between phantasy and identity that provides a space for exploring a number of issues which surface at the intersection of feminism and film.

By way of conclusion, I shall suggest what some of these issues might be. The suggestions do not even approximate a theorization of pornography – feminist or otherwise; they are more in the nature of spin-offs from thinking about porn, and they spin into questions about a cinematic politics of pleasure. The questions revolve around phantasy. How does phantasy articulate with fiction? What is the relation between sexual identity and identification in the viewing process? Is there a feminine desire commensurate with feminism that can be satisfied by a pleasure articulated through textual strategy? If the question of pleasure arises, how is a cinema of arousal conceived?

Much psychoanalytically oriented work on the cinema has dealt with phantasy, with the way in which the cinema harnesses unconscious drives and desires. Where the cinema is seen to be structured by the unconscious, in a simultaneous movement the viewer's unconscious is seen to be structured by the filmic work. The understanding of 'phantasy' used in this theoretical work is fairly broad, and indeed capitalizes on a lack of clarity in Freud's own work. Freud uses the term in three ways: first to denote conscious imaginings or daydreams (in less specialized writings this is often spelt 'fantasy'); second, to denote unconscious phantasies which have a similar structure to dreams in that their origin lies in repressed material – analysis of the manifest content should reveal the way in which the prohibition is present in the actual formation of the wish that motivates the dream or the phantasy; and third to denote primal phantasies, fundamental unconscious structures which transcend individual experience. Freud draws an analogy between daydreams and nocturnal dreams; in both cases the primary material lends itself to 'scripting', to organized scenes and dramatization. Daydreams differ from nocturnal dreams in that a greater degree of secondary revision is brought to bear so that the scenarios have more consistency, but both are subject to the same psychical mechanisms which organize wish-fulfilment and concomitant defensive strategies. The relation between desire and phantasy is much harder to work out in Freud; sometimes the terms seem to conflate, at others desire is seen as a way of articulating phantasy, or vice versa.

Within film theory, phantasy seems most often to be used as an approximation of desire, so that the film text is either seen as working upon the unconscious desires/phantasies (usually primal) of the viewer or the text is given the same status as dreams/daydreams/phantasies, and analysed according to a symptomatic reading which charts the return of the repressed through defensive operations and wish-fulfilment strategies. The generalized way in which phantasy is employed in cinematic theory gives rise to some problems which become particularly pronounced when trying to deal with a cinema which more specifically registers the phantastic. Most theory has concentrated on narrative, posing the narrative text as akin to the dream in 'working' towards wish-fulfilment by providing satisfaction, a happy ending; but also, as representation, akin to ideological processes, working towards unification, securing identity and resolution, both of the film and the viewing subject. Realism and narrative have been privileged sites for the return of the repressed, and breaks with them have been advocated as ways of fracturing the false unity of the viewing subject, provoking a more self-conscious and active subject. What has been glaringly absent from much of this discourse is a conceptualization of fiction. Fiction is most often collapsed into narrative or seen as shaped by and subordinate to realism: even where we know that we are watching something unreal we are structured into 'belief' through the strategies of realism. But it might be important to explore the way in which *disbelief* operates in film viewing and to ask how this relates to pleasure. A partial explanation for the lack of specification given to fiction seems to me to lie with the very generalized and often confused way that phantasy has been used, along with the rationale for its utilization – to explain narrative.

At a certain level it seems useful to make a distinction between, on the one hand *fantasy* as conscious imaginings, daydreams, inventions, make-believe, reverie; and on the other hand, the various other senses in which *phantasy* is used. This is not to make a strict demarcation between the conscious on one hand and the unconscious on the other, for clearly daydreams can tell us about the unconscious and are indeed structured by psychic mechanisms. However, the functioning of different kinds of phantasy needs to be distinguished.

Fantasy performs a particular function in waking life, in that the fantastic scenario can be evoked voluntarily, affords a certain pleasure, though not necessarily satisfaction, since fantasies tend to recur and be repetitious.

They are also frequently characterized by a delimitation of defensive operations, so that the fantasizer can clearly recognize that, although located in the daytime, the fantasies are removed from everyday life. They might express wishes, but in a mediated way: gratification is to be achieved not through acting out the fantasies, but through the activity of fantasizing itself. However, if there is a delimitation of defensive operations within fantasy it is likely that the defence mechanism is transferred – there exists paradoxically a compulsion to repeat fantasies and a prohibition on repeating, a defensiveness about 'telling'. Fantasies are illicit in a way that dreams are not – they span a space between self-indulgence and public restraint.

FICTION: ELICITING THE ILLICIT

Fiction *differs* from fantasy in that it is constituted by a process of telling, and in the process elicits a response, asks to be read, looked, at, listened to, but not necessarily believed. It is also *related* to fantasy – not because it is a direct representation or manifestation, but in terms of function. Fiction also relates to phantasy in the other senses that have been noted, but for the moment I shall hold these relations in abeyance. It is perhaps more important to start thinking about how to distinguish fiction from narrative and realism. A commonsense understanding of fiction is that which is imaginary, feigned, invented. It is the antithesis of fact, truth, reality. Fiction involves a shaping, a moulding, indeed a structuring. The raw material which fiction shapes, structures into a discourse, is something like fantasy. Where fantasy lends itself to scripting, to organized scenes and dramatization, it does not necessarily involve a logical sequencing, nor a logical relation to the real world, to everyday life. The work fiction performs upon this raw material is not necessarily a correction of these 'mismatches', it is more in the nature of a realization – in words or pictures. This process of realization poses problems for the reading of fiction, since realization tends towards an anchorage in realism, representation towards an anchorage in meaning. However, it strikes me that the reading of fiction in film has been largely determined by the theoretical preoccupation with realism, which has nurtured a realist mode of reading. The delimitation of defensive operations in fiction has been compensated for by highly defensive reading practices which in effect work to censor the fictionality of filmic texts. A will to knowledge has erected barricades against the pleasures of disbelief.

Part of the problem of dealing with fiction in film has no doubt to do with the status of the moving image, its referentiality, its visibility, its explicitness. The image can be identified, and this has led to elaborate arguments about identification, the tyranny of the cinematic apparatus in constructing an identity for the viewer through mechanisms of identification. Curiously, much film theory of this nature coincides with the 'body of evidence' used by the prosecution in anti-porn campaigns. If all movies construct meanings, promote certain readings, what is interesting about fiction is the kind of reading that it elicits (and which is often refused). There is a difference between fantasizing and reading or watching fiction. Where the fantastic scenario can be voluntarily evoked in the activity of fantasizing, the reader-spectator does not have the same freedom, is denied originality, refused as origin of the scenario. However, if there is a delimitation of defensive operations in the activity of fantasizing, there is also a prohibition, a defensiveness about 'telling', about revealing.

For the spectator of fiction this prohibition is in a sense lifted, since the telling can be identified as originating elsewhere. This identification of the 'elsewhere' is important for it allows an identification of the seen as other, and so foregrounds the gap between fiction and reality. Fiction does not ask to be believed, does not seek to establish a relation of identity between the real and the image, or the viewer and the narrative voice. Rather than suturing the viewer into the text, it proffers a possibility of pleasure by stimulating the imaginative capacity. This projection of an other scene does not involve a looking ahead, a desire to fulfil a lack by jumping the metonymic gun. It is not motivated by the incompleteness of the image (which implies that completion may be achieved in the next image). Rather, the fiction declares the limits of its imagery in relation to the real. Fiction is posited on pretence, but not a pretence of plenitude: instead of the image asserting its presence as the only possibility (or obversely signalling absence) it provokes other possibilities, substitutions. The projection of images on to the screen elicits the viewer's projection or superimposition of images, of the Imaginary, of fantasy.

Fiction does not constitute a category exclusive of narrative, independent of realism. I am not even sure that it is possible to speak of a structure of fiction. Most films contain fictional elements, and I have simply attempted a tentative sketch of some relation between fiction and fantasy. Once a move is made from 'most films' to those which extend beyond the incorporation of fictional elements, which more specifically register the fantastic, it seems important to understand how those films function as fiction – not just as animated phantasies. For feminists it might be more productive to explore both the kinds of reading elicited by fiction and the possibilities for using fiction to exploit pleasure. The 'intention to arouse' which seems to characterize porn films has proved problematic for feminism, since in the porn industry this means a promotion of the male consumer's erection and masturbation. Analysis has usually pointed to the way that this is dependent on an objectification (if not assault upon) the female body. So, much exploration of feminine pleasure in feminist cinema has been premised on an elimination from the image of the naked or sexualized female body. In a curious way this has also frequently involved a desexualization of pleasure, a suspicion of all pleasure promoted by cinema. But questions beginning to surface within the movement, questions about what women find a turn-on, what kind of fantasies are mobilized, could productively be explored in cinema, by looking at pornography and its relation to fiction. In other words it is possible to explore questions of stimulation and arousal without submitting to a Pavlovian notion of the cinema, to look at *processes* which might potentially involve a structuring of diverse sexualities *for* feminism.

THE BODY IN EVIDENCE

I began this paper by contesting the way in which anti-porn movements have focused the visibility of pornography as a target, have taken the explicit sex of pornography to demonstrate that it constitutes evidence of explicit sexism. I am convinced that such an approach is strategically inappropriate. However, although pornography is neither explained nor accounted for by its explicitness (as has often enough been pointed out, porn titillates by leaving out elements, by heightening expectations), for the development of a feminist politics of pleasure it might be necessary to reverse the process and account for how the explicitness does operate. One explanation revolves around substitution: 'The substitution of the look for physical contact is precisely the essential precondition for porn and the specific difference which distinguishes it from other scopophilic regimes such as looking at family snapshots or Hollywood movies.'[30]

Willemen goes on to argue that it is 'the loss generated by the friction between the phantasy looked for and the phantasy offered' that provokes the 'compensatory activity associated with porn, that is masturbation'.[31] Fiction, I have argued, evokes a response of superimposition, the projection of fantasy involves a process of substitution, an imaginary image for the present image. Pornography is a particularly condensed version of fiction and is also overdetermined by sexual fantasy, by the figuring out of body space, the spacing out of bodies. But the substitution is not necessarily that of the look for physical contact. A desire to appropriate both the body and the image can only be frustrated since the phantasy can only embody desire, it cannot satisfy desire by offering the body. And if fiction declares the limits of its imagery in relation to the real, porn does so to an even greater extent – gratification is not achieved through acting out the fantasies or through the enactment on the screen of fantasies but through the activity of fantasizing itself. This obviously involves the activity of looking, but not the look itself as substitution. The viewer does not necessarily work to confirm sexual identity but to disperse it. The body is very much in evidence in porn but its fictionality, its distance from the real, is potentially heightened.

To reinstate the body in a feminist cinema of fictionality, then, is not necessarily to reduce woman to body, to use the image as evidence of woman *as* body. Rather, viewing processes could be generated to disperse rather than confirm sexual identity, to explore sexuality by paradoxically refusing the sight of the body as a site of realism. Which is not to withhold from sight. The body in evidence is not the body as evidence.

COMING TO AN INCONCLUSION

Many of the critiques of pornography argue that porn is a representation of male phantasy, of the collective male unconscious, and as such reveals a conjunction of sex and death expressed in a desire to destroy the feminine principle. When women admit to being turned on by porn images, or having fantasies which may involve violence or submission, the confession is often qualified by an acknowledgement of conditioning – patriarchy writes the scripts and we are all assigned roles. The problem with this approach is that it rests on a notion of sexuality as given, as fixed, so that fantasy is seen as a confirmation of belief, or in the case of 'incorrect' female fantasies as a defence against disbelief. However, in so far as this approach removes fantasy from the realm of the purely personal and idiosyncratic it does indirectly raise questions about the way in which sexual difference is structured on an unconscious level. This is where various notions of phantasy, rather than fantasy, need to be employed.

I do not wish to locate porn films as pure fiction or innocent fantasy. Certainly the fantasies of porn are articulated together with a structuring of phantasies which privilege a male view of female sexuality. But if we are to challenge the notion of fixed sexual identities, if we are concerned with processes of construction in the cinema, then it is worth the risk of exploring female fantasy, of exploiting the possibilities of filmic fiction. For it may well turn out that female fantasy is not singular and certainly contradictory, that the intertwinings of sex and death and violence are not uniquely male properties. There is no formula for a feminist pornography, nor would it be desirable to pose the love story (as in 'not a love story') as a feminine opposition, or erotica as a feminine truth. Phantasy, on the level of the unconscious, does not make neat distinctions between sex and love, between clean and dirty, between pacifism and aggression. On the more conscious level fantasies might well be mobilized to focus in particular ways, but this is not to say that fantasies about masochism or life-nurturing love have nothing to do with sadism or death.

A shift of attention from pornography to the possibilities of fiction might provide a way of constructing and exploring diverse sexualities *for* feminism. This is certainly not to suggest that a feminine desire commensurate with feminism will be found and returned to its proper place. Rather, the hope, and the risk, is that in the gap between sexual identity and fantasy opened up by fiction, improper places – spaces of impropriety – might be sighted.

218

NOTES

First published in *Screen*, November–December 1982, vol. 23, no. 5, pp. 39–60.

1 Valerie Miner, 'Fantasies and Nightmares: The Red-Blooded Media', *Jump Cut*, 1981, no. 26, pp. 48–50. This issue also includes an annotated bibliography on Women and Pornography, pp. 56–60.
2 *The Home Office Report of the Committee on Obscenity and Film Censorship*, London, HMSO, 1979, p. 103.
3 Miner, op. cit., p. 48.
4 Rosalind Coward, 'Sexual Violence and Sexuality', *Feminist Review*, Summer 1982, no. 11, p. 11.
5 Helen Longino, 'Pornography, Oppression and Freedom: A Closer Look' in Laura Lederer (ed.), *Take Back the Night*, New York, William Morrow & Co., 1980.
6 New York, Bantam Books 1975, London, Secker & Warburg, 1975.
7 Noreen Connell and Cassandra Wilson (eds), New York, New American Library, 1974.
8 New York, Grosset & Dunlap, 1976.
9 Ros Innes, ' "What She Needs is a Good Fuck" – Rape and Femininity', *Hecate*, July 1976, vol. 2, no. 2; Lesley Stern, 'The Language of Rape', *Intervention*, March 1977. no. 8.
10 Monique Plaza, 'Our Costs and Their Benefits', *m/f*, 1980, no. 4, pp. 28–40; Delia Dumaresq, 'Rape: Sexuality in the Law', *m/f*, 1981, nos. 5–6, pp. 41–60.
11 New York, E. P. Dutton, 1974.
12 Boston, Beacon Press, 1978.
13 In Robin Morgan, *Going Too Far: the Personal Chronicle of a Feminist*, New York, Vintage, 1978.
14 *MS* Magazine, November 1978.
15 ibid.
16 *MS* Magazine, August 1977.
17 London, Virago, 1979.
18 See Longino, op. cit.
19 Beatrice Faust, New York, Macmillan, 1980.
20 Paula Webster, 'Pornography and Pleasure', *Heresies*, 1981, no. 12 (Sex Issue), p. 48. She is referring to Deirdre English, 'The Politics of Porn', *Mother Jones*, April 1980, vol. 5, no. 3, p. 20; and Ellen Willis, *Village Voice*, 15 October 1979.
21 Available from WAP, 579 9th Avenue, New York, NY 10036.
22 See Jeanne Cordova and Kerry Lobel, 'Feminists and the Right – Merging over Porn?', *Lesbian Tide*, May–June 1980; and Mandy Merck, 'Pornography', *City Limits*, 13–19 November 1981, p. 49.
23 *Diary of a Conference*: documentation of the planning of Towards a Politics of Sexuality, held at Barnard College, April 1982, p. 19.
24 Diana Hume George, 'The Myth of Mythlessness and the New Mythology of Love: Feminist Theory on Rape and Pornography', *Enclitic*, Fall 1980, vol. 4, no. 2, p. 31.
25 See Zillah R. Eisenstein, 'The Sexual Politics of the New Right: Understanding the Crisis of Liberalism for the 1980s', *Signs*, Spring 1982, vol. 7, no. 3, pp. 567–88; June Kress, 'Austerity and the Right Wing Attack on Women', *Contemporary Marxism*, Winter 1981–2, no. 4; and Judith R. Walkowitz, 'Male Vice and Feminist Virtue: Feminism and the Politics of Prostitution in Nineteenth Century Britain', *History Workshop*, Spring 1982, no. 13, pp. 77–94.
26 Kathy Myers, 'Towards a Feminist Erotica', *Camerawork*, March 1982, pp. 14–19.

27 See Coward, op. cit.; Beverley Brown, 'A Feminist Interest in Pornography: Some Modest Proposals', *m/f*, 1981, nos. 5–6, pp. 5–18; John Ellis, 'On Pornography', chapter 6 pp. 146–70 in this volume; originally published in *Screen*, Spring 1980, vol. 21, no. 1, pp. 81–108; Annette Kuhn, *Women's Pictures: Feminism and Cinema*, London, Routledge & Kegan Paul, 1982, pp. 109–28.

28 Deirdre English, Amber Hollibaugh and Gayle Rubin, 'Talking Sex: A Conversation on Sexuality and Feminism', *Feminist Review*, Summer 1982, no. 11, p. 44.

29 See *Heresies*, no. 12 (Sex Issue), 1981 and *Diary of a Conference*, op. cit.

30 Paul Willemen, 'Letter to John', chapter 7 in this volume, p. 177; originally published in *Screen*, Summer 1980, vol. 21, no. 2, pp. 53–65.

31 ibid, pp. 179–80.

Part III

THE FEMALE
SPECTATOR

INTRODUCTION

Who is the female spectator? Is she a pseudo-male? Is she a viewer in her own right? What kinds of pleasure do mainstream cinema and television genres offer the female spectator? An analysis of the female spectator as the figure in the auditorium draws on at least three related areas: the spectator as constituted by the processes of subjectivity; the spectator as a socially and historically constructed figure; and the female audience. Early analyses of the female spectator largely addressed the spectator as constituted by the psychic processes of subject formation. The two chapters in this section are mainly concerned with this area. The authors, Mary Ann Doane and Jackie Stacey, both address problems raised by Mulvey's theory of spectatorship. Before considering these two important contributions, it may be useful to examine briefly several of the key writings in the area of female spectatorship.

Shortly after the publication of Mulvey's article on 'Visual Pleasure' feminist critics, unhappy with the masculinization of the female spectator, turned their attention to Freud's theory of female bisexuality, which Freud saw as based in the girl's pre-oedipal attachment to the mother. They hoped to posit the notion of a female gaze in relation to woman's erotic desires and relationships with other women. In 1978 *New German Critique* published a discussion among feminists in which attention was drawn to the possibility of an erotic gaze between women in the diegesis and the implications of this for the female spectator in the auditorium.[1] Jackie Stacey takes up this issue in 'Desperately Seeking Difference'. E. Ann Kaplan explores this topic in a later analysis of Sternberg's *Blonde Venus*. She argues that the female spectator relates sexually to Dietrich's masculinized image in a way that excludes men. Dietrich's image becomes a 'resisting' one for the female spectator.[2]

In 1981 Mulvey explored the question of female spectatorship in her article, 'Afterthoughts on "Visual Pleasure and Narrative Cinema"'.[3] Here Mulvey analysed the position of the female spectator when called upon to identify with a woman as the central protagonist where the woman was an active, strong figure. Mulvey concluded that in this context the female spectator undergoes an impossible 'phantasy of masculinisation'. In a response to this notion, Teresa de Lauretis argued that the nature of female identification is neither single or simple. She argues that identification is 'itself a movement, a subject-process, a relation . . .'.[4] She concludes that female identification is more complex than Mulvey allows, and that the female spectator is always involved in a 'double identification' in which she identifies with both the passive object (woman, body, landscape) and the active subject positions (the look of the male and the camera).[5]

In her influential essay, 'Film and the Masquerade: Theorizing the Female Spectator', Mary Ann Doane uses the notion of masquerade to discuss female spectatorship. First she draws attention to the way in which woman's image is represented in the cinema (larger than life, glamorous, consumable) as an object of desire for the male spectator. Doane asks the important question – 'What, then, of the female spectator?' In what sense is the woman in the auditorium given 'access' to her own objectified and fetishized image? Does woman simply appropriate the 'male' gaze and subject woman to her voyeuristic and/or fetishistic look? In Doane's view the situation is more complex than this explanation, based on a simple reversal of roles, would allow.

In theorizing the female gaze, Doane suggests a different way of conceptualizing the screen–spectator relationship. Whereas Mulvey drew on the dichotomy of active/male and passive/female, Doane proposes the binary opposition of proximity and distance discussed by Metz. 'For the female spectator there is a certain over-presence of the image – she *is* the image.'[6] To support her theory, Doane refers to the daughter's pre-Oedipal relationship with the mother, which she sees as posing a number of difficulties for the female spectator. It is woman's inability to separate fully from the maternal body which makes it difficult for her to achieve a distance from the text; in this instance the image on the cinema screen. There is a further reason why she finds it difficult to establish distance from the image. Unlike the boy, the girl has no need to use her body to symbolize difference. The boy's early experiences, including the possibility of losing the penis, help him to construct a distance from his body while also largely pre-determining his destiny as a fetishist. For the two reasons discussed above, woman's experiences make it virtually impossible for her to preserve a distance from her body or adopt the position of a fetishist. Doane concludes that one avenue open to the female spectator is to identify so closely with the image that she is unable to step back, to adopt a critical distance. The female spectator finds herself adopting a masochistic position of overidentification.

The position which Doane sees as having radical implications for female spectatorship is that of masquerade. Drawing on Joan Riviere's essay 'Womanliness as a Masquerade', Doane argues that masquerade provides a way of conceptualizing the female spectator in terms other than those usually associated with the male spectator, such as voyeurism and fetishism.[7] Because of her problematic status in a man's world, woman more easily dons the clothes of the 'other', in fact, finds it necessary in order to get on in a man's world. Feminine masquerade is represented in two forms in the diegetic world of the film. First the female protagonist in the diegesis can appropriate the gaze, can masquerade as controller of the look and hence threaten the conventional system of looking in which the gaze is usually aligned with masculinity. Second, the female protagonist, in the case of the *femme fatale*, can masquerade the feminine by presenting femininity in excess. The female spectator in the auditorium who sees through the masquerade understands that femininity can be a performance, is better able to stand back from the image, adopt a critical attitude. The value of the latter position is that it enables the female spectator to construct a distance from the image, to generate a problematic within which the image is manipulable, producible, and readable by the woman.

Jackie Stacey takes up the question of spectatorship in relation to female homoeroticism. She considers a number of ways in which the general topic of female spectatorship has been be approached, but concludes that the findings are too restricted and restrictive. Raymond Bellour sees women as total victims of a patriarchal system; Mary Ann Doane marginalizes the female spectator; and Mulvey defines her primarily in male terms. Stacey points out that psychoanalytic theories of identification which are based on binary oppositions tend to masculinize the homosexual woman. In order to establish a more complex model of spectatorship, Stacey argues that sexuality and gender should be seen as separate categories. In order to explore the pleasures on offer for the female spectator, Stacey presents an interesting critique of two films: *All About Eve* and *Desperately Seeking Susan*. Both films explore the same theme – one woman's obsession with another woman.

Stacey suggests a number of possible pleasures of spectatorship for the female viewer: representation of woman's desire for another woman which constitutes a re-enactment of an experience common to all women in their childhood relationship with the mother; representation of woman's desire to identify with a female ideal; representation of woman as the active bearer of the look. Stacey concludes that existing theories of difference which separate out desire from identification fail to provide an adequate understanding of the pleasures offered to the female spectator in these two films, in which desire and identification are interwoven. Although Stacey does not discuss a text which deals explicitly with a lesbian relationship, it would be interesting to relate some of the questions she raises to a narrative about lesbian desire. How might a narrative about lesbian desire differ from the two films Stacey discusses? What kind of pleasure does an explicitly lesbian text offer the viewer? How might different spectators –

female and male homosexuals as well as heterosexuals – respond to such a film? Is narcissism inflected differently in films which deal with desire between people of the same sex?

NOTES

1 Michelle Citron, Julia Lesage, Judith Mayne, B. Ruby Rich and Anna Maria Taylor, 'Women and Film: A Discussion of Feminist Aesthetics', *New German Critique*, Winter 1978, no. 13, pp. 83–107.
2 E. Ann Kaplan, *Women and Film – Both Sides of the Camera*, New York, Methuen, 1983, p. 5
3 Laura Mulvey, 'Afterthoughts on "Visual Pleasure and Narrative Cinema" inspired by *Duel in the Sun*', in *Visual and Other Pleasures*, London, Macmillan, 1989, pp. 29–39.
4 Teresa de Lauretis, *Alice Doesn't*, Bloomington, Indiana University Press, 1984, p. 141.
5 ibid., p. 144.
6 Mary Ann Doane, 'Film and the Masquerade', chapter 10 in this volume, p. 231.
7 Joan Riviere, 'Womanliness as a Masquerade', in Hendrik M. Rvitenbeek (ed.), *Psychoanalysis and Female Sexuality*, New Haven, College and University Press, 1966.

10

FILM AND THE MASQUERADE: THEORIZING THE FEMALE SPECTATOR

Mary Ann Doane

I HEADS IN HIEROGLYPHIC BONNETS

In his lecture on 'Femininity', Freud forcefully inscribes the absence of the female spectator of theory in his notorious statement, 'to those of you who are women this will not apply – you are yourselves the problem . . .'.[1] Simultaneous with this exclusion operated upon the female members of his audience, he invokes, as a rather strange prop, a poem by Heine. Introduced by Freud's claim concerning the importance and elusiveness of his topic – 'Throughout history people have knocked their heads against the riddle of the nature of femininity' – are four lines of Heine's poem:

Heads in hieroglyphic bonnets,
Heads in turbans and black birettas,
Heads in wigs and thousand other
Wretched, sweating heads of humans . . .[2]

The effects of the appeal to this poem are subject to the work of over-determination Freud isolated in the text of the dream. The sheer proliferation of heads and hats (and hence, through a metonymic slippage, minds), which are presumed to have confronted this intimidating riddle before Freud, confers on his discourse the weight of an intellectual history, of a tradition of interrogation. Furthermore, the image of hieroglyphics strengthens the association made between femininity and the enigmatic, the indecipherable, that which is 'other'. And yet Freud practises a slight deception here, concealing what is elided by removing the lines from their context, castrating, as it were, the stanza. For the question over which Heine's heads brood is not the same as Freud's – it is not 'What is Woman?', but instead, 'what signifies Man?' The quote is taken from the seventh section (entitled 'Questions') of the second cycle of *The North Sea*. The full stanza, presented as the words of 'a young man,/ His breast full of sorrow, his head full of doubt', reads as follows:

O solve me the riddle of life,
The teasingly time-old riddle,

Over which many heads already have brooded,
Heads in hats of hieroglyphics,
Turbaned heads and heads in black skull-caps,
Heads in perrukes and a thousand other
Poor, perspiring human heads –
Tell me, what signifies Man?
Whence does he come? Whither does he go?
Who lives up there upon golden stars?[3]

The question in Freud's text is thus a disguise and a displacement of that other question, which in the pre-text is both humanistic and theological. The claim to investigate an otherness is a pretence, haunted by the mirror effect by means of which the question of the woman reflects only the man's own ontological doubts. Yet what interests me most in this intertextual mis-representation is that the riddle of femininity is initiated from the beginning in Freud's text as a question in masquerade. But I will return to the issue of masquerade later.

More pertinently, as far as the cinema is concerned, it is not accidental that Freud's eviction of the female spectator/auditor is co-present with the invocation of a hieroglyphic language. The woman, the enigma, the hieroglyphic, the picture, the image – the metonymic chain connects with another: the cinema, the theatre of pictures, a writing in images of the woman but not *for* her. For she *is* the problem. The semantic valence attributed to a hieroglyphic language is two-edged. In fact, there is a sense in which the term is inhabited by a contradiction. On the one hand, the hieroglyphic is summoned, particularly when it merges with a discourse on the woman, to connote an indecipherable language, a signifying system which denies its own function by failing to signify anything to the uninitiated, to those who do not hold the key. In this sense, the hieroglyphic, like the woman, harbours a mystery, an inaccessible though desirable otherness. On the other hand, the hieroglyphic is the most readable of languages. Its immediacy, its accessibility are functions of its status as a *pictorial* language, a writing in images. For the image is theorized in terms of a certain *closeness*, the lack of a distance or gap between sign and referent. Given its iconic characteristics, the relationship between signifier and signified is understood as less arbitrary in imagistic systems of representation than in language 'proper'. The intimacy of signifier and signified in the iconic sign negates the distance which defines phonetic language. And it is the absence of this crucial distance or gap which also, simultaneously, specifies both the hieroglyphic and the female. This is precisely why Freud evicted the woman from his lecture on femininity. Too close to herself, entangled in her own enigma, she could not step back, could not achieve the necessary distance of a second look.[4]

Thus, while the hieroglyphic is an indecipherable or at least enigmatic language, it is also and at the same time potentially the most universally understandable, comprehensible, appropriable of signs.[5] And the woman shares this contradictory status. But it is here that the analogy slips. For hieroglyphic languages are *not* perfectly iconic. They would not achieve the status of languages if they were – due to what Todorov and Ducrot refer to as a certain non-generalizability of the iconic sign:

> Now it is the impossibility of generalizing this principle of represen-
> tation that has introduced even into fundamentally morphemo-
> graphic writing systems such as Chinese, Egyptian, and Sumerian,
> the phonographic principle. We might almost conclude that every
> logography [the graphic system of language notation] grows out of *the
> impossibility of a generalized iconic representation*; proper nouns and
> abstract notions (including inflections) are then the ones that will be
> noted phonetically.[6]

The iconic system of representation is inherently deficient – it cannot disengage itself from the 'real', from the concrete; it lacks the gap necessary for generalizability (for Saussure, this is the idea that, 'Signs which are arbitrary realise better than others the ideal of the semiotic process'). The woman, too, is defined by such an insufficiency. My insistence upon the congruence between certain theories of the image and theories of femininity is an attempt to dissect the *episteme* which assigns to the woman a special place in cinematic representation while denying her access to that system.

The cinematic apparatus inherits a theory of the image which is not conceived outside of sexual specifications. And historically, there has always been a certain imbrication of the cinematic image and the representation of the woman. The woman's relation to the camera and the scopic regime is quite different from that of the male. As Noël Burch points out, the early silent cinema, through its insistent inscription of scenarios of voyeurism, conceives of its spectator's viewing pleasure in terms of that of the Peeping Tom, behind the screen, reduplicating the spectator's position in relation to the woman as screen.[7] Spectatorial desire, in contemporary film theory, is generally delineated as either voyeurism or fetishism, as precisely a pleasure in seeing what is prohibited in relation to the female body. The image orchestrates a gaze, a limit, and its pleasurable transgression. The woman's beauty, her very desirability, becomes a function of certain practices of imaging – framing, lighting, camera movement, angle. She is thus, as Laura Mulvey has pointed out, more closely associated with the surface of the image than its illusory depths, its constructed three-dimensional space which the man is destined to inhabit and hence control.[8] In *Now Voyager*, for instance, a single image signals the momentous transformation of the Bette Davis character from ugly spinster aunt to glamorous single woman. Charles Affron describes the specifically cinematic aspect of this operation as a 'stroke of genius':

> The radical shadow bisecting the face in white/dark/white strata creates a visual phenomenon quite distinct from the makeup transformation of lipstick and plucked eyebrows. . . . This shot does not reveal what we commonly call acting, especially after the most recent exhibition of that activity, but the sense of face belongs to a plastique pertinent to the camera. The viewer is allowed a different perceptual referent, a chance to come down from the nerve-jarring, first sequence and to use his eyes anew.[9]

A 'plastique pertinent to the camera' constitutes the woman not only as the image of desire but as the desirous image – one which the devoted *cinéphile* can cherish and embrace. To 'have' the cinema is, in some sense, to 'have' the woman. But *Now Voyager* is, in Affron's terms, a 'tearjerker', in others, a 'woman's picture', that is, a film purportedly produced for a female audience. What, then, of the female spectator? What can one say about her desire in relation to this process of imaging? It would seem that what the cinematic institution has in common with Freud's gesture is the eviction of the female spectator from a discourse purportedly about her (the cinema, psychoanalysis) – one which, in fact, narrativizes her again and again.

II A LASS BUT NOT A LACK

Theories of female spectatorship are thus rare, and when they are produced, seem inevitably to confront certain blockages in conceptualization. The difficulties in thinking female spectatorship demand consideration. After all, even if it is admitted that the woman is frequently the object of the voyeuristic or fetishistic gaze in the cinema, what is there to prevent her from reversing the relation and appropriating the gaze for her own pleasure? Precisely the fact that the reversal itself remains locked within the same logic. The male striptease, the gigolo – both inevitably signify the mechanism of reversal itself, constituting themselves as aberrations whose acknowledgement simply reinforces the dominant system of aligning sexual difference with a subject/object dichotomy. And an essential attribute of that dominant system is the matching of male subjectivity with the agency of the look.

The supportive binary opposition at work here is not only that utilized by Laura Mulvey – an opposition between passivity and activity – but perhaps more importantly, an opposition between proximity and distance in relation to the image.[10] It is in this sense that the very logic behind the structure of the gaze demands a sexual division. While the distance between image and signified (or even referent) is theorized as minimal, if not non-existent, that between the film and the spectator must be maintained, even measured. One need only think of Noël Burch's mapping of spectatorship as a perfect distance from the screen (two times the width of the image) – a point in space from which the filmic discourse is most accessible.[11]

But the most explicit representation of this opposition between proximity and distance is contained in Christian Metz's analysis of voyeuristic desire in terms of a kind of social hierarchy of the senses: 'It is no accident that the main socially acceptable arts are based on the senses at a distance, and that those which depend on the senses of contact are often regarded as "minor" arts (=culinary arts, art of perfumes, etc.).'[12] The voyeur, according to Metz, must maintain a distance between himself and the image – the *cinéphile needs* the gap which represents for him the very distance between desire and its object. In this sense, voyeurism is theorized as a type of meta-desire:

> If it is true of all desire that it depends on the infinite pursuit of its absent object, voyeuristic desire, along with certain forms of sadism, is the only desire whose principle of distance symbolically and spatially evokes this fundamental rent.[13]

Yet even this status as meta-desire does not fully characterize the cinema for it is a feature shared by other arts as well (painting, theatre, opera, etc.). Metz thus adds another reinscription of this necessary distance. What specifies the cinema is a further reduplication of the lack which prompts desire. The cinema is characterized by an illusory sensory plenitude (there is 'so much to see') and yet haunted by the absence of those very objects which are there to be seen. Absence is an absolute and irrecoverable distance. In other words, Noël Burch is quite right in aligning spectatorial desire with a certain spatial configuration. The viewer must not sit either too close or too far from the screen. The result of both would be the same – he would lose the image of his desire.

It is precisely this opposition between proximity and distance, control of the image and its loss, which locates the possibilities of spectatorship within the problematic of sexual difference. For the female spectator there is a certain over-presence of the image – she *is* the image. Given the closeness of this relationship, the female spectator's desire can be described only in terms of a kind of narcissism – the female look demands a becoming. It thus appears to negate the very distance or gap specified by Metz and Burch as the essential precondition for voyeurism. From this perspective, it is important to note the constant recurrence of the motif of proximity in feminist theories (especially those labelled 'new French feminisms') which purport to describe a feminine specificity. For Luce Irigaray, female anatomy is readable as a constant relation of the self to itself, as an auto-eroticism based on the embrace of the two lips which allow the woman to

231

touch herself without mediation. Furthermore, the very notion of property, and hence possession of something which can be constituted as other, is antithetical to the woman:

> Nearness however, is not foreign to woman, a nearness so close that any identification of one or the other, and therefore any form of property, is impossible. Woman enjoys a closeness with the other that is so near she cannot possess it any more than she can possess herself.[14]

Or, in the case of female madness or delirium, 'women do not manage to articulate their madness: they suffer it directly in their body'.[15] The distance necessary to detach the signifiers of madness from the body in the construction of even a discourse which exceeds the boundaries of sense is lacking. In the words of Hélène Cixous, 'More so than men who are coaxed toward social success, toward sublimation, women are body.'[16]

This theme of the overwhelming presence-to-itself of the female body is elaborated by Sarah Kofman and Michèle Montrelay as well. Kofman describes how Freudian psychoanalysis outlines a scenario whereby the subject's passage from the mother to the father is simultaneous with a passage from the senses to reason, nostalgia for the mother henceforth signifying a longing for a different positioning in relation to the sensory or the somatic, and the degree of civilization measured by the very distance from the body.[17] Similarly, Montrelay argues that while the male has the possibility of displacing the first object of desire (the mother), the female must become that object of desire:

> Recovering herself as maternal body (and also as phallus), the woman can no longer repress, 'lose', the first stake of representation. . . . From now on, anxiety, tied to the presence of this body, can only be insistent, continuous. This body, so close, which she has to occupy, is an object in excess which must be 'lost', that is to say, repressed, in order to be symbolised.[18]

This body so close, so excessive, prevents the woman from assuming a position similar to the man's in relation to signifying systems. For she is haunted by the loss of a loss, the lack of that lack so essential for the realization of the ideals of semiotic systems.

Female specificity is thus theorized in terms of spatial proximity. In opposition to this 'closeness' to the body, a spatial distance in the male's relation to his body rapidly becomes a temporal distance in the service of knowledge. This is presented quite explicitly in Freud's analysis of the construction of the 'subject supposed to know'. The knowledge involved here is a knowledge of sexual difference as it is organized in relation to the structure of the look, turning on the visibility of the penis. For the little girl in Freud's description seeing and knowing are simultaneous – there is no temporal gap between them. In 'Some Psychological Consequences of the Anatomical Distinction Between the Sexes', Freud claims that the girl, upon seeing the penis for the first time, 'makes her judgement and her decision in a flash. She has seen it and knows that she is without it and wants to have it.'[19] In the lecture on 'Femininity' Freud repeats this gesture, merging perception and intellection: 'They [girls] at once notice the difference and, it must be admitted, its significance too.'[20]

The little boy, on the other hand, does not share this immediacy of understanding. When he first sees the woman's genitals he 'begins by showing irresolution and lack of interest; he sees nothing or disowns what he has seen, he softens it down or looks about for expedients for bringing it into line with his expectations'.[21] A second event, the threat of castration, is necessary to prompt a rereading of the image, endowing it with a meaning in relation to the boy's own subjectivity. It is in the distance between the look and the threat that the boy's relation to knowledge of sexual difference is formulated. The boy, unlike the girl in Freud's description, is capable of re-vision of earlier events, a retrospective understanding which invests the events with a significance which is in no way linked to an immediacy of sight. This gap between the visible and the knowable, the very possibility of disowning what is seen, prepares the ground for fetishism. In a sense, the male spectator is destined to be a fetishist, balancing knowledge and belief.

The female, on the other hand, must find it extremely difficult, if not impossible, to assume the position of fetishist. That body which is so close continually reminds her of the castration which cannot be 'fetishised away'. The lack of a distance between seeing and understanding, the mode of judging 'in a flash', is conducive to what might be termed as 'over-identification' with the image. The association of tears and 'wet wasted afternoons' (in Molly Haskell's words)[22] with genres specified as feminine (the soap opera, the 'woman's picture') points very precisely to this type of over-identification, this abolition of a distance, in short, this inability to fetishize. The woman is constructed differently in relation to processes of looking. For Irigaray, this dichotomy between distance and proximity is described as the fact that:

> The masculine can partly look at itself, speculate about itself, represent itself and describe itself for what it is, whilst the feminine can try to speak to itself through a new language, but cannot describe itself from outside or in formal terms, except by identifying itself with the masculine, thus by losing itself.[23]

Irigaray goes even further: the woman always has a problematic relation to the visible, to form, to structures of seeing. She is much more comfortable with, closer to, the sense of touch.

The pervasiveness, in theories of the feminine, of descriptions of such a claustrophobic closeness, a deficiency in relation to structures of seeing and the visible, must clearly have consequences for attempts to theorize female spectatorship. And, in fact, the result is a tendency to view the female spectator as the site of an oscillation between a feminine position and a masculine position, invoking the metaphor of the transvestite. Given the structures of cinematic narrative, the woman who identifies with a female character must adopt a passive or masochistic position, while identification with the active hero necessarily entails an acceptance of what Laura Mulvey refers to as a certain 'masculinization' of spectatorship.

> . . . as desire is given cultural materiality in a text, for women (from childhood onwards) trans-sex identification is a *habit* that very easily becomes *second Nature*. However, this Nature does not sit easily and shifts restlessly in its borrowed transvestite clothes.[24]

The transvestite wears clothes which signify a different sexuality, a sexuality which, for the woman, allows a mastery over the image and the very possibility of attaching the gaze to desire. Clothes make the man, as they say. Perhaps this explains the ease with which women can slip into male clothing. As both Freud and Cixous point out, the woman seems to be *more* bisexual than the man. A scene from Cukor's *Adam's Rib* graphically demonstrates this ease of female transvestism. As Katherine Hepburn asks the jury to imagine the sex role reversal of the three major characters involved in the case, there are three dissolves linking each of the characters successively to shots in which they are dressed in the clothes of the opposite sex. What characterizes the sequence is the marked facility of the transformation of the two women into men in contradistinction to a certain resistance in the case of the man. The acceptability of the female reversal is quite distinctly opposed to the male reversal, which seems capable of representation only in terms of farce. Male transvestism is an occasion for laughter; female transvestism only another occasion for desire.

Thus, while the male is locked into sexual identity, the female can at least pretend that she is other – in fact, sexual mobility would seem to be a distinguishing feature of femininity in its cultural construction. Hence, transvestism would be fully recuperable. The idea seems to be this: it is understandable that women would want to be men, for everyone wants to be elsewhere than in the feminine position. What is not understandable within the given terms is why a woman might flaunt her femininity, produce herself as an excess of femininity, in other words, foreground the masquerade. Masquerade is not as recuperable as transvestism precisely because it constitutes an acknowledgement that it is femininity itself which is constructed as mask – as the decorative layer which conceals a non-identity. For Joan Riviere, the first to theorize the concept, the masquerade of femininity is a kind of reaction-formation against the woman's trans-sex identification, her transvestism. After assuming the position of the subject of discourse rather than its object, the intellectual woman whom

Riviere analyses felt compelled to compensate for this theft of masculinity by overdoing the gestures of feminine flirtation.

> Womanliness therefore could be assumed and worn as a mask, both to hide the possession of masculinity and to avert the reprisals expected if she was found to possess it – much as a thief will turn out his pockets and ask to be searched to prove that he has not the stolen goods. The reader may now ask how I define womanliness or where I draw the line between genuine womanliness and the masquerade. My suggestion is not, however, that there is any such difference; whether radical or superficial, they are the same thing.[25]

The masquerade, in flaunting femininity, holds it at a distance. Womanliness is a mask which can be worn or removed. The masquerade's resistance to patriarchal positioning would therefore lie in its denial of the production of femininity as closeness, as presence-to-itself, as, precisely, imagistic. The transvestite adopts the sexuality of the Other – the woman becomes a man in order to attain the necessary distance from the image. Masquerade, on the other hand, involves a realignment of femininity, the recovery, or more accurately, simulation, of the missing gap or distance. To masquerade is to manufacture a lack in the form of a certain distance between oneself and one's image. If, as Moustafa Safouan points out, 'to wish to include in oneself as an object the cause of the desire of the Other is a formula for the structure of hysteria',[26] then masquerade is anti-hysterical for it works to effect a separation between the cause of desire and oneself. In Montrelay's words, 'the woman uses her own body as a disguise.'[27]

The very fact that we can speak of a woman 'using' her sex or 'using' her body for particular gains is highly significant – it is not that a man cannot use his body in this way, but that he doesn't have to. The masquerade doubles representation; it is constituted by a hyperbolization of the accoutrements of femininity. *A propos* of a recent performance by Marlene Dietrich, Silvia Bovenschen claims, 'we are watching a woman demonstrate the representation of a woman's body'.[28] This type of masquerade, an excess of femininity, is aligned with the *femme fatale* and, as Montrelay explains, is necessarily regarded by men as evil incarnate: 'It is this evil which scandalises whenever woman plays out her sex in order to evade the word and the law. Each time she subverts a law or a word which relies on the predominantly masculine structure of the look.'[29] By destabilizing the image, the masquerade confounds this masculine structure of the look. It effects a defamiliarization of female iconography. Nevertheless, the preceding account simply specifies masquerade as a type of representation which carries a threat, disarticulating male systems of viewing. Yet it specifies nothing with respect to female spectatorship. What might it mean to masquerade as spectator? To assume the mask in order to see in a different way?

III 'MEN SELDOM MAKE PASSES AT GIRLS WHO WEAR GLASSES'

The first scene in *Now Voyager* depicts the Bette Davis character as repressed, unattractive and undesirable or, in her own words, as the spinster aunt of the family. ('Every family has one.') She has heavy eyebrows, keeps her hair bound tightly in a bun, and wears glasses, a drab dress and heavy shoes. By the time of the shot discussed earlier, signalling her transformation into beauty, the glasses have disappeared, along with the other signifiers of unattractiveness. Between these two moments there is a scene in which the doctor who cures her actually confiscates her glasses (as a part of the cure). The woman who wears glasses constitutes one of the most intense visual clichés of the cinema. The image is a heavily marked condensation of motifs concerned with repressed sexuality, knowledge, visa-bility and vision, intellectuality, and desire. The woman with glasses signifies simultaneously intellectuality and undesirability; but the moment she re-moves her glasses (a moment which, it seems, must almost always be *shown* and which is itself linked with a certain sensual quality), she is transformed into spectacle, the very picture of desire. Now, it must be remembered that the cliché is a heavily loaded moment of signification, a social knot of meaning. It is characterized by an effect of ease and naturalness. Yet, the cliché has a binding power so strong that it indicates a precise moment of ideological danger or threat – in this case, the woman's appropriation of the gaze. Glasses worn by a woman in the cinema do not generally signify a deficiency in seeing but an active looking, or even simply the fact of seeing as opposed to being seen. The intellectual woman looks and analyses, and in usurping the gaze she poses a threat to an entire system of representation. It is as if the woman had forcefully moved to the other side of the specular. The overdetermination of the image of the woman with glasses, its status as a cliché, is a crucial aspect of the cinematic alignment of structures of seeing and being seen with sexual difference. The cliché, in assuming an immediacy of understanding, acts as a mechanism for the naturalization of sexual difference.

But the figure of the woman with glasses is only an extreme moment of a more generalized logic. There is always a certain excessiveness, a difficulty associated with women who appropriate the gaze, who insist upon looking. Linda Williams has demonstrated how, in the genre of the horror film, the woman's active looking is ultimately punished. And what she sees, the monster, is only a mirror of herself – both woman and monster are freakish in their difference – defined by either 'too much' or 'too little'.[30] Just as the dominant narrative cinema repetitively inscribes scenarios of voyeurism, internalizing or narrativizing the film–spectator relationship (in films like *Psycho*, *Rear Window*, *Peeping Tom*), taboos in seeing are insistently formulated in relation to the female spectator as well. The man with binoculars is countered by the woman with glasses. The gaze must be dissociated from mastery. In *Leave Her to Heaven* (John Stahl, 1945), the female protagonist's (Gene Tierney's) excessive desire and over-possessiveness are signalled from the very beginning of the film by her intense and sustained stare at the major male character, a stranger she first encounters on a train. The discomfort her look causes is graphically depicted. The Gene Tierney character is ultimately revealed to be the epitome of evil – killing her husband's crippled younger brother, her unborn child and ultimately herself in an attempt to brand her cousin as a murderess in order to ensure her husband's future fidelity. In *Humoresque* (Jean Negulesco, 1946), Joan Crawford's problematic status is a result of her continual attempts to assume the position of spectator – fixing John Garfield with her gaze. Her transformation from spectator to spectacle is signified repetitively by the gesture of removing her glasses. Rosa, the character played by Bette Davis in *Beyond the Forest* (King Vidor, 1949) walks to the station every day simply to *watch* the train departing for Chicago. Her fascination with the train is a fascination with its phallic power to transport her to 'another place'. This character is also specified as having a 'good eye' – she can shoot, both pool and guns. In all three films the woman is constructed as the site of an excessive and dangerous desire. This desire mobilizes extreme efforts of containment and unveils the sadistic aspect of narrative. In all three films the woman dies. As Claire Johnston points out, death is the 'location of all impossible signs',[31] and the films demonstrate that the woman as subject of the gaze is clearly an impossible sign. There is a perverse rewriting of this logic of the gaze in *Dark Victory* (Edmund Goulding, 1939), where the woman's story achieves heroic and tragic proportions not only in blindness, but in a blindness which mimes sight – when the woman pretends to be able to see.

IV OUT OF THE CINEMA AND INTO THE STREETS: THE CENSORSHIP OF THE FEMALE GAZE

This process of narrativizing the negation of the female gaze in the classical Hollywood cinema finds its perfect encapsulation in a still photograph taken in 1948 by Robert Doisneau, *Un Regard oblique*. Just as the Hollywood narratives discussed above purport to centre a female protago-nist, the photograph appears to give a certain prominence to a woman's look. Yet both the title of the photograph and its organization of space indicate that the real site of scopophiliac power is on the margins of the frame. The man is not centred; in fact, he occupies a very narrow space on the extreme right of the picture. Nevertheless, it is his gaze which defines the problematic of the photograph; it is his gaze which effectively erases that of the woman. Indeed, as subject of the gaze, the woman looks intently. But not only is the object of her look concealed from the specta-tor, her gaze is encased by the two poles defining the masculine axis of vision. Fascinated by nothing visible – a blankness or void for the spectator

237

Figure 10:1 Un Regard oblique: a dirty joke at the expense of the woman's look. Reproduced by kind permission of The Metropolitan Museum of Art, Warner Communications Inc. Purchase Fund, 1981 (1981.1199).

– unanchored by a 'sight' (there is nothing 'proper' to her vision – save, perhaps, the mirror), the female gaze is left free-floating, vulnerable to subjection. The faint reflection in the shop window of only the frame of the picture at which she is looking serves merely to rearticulate, *en abŷme*, the emptiness of her gaze, the absence of her desire in representation.

On the other hand, the object of the male gaze is fully present, *there* for the spectator. The fetishistic representation of the nude female body, fully in view, ensures a masculinization of the spectatorial position. The woman's look is literally outside the triangle which traces a complicity between the man, the nude and the spectator. The feminine presence in the photograph, despite a diegetic centring of the female subject of the gaze, is taken over by the picture as object. And, as if to doubly 'frame' her in the act of looking, the painting situates its female figure as a spectator (although it is not clear whether she is looking at herself in a mirror or peering through a door or window). While this drama of seeing is played out at the surface of the photograph, its deep space is activated by several young boys, out-of-focus, in front of a belt shop. The opposition out-of-focus/in-focus reinforces the supposed clarity accorded to the represen-tation of the woman's 'non-vision'. Furthermore, since this out-of-focus area constitutes the precise literal centre of the image, it also demonstrates how the photograph makes figurative the operation of centring – draining the actual centre point of significance in order to deposit meaning on the margins. The male gaze is centred, in control – although it is exercised from the periphery.

The spectator's pleasure is thus produced through the framing/negation of the female gaze. The woman is there as the butt of a joke – a 'dirty joke' which, as Freud has demonstrated, is always constructed at the expense of a woman. In order for a dirty joke to emerge in its specificity in Freud's description, the object of desire – the woman – must be absent and a third person (another man) must be present as witness to the joke – 'so that gradually, in place of the woman, the onlooker, now the listener, becomes the person to whom the smut is addressed'.[32] The terms of the photograph's address as joke once again ensure a masculinization of the place of the spectator. The operation of the dirty joke is also inextricably linked by Freud to scopophilia and the exposure of the female body:

> Smut is like an exposure of the sexually different person to whom it is directed. By the utterance of the obscene words it compels the person who is assailed to imagine the part of the body or the procedure in question and shows her that the assailant is himself imagining it. It cannot be doubted that the desire to see what is sexual exposed is the original motive of smut.[33]

From this perspective, the photograph lays bare the very mechanics of the joke through its depiction of sexual exposure and a surreptitious act of seeing (and desiring). Freud's description of the joke-work appears to constitute a perfect analysis of the photograph's orchestration of the gaze. There is a 'voice-off' of the photographic discourse, however – a component of the image which is beyond the frame of this little scenario of voyeurism. On the far left-hand side of the photograph, behind the wall holding the painting of the nude, is the barely detectable painting of a woman imaged differently, in darkness – *out of sight* for the male, blocked by his fetish. Yet to point to this almost invisible alternative in imaging is also only to reveal once again the analyst's own perpetual desire to find a not-seen that might break the hold of representation. Or to laugh last.

There is a sense in which the photograph's delineation of a sexual politics of looking is almost uncanny. But, to counteract the very possibility of such a perception, the language of the art critic effects a naturalization of this joke on the woman. The art-critical reception of the picture emphasizes a natural but at the same time 'imaginative' relation between photography and life, ultimately subordinating any formal relation to a referential ground: 'Doisneau's lines move from right to left, directed by the man's glance; the woman's gaze creates a line of energy like a hole in space. . . . The creation of these relationships from life itself is imagination in photography.'[34] 'Life itself', then, presents the material for an 'artistic' organization of vision along the lines of sexual difference. Furthermore, the critic would have us believe that chance events and arbitrary clicks of the shutter cannot be the agents of a generalized sexism because they are particular, unique – 'Keitesz and Doisneau depend entirely upon our recognition that they were present at the instant of the unique intersection of events.'[35] Realism seems always to reside in the streets and, indeed, the out-of-focus boy across the street, at the centre of the photograph, appears to act as a guarantee of the 'chance' nature of the event, its arbitrariness, in short – its realism. Thus, in the discourse of the art critic the photograph, in capturing a moment, does not construct it; the camera finds a naturally given series of subject and object positions. What the critic does not consider are the conditions of reception of photography as an art form, its situation within a much larger network of representation. What is it that makes the photograph not only readable but pleasurable – at the expense of the woman? The critic does not ask what makes the photograph a negotiable item in a market of signification.

V THE MISSING LOOK

The photograph displays insistently, in microcosm, the structure of the cinematic inscription of a sexual differentiation in modes of looking. Its process of framing the female gaze repeats that of the cinematic narratives described above, from *Leave Her to Heaven* to *Dark Victory*. Films play out scenarios of looking in order to outline the terms of their own understanding. And given the divergence of masculine and feminine scenarios, those terms would seem to be explicitly negotiated as markers of sexual difference. Both the theory of the image and its apparatus, the cinema, produce a position for the female spectator – a position which is ultimately untenable because it lacks the attribute of distance so necessary for an adequate reading of the image. The entire elaboration of femininity as a closeness, a nearness, as present-to-itself is not the definition of an essence but the delineation of a *place* culturally assigned to the woman. Above and beyond a simple adoption of the masculine position in relation to the cinematic sign, the female spectator is given two options: the masochism of over-identification or the narcissism entailed in becoming one's own object of desire, in assuming the image in the most radical way. The effectivity of masquerade lies precisely in its potential to manufacture a distance from the image, to generate a problematic within which the image is manipulable, producible, and readable by the woman. Doisneau's photograph is not readable by the female spectator – it can give her pleasure only in masochism. In order to 'get' the joke, she must once again assume the position of transvestite.

It is quite tempting to foreclose entirely the possibility of female spectatorship, to repeat at the level of theory the gesture of the photograph, given the history of a cinema which relies so heavily on voyeurism, fetishism, and identification with an ego ideal conceivable only in masculine terms. And, in fact, there has been a tendency to theorize femininity and hence the feminine gaze as repressed, and in its repression somehow irretrievable, the enigma constituted by Freud's question. Yet, as Michel Foucault has demonstrated, the repressive hypothesis on its own entails a very limited and simplistic notion of the working of power.[36] The 'no' of the father, the prohibition, is its only technique. In theories of repression there is no sense of the productiveness and positivity of power. Femininity is produced very precisely as a position within a network of power relations. And the growing insistence upon the elaboration of a theory of female spectatorship is indicative of the crucial necessity of understanding that position in order to dislocate it.

NOTES

This article is an expanded version of a paper presented at a symposium on recent film theory at Yale University, February 1982, organized by Miriam Hansen and Donald Crafton. It was first published in *Screen*, September–October 1982, vol. 23, nos. 3–4, pp. 74–87.

1 Sigmund Freud, 'Femininity', in James Strachey (ed.), *The Standard Edition of the Complete Psychological Words of Sigmund Freud*, London, Hogarth Press and the Institute of Psychoanalysis, 1964, vol. XXII, p. 113.
2 This is the translation given in a footnote in *Standard Edition*, ibid., p. 113.
3 Heinrich Heine, *The North Sea*, trans. Vernon Watkins, New York, New Direction Books, 1951, p. 77.
4 In other words, the woman can never ask her own ontological question. The absurdity of such a situation within traditional discursive conventions can be demonstrated by substituting a 'young woman' for the 'young man' of Heine's poem.
5 As Oswald Ducrot and Tzvetan Todorov point out in *Encyclopedic Dictionary of the Sciences of Language*, trans. Catherine Porter, Baltimore and London, Johns Hopkins University Press, 1979, p. 195, the potentially universal understandability of the hieroglyphic is highly theoretical and can only be thought as the unattainable ideal of an imagistic system: 'It is important of course not to exaggerate either the resemblance of the image with the object – the design is stylized very rapidly – or the "natural" and "universal" character of the signs: Sumerian, Chinese, Egyptian and Hittite hieroglyphics for the same object have nothing in common.'
6 ibid., p. 194; emphasis added.
7 See Noël Burch's film, *Correction Please, or How We Got Into Pictures* (1979).
8 Laura Mulvey, 'Visual Pleasure and Narrative Cinema', chapter 1, pp. 27–8 in this volume; originally published in *Screen*, Autumn 1975, vol. 16, no. 3, pp. 6–18.
9 Charles Affron, *Star Acting: Gish, Garbo, Davis*, New York, E. P. Dutton, 1977, pp. 281–2.
10 This argument focuses on the image to the exclusion of any consideration of the soundtrack primarily because it is the process of imaging which seems to constitute the major difficulty in theorizing female spectatorship. The image is also popularly understood as metonymic signifier for the cinema as a whole and

for good reason: historically, sound has been subordinate to the image within the dominant classical system. For more on the image/sound distinction in relation to sexual difference see my article, 'The Voice in the Cinema: The Articulation of Body and Space', *Yale French Studies*, 1980, no. 60, pp. 33–50.

11 Noël Burch, *Theory of Film Practice*, trans. Helen R. Lane, New York and Washington, Praeger, 1973, p. 35.

12 Christian Metz, 'The Imaginary Signifier', *Screen*, Summer 1975, vol. 16, no. 2, p. 60.

13 ibid., p. 61.

14 Luce Irigaray, 'This Sex Which is Not One', in Elaine Marks and Isabelle de Courtivron (eds), *New French Feminisms*, Amherst, University of Massachusetts Press, 1980, pp. 104–5; Brighton, Harvester Press, 1981.

15 Luce Irigaray, 'Women's Exile', *Ideology and Consciousness*, May 1977, no. 1, p. 74.

16 Hélène Cixous, 'The Laugh of the Medusa', in Marks and de Courtivron, op. cit., p. 257.

17 Sarah Kofman, 'Ex: The Woman's Enigma', *Enclitic*, Fall 1980, vol. 4, no. 2, p. 20.

18 Michèle Montrelay, 'Inquiry into Femininity', *m/f*, 1978, no. 1, pp. 91–2.

19 Freud, 'Some Psychological Consequences of the Anatomical Distinction Between the Sexes', in Philip Rieff (ed.), *Sexuality and the Psychology of Love*, New York, Collier Books, 1963, pp. 187–8.

20 Freud, 'Femininity', op. cit., p. 125.

21 Freud, 'Some Psychological Consequences', op. cit., p. 187.

22 Molly Haskell, *From Reverence to Rape*, Baltimore, Penguin Books, 1974, p. 154.

23 Irigaray, 'Women's Exile', op. cit., p. 65.

24 Laura Mulvey, 'Afterthoughts . . . Inspired by *Duel in the Sun*', *Framework*, Summer 1981, nos. 15–17, p. 13.

25 Joan Riviere, 'Womanliness as a Masquerade', in Hendrik M. Ruitenbeek (ed.), *Psychoanalysis and Female Sexuality*, New Haven, College and University Press, 1966, p. 213. My analysis of the concept of masquerade differs markedly from that of Luce Irigaray. See *Ce sexe qui n'en est pas un*, Paris, Editions de Minuit, 1977, pp. 131–2. It also diverges to a great extent from the very important analysis of masquerade presented by Claire Johnston in 'Femininity and the Masquerade: Anne of the Indies', in Claire Johnston and Paul Willemen (eds), *Jacques Tourneur*, Edinburgh, Edinburgh Film Festival, 1975, pp. 36–44. I am indebted to her for the reference to Riviere's article.

26 Moustafa Safouan, 'Is the Oedipus Complex Universal?', *m/f*, 1981, nos. 5–6, pp. 84–5.

27 Montrelay, op. cit., p. 93.

28 Silvia Bovenschen, 'Is There a Feminine Aesthetic?', *New German Critique*, Winter 1977, no. 10, p. 129.

29 Montrelay, op. cit., p. 93.

30 Linda Williams, 'When the Woman Looks . . .', in Mary Ann Doane, Patricia Mellencamp and Linda Williams (eds), *Re-vision: Essays in Feminist Film Criticism*, Los Angeles, American Film Institute, 1984.

31 Johnston, op. cit., p. 40.

32 Sigmund Freud, *Jokes and Their Relation to the Unconscious*, trans. James Strachey, New York, W. W. Norton, 1960, p. 99.

33 ibid., p. 98.

34 Weston J. Naef, *Counterparts: Form and Emotion in Photographs*, New York, E. P. Dutton and the Metropolitan Museum of Art, 1982, pp. 48–9.

242

35 ibid.
36 Michel Foucault, *The History of Sexuality*, trans. Robert Hurley, New York, Pantheon Books, 1978.

11

DESPERATELY SEEKING
DIFFERENCE

Jackie Stacey

During the last decade, feminist critics have developed an analysis of the constructions of sexual difference in dominant narrative cinema, drawing on psychoanalytic and poststructuralist theory. One of the main indictments of Hollywood film has been its passive positioning of the woman as sexual spectacle, as there 'to be looked at', and the active positioning of the male protagonist as bearer of the look. This pleasure has been identified as one of the central structures of dominant cinema, constructed in accordance with masculine desire. The question which has then arisen is that of the pleasure of the woman spectator. While this issue has hardly been addressed, the specifically homosexual pleasures of female spectatorship have been ignored completely. This article will attempt to suggest some of the theoretical reasons for this neglect.

THEORIES OF FEMININE SPECTATORSHIP:
MASCULINIZATION, MASOCHISM OR MARGINALITY

Laura Mulvey's 'Visual Pleasure and Narrative Cinema'[1] has been the springboard for much feminist film criticism during the last decade. Using psychoanalytic theory, Mulvey argued that the visual pleasures of Hollywood cinema are based on voyeuristic and fetishistic forms of looking. Because of the ways these looks are structured, the spectator necessarily identifies with the male protagonist in the narrative, and thus with his objectification of the female figure via the male gaze. The construction of woman as spectacle is built into the apparatus of dominant cinema, and the spectator position which is produced by the film narrative is necessarily a masculine one.

Mulvey maintained that visual pleasure in narrative film is built around two contradictory processes: the first involves objectification of the image and the second identification with it. The first process depends upon 'direct scopophilic contact with the female form displayed for [the spectator's] enjoyment'[2] and the spectator's look here is active and feels powerful. This form of pleasure requires the separation of the 'erotic identity of the subject from the object on the screen'.[3] This 'distance' between spectator and screen contributes to the voyeuristic pleasure of looking in on a private world. The second form of pleasure depends upon the opposite process, an identification with the image on the screen 'developed through narcissism and the constitution of the ego'.[4] The process of identification in the cinema, Mulvey argues, like the process of objectification, is structured by the narrative. It offers the spectator the pleasurable identification with the main male protagonist, and through him the power to indirectly possess the female character displayed as sexual object for his pleasure. The look of the male character moves the narrative forward and identification with it thus implies a sense of sharing in the power of his active look.

Two absences in Mulvey's argument have subsequently been addressed in film criticism. The first raises the question of the male figure as erotic object,[5] the second that of the feminine subject in the narrative, and, more specifically in relation to this article, women's active desire and the sexual aims of women in the audience in relationship to the female protagonist on the screen. As David Rodowick points out:

> her discussion of the female figure is restricted only to its function as masculine object-choice. In this manner, the place of the masculine is discussed as both the subject and object of the gaze: and the feminine is discussed only as an object which structures the masculine look according to its active (voyeuristic) and passive (fetishistic) forms. So where is the place of the feminine subject in this scenario?[6]

There are several possible ways of filling this theoretical gap. One would use a detailed textual analysis to demonstrate that different gendered spectator positions are produced by the film text, contradicting the unified masculine model of spectatorship. This would at least provide some space for an account of the feminine subject in the film text and in the cinema audience. The relationship of spectators to these feminine and masculine positions would then need to be explored further: do women necessarily take up a feminine and men a masculine spectator position?

Alternatively, we could accept a theory of the masculinization of the spectator at a textual level, but argue that spectators bring different subjectivities to the film according to sexual difference,[7] and therefore respond differently to the visual pleasures offered in the text. I want to elaborate these two possibilities briefly, before moving on to discuss a third which offers a more flexible or mobile model of spectatorship and cinematic pleasure.

The first possibility is, then, arguing that the film text can be read and enjoyed from different gendered positions. This problematizes the monolithic model of Hollywood cinema as an 'anthropomorphic male machine'[8] producing unified and masculinized spectators. It offers an explanation of women's pleasure in narrative cinema based on different processes of spectatorship, according to sexual difference. What this 'difference' signifies, however, in terms of cinematic pleasure, is highly contestable.

Raymond Bellour has explored the way the look is organized to create filmic discourse through detailed analyses of the system of enunciation in Hitchcock's work.[9] The mechanisms for eliminating the threat of sexual difference represented by the figure of the woman, he argues, are built into the apparatus of the cinema. Woman's desire only appears on the screen to be punished and controlled by assimilation to the desire of the male character. Bellour insists upon the masochistic nature of the woman spectator's pleasure in Hollywood film.

> I think that a woman can love, accept, and give positive value to these films only from her own masochism, and from a certain sadism that she can exercize in return on the masculine subject, within a system loaded with traps.[10]

Bellour, then, provides an account of the feminine subject and women's spectatorship which offers a different position from the masculine one set up by Mulvey. However, he fixes these positions within a rigid dichotomy which assumes a biologically determined equivalence between male/female and the masculine/feminine, sadistic/masochistic positions he believes to be set up by the cinematic apparatus. The apparatus here is seen as determining, controlling the meaning produced by a film text unproblematically:

> the resulting picture of the classical cinema is even more totalistic and deterministic than Mulvey's. Bellour sees it as a logically consistent, complete and closed system.[11]

The problem here is that Bellour's analysis, like those of many structural functionalists, leaves no room for subjectivity. The spectator is presumed to be an already fully constituted subject and is fixed by the text to a predetermined gender identification. There is no space for subjectivity to be seen as a process in which identification and object choice may be shifting, contradictory or precarious.

A second challenge to the model of the masculinized spectator set up by Mulvey's 1975 essay comes from the work of Mary Ann Doane. She draws on Freud's account of asymmetry in the development of masculinity and femininity to argue that women's pleasures are not motivated by fetishistic and voyeuristic drives.

> For the female spectator there is a certain over-presence of the image – she *is* the image. Given the closeness of this relationship, the female spectator's desire can be described only in terms of a kind of narcissism – the female look demands a becoming. It thus appears to negate the very distance or gap specified . . . as the essential precondition for voyeurism.[12]

Feminist critics have frequently challenged the assumption that fetishism functions for women in the same way that it is supposed to for men. Doane argues that the girl's understanding of the meaning of sexual difference occurs simultaneously with seeing the boy's genitals; the split between seeing and knowing, which enables the boy to disown the difference which is necessary for fetishism, does not occur in girls.

> It is in the distance between the look and the threat that the boy's relation to the knowledge of sexual difference is formulated. The boy, unlike the girl in Freud's description, is capable of a re-vision. . . . This gap between the visible and the knowable, the very possibility of disowning what is seen, prepares the ground for fetishism.[13]

This argument is useful in challenging the hegemony of the cinema apparatus and in offering an account of visual pleasure which is based neither on a phallic model, nor on the determinacy of the text. It allows for an account of women's potential resistance to the dominant masculine spectator position. However, it also sets women outside the problematic pleasures of looking in the cinema, as if women do not have to negotiate within patriarchal regimes. As Doane herself has pointed out:

> The feminist theorist is thus confronted with something of a double bind: she can continue to analyse and interpret various instances of the repression of woman, of her radical absence in the discourses of men – a pose which necessitates remaining within that very problema-tic herself, repeating its terms; or she can attempt to delineate a feminine specificity, always risking a recapitulation of patriarchal constructions and a naturalization of 'woman'.[14]

In fact, this is a very familiar problem in feminist theory: how to argue for a feminine specificity without falling into the trap of biological essentialism. If we do argue that women differ from men in their relation to visual constructions of femininity, then further questions are generated for femi-nist film theory: do all women have the same relationship to images of themselves? Is there only one feminine spectator position? How do we account for diversity, contradiction or resistance within this category of feminine spectatorship?

The problem here is one which arises in relation to all cultural systems in which women have been defined as 'other' within patriarchal discourses: how can we express the extent of women's oppression without denying femininity any room to manoeuvre (Mulvey, 1975), defining women as complete victims of patriarchy (Bellour, 1979), or as totally other to it (Doane, 1982)? Within the theories discussed so far, the female spectator is offered only the three rather frustrating options of masculinization, masochism or marginality.

TOWARDS A MORE CONTRADICTORY MODEL OF SPECTATORSHIP

A different avenue of exploration would require a more complex and contradictory model of the relay of looks on the screen and between the audience and the diegetic characters.

> It might be better, as Barthes suggests, neither to destroy difference nor to valorize it, but to multiply and disperse differences, to move towards a world where differences would not be synonymous with exclusion.[15]

In her 1981 'Afterthoughts' on visual pleasure, Mulvey addresses many of the problems raised so far. In an attempt to develop a more 'mobile' position for the female spectator in the cinema, she turns to Freud's theories of the difficulties of attaining heterosexual femininity.[16] Required, unlike men, to relinquish the phallic activity and female object of infancy, women are argued to oscillate between masculine and feminine identifications. To demonstrate this oscillation between positions, Mulvey cites Pearl Chavez's ambivalence in *Duel in the Sun*, the splitting of her desire (to be Jesse's 'lady' or Lewt's tomboy lover), a splitting which also extends to the female spectator. Mulvey's revision is important for two reasons: it displaces the notions of the fixity of spectator positions produced by the text, and it focuses on the gaps and contradictions within patriarchal signification, thus opening up crucial questions of resistance and diversity. However, Mulvey maintains that fantasies of action 'can only find expression . . . through the metaphor of masculinity'. In order to identify with active desire, the female spectator must assume an (uncomfortably) masculine position:

> the female spectator's phantasy of masculinisation is always to some extent at cross purposes with itself, restless in its transvestite clothes.[17]

OPPRESSIVE DICHOTOMIES

Psychoanalytic accounts which theorize identification and object choice within a framework of linked binary oppositions (masculinity/femininity: activity/passivity) necessarily masculinize female homosexuality. Mary Ann Doane's reading of the first scene in the film *Caught* demonstrates the limitations of this psychoanalytic binarism perfectly.

> The woman's sexuality, as spectator, must undergo a constant pro-cess of transformation. She must look, as if she were a man with the phallic power of the gaze, at a woman who would attract that gaze, in order to be that woman. . . . The convolutions involved here are analogous to those described by Julia Kristeva as 'the double or triple twists of what we commonly call female homosexuality': 'I am look-

248

ing, as a man would, for a woman'; or else, 'I submit myself, as if I were a man who thought he was a woman, to a woman who thinks she is a man.'[18]

Convolutions indeed. This insistence upon a gendered dualism of sexual desire maps homosexuality on to an assumed antithesis of masculinity and femininity. Such an assumption precludes a description of homosexual positionality without resorting to the manoeuvres cited by Doane. In arguing for a more complex model of cinematic spectatorship, I am suggesting that we need to separate gender identification from sexuality, too often conflated in the name of sexual difference.

In films where the woman is represented as sexual spectacle for the masculine gaze of the diegetic and the cinematic spectator, an identification with a masculine heterosexual desire is invited. The spectator's response can vary across a wide spectrum between outright acceptance and refusal. It has proved crucial for feminist film theorists to explore these variations. How might a woman's look at another woman, both within the diegesis and between spectator and character, compare with that of the male spectator?

This article considers the pleasures of two narrative films which develop around one woman's obsession with another woman, *All About Eve* (directed by Joseph Mankiewicz, 1950) and *Desperately Seeking Susan* (directed by Susan Seidelman, 1984). I shall argue that these films offer particular pleasures to the women in the audience which cannot simply be reduced to a masculine heterosexual equivalent. In so doing I am not claiming these films as 'lesbian films',[19] but rather using them to examine certain possibilities of pleasure.

I want to explore the representation of forms of desire and identification in these films in order to consider their implications for the pleasures of female spectatorship. My focus is on the relations between women on the screen, and between these representations and the women in the audience. Interestingly, the fascinations which structure both narratives are precisely about difference – forms of otherness between women characters which are not merely reducible to sexual difference, so often seen as the sole producer of desire itself.

THE INSCRIPTION OF ACTIVE FEMININE DESIRE

In *Alice Doesn't*, Teresa de Lauretis explores the function of the classic masculine Oedipal trajectory in dominant narrative. The subjects which motivate the narrative along the logic of the 'Oedipus', she argues, are necessarily masculine.

However varied the conditions of the presence of the narrative form in fictional genres, rituals or social discourses, its movement seems to be that of a passage, a transformation predicated on the figure of the

hero, a mythical subject . . . the *single* figure of the hero who crosses
the boundary and penetrates the other space. In so doing, the hero,
the mythical subject, is constructed as a human being and as male; he
is the active principle of culture, the establisher of distinction, the
creator of differences. Female is what is not susceptible to transformation, to life or death.[20]

De Lauretis then proceeds to outline the significance of this division
between masculine and feminine within the textual narrative in terms of
spectatorship.

Therefore, to say that narrative is the production of Oedipus is to say
that each reader – male or female – is constrained and defined within
the two positions of a sexual difference thus conceived: male-hero-
human, on the side of the subject; the female-obstacle-boundary-
space, on the other.[21]

As de Lauretis herself acknowledges later in the chapter, this analysis
leaves little space for either the question of the feminine subject in the
narrative, or the pleasures of desire and identification of the women in the
audience. In order to explore these questions more concretely, I want to
discuss two texts – one a Hollywood production of 1950, the other a recent
US 'independent' – whose central narrative concern is that of female
desire. Both *All About Eve* and *Desperately Seeking Susan* have female
protagonists whose desire and identifications move the narratives forward.
In de Lauretis's terms, these texts construct not only a feminine object of
desire in the narrative, but also a feminine subject of that desire.

All About Eve is particularly well suited to an analysis of these questions, as
it is precisely about the pleasures and dangers of spectatorship for women.
One of its central themes is the construction and reproduction of feminine
identities, and the activity of looking is highlighted as an important part of
these processes. The narrative concerns two women, a Broadway star and her
most adoring spectator, Eve. In its course, we witness the transformation of
Eve Butler (Anne Baxter) from spectator to star herself. The pleasures of
spectatorship are emphasized by Eve's loyal attendance at every one of
Margot Channing's (Bette Davis's) performances. Its dangers are also made
explicit as an intense rivalry develops between them. Eve emerges as a greedy
and ambitious competitor, and Margot steps down from stardom into marriage, finally enabling her protégée to replace her as 'actress of the year' in a
part originally written for Margot.

Eve's journey to stardom could be seen as the feminine equivalent to the
masculine Oedipal trajectory described by de Lauretis above. Freud's later
descriptions of the feminine Oedipal journey[22] contradict his previous
symmetrical model wherein the girl's first love object is her father, as the
boy's is his mother. In his later arguments Freud also posited the mother as

the girl's first love object. Her path to heterosexuality is therefore difficult and complex, since it requires her not only to relinquish her first object, like the boy, but to transform both its gender (female to male) and the aim (active to passive) directed at it. Up to this point, active desire towards another woman is an experience of all women, and its re-enactment in *All About Eve* may constitute one of the pleasures of spectatorship for the female viewer.

Eve is constantly referred to as innocent and childlike in the first half of the film and her transformation involves a process of maturation, of becoming a more confident adult. First she is passionately attached to Margot, but then she shifts her affection to Margot's lover Bill, attempting unsuccessfully to seduce him. Twice in the film she is shown interrupting their intimacy: during their farewell at the airport and then during their fierce argument about Margot's jealousy, shortly before Bill's welcome-home party. Eve's third object of desire, whom she actively pursues, is the married playwright, Lloyd Richards, husband to Margot's best friend. In both cases the stability of the older heterosexual couples, Margot and Bill, Karen and Lloyd, are threatened by the presence of the younger woman who completes the Oedipal triangle. Eve is finally punished for her desires by the patriarchal power of the aptly named Addison de Wit, who proves to be one step ahead of her manipulations.

The binary opposition between masculinity and femininity offers a limited framework for the discussion of Eve's fascination with Margot, which is articulated actively through an interplay of desire and identification during the film. In many ways, Margot is Eve's idealized object of desire. She follows Margot from city to city, never missing any of her performances. Her devotion to her favourite Broadway star is stressed at the very start of the film.

Karen   But there are hundreds of plays on Broadway
             . . .

Eve   Not with Margot Channing in them!

Margot is moved by Eve's representation of her 'tragic' past, and flattered by her adoration, so she decides to 'adopt' her.

Margot (voiceover)   We moved Eve's few pitiful possessions into my
                     apartment . . . Eve became my sister, mother,
                     lawyer, friend, psychiatrist and cop. The honey-
                     moon was on!

Eve acts upon her desire to become more like her ideal. She begins to wear Margot's cast-off clothes, appearing in Margot's bedroom one morning in her old black suit. Birdie, Margot's personal assistant, responds suspiciously to Eve's behaviour.

Margot   She thinks only of me.

Birdie	She thinks only *about* you – like she's studying you – like you was a book, or a play, or a set of blueprints – how you walk, talk, eat, think, sleep.
Margot	I'm sure that's very flattering, Birdie, and I'm sure there's nothing wrong with it.

The construction of Bette Davis as the desirable feminine ideal in this narrative has a double significance here. As well as being a 'great star' for Eve, she is clearly the same for the cinema audience. The film offers the fictional fulfilment of the spectator's dreams as well as Eve's, to be a star like Bette Davis, like Margot. Thus the identifications and desires of Eve, to some extent, narrativize a traditional pleasure of female spectatorship.

Margot is not only a star, she is also an extremely powerful woman who intimidates most of the male characters in the film. Her quick wit and disdain for conventional politeness, together with her flare for drama offstage as much as on, make her an attractive figure for Eve, an 'idealistic dreamy-eyed kid', as Bill describes her. It is this *difference* between the two women which motivates Eve, but which Eve also threatens. In trying to 'become as much like her ideal as possible', Eve almost replaces Margot in both her public and her private lives. She places a call to Bill on Margot's behalf, and captures his attention when he is on his way upstairs to see Margot before his coming-home party. Margot begins to feel dispensable.

Margot	I could die right now and nobody would be confused. My inventory is all in shape and the merchandise all put away.

Yet even dressed in Margot's costume, having taken her role in the evening's performance, Eve cannot supplant her in the eyes of Bill, who rejects her attempt at seduction. The difference between the two women is repeatedly stressed and complete identification proves impossible.

All About Eve offers some unusual pleasures for a Hollywood film, since the active desire of a female character is articulated through looking at the female star. It is by watching Margot perform on the stage that Eve becomes intoxicated with her idol. The significance of active looking in the articulation of feminine desire is foregrounded at various points in the narrative. In one scene, we see Eve's devoted spectatorship in progress during one of Margot's performances. Eve watches Margot from the wings of the stage, and Margot bows to the applause of her audience. In the next scene the roles are reversed, and Margot discovers Eve on the empty stage bowing to an imaginary audience. Eve is holding up Margot's costume to sample the pleasures of stardom for herself. This process is then echoed in the closing scene of the film with Eve, now a Broadway star herself, and the newly introduced Phoebe, an adoring schoolgirl fan. The final shot shows Phoebe, having covertly donned Eve's bejewelled evening cloak, holding Eve's award and gazing at her reflection in the mirror. The reflected image, infinitely multiplied in the triptych of the glass, creates a spectacle of stardom that is the film's final shot, suggesting a perpetual regeneration of intra-feminine fascinations through the pleasure of looking.

THE DESIRE TO BE DESPERATE

Like *All About Eve*, *Desperately Seeking Susan* concerns a woman's obsession with another woman. But instead of being punished for acting upon her desires, like Eve, Roberta (Rosanna Arquette) acts upon her desires, if in a rather more haphazard way, and eventually her initiatives are rewarded with the realization of her desires. Despite her classic feminine behaviour, forgetful, clumsy, unpunctual and indecisive, she succeeds in her quest to find Susan (Madonna).

Even at the very beginning of the film, when suburban housewife Roberta is represented at her most dependent and childlike, her actions propel the narrative movement. Having developed her own fantasy narrative about Susan by reading the personal advertisements, Roberta acts upon her desire to be 'desperate' and becomes entangled in Susan's life. She anonymously attends the romantic reunion of Susan and Jim, and then pursues Susan through the streets of Manhattan. When she loses sight of her quarry in a second-hand shop, she purchases the jacket which Susan has just exchanged. The key found in its pocket provides an excuse for direct contact, and Roberta uses the personals to initiate another meeting.

Not only is the narrative propelled structurally by Roberta's desire, but almost all the spectator sees of Susan at the beginning of the film is revealed through Roberta's fantasy. The narrativization of her desires positions her as the central figure for spectator identification: through her desire we seek, and see, Susan. Thus, in the opening scenes, Susan is introduced by name when Roberta reads the personals aloud from under the dryer in the beauty salon. Immediately following Roberta's declaration 'I wish I was desperate', there is a cut to the first shot of Susan.

The cuts from the Glasses' party to Susan's arrival in New York City work to the same effect. Repelled by her husband's TV commercial for his bathroom wares, Roberta leaves her guests and moves towards the window, as the ad's voiceover promises 'At Gary's Oasis, all your fantasies can come true.' Confronted with her own image in the reflection, she pushes it away by opening the window and looking out longingly on to Manhattan's skyline. The ensuing series of cuts between Roberta and the bridge across the river to the city link her desiring gaze to Susan's arrival there via the same bridge.

At certain points within *Desperately Seeking Susan*, Roberta explicitly becomes the bearer of the look. The best illustration of this transgression of traditional gender positionalities occurs in the scene in which she first catches sight of Susan. The shot sequence begins with Jim seeing Susan and is immediately followed with Roberta seeing her. It is, however, Roberta's point of view which is offered for the spectator's identification. Her look is specified by the use of the pay-slot telescope through which Roberta, and the spectator, see Susan.

In accordance with classic narrative cinema, the object of fascination in *Desperately Seeking Susan* is a woman – typically, a woman coded as a sexual spectacle. As a star Madonna's image is saturated in sexuality. In many ways she represents the 1980s 'assertive style' of heterosexual spectacle, inviting masculine consumption. This is certainly emphasized by shots of Susan which reference classic pornographic poses and camera angles; for example, the shot of Susan lying on Roberta's bed reading her diary, which shows Susan lying on her back, wearing only a vest and a pair of shorts over her suspenders and lacy tights. (Although one could argue that the very next shot, from Susan's point of view, showing Gary upside down, subverts the conventional pornographic codes.) My aim is not to deny these meanings in *Desperately Seeking Susan* in order to claim it as a 'progressive text', but to point to cinematic pleasures which may be available to the spectator *in addition* to those previously analysed by feminist film theory. Indeed, I believe such a project can only attempt to work within the highly contradictory constructions of femininity in mainstream films.

Susan is represented as puzzling and enigmatic to the protagonist, and to the spectator. The desire propelling the narrative is partly a desire to become more like her, but also a desire to know her, and to solve the riddle of her femininity. The protagonist begins to fulfil this desire by following the stranger, gathering clues about her identity and her life, such as her jacket, which, in turn, produces three other clues, a key, a photograph and a telephone number. The construction of her femininity as a riddle is emphasized by the series of intrigues and misunderstandings surrounding Susan's identity. The film partly relies on typical devices drawn from the mystery genre in constructing the protagonist's, and thus the spectator's, knowledge of Susan through a series of clues and coincidences. Thus, in some ways, Susan is positioned as the classic feminine enigma; she is, however, investigated by another woman.

One line of analysis might simply see Roberta as taking up the position of the masculine protagonist in expressing a desire to be 'desperate', which, after all, can be seen as identifying with Jim's position in relation to Susan, that of active, desiring masculinity. Further legitimation for this reading could be seen in Jim's response to Roberta's advertisement to Susan in the personals. He automatically assumes it has been placed there by another man, perhaps a rival. How can we understand the construction of the female protagonist as the agent and articulator of desire for another woman in the narrative within existing psychoanalytic theories of sexual

difference? The limitations of a dichotomy which offers only two significant categories for understanding the complex interplay of gender, sexual
aim and object choice is clearly demonstrated here.

DIFFERENCE AND DESIRE BETWEEN WOMEN

The difference which produces the narrative desire in *Desperately Seeking
Susan* is not sexual difference, but the difference between two women in
the film. It is the difference between suburban marriage and street credibility. Two sequences contrast the characters, using smoking as a signifier of
difference. The first occurs in Battery Park, where Roberta behaves awk-
wardly in the unfamiliar territory of public space. She is shown sitting on a
park bench, knees tightly clenched, looking around nervously for Susan.
Jim asks her for a light, to which she timidly replies that she does not
smoke. The ensuing cut shows Susan, signalled by Jim's shout of recognition. Susan is sitting on the boat rail, striking a match on the bottom of
her raised boot to light a cigarette.

Smoking is used again to emphasize difference in a subsequent sequence. This time, Roberta, having by now lost her memory and believing
she may be Susan, lights a cigarette from Susan's box. Predictably, she
chokes on the smoke, with the unfamiliarity of an adolescent novice. The
next cut shows us Susan, in prison for attempting to skip her cab fare,
taking a light from the prison matron and blowing the smoke defiantly
straight back into her face. The contrast in their smoking ability is only one
signifier of the characters' very different femininities. Roberta is represented as young, inexperienced and asexual, while Susan's behaviour
and appearance are coded as sexually confident and provocative. Rhyming
sequences are used to emphasize their differences even after Roberta has
taken on her new identity as Susan. She ends up in the same prison cell, but
her childlike acquiescence to authority contrasts with Susan's defiance of
the law.

Susan transgresses conventional forms of feminine behaviour by appropriating public space for herself. She turns the public lavatory into her own
private bathroom, drying her armpits with the hand blower, and changing
her clothes in front of the mirror above the washbasins as if in her own
bedroom. In the streets, Susan challenges the patronizing offer of a free
newspaper from a passer-by by, dropping the whole pile at his feet and
taking only the top copy for herself. In contrast to Susan's supreme public
confidence, Roberta is only capable in her own middle-class privacy.
Arriving home after her day of city adventures, she manages to synchro-
nize with a televised cooking show, catching up on its dinner preparations
with confident dexterity in her familiar domestic environment.

As soon as Roberta becomes entangled in Susan's world, her respectable
sexuality is thrown into question. First she is assumed to be having an

affair, then she is arrested for suspected prostitution, and finally Gary asks her if she is a lesbian. When the two photographs of Roberta, one as a bride and one as a suspected prostitute, are laid down side by side at the police station, her apparent transformation from virgin to whore shocks her husband. The ironic effect of these largely misplaced accusations about Roberta's sexuality works partly in relation to Susan, who is represented as the epitome of opposition to acceptable bourgeois feminine sexuality. She avoids commitment, dependency or permanence in her relationships with men, and happily takes their money, while maintaining an intimate friendship with the woman who works at the Magic Box.

Roberta's desire is finally rewarded when she meets Susan in an almost farcical chase scene at that club during the chaotic film finale. Gary finds Roberta, Des finds 'Susan' (Roberta), Jim finds Susan, the villain finds the jewels (the earrings which Susan innocently pocketed earlier in the film), Susan and Roberta catch the villain, and Susan and Roberta find each other. . . . The last shot of the film is a front-page photograph of the two women hand in hand, triumphantly waving their reward cheque in return for the recovery of the priceless Nefertiti earrings. In the end, both women find what they were searching for throughout the narrative: Roberta has found Susan, and Susan has found enough money to finance many future escapades.

Roberta's desire to become more like her ideal – a more pleasingly co-ordinated, complete and attractive feminine image[23] – is offered temporary narrative fulfilment. However, the pleasures of this feminine desire cannot be collapsed into simple identification, since difference and otherness are continuously played upon, even when Roberta 'becomes' her idealized object. Both *Desperately Seeking Susan* and *All About Eve* tempt the woman spectator with the fictional fulfilment of becoming an ideal feminine other, while denying complete transformation by insisting upon differences between women. The rigid distinction between *either* desire *or* identification, so characteristic of psychoanalytic film theory, fails to address the construction of desires which involve a specific interplay of both processes.

NOTES

I would like to thank Sarah Franklin, Richard Dyer, Alison Light, Chris Healey and the Women Thesis Writers Group in Birmingham for their inspiration, support and helpful comments during the writing of this article. It was first published in *Screen*, Winter 1987, vol. 28, no. 1, pp. 48–61.

1 Laura Mulvey, 'Visual Pleasure and Narrative Cinema', chapter 1, pp. 22–34 in this volume; originally published in *Screen*, Autumn 1975, vol. 16, no. 3, pp. 6–18.
2 ibid., p. 28.
3 ibid., p. 26.

4 ibid.
5 There have been several attempts to fill this theoretical gap and provide analyses of masculinity as sexual spectacle: see Richard Dyer, 'Don't Look Now – The Male Pin-Up', chapter 12, pp. 265–76 in this volume; originally published in *Screen*, September–October 1982; vol. 23, nos. 3–4; Steve Neale, 'Masculinity as Spectacle', chapter 13, pp. 279–90 in this volume; originally published in *Screen*, Winter 1983, vol. 24, no. 6; and Andy Medhurst, 'Can Chaps Be Pin-Ups?' *Ten*, 1985, vol. 8, no. 17.
6 David Rodowick, 'The Difficulty of Difference', *Wide Angle*, 1982, vol. 5, no. 1, p. 8.
7 Mary Ann Doane, 'Film and the Masquerade: Theorizing the Female Spectator', chapter 10 pp. 227–43 in this volume; first published in *Screen*, September–October 1982, vol. 23, nos. 3–4, pp. 74–87. Page numbers cited in the following notes refer to this volume.
8 Constance Penley, 'Feminism, Film Theory and the Bachelor Machines', *m/f*, 1985, no. 10, pp. 39–56.
9 *Enunciator*: 'the term . . . marks both the person who possesses the right to speak within the film, and the source (instance) towards which the series of representations is logically channelled back' (Raymond Bellour, 'Hitchcock the Enunciator', *Camera Obscura*, 1977, no. 2, p. 94).
10 Raymond Bellour, 'Psychosis, Neurosis, Perversion', *Camera Obscura*, 1979, nos. 3–4, p. 97.
11 Janet Bergstrom, 'Enunciation and Sexual Difference', *Camera Obscura*, 1979, nos. 3–4, p. 57. See also Janet Bergstrom, 'Alternation, Segmentation, Hypnosis: An Interview with Raymond Bellour', *Camera Obscura*, 1979, nos. 3–4.
12 Doane, op. cit., p. 231.
13 ibid., p. 233.
14 Mary Ann Doane, Patricia Mellencamp and Linda Williams, 'Feminist Film Criticism: An Introduction', in Mary Ann Doane, Patricia Mellencamp and Linda Williams (eds), *Re-Vision: Essays in Feminist Film Criticism*, Los Angeles, American Film Institute, 1984, p. 9.
15 ibid., p. 14.
16 Laura Mulvey, 'Afterthoughts on "Visual Pleasure and Narrative Cinema" . . . Inspired by *Duel in the Sun*', *Framework*, 1981, nos. 15–17, pp. 12–15.
17 ibid., p. 15.
18 Mary Ann Doane citing Julia Kristeva, *About Chinese Women*, in '*Caught* and *Rebecca*: The Inscription of Femininity as Absence', *Enclitic*, Fall 1981/Spring 1982, vol. 5, no. 2/vol. 6, no. 1, p. 77.
19 For a discussion of films which might be included under this category, see Caroline Sheldon, 'Lesbians and Film: Some Thoughts', in Richard Dyer (ed.), *Gays and Film*, New York, Zoetrope, revised edn 1984.
20 Teresa de Lauretis, *Alice Doesn't: Feminism, Semiotics and the Cinema*, London, Macmillan, 1984, pp. 113, 119.
21 ibid., p. 121.
22 See, for example, Sigmund Freud, 'Some Psychical Consequences of the Anatomical Distinction Between the Sexes' (1925), in *On Sexuality*, Pelican Freud Library, vol. VII, Harmondsworth, Penguin Books, 1977, pp. 331–43.
23 See Jacques Lacan, 'The Mirror Stage as Formative of the Function of the I as Revealed in Psychoanalytic Experience', *Ecrits*, trans. Alan Sheridan, London, Tavistock, 1977, pp. 1–7.

Part IV
IMAGES OF MEN

INTRODUCTION

What is 'masculinity?' The title of a recent book on the subject, *The Darker Continent*,[1] suggests it may pose even more mysteries than the enigma of femininity immortalized by Freud as 'the dark continent'. Discussions of masculinity, which had begun to appear by the early 1980s, were written largely in reponse to issues raised by Laura Mulvey's 'Visual Pleasure' article. Committed to exploring these issues, *Screen* provided a forum for debates about masculinity: two of these pioneering articles appear in this part. A number of important issues were central to these early discussions: the conditions under which the male body could be eroticized and presented as an object of the voyeuristic female gaze; the male body as erotic object of another male gaze; male masochism; the male body as signifier of the phallus; the relationship between the representation of images of men and discourses of sexism and racism. The following two chapters explore all of these issues.

One of the most interesting and important debates which has arisen from a concern with masculinity is that of homosexual desire. Most articles which explore questions of identification and spectatorship for men are, almost inevitably, faced with the relationship of the male spectator to his cinematic counterpart. If the dominant look in mainstream cinema is 'male' then the way in which this look is positioned in relation to the male face and form on the screen should be considered in all discussions of the male spectatorial relations. Whereas *Screen* published articles which explored male homosexual desire, there was little discussion from women on lesbian desire in relation to the female spectator. Until recently very few writers have addressed this neglected but important area.

In recent years the debate involving masculinity has taken a new direction. Initially male theorists drew on feminist film theory to explore the representation of masculinity in the cinema. Like feminist writers, male critics also wished to challenge existing preconceptions about the nature of gender and its representation in cinema. They sought to question the assumption that images of men in film were unproblematic and simply 'reflected' the way masculinity was presented in the real world. They were

261

also concerned about the relationship between representation and the workings of patriarchal ideology. Recently, a number of seminars and papers have explored the whole question of 'men in feminism'.[2] Can men critique masculinity without drawing on feminist theories of gender and representation? To what extent are male theorists prepared to use feminist theory to challenge the very nature of their theoretical approaches? Given that feminist theory is subversive of phallocentric theory, this is an important question. The two articles reprinted below do not anticipate these debates; nevertheless they provide us with an understanding of the issues central to a critique of the representation of men in the cinema.

Richard Dyer's 'Don't Look Now: The Male Pin-up' examines the conditions under which the eroticization of the male body becomes acceptable, as well as the conditions under which women are permitted to look. Dyer is particularly interested in the way in which codes of looking are used to reaffirm gender roles, particularly those which reinforce male power. Drawing on Nancy Henley's *Body Politics*, specifically on her research on eye contact and its relation to power, Dyer makes a series of interesting observations about the male pin-up of women's magazines. He concludes that the practice of putting men on display for the female gaze tends to violate conventional codes of looking which have been built up around the socially sanctioned practice whereby men look and women are looked at. Dyer isolates three different approaches which are designed to deal with this violation: these have resulted in what Dyer terms the 'instabilities' of the male pin-up.

The first instability arises from the model's attempt to deny he is the object of a female gaze. Whereas the female pin-up deals with the controlling male gaze by averting her eyes in order to suggest modesty, the male looks either up or away. The look off or away suggests that something important has captured his attention, while the look up implies he is thinking of higher, spiritual matters. Whereas the woman's averted look always acknowledges the gaze of the viewer, his look (always elsewhere) ignores the viewer altogether. When he does return the look, Dyer observes, it is usually a penetrating/castrating look. The second instability arises from the violation of the active/passive structure of looking which is based on notions of proper gender conduct. To overcome the problem of being looked at, that is, placed in a passive position (Dyer disagrees that this position is passive), the male model is usually represented either as engaged in some form of physical activity or holding his body taut, tightening his muscles, so as to suggest a readiness for action. The third and most marked instability of the male pin-up arises from the impossible male desire of wanting to be the phallus. Dyer points out it is no accident that the penis has been chosen as the model for the symbol of the phallus – only men possess this organ. The problem is that the penis, particularly the flaccid penis of the male nude, can never match the mystique and power implied by the phallus. 'Hence the excessive, even hysterical, quality of so much male imagery. The clenched fists, the bulging muscles, the hardened jaws . . .'.

Dyer's analysis of the male pin-up raises important questions for those interested in the nature of the female gaze. Does the female gaze, like the male gaze, contain a controlling, even sadistic, component? How do the instabilities produced in the representation of the male influence the female gaze? Do these instabilities undermine or intensify the voyeuristic potential of the female gaze? Or are other structures at work? For instance, when the woman looks at the 'hysterical quality' of those male bodies which attempt to represent the phallus, is she aware of the contradictions involved? Is she amused? Dyer states that male pin-ups do not 'work' for women, but he does not really explore this area.

Steve Neale's 'Masculinity as Spectacle' explores the homoerotic component of the male gaze. He is interested in the implications of Laura Mulvey's 'Visual Pleasure' article for questions of masculinity. Neale agrees with Mulvey that the dominant look in mainstream cinema is male; he examines three central structures discussed by Mulvey in her analysis of visual representation: identification, and voyeuristic and fetishistic modes of looking. Neale argues that all three forms, associated with the representation of male images, are not only marked by eroticism but the cinematic processes at work also seek to deny this play of eroticism. Denial takes two main forms. In scenes of voyeuristic looking in which the male body is put on display, as in the action scenes of the western or war film, the look is ultimately deflected from its object, the male body. While such scenes might initially appear to encourage objectification, the spectator's voyeuristic gaze is displaced from an appreciation of the male face and figure to an appreciation of the ritual elements of the scene itself. Narrative flow is interrupted as the spectacle takes over. In scenes of fetishistic looking, as in a shoot-out between two men, the male body is often fetishized through editing and close-up shots, but the viewer is denied a look of direct access; instead the spectator's look is mediated by the looks of other characters, looks characterized not by desire but by fear and aggression.

Neale states that mainstream cinema cannot afford to acknowledge openly the presence of an erotic relationship between the male spectator and the image of his gender counterpart, as this would open up threatening questions about the nature of male desire. It would also raise questions about the nature of the female gaze, which may also explain the absence of an open eroticization of men; but it is not Neale's intention to explore this area. Neale concludes that mainstream cinema naturalizes the representation of masculinity as if it were known and knowable, an open-and-shut case; it is only femininity which is posed as enigmatic and problematic. By presenting femininity as a mystery, attention is diverted from the problem of masculinity. Nevertheless, male homosexual desire is present in a

263

repressed form in many films – a troubling element in the cinematic representation of men. These articles by Dyer and Neale anticipated debates about masculinity which are only now being fully explored.

NOTES

1 Heather Formaini, *Men – The Darker Continent*, London, Heinemann, 1990.
2 See Antony Easthope, *What a Man's Gotta Do – The Masculine Myth in Popular Culture*, London, Paladin, 1986; Andy Metcalf and Martin Humphries (eds), *The Sexuality of Men*, London, Pluto Press, 1985; Paul Patton and Ross Poole (eds), *War/Masculinity*, Sydney, Intervention Publications, 1985; Alice Jardine and Paul Smith, *Men in Feminism*, New York, Methuen, 1987; Gaylyn Studlar, 'Masochism and the Perverse Pleasures of the Cinema', in Bill Nichols (ed.), *Movies and Methods*, vol. II, Berkeley and Los Angeles, University of California Press, 1985; *Camera Obscura*, Special Issue on 'Male Trouble', May 1988, no. 17.

12

DON'T LOOK NOW: THE MALE PIN-UP

Richard Dyer

'One of the things I really envy about men', a friend once said to me, 'is the right to look'. She went on to point out how in public places, on the street, at meetings, men could look freely at women, but that women could only look back surreptitiously, against the grain of their upbringing. It is a point that has been reiterated in many of the personal-political accounts that have emerged from the consciousness-raising of the Women's Movement. And it is a fact that we see endlessly reworked in movies and on television. We have all seen, countless times, that scene of Young Love, where, in the canteen, at school, in church, the Boy and the Girl first see each other. The precise way it is done is very revealing. We have a close-up of him looking off camera, followed by one of her looking downwards (in a pose that has, from time immemorial, suggested maidenliness). Quite often, we move back and forth between these two close-ups, so that it is very definitely established that he looks at her and she is looked at. Then, she may look up and off camera, and we may go back briefly to the boy still looking – but it is only briefly, for no sooner is it established that she sees him than we must be assured that she at once averts her eyes. She has seen him, but she doesn't look at him as he looks at her – having seen him, she quickly resumes being the one who is looked at.

So utterly routine is this kind of scene that we probably don't remark on it, yet it encapsulates, and effectively reinforces, one of the fundamental ways by which power relations between the sexes are maintained. In her book *Body Politics*, Nancy M. Henley examines the very many different non-verbal ways that gender roles and male power are constantly being rebuilt and reaffirmed.[1] She does for gesture, body posture, facial expressions and so on what, most recently, Dale Spender's *Man Made Language*[2] does for verbal communication, and shows how non-verbal communication is both a register of male–female relations and one of the means by which those relations are kept the way they are. Particularly relevant here is her discussion of eye contact.

Henley argues that it is not so much a question of whether women or men look at each other, but how they do. In fact, her evidence suggests

Figure 12:1 Montgomery Clift strikes an uplifting pose for a Hollywood publicity photo.

that in face-to-face interactions, women look at men more than men do at women – but then this is because women listen more to men, pay more attention to them. In other words, women do not so much look at men as watch them. On the other hand, in crowd situations, men look more at women – men stare at women, whereas women avert their eyes. In both cases, this (re-)establishes male dominance. In the first case (one-to-one), 'superior position . . . is communicated by visually ignoring the other person – *not* looking while listening, but looking into space as if the other isn't there'; whereas in the second case (crowds), 'staring is used to *assert* dominance – to establish, to maintain, and to regain it'.[3]

Images of men aimed at women – whether star portraits, pin-ups or drawings and paintings of men – are in a particularly interesting relation to these eye contact patterns. A certain instability is produced – the first of several we encounter when looking at images of men that are offered as sexual spectacle. On the one hand, this is a visual medium, these men are there to be looked at by women. On the other hand, this does violence to the codes of who looks and who is looked at (and how), and some attempt is instinctively made to counteract this violation. Much of this centres on the model or star's own 'look' – where and how he is looking in relation to the woman looking at him, in the audience or as she leafs through the fan or women's magazine (not only *Playgirl*, which has male nudes as *Playboy* has female ones, but also teenage magazines like *Oh Boy!* and *My Guy*, with their half-dressed pin-ups, and such features as 'Your Daily Male' in the *Sun* and 'She-Male' in *She*).

To repeat, it is not a question of whether or not the model looks at his spectator(s), but how he does or does not. In the case of not looking, where the female model typically averts her eyes, expressing modesty, patience and a lack of interest in anything else, the male model looks either off or up. In the case of the former, his look suggests an interest in something else that the viewer cannot see – it certainly doesn't suggest any interest in the viewer. Indeed, it barely acknowledges the viewer, whereas the woman's averted eyes do just that – they are averted from the viewer. In the cases where the model is looking up, this always suggests a spirituality: he might be there for his face and body to be gazed at, but his mind is on higher things, and it is this upward striving that is most supposed to please. This pose encapsulates the kind of dualism that Paul Hoch analyses in his study of masculinity, *White Hero Black Beast* – higher is better than lower, the head above is better than the genitals below.[4] At the same time, the sense of straining and striving upwards does also suggest analogies with the definition of the very sexuality supposedly relegated to an inferior place – straining and striving are the terms most often used to describe male sexuality in this society.

It may be, as is often said, that male pin-ups more often than not do not look at the viewer, but it is by no means the case that they never do. When

Figure 12:2 Arnold Schwarzenegger demonstrates the merits of the master race.

they do, what is crucial is the kind of look it is, something very often determined by the set of the mouth that accompanies it. When the female pin-up returns the viewer's gaze, it is usually some kind of smile, inviting. The male pin-up, even at his most benign, still stares at the viewer. Even Paul Newman's frank face-on to the camera or the *Oh Boy!* coverboy's yearning gaze at us still seems to reach beyond the boundary marked, when the photo was taken, by the camera, as if he wants to reach beyond and through and establish himself. The female model's gaze stops at that boundary, the male's looks right through it.

Freud noticed a similar sort of look on Michelangelo's statue of Moses – though Moses is not looking at us but at the Jews' worship of the Golden Calf. Since Freud, it is common to describe such a look as 'castrating' or 'penetrating' – yet to use such words to describe the look of a man at a woman is revealing in ways that Freudians do not always intend. What, after all, have women to fear from the threat of castration? And why, come to that, should the possibility of penetration be *necessarily* fearful to women? It is clear that castration can only be a threat to men, and more probable that it is the taboo of male anal eroticism that causes masculine-defined men to construct penetration as frightening and the concept of male (hetero)sexuality as 'taking' a woman that constructs penetration as an act of violence. In looking at and dealing with these castrating/ penetrating looks, women are caught up in a system that does not so much address them as work out aspects of the construction of male sexuality in men's heads.

If the first instability of the male pin-up is the contradiction between the fact of being looked at and the attempt of the model's look to deny it, the second is the apparent address to women's sexuality and the actual working out of male sexuality (and this may be one of the reasons why male pin-ups notoriously don't 'work' for women). What is at stake is not just male and female sexuality, but male and female power. The maintenance of power underpins further instabilities in the image of men as sexual spectacle, in terms of the active/passive nexus of looking, the emphasis on muscularity and the symbolic association of male power and the phallus.

The idea of looking (staring) as power and being looked at as powerlessness overlaps with ideas of activity/passivity. Thus to look is thought of as active; whereas to be looked at is passive. In reality, this is not true. The model prepares her- or himself to be looked at, the artist or photographer constructs the image to be looked at; and, on the other hand, the image that the viewer looks at is not summoned up by his or her act of looking but in collaboration with those who have put the image there. Most of us probably experience looking and being looked at, in life as in art, somewhere among these shifting relations of activity and passivity. Yet it remains the case that images of men must disavow this element of passivity if they are to be kept in line with dominant ideas of masculinity-as-activity.

269

For this reason images of men are often images of men doing something. When, before the full invention of cinematography, Eadweard Muybridge took an enormous series of photographic sequences, each one in the sequence taken a few seconds after the other, one of his intentions was to study the nature of movement. Muybridge photographed sequences of naked male and female figures. In a study of these sequences, Linda Williams shows how, even in so 'scientific' an undertaking and at such a comparatively 'primitive' stage in the development of photography, Muybridge established a difference between the female subjects, who are just there to be looked at, and the male subjects, who are doing something (carrying a boulder, sawing wood, playing baseball) which we can look in on.[5] This distinction is maintained in the history of the pin-up, where time and again the image of the man is one caught in the middle of an action, or associated, through images in the pictures, with activity.

Even when not actually caught in an act, the male image still promises activity by the way the body is posed. Even in an apparently relaxed, supine pose, the model tightens and tautens his body so that the muscles are emphasized, hence drawing attention to the body's potential for action. More often, the male pin-up is not supine anyhow, but standing taut ready for action.

Figure 12:3 Ready for action: a supine model tautens his muscles for *Playgirl*.

There is an interesting divergence here in ethnic and class terms, a good example of the way that images of male power are always and necessarily

270

inflected with other aspects of power in society. In relation to ethnicity, it is generally the case that the activity shown or implied in images of white men is clearly related to the split in western society between leisure and work activity, whereas black men, even though they are in fact American or European, are given a physicality that is inextricably linked to notions of 'the jungle', and hence 'savagery'. This is done either by a natural setting, in which a generalized physical exertion is conflated with the energies of nature (and, doubtless, the beat of drums), or else, more recently, in the striking use of 'black power' symbolism. This might seem like an acknowledgement of ethnic politics, and perhaps for some viewers it is, but the way the media constructed black power in fact tended to reproduce the idea of a savage energy rather than a political movement – hence the stress on back-to-Africa (in the white western imagination still an amorphous jungle), or the 'senseless' violence erupting from the jungle of the ghetto.

Such images also put black men 'outside of' class (though there has been the promotion of specifically middle-class black images, as with, especially, Sidney Poitier). White men are more likely to be class differentiated, but this does overlap with the work/leisure distinction. Work is in fact almost suppressed from dominant imagery in this society – it is mainly in socialist imagery that its images occur. In nineteenth-century socialist and trade union art and in Soviet socialist realism the notions of the dignity and heroism of labour are expressed through dynamically muscular male bodies. As Eric Hobsbawm has pointed out, what this tradition has done, in effect, is to secure for masculinity the definition of what is finest in the proletarian and socialist traditions – women have been marginalized to the ethereal role of 'inspiration'.[6] Moreover, it is certainly no *conscious* part of this tradition that these male bodies should be a source of erotic visual pleasure, for men and women.

Sport is the area of life that is the most common contemporary source of male imagery – not only in pin-ups of sportsmen, but in the sports activities of film stars, pop stars and so on. (*She* magazine recently ran a series of pin-ups of wrestlers.) Although certain sports have very clear class associations (the Prince of Wales plays polo, not football), there is a sense in which sport is a 'leveller'. Running, swimming, ball games are pretty well open to anyone in any class, and so imagery derived from these activities does not have immediate class associations. What all imply, however, is leisure, and the strength and vitality to use it. The celebration of the body in sport is also a celebration of the relative affluence of western society, where people have time to dedicate themselves to the development of the body for its own sake.

Whether the emphasis is on work or sport or any other activity, the body quality that is promoted is muscularity. In the copy accompanying the pin-ups in *Oh Boy!*, for instance, the female readers are called on to 'getta load of his muscles' and other such invitations. Although the hyper-developed

Figure 12:4 From savagery to the black bourgeoisie: a short Afro and modern jewellery.

Figure 12:5 The naked civil servant: a muscular motorcycle cop naturalizes sexual and state power.

muscularity of an Arnold Schwarzenegger is regarded by most people as excessive, and perhaps bordering on the fascist, it is still the case that muscularity is a key term in appraising men's bodies. This again probably comes from men themselves. Muscularity is the *sign* of power – natural, achieved, phallic.

At a minimum, developed muscles indicate a physical strength that women do not generally match (although recent developments in women's sport and physical conditioning suggest that differences between the sexes here may not be so fixed). The potential for muscularity in men is seen as a biological given, and is also the means of dominating both women and other men who are in the competition for the spoils of the earth – and women. The point is that muscles are biological, hence 'natural', and we persist in habits of thought, especially in the area of sexuality and gender, whereby what can be shown to be natural must be accepted as given and inevitable. The 'naturalness' of muscles legitimizes male power and domination.

However, developed muscularity – muscles that *show* – is not in truth natural at all, but is rather achieved. The muscle man is the end product of his own activity of muscle-building. As always, the comparison with the female body beautiful is revealing. Rationally, we know that the beauty queen has dieted, exercised, used cleansing creams, solariums and cosmetics – but none of this really shows in her appearance, and is anyway generally construed as something that has been *done to* the woman. Conversely, a man's muscles constantly bespeak this achievement of his beauty/power.

Muscles, as well as being a sign of activity and achievement, are hard. We've already seen how even not overly developed male pin-ups harden their bodies to be looked at. This hardness may then be reinforced by aspects of setting or symbolic references, or by poses that emphasize hard lines and angular shapes (not the soft roundness of the feminine aesthetic). In her book *The Nude Male*, Margaret Walters suggests this hardness is phallic, not in the direct sense of being like an erect penis but rather in being symbolic of all that the phallus represents of 'abstract paternal power'.[7] There is no doubt that the image of the phallus as power is widespread to the point of near-universality, all the way from tribal and early Greek fertility symbols to the language of pornography, where the penis is endlessly described as a weapon, a tool, a source of terrifying power.

There is a danger of casual thought here. The phallus is not just an arbitrarily chosen symbol of male power; it is crucial that the penis has provided the model for this symbol. Because only men have penises, phallic symbols, even if in some sense possessed by a woman (as may be the case with female rulers, for instance), are always symbols of ultimately male power. The woman who wields 'phallic' power does so in the interests of men.[8]

This leads to the greatest instability of all for the male image. For the fact is that the penis isn't a patch on the phallus. The penis can never live up to the mystique implied by the phallus. Hence the excessive, even hysterical quality of so much male imagery. The clenched fists, the bulging

274

Figure 12:6 The masculine mystique: Warner's hysterically phallic portrait of the young Bogie.

muscles, the hardened jaws, the proliferation of phallic symbols – they are all straining after what can hardly ever be achieved, the embodiment of the phallic mystique. This is even more the case with the male nude. The limp penis can never match up to the mystique that has kept it hidden from view for the last couple of centuries, and even the erect penis often looks

275

awkward, stuck on to the man's body as if it is not a part of him.

Like so much else about masculinity, images of men, founded on such multiple instabilities, are such a strain. Looked at but pretending not to be, still yet asserting movement, phallic but weedy – there is seldom anything easy about such imagery. And the real trap at the heart of these instabilities is that it is precisely *straining* that is held to be the great good, what makes a man a man. Whether head held high reaching up for an impossible transcendence or penis jerking up in a hopeless assertion of phallic mastery, men and women alike are asked to value the very things that make masculinity such an unsatisfactory definition of being human.

NOTES

First published in *Screen*, September–October 1982, vol. 23, nos. 3–4, pp. 61–73.

1 Nancy M. Henley, *Body Politics*, Englewood Cliffs, New Jersey, Prentice-Hall, 1977.
2 Dale Spender, *Man Made Language*, London, Routledge & Kegan Paul, 1980.
3 Henley, op. cit., p. 166.
4 Paul Hoch, *White Hero Black Beast*, London, Pluto Press, 1979.
5 Linda Williams, 'Film Body, an Implantation of Perversions', *Cinetracts*, Winter 1981, vol. 3, no. 4, pp. 19–35.
6 Eric Hobsbawm, 'Man and Woman in Socialist Iconography', *History Workshop Journal*, 1978, no. 6, pp. 121–38.
7 Margaret Walters, *The Nude Male*, London, Paddington Press, 1978.
8 See, for example, Alison Heisch, 'Queen Elizabeth I and the Persistence of Patriarchy', *Feminist Review*, 1980, no. 4, pp. 45–56.

13

MASCULINITY AS SPECTACLE

Steve Neale

Over the past ten years or so, numerous books and articles have appeared discussing the images of women produced and circulated by the cinematic institution. Motivated politically by the development of the Women's Movement, and concerned therefore with the political and ideological implications of the representations of women offered by the cinema, a number of these books and articles have taken as their basis Laura Mulvey's 'Visual Pleasure and Narrative Cinema', first published in *Screen* in 1975.[1] Mulvey's article was highly influential in its linking together of psychoanalytic perspectives on the cinema with a feminist perspective on the ways in which images of women figure within mainstream film. She sought to demonstrate the extent to which the psychic mechanisms cinema has basically involved are profoundly patriarchal, and the extent to which the images of women that mainstream film has produced lie at the heart of those mechanisms.

Inasmuch as there has been discussion of gender, sexuality, representation and the cinema over the past decade then, that discussion has tended overwhelmingly to centre on the representation of women, and to derive many of its basic tenets from Mulvey's article. Only within the Gay Movement have there appeared specific discussions of the representation of men. Most of these, as far as I am aware, have centred on the representations and stereotypes of gay men. Within both the Women's Movement and the Gay Movement there is an important sense in which the images and functions of heterosexual masculinity within mainstream cinema have been left undiscussed. Heterosexual masculinity has been identified as a structuring norm in relation to images both of women and of gay men. It has to that extent been profoundly problematized, rendered visible. But it has rarely been discussed and analysed as such. Outside these movements, it has been discussed even less. It is thus very rare to find analyses that seek to specify in detail, in relation to particular films or groups of films, how heterosexual masculinity is inscribed and the mechanisms, pressures and contradictions that inscription may involve. Aside from a number of recent pieces in *Screen*[2] and *Framework*[3] Raymond Bellour's article on *North by*

Northwest is the only example that springs readily to mind. Bellour's article follows in some detail the Oedipal trajectory of Hitchcock's film, tracing the movement of its protagonist, Roger Thornhill (Cary Grant) from a position of infantile dependence on the mother to a position of 'adult', 'male', heterosexual masculinity, sealed by his marriage to Eve Kendall (Eva Marie Saint) and by his acceptance of the role and authority of the father. However, the article is concerned as much with the general workings of a classical Hollywood film as it is with the specifics of a set of images of masculinity.[4]

Although, then, there is a real need for more analyses of individual films, I intend in this article to take another approach to some of the issues involved. Using Laura Mulvey's article as a central, structuring reference point, I want to look in particular at identification, looking and spectacle as she has discussed them and to pose some questions as to how her remarks apply directly or indirectly to images of men, on the one hand, and to the male spectator on the other. The aim is less to challenge fundamentally the theses she puts forward than to open a space within the framework of her arguments and remarks for a consideration of the representation of masculinity as it can be said to relate to the basic characteristics and conventions of the cinematic institution.

IDENTIFICATION

To start with, I want to quote from John Ellis's book *Visible Fictions*.[5] Writing very much in the light of Mulvey's article, Ellis is concerned both to draw on her arguments and to extend and qualify some of the theses she puts forward *vis-à-vis* gender and identification in the cinema. Ellis argues that identification is never simply a matter of men identifying with male figures on the screen and women identifying with female figures. Cinema draws on and involves many desires, many forms of desire. And desire itself is mobile, fluid, constantly transgressing identities, positions and roles. Identifications are multiple, fluid, at points even contradictory. Moreover, there are different forms of identification. Ellis points to two such forms, one associated with narcissism, the other with phantasies and dreams. He sums up as follows:

> Cinematic identification involves two different tendencies. First, there is that of dreaming and phantasy that involve the multiple and contradictory tendencies within the construction of the individual. Second, there is the experience of narcissistic identification with the image of a human figure perceived as other. Both these processes are invoked in the conditions of entertainment cinema. The spectator does not therefore 'identify' with the hero or heroine: an identification that would, if put in its conventional sense, involve socially constructed males identifying with male heroes, and socially con-

structed males identifying with male heroes, and socially constructed females identifying with women heroines. The situation is more complex than this, as identification involves both the recognition of self in the image on the screen, a narcissistic identification, and the identification of self with the various positions that are involved in the fictional narration: those of hero and heroine, villain, bit-part player, active and passive character. Identification is therefore multiple and fractured, a sense of seeing the constituent parts of the spectator's own psyche paraded before her or him.[6]

A series of identifications is involved, then, each shifting and mobile. Equally, though, there is constant work to channel and regulate identification in relation to sexual division, in relation to the orders of gender, sexuality and social identity and authority marking patriarchal society. Every film tends both to assume and actively to work to renew those orders, that division. Every film thus tends to specify identification in accordance with the socially defined and constructed categories of male and female.

In looking specifically at masculinity in this context, I want to examine the process of narcissistic identification in more detail. Inasmuch as films *do* involve gender identification, and inasmuch as current ideologies of masculinity involve so centrally notions and attitudes to do with aggression, power and control, it seems to me that narcissism and narcissistic identification may be especially significant.

Narcissism and narcissistic identification both involve phantasies of power, omnipotence, mastery and control. Laura Mulvey makes the link between such phantasies and patriarchal images of masculinity in the following terms:

> As the spectator identifies with the main male protagonist, he projects his look on to that of his like, his screen surrogate, so that the power of the male protagonist as he controls events coincides with the active power of the erotic look, both giving a satisfying sense of omnipotence. A male movie star's glamorous characteristics are thus not those of the erotic object of his gaze, but those of the more perfect, more complete, more powerful ideal ego conceived in the original moment of recognition in front of the mirror.[7]

I want to turn to Mulvey's remarks about the glamorous male movie star below. But first it is worth extending and illustrating her point about the male protagonist and the extent to which his image is dependent upon narcissistic phantasies, phantasies of the 'more perfect, more complete, more powerful ideal ego'.

It is easy enough to find examples of films in which these phantasies are heavily prevalent, in which the male hero is powerful and omnipotent to an extraordinary degree: the Clint Eastwood character in *A Fistful of Dollars*,

For a Few Dollars More and *The Good, the Bad and the Ugly*, the Tom Mix westerns, Charlton Heston in *El Cid*, the *Mad Max* films, the Steve Reeves epics, *Superman*, *Flash Gordon* and so on. There is generally, of course, a drama in which that power and omnipotence are tested and qualified (*Superman 2* is a particularly interesting example as are Howard Hawks's westerns and adventure films), but the Leone trilogy, for example, is marked by the extent to which the hero's powers are rendered almost godlike, hardly qualified at all. Hence, perhaps, the extent to which they are built around ritualized scenes which in many ways are devoid of genuine suspense. A film like Melville's *Le Samourai*, on the other hand, starts with the image of self-possessed, omnipotent masculinity and traces its gradual and eventual disintegration. Alain Delon plays a lone gangster, a hit-man. His own narcissism is stressed in particular through his obsessive concern with his appearance, marked notably by a repeated and ritualized gesture he makes when putting on his hat, a sweep of the hand across the rim. Delon is sent on a job, but is spotted by a black female singer in a club. There is an exchange of looks. From that point on his omnipotence, silence and inviolability are all under threat. He is shot and wounded; his room is broken into and bugged; he is nearly trapped on the Métro. Eventually he is gunned down, having returned to the club to see the singer again. The film is by no means a critique of the male image it draws upon. On the contrary, it very much identifies (and invites us to identify) with Delon. Nevertheless, the elements both of that image and of that to which the image is vulnerable are clearly laid out. It is no accident that Delon's downfall is symptomatically inaugurated in his encounter with the black woman. Difference (double difference) is the threat. An exchange of looks in which Delon's cold commanding gaze is troubled, undermined and returned is the mark of that threat.

The kind of image that Delon here embodies, and that Eastwood and the others mentioned earlier embody too, is one marked not only by emotional reticence, but also by silence, a reticence with language. Theoretically this silence, this absence of language, can further be linked to narcissism and to the construction of an ideal ego. The acquisition of language is a process profoundly challenging to the narcissism of early childhood. It is productive of what has been called 'symbolic castration'. Language is a process (or set of processes) involving absence and lack, and these are what threaten any image of the self as totally enclosed, self-sufficient, omnipotent. The construction of an ideal ego, meanwhile, is a process involving profound contradictions. While the ideal ego may be a 'model' with which the subject identifies and to which it aspires, it may also be a source of further images and feelings of castration, inasmuch as that ideal is something to which the subject is never adequate.[8]

If this is the case, there can be no simple and unproblematic identification on the part of the spectator, male or female, with Mulvey's 'ideal ego' on the screen. In an article published in *Wide Angle*, D. N. Rodowick has made a similar point. He goes on to argue both that the narcissistic male image – the image of authority and omnipotence – can entail a concomitant masochism in the relations between the spectator and the image, and further that the male image can involve an eroticism, since there is always a constant oscillation between that image as a source of identification, and as an other, a source of contemplation. The image is a source both of narcissistic processes and drives, and, inasmuch as it is other, of object-oriented processes and drives:

> Mulvey discusses the male star as an object of the look but denies him the function of an erotic object. Because Mulvey conceives the look to be essentially active in its aims, identification with the male protagonist is only considered from a point of view which associates it with a sense of omnipotence, of assuming control of the narrative. She makes no differentiation between identification and object choice in which sexual aims may be directed towards the male figure, nor does she consider the signification of authority in the male figure from the point of view of an economy of masochism.[9]

Given Rodowick's argument, it is not surprising either that 'male' genres and films constantly involve sado-masochistic themes, scenes and phantasies or that male heroes can at times be marked as the object of an erotic gaze. These are both points I wish to discuss below. However, it is worth mentioning here that they have also been discussed in Paul Willemen's article 'Anthony Mann: Looking at the Male'.[10]

Willemen argues that spectacle and drama in Mann's films tend both to be structured around the look at the male figure:

> The viewer's experience is predicated on the pleasure of seeing the male 'exist' (that is walk, move, ride, fight) in or through cityscapes, landscapes or, more abstractly, history. And on the unquiet pleasure of seeing the male mutilated (often quite graphically in Mann) and restored through violent brutality.[11]

These pleasures are founded upon a repressed homosexual voyeurism, a voyeurism 'not without its problems: the look at the male produces just as much anxiety as the look at the female, especially when it's presented as directly as in the killing scenes in *T-Men* and *Border Incident*'.[12] The (unstated) thesis behind these comments seems to be that in a heterosexual and patriarchal society the male body cannot be marked explicitly as the erotic object of another male look: that look must be motivated in some other way, its erotic component repressed. The mutilation and sadism so often involved in Mann's films are marks both of the repression involved and of a means by which the male body may be disqualified, so to speak, as an object of erotic contemplation and desire. The repression and disavowal involved are figured crucially in the scenes in *T-Men* and *Border Incident* to which Willemen refers, in which 'an undercover agent must look on, impassively, while his close (male) friend and partner is being killed'.[13]

There is one final and important contradiction involved in the type of narcissistic images of masculinity discussed above to which I'd like to refer. It is the contradiction between narcissism and the Law, between an image of *narcissistic* authority on the one hand and an image of *social* authority on the other. This tension or contradiction is discussed at some length by Laura Mulvey in an article seeking to reconsider her 'Visual Pleasure' piece with particular reference to *Duel in the Sun*.[14] It is a tension she sees as especially evident in the western. Using a narrative model derived from Vladimir Propp's analyses of folktales,[15] Mulvey points to two narrative functions, 'marriage' (and hence social integration) and 'not marriage', a refusal by the hero to enter society, a refusal motivated by a nostalgic narcissism:

> In the Proppian tale, an important aspect of narrative closure is 'marriage', a function characterised by the 'princess' or equivalent. This is the only function that is sex specific and thus essentially relates to the sex of the hero and his marriageability. This function is very commonly reproduced in the Western, where once again 'marriage' makes a crucial contribution to narrative closure. However, the function's presence also has come to allow a complication in the Western, its complementary opposite 'not marriage'. Thus, while the social integration represented by marriage is an essential aspect of the folk-tale, in the Western it can be accepted . . . or not. A hero can gain in stature by refusing the princess and remaining alone (Randolph Scott in the Ranown series of movies). As the resolution of the Proppian tale can be seen to represent the resolution of the Oedipus complex (integration into the symbolic), the rejection of marriage personifies a nostalgic celebration of phallic, narcissistic omnipotence.[16]

There are thus two diverging images of masculinity commonly at play in the western:

> The tension between two points of attraction, the symbolic (social integration and marriage) and nostalgic narcissism, generates a common splitting of the Western hero into two, something unknown in the Proppian tale. Here two functions emerge, one celebrating integration into society through marriage, the other celebrating resistance to social standards and responsibilities, above all those of marriage and the family, the sphere represented by women.[17]

Mulvey goes on to discuss John Ford's western, *The Man Who Shot Liberty Valance*, noting the split there between Tom Doniphon, played by

John Wayne, who incarnates the narcissistic function of the anachronistic social outsider, and Ranse Stoddart, played by James Stewart, who incarnates the civilizing functions of marriage, social integration and social responsibility. The film's tone is increasingly nostalgic, in keeping with its mourning for the loss of Doniphon and what he represents. The nostalgia, then, is not just for an historical past, for the Old West, but also for the masculine narcissism that Wayne represents.

Taking a cue from Mulvey's remarks about nostalgia in *Liberty Valance*, one could go on to discuss a number of nostalgic westerns in these terms, in terms of the theme of lost or doomed male narcissism. The clearest examples would be Peckinpah's westerns: *Guns in the Afternoon*, *Major Dundee* (to a lesser extent), *The Wild Bunch* and, especially, *Pat Garrett and Billy the Kid*. These films are shot through with nostalgia, with an obsession with images and definitions of masculinity and masculine codes of behaviour, and with images of male narcissism and the threats posed to it by women, society and the Law. The threat of castration is figured in the wounds and injuries suffered by Joel McCrea in *Guns in the Afternoon*, Charlton Heston in *Major Dundee* and William Holden in *The Wild Bunch*. The famous slow-motion violence, bodies splintered and torn apart, can be viewed at one level at least as the image of narcissism in its moment of disintegration and destruction. Significantly, Kris Kristofferson as Billy in *Pat Garrett and Billy the Kid*, the ultimate incarnation of omnipotent male narcissism in Peckinpah's films, is spared any bloody and splintered death. Shot by Pat Garrett, his body shows no sign either of wounds or blood: narcissism transfigured (rather than destroyed) by death.

I want now to move on from identification and narcissism to discuss in relation to images of men and masculinity the two modes of looking addressed by Mulvey in 'Visual Pleasure', voyeuristic looking, on the one hand, and fetishistic looking on the other.

LOOKING AND SPECTACLE

In discussing these two types of looking, both fundamental to the cinema, Mulvey locates them solely in relation to a structure of activity/passivity in which the look is male and active and the object of the look female and passive. Both are considered as distinct and variant means by which male castration anxieties may be played out and allayed.

Voyeuristic looking is marked by the extent to which there is a distance between spectator and spectacle, a gulf between the seer and the seen. This structure is one which allows the spectator a degree of power over what is seen. It hence tends constantly to involve sado-masochistic phantasies and themes. Here is Mulvey's description:

voyeurism . . . has associations with sadism: pleasure lies in ascertaining guilt (immediately associated with castration), asserting control and subjecting the guilty person through punishment and forgiveness. This sadistic side fits in well with narrative. Sadism demands a story, depends on making something happen, forcing a change in another person, a battle of will and strength, victory and defeat, all occurring in a linear time with a beginning and an end.[18]

Mulvey goes on to discuss these characteristics of voyeuristic looking in terms of the *film noir* and of Hitchcock's movies, where the hero is the bearer of the voyeuristic look, engaged in a narrative in which the woman is the object of its sadistic components. However, if we take some of the terms used in her description – 'making something happen', 'forcing a change in another person', 'a battle of will and strength', 'victory and defeat' – they can immediately be applied to 'male' genres, to films concerned largely or solely with the depiction of relations between men, to any film, for example, in which there is a struggle between a hero and a male villain. War films, westerns and gangster movies, for instance, are all marked by 'action', by 'making something happen'. Battles, fights and duels of all kinds are concerned with struggles of 'will and strength', 'victory and defeat', between individual men and/or groups of men. All of which implies that male figures on the screen are subject to voyeuristic looking, both on the part of the spectator and on the part of other male characters.

Paul Willemen's thesis on the films of Anthony Mann is clearly relevant here. The repression of any explicit avowal of eroticism in the act of looking at the male seems structurally linked to a narrative content marked by sado-masochistic phantasies and scenes. Hence both forms of voyeuristic looking, intra- and extra-diegetic, are especially evident in those moments of contest and combat referred to above, in those moments at which a narrative outcome is determined through a fight or gunbattle, at which male struggle becomes pure spectacle. Perhaps the most extreme examples are to be found in Leone's westerns, where the exchange of aggressive looks marking most western gun duels is taken to the point of fetishistic parody through the use of extreme and repetitive close-ups. At this point the look begins to oscillate between voyeurism and fetishism as the narrative starts to freeze and spectacle takes over. The anxious 'aspects' of the look at the male to which Willemen refers are here both embodied and allayed not just by playing out the sadism inherent in voyeurism through scenes of violence and combat, but also by drawing upon the structures and processes of fetishistic looking, by stopping the narrative in order to recognize the pleasure of display, but displacing it from the male body as such and locating it more generally in the overall components of a highly ritualized scene.

John Ellis has characterized fetishistic looking in the following terms:

> where voyeurism maintains (depends upon) a separation between the

seer and the object seen, fetishism tries to abolish the gulf . . . This process implies a different position and attitude of the spectator to the image. It represents the opposite tendency to that of voyeurism. . . . Fetishistic looking implies the direct acknowledgement and participation of the object viewed . . . with the fetishistic attitude, the look of the character towards the viewer . . . is a central feature. . . . The voyeuristic look is curious, inquiring, demanding to know. The fetishistic gaze is captivated by what it sees, does not wish to inquire further, to see more, to find out. . . . The fetishistic look has much to do with display and the spectacular.[19]

Mulvey again centrally discusses this form of looking in relation to the female as object: 'This second avenue, fetishistic scopophilia, builds up the physical beauty of the object, transforming it into something satisfying in in itself.'[20] Physical beauty' is interpreted solely in terms of the female body. It is specified through the example of the films of Sternberg:

While Hitchcock goes into the investigative side of voyeurism, Sternberg produces the ultimate fetish, taking it to the point where the powerful look of the male protagonist is broken in favour of the image in direct erotic rapport with the spectator. The beauty of the woman as object and the screen space coalesce; she is no longer the bearer of guilt but a perfect product, whose body, stylised and fragmented by close-ups, is the content of the film and the direct recipient of the spectator's look.[21]

If we return to Leone's shoot-outs, we can see that some elements of the fetishistic look as here described are present, others not. We are offered the spectacle of male bodies, but bodies unmarked as objects of erotic display. There is no trace of an acknowledgement or recognition of those bodies as displayed solely for the gaze of the spectator. They are on display, certainly, but there is no cultural or cinematic convention which would allow the male body to be presented in the way that Dietrich so often is in Sternberg's films. We see male bodies stylized and fragmented by close-ups, but our look is not direct, it is heavily mediated by the looks of the characters involved. And those looks are marked not by desire, but by fear, or hatred, or aggression. The shoot-outs are moments of spectacle, points at which the narrative hesitates, comes to a momentary halt, but they are also points at which the drama is finally resolved, a suspense in the culmination of the narrative drive. They thus involve an imbrication of *both* forms of looking, their intertwining designed to minimize and displace the eroticism they each tend to involve, to disavow any explicitly erotic look at the male body.

There are other instances of male combat which seem to function in this way. Aside from the western, one could point to the epic as a genre, to the gladiatorial combat in *Spartacus*, to the fight between Christopher

Plummer and Stephen Boyd at the end of *The Fall of the Roman Empire*, to the chariot race in *Ben Hur*. More direct displays of the male body can be found, though they tend either to be fairly brief or else to occupy the screen during credit sequences and the like (in which case the display is mediated by another textual function). Examples of the former would include the extraordinary shot of Gary Cooper lying under the hut toward the end of *Man of the West*, his body momentarily filling the Cinemascope screen. Or some of the images of Lee Marvin in *Point Blank*, his body draped over a railing or framed in a doorway. Examples of the latter would include the credit sequence of *Man of the West* again (an example to which Willemen refers), and *Junior Bonner*.

The presentation of Rock Hudson in Sirk's melodramas is a particularly interesting case. There are constantly moments in these films in which Hudson is presented quite explicitly as the object of an erotic look. The look is usually marked as female. But Hudson's body is *feminized* in those moments, an indication of the strength of those conventions which dictate that only women can function as the objects of an explicitly erotic gaze. Such instances of 'feminization' tend also to occur in the musical, the only genre in which the male body has been unashamedly put on display in mainstream cinema in any consistent way. (A particularly clear and interesting example would be the presentation of John Travolta in *Saturday Night Fever*.)

It is a refusal to acknowledge or make explicit an eroticism that marks all three of the psychic functions and processes discussed here in relation to images of men: identification, voyeuristic looking and fetishistic looking. It is this that tends above all to differentiate the cinematic representation of images of men and women. Although I have sought to open up a space within Laura Mulvey's arguments and theses, to argue that the elements she considers in relation to images of women can and should also be considered in relation to images of men, I would certainly concur with her basic premiss that the spectatorial look in mainstream cinema is implicitly male: it is one of the fundamental reasons why the erotic elements involved in the relations between the spectator and the male image have constantly to be repressed and disavowed. Were this not the case, mainstream cinema would openly have to come to terms with the male homosexuality it so assiduously seeks either to denigrate or deny. As it is, male homosexuality is constantly present as an undercurrent, as a potentially troubling aspect of many films and genres, but one that is dealt with obliquely, symptomatically, and that has to be repressed. While mainstream cinema, in its assumption of a male norm, perspective and look, can constantly take women and the female image as its object of investigation, it has rarely investigated men and the male image in the same kind of way: women are a problem, a source of anxiety, of obsessive inquiry; men are not. Where women are investigated, men are tested. Masculinity, as an ideal at least, is implicitly known. Femininity is, by contrast, a mystery. This is one of the reasons why the representation of masculinity, both inside and outside the cinema, has been so rarely discussed. Hopefully, this article will contribute towards such a discussion.

NOTES

I would like to thank John Ellis and Andrew Higson for their comments on an earlier draft of this article, which is based on a talk given during the course of a Society for Education in Film and Television Day Event on Masculinity held at Four Corners Film Workshop, London, 19 March 1983. It was first published in *Screen*, Winter 1983, vol. 24, no. 6, pp. 2–16.

1 Laura Mulvey, 'Visual Pleasure and Narrative Cinema', chapter 1, pp. 22–34 in this volume; originally published in *Screen*, Autumn 1975, vol. 16, no. 3, pp. 6–18.
2 Pam Cook, 'Masculinity in Crisis?', *Screen*, Autumn 1982, vol. 23, nos, 3–4, pp. 39–46; Steve Neale, 'Chariots of Fire, Images of Men', ibid., pp. 47–53; John Caughie and Gillian Skirrow, 'Ahab Ishmael . . . and Mo', ibid., pp. 54–9; Tania Modleski, 'Film Theory's Detour', *Screen*, Winter 1982, vol. 23, no. 5, pp. 72–9.
3 Paul Willemen, 'Anthony Mann: Looking at the Male', *Framework*, Summer 1981, nos. 15–17, p. 16.
4 Raymond Bellour, 'Le blocage symbolique', *Communications*, 1975, no. 23, pp. 235–350.
5 John Ellis, *Visible Fictions*, London, Routledge & Kegan Paul, 1982.
6 ibid., p. 43.
7 Mulvey, op. cit., p. 28.
8 For further elaboration of these two related points see Moustapha Safouan, 'Is the Oedipus Complex Universal?', *m/f*, 1981, nos. 5–6, pp. 85–7.
9 D. N. Rodowick, 'The Difficulty of Difference', *Wide Angle*, 1982, vol. 5, no. 1, p. 8.
10 Willemen, op. cit.
11 ibid., p. 16.
12 ibid.
13 ibid.
14 Laura Mulvey, 'Afterthoughts . . . Inspired by *Duel in the Sun*', *Framework*, Summer 1981, nos. 15–17, pp. 12–15.
15 Vladimir Propp, *Morphology of the Folktale*, Austin, University of Texas Press, 1968.
16 Mulvey, 'Afterthoughts', op. cit., p. 14.
17 ibid., p. 18.
18 Mulvey, 'Visual Pleasure', op. cit., p. 29.
19 Ellis, op. cit., p. 47.
20 Mulvey, 'Visual Pleasure' op. cit., p. 30.
21 ibid.

Part V
THE SOCIAL SUBJECT

INTRODUCTION

Looking back over the chapters in the previous four parts we can see that certain terms recur – subjectivity, difference, man, woman, gender. This is because the concept of sexual difference dominated film debates from the mid-1970s to mid-1980s. Initiated by feminist theorists working on questions of spectatorship in the cinema, debates about sexual difference sought to pose subjectivity in contexts other than those incorporated by the notion of the ubiquitous male subject. The topic of sexual difference covered areas such as viewing and pleasure, female spectatorship, objectification of the male body, fantasy and pornography. Despite the variety of topics addressed, debates about sexual difference and subjectivity largely ignored other crucial differences – race, colour, class, age, sexual preference. Similarly, forms of popular culture such as television were neglected in favour of the more glamorous object: cinema. In the editorial statement of the 'Deconstructing Difference' issue of *Screen* (Winter 1987) Mandy Merck analysed many of the problems which had beset difference theory by the mid-1980s – its neglect of differences other than those posed in terms of male/female; and its neglect of the subject as a site of differences other than the sexual.

The articles reprinted in part V draw attention to those subjects, whose voices have been repressed and ignored in dominant discourses – including the discourse of sexual difference. These articles offer a new way of thinking about subjectivity which involves a consideration of such issues as race, class and colour. The authors draw our attention to the importance of redefining the boundaries of what constitutes subjectivity. Unlike theories of sexual difference, which constantly return to the figure of man as the central term of reference, these articles are careful not to elevate one particular concept or image as the standard from which to evaluate all other differences.

In 'The Subject of Feminist Film Theory/Practice', Claire Johnston brings together a number of crucial issues which were central to 1970s debates about the usefulness of psychoanalytic theory for an understanding of sexual difference. Her article addresses issues raised, mainly by Christine Gledhill's paper, at the Feminism and Cinema Event held at the

1979 Edinburgh Film Festival. Gledhill's criticisms focused on the fact that feminist film theory had failed to address the relationship between theory and practice. Feminist theory placed too much emphasis on the closed relationship of the individual reader and the subject in the text at the expense of the reader as a subject in history and society. Gledhill's concerns about the increasingly ahistorical approach of much feminist criticism, influenced by poststructuralism and psychoanalytic theory, were shared by others at the time.

Johnston carefully evaluates her arguments while drawing an important distinction between theory and theoreticism. She also supports the crucial role played by semiotics and psychoanalysis in the early development of feminist theory. Johnston stresses the important point that this early work, which consisted mainly of feminist readings of the classic realist text, should be seen as a necessary intervention which occurred at a particular historical moment. Johnston also urges the need to discard approaches which see the text–reader relationship as a purely theoretical construct, and adopt instead those which locate subjectivity in its social and historical contexts. She proposes a new form of conjunctural analysis which would incorporate the notion of the text as a specific signifying practice which is also situated in the wider sociopolitical formation.

In 'Women's Genres' Annette Kuhn takes up the issues raised by Johnston in relation to popular culture. Her article provided an important contribution to a growing feminist interest of the early 1980s in forms of popular culture directed at women. Whereas feminist writings on the cinema concentrated on melodrama and the woman's film, feminist analyses of television privileged the soap opera as the cultural form directed most clearly at a female audience. Feminist writings on television, however, did not simply duplicate the psychoanalytic-based feminist critique of the cinema. From the beginning, more attention was given to the sociocultural context of television production and reception. An important aim of the feminist critique of film and television at this time was to reject the relatively negative psychoanalytic approach to mainstream cinema, in which woman was almost always produced as the lack in male discourse, and concentrate on women's cultural forms such as the women's film and the soap opera.

Here Annette Kuhn discusses problems of female spectatorship in relation to the melodrama and soap opera which she situates as 'gynocentric genres', that is, films and television programmes that are addressed to the female spectator and have woman-centred narratives. Kuhn argues that it is not appropriate to draw on sexual difference theories developed in relation to film and television in order to understand these genres. She is primarily concerned with questions of audience, particularly those of gendered spectatorship. Kuhn's intention is to avoid universalizing the spectator – a problem endemic to existing psychoanalytic theories of cinema spectatorship. She draws attention to the specificities involved – sexual identity, social, historical and institutional contexts – and argues that psychoanalysis cannot adequately theorize subjectivity in specific cultural or historical contexts. Consequently, most existing theories of the cinema suffer from a text–context split.

In Kuhn's view the text–context dualism has not bedevilled television theory in the same way; television theory has almost always considered both texts and contexts of production and reception. Kuhn stresses, however, the crucial importance of separating out, for the purposes of analysis, not only text and context but also social audience and spectator. In her interesting discussion of current feminist writing on gynocentric genres, Kuhn draws attention to the vital importance for a feminist cultural politics of paying close attention to all structures and contexts – subjective, social, economic – which impinge on the screen–spectator relationship.

In 'The Other Question' Homi K. Bhabha uses psychoanalytic theory to explore the representation of racial difference as otherness in the discourse of colonialism. His approach provides an interesting example of conjunctural analysis, as proposed by Johnston, but applied to racist rather than sexist discourses. In particular, Bhabha concentrates on the construction and function of the stereotype as an ambiguous form which works by continually repeating information about the 'other' that is already known. It is 'as if the essential duplicity of the Asiatic or the bestial sexual licence of the African that needs no proof, can never really, in discourse, be proved'.[1] Bhabha sees the *ambivalent* nature of the stereotype – whether employed in discourses of racism or sexism – as one of its most insidious aspects. 'The Other Question' presents a sustained and complex critique of the ideological functioning of the stereotype as a discursive strategy. Bhabha is specifically interested not in the positive or negative images afforded by the stereotype of the colonial subject (colonizer and colonized), but in the *range of positions* that the stereotype constructs and allows in relation to questions of power and dependence. In the past the notion of the colonial subject has not been sufficiently problematized.

Like Kuhn's discussion of women's cultural forms, Bhabha's analysis of the colonial discourse stresses the importance of social/cultural/historical structures – class, gender, ideology – in the construction of the stereotype of the colonial subject. Differences are repressed in favour of a generalized image of the colonized subject as 'other', in this instance, a 'degenerate' who must be controlled by and subjected to the colonizer. Like the discourse of narrative realism in the cinema, the colonial discourse renders invisible its codes of construction and presents the colonized subject as transparently and immutably 'other'. Bhabha also argues that the racial stereotype of the colonial discourse can be read as a fetish in that it serves to mask difference, the difference of skin and colour, and affirm wholeness, in this instance the sameness of skin and colour, the fantasy of a pure origin. The fetishized stereotype functions to reactivate in the colonial subject the Imaginary fantasy of 'an ideal ego that is white and whole'. Bhabha draws on his theory of the colonial discourse, which he sees as constructed through fetishism and the play of Imaginary desires, to analyse the workings of racial discrimination. This approach ensures that the subject positions available to both colonizer and colonized are seen as multiple and shifting, occupying a number of positions rather than as fixed and contained, as is usually implied by the stereotype. By drawing on psychoanalytic theory to explicate the workings of the racist discourse in the context of the political and social formation, Bhabha is able to adopt a more complex approach to the question of different subjectivities.

NOTE

1 Homi K. Bhabha, 'The Other Question: The Stereotype and Colonial Discourse', chapter 16, p. 312 in this volume.

14

THE SUBJECT OF FEMINIST FILM THEORY/PRACTICE

Claire Johnston

The major focus of the discussions at the Feminism and Cinema Event held at the 1979 Edinburgh Film Festival turned on the terms in which we could talk about the emergence of a 'feminist film culture' within the present conjuncture. Throughout the week emphasis was placed on the need to locate feminist politics within a conception of film as a social practice, on the dialectic of making and viewing and on film as process rather than object. The aim of the event was to bring together filmmakers, film theorists and women involved in distribution and exhibition, and through the papers, forums and workshops, to generate discussion and analysis of the conditions of existence of each of these practices, their forms and their relation to each other. The event provided a useful starting point for developing a new space in which the transformation of the relationship between production, distribution, exhibition and criticism could be worked through and from which strategies could be forged.

In redefining cinema as social practice the central question which had to be addressed was that of political effectivity. In her paper (and in the article on which it is based)[1] Christine Gledhill identified a number of key problems for feminist film theory which I would like to take up and explore here. First, she argued that, so far, work on subjectivity and the text has ignored the crucial question of the audience as constituted socially, outside the text, in different sets of social relations. She criticized the emphasis on the individual reader, on the place of the subject in the text and positionality in language at the expense of attention to historical and social processes and to a concept of the subject in history – the extra-textual. Second, she raised the equally important question of the need to assess the power and role of recognition and identification as political strategies in feminist film practice. These problems seem to me to be the most urgent theoretical questions we have to address at the present time if we see ourselves as seriously engaged in ideological struggle rather than in the cosy business of providing cultural enlightenment from the margins of academia. Indeed, the process of addressing such problems points to the need to formulate a new project for theory as a practice which aims to transform the way in which film is perceived and used and which accounts for the ways in which other practices determine the production of theory itself.

The struggle in the Women's Movement to establish theoretical work as a valid enterprise has been an important one. In fact it could be argued that, at least in this country, theory has always been present in the politics of feminism, since the question of how to combine theory and politics has always been a subject of debate. In this sense, theory and politics have not been seen as two separate realms. The relationship between theory and practice has posed itself acutely for the Women's Movement because one of the projects of the movement is to construct knowledge of the nature and causes of women's oppression in order to devise strategies for social transformation. Indeed, this is the point of any theoretical work. In this context it is important to make a distinction between theory and theoreticism. Theoreticism assumes the autonomy of theory as a discourse and tends to have its operation within certain institutional practices (for example academia), and a mode of address which produces the theoretician as the authoritative source of knowledge. It poses itself as a discourse of mastery, and anything which falls outside the realm of the discourse – the real (in the Lacanian sense of the constant limit of the subject's 'reality') – is decreed to be unavailable for knowledge. I would suggest that the process involved in the production of theory could be seen as analogous to the Lacanian notion of desire: an endless and dialectical discursive activity, embedded in the real, and always exceeded and transformed by practice – a constant dialectic with the aim of breaking of exchange for *use*. In this sense, I would argue that the reason why the problems Christine Gledhill raised have not been seriously addressed until now has to to with the necessary disjuncture between theory and practice as much as it does to the institutional sources of much theoretical work.

However, we are now at a stage when it is becoming possible to theorize a conception of ideological struggle within feminist film theory and practice more concretely, and to ignore these problems at this point could constitute a move towards theoreticism. What is most useful about an event like the Feminism and Cinema Event is that it helps us to understand more fully the ways in which cultural practices themselves determine the production of theory and to see more clearly the danger of seeing a film text as having a specific effectivity regardless of the context in which it is being viewed. I would argue that while the emphasis on textual analysis in feminist film criticism has been productive, and while strategic work of this kind (particularly on the specificity of the relations of subjectivity set up in different genres) still remains important, theoretical work on the relationship between text and subject and the historical conjuncture is now more important. This paper, then, is a tentative outline for such a project.

The importance of the work within the field of semiotics and psychoanalysis for feminist film theory had been twofold. First it has laid emphasis on the activity of reading films, of seeing film as a textual practice rather than an autonomous object of study or consumption, so that the effectivity of a film has to be seen as a function both of the mode of reading and of the text itself. Second, work on text/subject relations has established that a transformation of the relationship between text and viewer is a prerequisite for political work on cinema as an institution. It has therefore opened up a way of seeing film practice as a practice of meaning-production involving both filmmaker and film viewer in a dialectical relationship – as a *social practice*. In her paper, Christine Gledhill pointed to what she considered to be the 'negativeness' and 'prescriptive, anti-realist' stance of some of this work, in particular the article by Pam Cook and myself on Raoul Walsh's *The Revolt of Mamie Stover*.[2] The point she missed, I think, is that that work was an intervention at a particular historical moment within feminist film theory, an appropriation of psychoanalysis for feminism at a time when work which had been undertaken in the field (such as Metz's 'The Imaginary Signifier') had failed to address questions of sexual difference in relation to the cinematic apparatus. The major point of disagreement I have with her critique is her rejection of psychoanalysis as at all useful in helping us to grasp more concretely some key problems for feminist film theory. It is not that psychoanalysis provides ready answers or that there are no limits to the theory. As Stephen Heath has pointed out,[3] the Lacanian notion of the phallus as essence in nature, and castration as a scenario of vision, constitute decisive limits to the theory which foreclose questions of social and political transformation. Nevertheless, feminist readings of this kind of the classic realist text, I would argue, were a necessary starting point for feminist film theory and practice, because they revealed how the economy of the classic realist text works towards the unquestioned Imaginary of the patriarchal order.

Clearly, however, work on text/subject relations which aims to transform the relationship between text and viewer cannot be seen as a goal in itself, nor is that work alone able to answer political questions about cinema as an institution. As Paul Willemen has pointed out, the danger is that it can indeed become a prescriptive and essentialist dogma, 'a strategy of attack against all imaginary unity as such, thus condemning itself to a romantic, anarchist project of eternal and universal subversion/transgression'.[4]

Any political project such as feminism, while it must contain and pre-serve a heterogeneity of social practices, must at the same time involve a form of imaginary unity for it to be at all effective. The struggle to maintain the Women's Movement as an autonomous movement around a network system and a platform of political demands for social change bears witness to this. As Christine Gledhill suggested, recognition and identification at some level are vital for political effectivity in feminist film practice.

Any theory of ideological struggle, therefore, in relation to feminist film theory and practice must engage with both aspects of this problematic at the same time in a dialectical movement. This would involve a move away from work on subjectivity which concentrates exclusively on the notion of subject production and on the text with its inscribed reader/author and towards the more complex question of subjectivity seen in historical and social terms. In this way feminist film practice can no longer be seen simply in terms of the effectivity of a system of representation, but rather as a production of and by subjects already in social practices which always involve heterogeneous and often contradictory positions in ideologies. In other words, feminist film practice is determined by the conjuncture of discursive, economic and political practices which produce subjects in history. As Stuart Hall and others have argued,

> The proposition that ideology is grounded entirely through the inscription of subject positions, through discursive practices which are wholly autonomous, which have neither determinacy in, articulation with nor pertinent specific effects for other levels of the social formation, is difficult to found within a problematic which at the same time declares itself to be marxist.[5]

The notion of the 'reader' is a purely theoretical construct. Real readers are subjects in history rather than mere subjects of a single text.[6] As those of us who have worked with audiences know, this has proved an important problem in relation to the development of an oppositional practice involving the transformation of the relations of production, distribution, exhibition and criticism. Films are read unpredictably and can be pulled into a variety of ideological spaces and mobilized for diverse projects. Textual strategies have thus to be posed in conjunctural terms. The problem must be thought in terms of which set of discourses the text encounters and how this encounter may restructure the productivity of the text and the discourses with which it combines to form an intertexual field in ideology and history. Hence the importance of a film such as *The Song of the Shirt* (1979) which takes as its problematic precisely such an intervention in instructions and historical discourses, with the aim of activating contradictions within sets of discourses. In the film, which is set in the 1830s and 1840s, Jonathan Curling and Sue Clayton interrogate the way in which the history of a group of women workers, the 'distressed needlewomen', was constructed through the juxtaposing of different means of representation – government commissions, newspaper reports, lithographs, novels, music – utilizing the conventions of cinema and television history in order to deconstruct their operations by the use of montage. In so doing, the film not only questions its own process of construction, but also offers an investigation into historical modes of representation and the process of writing history itself.

An important point which emerges from these questions is that particular practices in the social formation should not be treated in isolation and designated as essentially 'reactionary' or 'progressive' once and for all. Their political function and effectivity will depend on the sociohistorical conjuncture and the conditions of existence of each practice – that is to say, which discourses and practices are being displaced and to what effect? The textual strategies of films like Jan Worth's *Taking A Part* (1979) or Michelle Citron's *Daughter Rite* (1979) which depend on identification processes and realism can only be assessed in these terms. Jan Worth's study of prostitutes is at one level a documentary which mobilizes identification processes but at the same time calls into question the notion that the way to understand the two women's oppression is to simply film them retelling their lived experience. The women read their interviews from a notebook in selected settings, which achieves a resituating of identification processes for the viewer. *Daughter Rite*, on the other hand, poses within itself the history of the forms within feminist film practice as it has developed (from *cinéma-vérité* to experimental film) and mobilizes this juxtaposition to question the dominance of documentary in feminist film practice now.

Conjunctural analysis, therefore, calls for a redefinition of the problem of subjectivity which, while accounting for intersubjective relations, at the same time offers an analysis of discourse which includes a consideration of ideological representations in relation to and in context of the political and the economic in the social formation – a following through of the implications of cinema as a social practice. The stress that semiotics and psychoanalysis has placed on film as a language, as a specific signifying practice, is crucial because it poses film as a process, a discourse which simultaneously puts into place an 'I' and a 'you'. But as I have argued, there is also an outside of discourse which has an effectivity and which must be taken into consideration if a productive strategy for ideological struggle in relation to feminist film theory and practice is to be developed. If institutions are an important site of struggle for feminism, I would agree with feminist critics[7] who have argued that women's art which poses itself as 'other', as negativity, as essentially feminine – a cultural feminism which is unified, non-contradictory and exclusive – could be seen as no longer a threat to the institutions of art and could be a way in which male dominance in art can be maintained. Feminist art, on the other hand, which asserts a woman's discourse about her position and the intersubjective relationships which constitute her as female subject in history, is far more problematic and far less easily assimilated into the conception of women as irrevocable 'other' by which patriarchy is maintained.

NOTES

First published in *Screen*, Summer 1980, vol. 21, no. 2, pp. 27–34.

1 Christine Gledhill, 'Recent Developments in Feminist Film Criticism', *Quarterly Review of Film Studies*, 1978, vol. 3, no. 4.
2 Pam Cook and Claire Johnston, 'The Place of Women in the Cinema of Raoul Walsh', in Phil Hardy (ed.), *Raoul Walsh*, Edinburgh Film Festival, 1974.
3 For a critique of Lacanian psychoanalysis and sexual difference see Stephen Heath, 'Difference', chapter 3, pp. 47–106 in this volume; originally published in *Screen*, Autumn 1974, vol. 19, no. 3, pp. 51– 113.
4 Paul Willemen, 'Notes on Subjectivity', *Screen*, Spring 1978, vol. 19, no. 1.
5 Iain Chambers, John Clarke, Ian Connell, Lidia Curti, Stuart Hall and Tony Jefferson, 'Marxism and Culture', *Screen*, Winter 1977–8, vol. 18, no. 4, pp. 109–19.
6 Willemen, op. cit.
7 For example, Griselda Pollock, 'Feminism, Femininity and the Hayward Annual Exhibition 1978', *Feminist Review*, 1979, no. 2, pp. 33–55.

15

WOMEN'S GENRES

Annette Kuhn

I

Television soap opera and film melodrama, popular narrative forms aimed at female audiences, are currently attracting a good deal of critical and theoretical attention. Not surprisingly, most of the work on these 'gynocentric' genres is informed by various strands of feminist thought on visual representation. Less obviously, perhaps, such work has also prompted a series of questions which relate to representation and cultural production in a more wide-ranging and thoroughgoing manner than a specifically feminist interest might suggest. Not only are film melodrama (and more particularly its subtype the 'woman's picture') and soap opera directed at female audiences, they are also actually enjoyed by millions of women. What is it that sets these genres apart from representations which possess a less gender-specific mass appeal?

One of the defining generic features of the woman's picture as a textual system is its construction of narratives motivated by female desire and processes of spectator identification governed by female point-of-view. Soap opera constructs woman-centred narratives and identifications, too, but it differs textually from its cinematic counterpart in certain other respects: not only do soaps never end, but their beginnings are soon lost sight of. And whereas in the woman's picture the narrative process is characteristically governed by the enigma-retardation-resolution structure which marks the classic narrative, soap opera narratives propose

> competing and intertwining plot lines introduced as the serial progresses. Each plot . . . develops at a different pace, thus preventing any clear resolution of conflict. The completion of one story generally leads into others, and ongoing plots often incorporate parts of semi-resolved conflicts.[1]

Recent work on soap opera and melodrama has drawn on existing theories, methods and perspectives in the study of film and television, including the structural analysis of narratives, textual semiotics and psychoanalysis, audience research, and the political economy of cultural institutions. At the same time, though, some of this work has exposed the limitations of existing approaches, and in consequence been forced if not actually to abandon them, at least to challenge their characteristic problematics. Indeed, it may be contended that the most significant developments in film and television theory in general are currently taking place precisely within such areas of feminist concern as critical work on soap opera and melodrama.

In examining some of this work, I shall begin by looking at three areas in which particularly pertinent questions are being directed at theories of representation and cultural production. These are, first, the problem of gendered spectatorship; second, questions concerning the universalism as against the historical specificity of conceptualizations of gendered spectatorship; and third, the relationship between film and television texts and their social, historical and institutional contexts. Each of these concerns articulates in particular ways with what seems to me the central issue here – the question of the audience, or audiences, for certain types of cinematic and televisual representation.

II

Film theory's appropriation to its own project of Freudian and post-Freudian psychoanalysis places the question of the relationship between text and spectator firmly on the agenda. Given the preoccupation of psychoanalysis with sexuality and gender, a move from conceptualizing the spectator as a homogeneous and androgynous effect of textual operations[2] to regarding her or him as a gendered subject constituted in representation seems in retrospect inevitable. At the same time, the interests of feminist film theory and film theory in general converge at this point in a shared concern with sexual difference. Psychoanalytic accounts of the formation of gendered subjectivity raise the question, if only indirectly, of representation and feminine subjectivity. This in turn permits the spectator to be considered as a gendered subject position, masculine or feminine: and theoretical work on soap opera and the woman's picture may take this as a starting point for its inquiry into spectator–text relations. Do these 'gyno-centric' forms address, or construct, a female or a feminine spectator? If so, how?

On the question of film melodrama, Laura Mulvey, commenting on King Vidor's *Duel in the Sun*,[3] argues that when, as in this film, a woman is at the centre of the narrative, the question of female desire structures the hermeneutic: 'what does *she* want?' This, says Mulvey, does not guarantee the constitution of the spectator as feminine so much as it implies a contradictory, and in the final instance impossible, 'phantasy of masculinisation' for the female spectator. This is in line with the author's earlier suggestion that cinema spectatorship involves masculine identification for spectators of either gender.[4] If cinema does thus construct a masculine subject, there can be no unproblematic feminine subject position for any spectator. Pam Cook, on the other hand, writing about a group of melo-dramas produced during the 1940s at the Gainsborough Studios, evinces greater optimism about the possibility of a feminine subject of classic cinema. She does acknowledge, though, that in a patriarchal society female desire and female point-of-view are highly contradictory, even if they have the potential to subvert culturally dominant modes of spectator–text re-lation. The characteristic 'excess' of the woman's melodrama, for example, is explained by Cook in terms of the genre's tendency to '[pose] problems for itself which it can scarcely contain'.[5]

Writers on television soap opera tend to take views on gender and spectatorship rather different from those advanced by film theorists. Tania Modleski, for example, argues with regard to soaps that their characteristic narrative patterns, their foregrounding of 'female' skills in dealing with personal and domestic crises, and the capacity of their programme formats and scheduling to key into the rhythms of women's work in the home, all address a female spectator. Furthermore, she goes so far as to argue that the textual processes of soaps are in some respects similar to those of certain 'feminine' texts which speak to a decentred subject, and so are 'not altogether at odds with . . . feminist aesthetics'.[6] Modleski's view is that soaps not only address female spectators, but in so doing construct femi-nine subject positions which transcend patriarchal modes of subjectivity.

Different though their respective approaches and conclusions may be, however, Mulvey, Cook and Modleski are all interested in the problem of gendered spectatorship. The fact, too, that this common concern is informed by a shared interest in assessing the progressive or transformative potential of soaps and melodramas is significant in light of the broad appeal of both genres to the mass audiences of women at which they are aimed.

But what precisely does it mean to say that certain representations are aimed at a female audience? However well theorized they may be, existing conceptualizations of gendered spectatorship are unable to deal with this question. This is because spectator and audience are distinct concepts which cannot – as they frequently are – be reduced to one another. Although I shall be considering some of its consequences more fully below (see p. 305), it is important to note a further problem for film and television theory, posed in this case by the distinction between spectator and audience. Critical work on the woman's picture and on soap opera has necessarily, and most productively, emphasized the question of gendered spectatorship. In doing this, film theory in particular has taken on board a conceptualization of the spectator derived from psychoanalytic accounts of the formation of human subjectivity.

Such accounts, however, have been widely criticized for their universa-lism. Beyond, perhaps, associating certain variants of the Oedipus complex with family forms characteristic of a patriarchal society and offering a

303

theory of the construction of gender, psychoanalysis seems to offer little scope for theorizing subjectivity in its cultural or historical specificity. Although in relation to the specific isues of spectatorship and representation there may, as I shall argue, be a way around this apparent impasse, virtually all film and television theory – its feminist variants included – is marked by the dualism of universalism and specificity.

Nowhere is this more evident than in the gulf between textual analysis and contextual inquiry. Each is done according to different rules and procedures, distinct methods of investigation and theoretical perspectives. In bringing to the fore the question of spectator–text relations, theories deriving from psychoanalysis may claim – to the extent that the spectatorial apparatus is held to be coterminous with the cinematic or televisual institution – to address the relationship between text and context. But as soon as any attempt is made to combine textual analysis with analysis of the concrete social, historical and institutional conditions of production and reception of texts, it becomes clear that the context of the spectator/subject of psychoanalytic theory is rather different from the context of production and reception constructed by conjunctural analyses of cultural institutions.

The disparity between these two 'contexts' structures Pam Cook's article on the Gainsborough melodrama, which sets out to combine an analysis of the characteristic textual operations and modes of address of a genre with an examination of the historical conditions of a particular expression of it. Gainsborough melodrama, says Cook, emerges from a complex of determinants, including certain features of the British film industry of the 1940s, the nature of the female cinema audience in the post World War II period, and the textual characteristics of the woman's picture itself.[7] While Cook is correct in pointing to the various levels of determination at work in this instance, her lengthy preliminary discussion of spectator–text relations and the woman's picture rather outbalances her subsequent investigation of the social and industrial contexts of the Gainsborough melodrama. The fact, too, that analysis of the woman's picture in terms of its interpellation of a female/feminine spectator is simply placed alongside a conjunctural analysis tends to vitiate any attempt to reconcile the two approaches, and so to deal with the broader issue of universalism as against historical specificity. But although the initial problem remains, Cook's article constitutes an important intervention in the debate because, in tackling the text–context split head-on, it necessarily exposes a key weakness of current film theory.

In work on television soap opera as opposed to film melodrama, the dualism of text and context manifests itself rather differently, if only because – unlike film theory – theoretical work on television has tended to emphasize the determining character of the contextual level, particularly the structure and organization of television institutions. Since this has often been at the expense of attention to the operation of television texts, television theory may perhaps be regarded as innovative in the extent to which it attempts to deal specifically with texts as well as contexts. Some feminist critical work has in fact already begun to address the question of television as text, though always with characteristic emphasis on the issue of gendered spectatorship. This emphasis constitutes a common concern of work on both television soaps and the woman's picture, but a point of contact between text and context in either medium emerges only when the concept of social audience is considered in distinction from that of spectator.

III

Each term – spectator and social audience – presupposes a different set of relations to representations and to the contexts in which they are received. Looking at spectators and at audiences demands different methodologies and theoretical frameworks, distinct discourses which construct distinct subjectivities and social relations. The *spectator*, for example, is a subject constituted in signification, interpellated by the film or television text. This does not necessarily mean that the spectator is merely an effect of the text, however, because modes of subjectivity which also operate outside spectator–text relations in film or television are activated in the relationship between spectators and texts.

This model of the spectator/subject is useful in correcting more deterministic communication models which might, say, pose the spectator not as actively constructing meaning but simply as a receiver and decoder of preconstituted 'messages'. In emphasizing spectatorship as a set of psychic relations and focusing on the relationship between spectator and text, however, such a model does disregard the broader social implications of filmgoing or televiewing. It is the social act of going to the cinema, for instance, that makes the individual cinemagoer part of an audience. Viewing television may involve social relations rather different from filmgoing, but in its own ways television does depend on individual viewers being part of an audience, even if its members are never in one place at the same time. A group of people seated in a single auditorium looking at a film, or scattered across thousands of homes watching the same television programme, is a *social audience*. The concept of social audience, as against that of spectator, emphasizes the status of cinema and television as social and economic institutions.

Constructed by discursive practices both of cinema and television and of social science, the social audience is a group of people who buy tickets at the box office, or who switch on their television sets; people who can be surveyed, counted and categorized according to age, sex and socioeconomic status.[8] The cost of a cinema ticket or television licence fee, or a readiness to tolerate commercial breaks, earns audiences the right to look at films and television programmes, and so to be spectators. Social audiences become spectators in the moment they engage in the processes and pleasures of meaning-making attendant on watching a film or television programme. The anticipated pleasure of spectatorship is perhaps a necessary condition of existence of audiences. In taking part in the social act of consuming representations, a group of spectators becomes a social audience.

The consumer of representations as audience member and spectator is involved in a particular kind of psychic and social relationship: at this point, a conceptualization of the cinematic or televisual apparatus as a regime of pleasure intersects with sociological and economic understandings of film and television as institutions. Because each term describes a distinct set of relationships, though, it is important not to conflate social audience with spectators. At the same time, since each is necessary to the other, it is equally important to remain aware of the points of continuity between the two sets of relations.

These conceptualizations of spectator and social audience have particular implications when it comes to a consideration of popular 'gynocentric' forms such as soap opera and melodrama. Most obviously, perhaps, these centre on the issue of gender, which prompts again the question: what does 'aimed at a female audience' mean? What exactly is being signalled in this reference to a gendered audience? Are women to be understood as a subgroup of the social audience, distinguishable through discourses which construct *a priori* gender categories? Or does the reference to a female audience allude rather to gendered spectatorship, to sexual difference constructed in relations between spectators and texts? Most likely it condenses the two meanings; but an examination of the distinction between them may nevertheless be illuminating in relation to the broader theoretical issues of texts, contexts, social audiences and spectators.

The notion of a female social audience, certainly as it is constructed in the discursive practices through which it is investigated, presupposes a group of individuals already formed as female. For the sociologist interested in such matters as gender and lifestyles, certain people bring a pre-existent femaleness to their viewing or film and television. For the business executive interested in selling commodities, television programmes and films are marketed to individuals already constructed as female. Both, however, are interested in the same kind of woman. On one level, then, soap operas and women's melodramas address themselves to a social audience of women. But they may at the same time be regarded as speaking to a female, or a feminine, spectator. If soaps and melodramas inscribe femininity in their address, women – as well as being already formed *for* such representations – are in a sense also formed *by* them.

In making this point, however, I intend no reduction of femaleness to femininity: on the contrary, I would hold to a distinction between femaleness as social gender and femininity as subject position. For example, it is possible for a female spectator to be addressed, as it were, 'in the masculine', and the converse is presumably also true. Nevertheless, in a cultur-ally pervasive operation of ideology, femininity is routinely identified with femaleness and masculinity with maleness. Thus, for example, an address 'in the feminine' may be regarded in ideological terms as privileging, if not necessitating, a socially constructed female gender identity.

The constitutive character of both the woman's picture and the soap opera has in fact been noted by a number of feminist commentators. Tania Modleski, for instance, suggests that the characteristic narrative structures and textual operations of soap operas both address the viewer as an 'ideal mother' – ever-understanding, ever-tolerant of the weaknesses and foibles of others – and also posit states of expectation and passivity as pleasurable: 'the narrative, by placing ever more complex obstacles between desire and fulfilment, makes anticipation of an end an end in itself'.[9] In our culture, tolerance and passivity are regarded as feminine attributes, and conse-quently as qualities proper in women but not in men.

Charlotte Brunsdon extends Modleski's line of argument to the extra-textual level: in constructing its viewers as competent within the ideological and moral frameworks of marriage and family life, soap opera, she implies, addresses both a feminine spectator and female audience.[10] Pointing to the centrality of intuition and emotion in the construction of the woman's point-of-view, Pam Cook regards the construction of a feminine spectator as a highly problematic and contradictory process: so that in the film melodrama's construction of female point-of-view, the validity of femini-nity as a subject position is necessarily laid open to question.[11]

This divergence on the question of gendered spectatorship within femi-nist theory is significant. Does it perhaps indicate fundamental differences between film and television in the spectator–text relations privileged by each? Do soaps and melodramas really construct different relations of gendered spectatorship, with melodrama constructing contradictory identi-fications in ways that soap opera does not? Or do these different positions on spectatorship rather signal an unevenness of theoretical development – or, to put it less teleologically, reflect the different intellectual histories and epistemological groundings of film theory and television theory?

Any differences in the spectator–text relations proposed respectively by soap opera and by film melodrama must be contingent to some extent on more general disparities in address between television and cinema. Thus film spectatorship, it may be argued, involves the pleasures evoked by looking in a more pristine way than does watching television. Whereas in classic cinema the concentration and involvement proposed by structures of the look, identification and point-of-view tend to be paramount, tele-vision spectatorship is more likely to be characterized by distraction and diversion.[12] This would suggest that each medium constructs sexual differ-ence through spectatorship in rather different ways: cinema through the look and spectacle, and television – perhaps less evidently – through a capacity to insert its flow, its characteristic modes of address, and the textual operations of different kinds of programmes into the rhythms and routines of domestic activities and sexual divisions of labour in the household at various times of day.

It would be a mistake, however, simply to equate current thinking on spectator–text relations in each medium. This is not only because theoretical work on spectatorship as it is defined here is newer and perhaps not so highly developed for television as it has been for cinema, but also because conceptualizations of spectatorship in film theory and in television theory emerge from quite distinct perspectives. When feminist writers on soap opera and on film melodrama discuss spectatorship, therefore, they are usually talking about different things. This has partly to do with the different intellectual histories and methodological groundings of theoretical work on film and on television. Whereas most television theory has until fairly recently existed under the sociological rubric of media studies, film theory has on the whole been based in the criticism-oriented tradition of literary studies. In consequence, while the one tends to privilege contexts over texts, the other usually privileges texts over contexts.

However, some recent critical work on soap opera, notably work produced within a cultural studies context, does attempt a *rapprochement* of text and context. Charlotte Brunsdon, writing about the British soap opera *Crossroads*, draws a distinction between subject positions proposed by texts and a 'social subject' who may or may not take up these positions.[13] In considering the interplay of 'social reader and social text', Brunsdon attempts to come to terms with problems posed by the universalism of the psychoanalytic model of the spectator/subject as against the descriptiveness and limited analytical scope of studies of specific instances and conjunctures. In taking up the instance of soap opera, then, one of Brunsdon's broader objectives is to resolve the dualism of text and context.

'Successful' spectatorship of a soap like *Crossroads*, it is argued, demands a certain cultural capital: familiarity with the plots and characters of a particular serial as well as with soap opera as a genre. It also demands wider cultural competence, especially in the codes of conduct of personal and family life. For Brunsdon, then, the spectator addressed by soap opera is constructed within culture rather than by representation. This, however, would indicate that such a spectator, a 'social subject', might – rather than being a subject in process of gender positioning – belong after all to a social audience already divided by gender.

The 'social subject' of this cultural model produces meaning by decoding messages or communications, an activity which is always socially situated.[14] Thus although such a model may move some way towards reconciling text and context, the balance of Brunsdon's argument remains weighted in favour of context: spectator–text relations are apparently regarded virtually as an effect of sociocultural contexts. Is there a way in which spectator/subjects of film and television texts can be thought in a historically specific manner, or indeed a way for the social audience to be rescued from social/historical determinism?

Although none of the feminist criticism of soap opera and melodrama reviewed here has come up with any solution to these problems, it all attempts, in some degree and with greater or lesser success, to engage with them. Brunsdon's essay possibly comes closest to an answer, paradoxically because its very failure to resolve the dualism which ordains that spectators are constructed by texts while audiences have their place in contexts begins to hint at a way around the problem. Although the hybrid 'social subject' may turn out to be more a social audience member than a spectator, this concept does suggest that a move into theories of discourse could prove productive.

Both spectators and social audience may accordingly be regarded as discursive constructs. Representations, contexts, audiences and spectators would then be seen as a series of interconnected social discourses, certain discourses possessing greater constitutive authority at specific moments than others. Such a model permits relative autonomy for the operations of texts, readings and contexts, and also allows for contradictions, oppositional readings and varying degrees of discursive authority. Since the state of a discursive formation is not constant, it can be apprehended only by means of inquiry into specific instances or conjunctures. In attempting to deal with the text–context split and to address the relationship between spectators and social audiences, therefore, theories of representation may have to come to terms with discursive formations of the social, cultural and textual.

IV

One of the impulses generating feminist critical and theoretical work on soap opera and the woman's picture is a desire to examine genres which are popular, and popular in particular with women. The assumption is usually that such popularity has to do mainly with the social audience: television soaps attract large numbers of viewers, many of them women, and in its heyday the woman's picture also drew in a mass female audience. But when the nature of this appeal is sought in the texts themselves or in relations between spectators and texts, the argument becomes rather more complex. In what specific ways do soaps and melodramas address or construct female/feminine spectators?

To some extent, they offer the spectator a position of mastery: this is certainly true as regards the hermeneutic of the melodrama's classic narrative, though perhaps less obviously so in relation to the soap's infinite process of narrativity. At the same time, they also place the spectator in a masochistic position of either – in the case of the woman's picture – identifying with a female character's renunciation or, as in soap opera, forever anticipating an endlessly held-off resolution. Culturally speaking, this combination of mastery and masochism in the reading competence constructed by soaps and melodramas suggests an interplay of masculine and feminine subject positions. Culturally dominant codes inscribe the masculine, while the feminine bespeaks a 'return of the repressed' in the form of codes which may well transgress culturally dominant subject positions, though only at the expense of proposing a position of subjection for the spectator.

At the same time, it is sometimes argued on behalf of both soap opera and film melodrama that in a society whose representations of itself are governed by the masculine, these genres at least raise the possibility of female desire and female point-of-view. Pam Cook advances such a view in relation to the woman's picture, for example.[15] But how is the oppositional potential of this to be assessed? Tania Modleski suggests that soap opera is 'in the vanguard not just of TV art but of all popular narrative art'.[16] But such a statement begs the question: in what circumstances can popular narrative art itself be regarded as transgressive? Because texts do not operate in isolation from contexts, any answer to these questions must take into account the ways in which popular narratives are read, the conditions under which they are produced and consumed, and the ends to which they are appropriated. As most feminist writing on soap opera and the woman's melodrama implies, there is ample space in the articulation of these various instances for contradiction and for struggles over meaning.

The popularity of television soap opera and film melodrama with women raises the question of how it is that sizeable audiences of women relate to these representations and the institutional practices of which they form part. It provokes, too, a consideration of the continuity between women's interpellation as spectators and their status as a social audience. In turn, the distinction between social audience and spectator/subject, and attempts to explore the relationship between the two, are part of a broader theoretical endeavour: to deal in tandem with texts and contexts. The distinction between social audience and spectator must also inform debates and practices around cultural production, in which questions of context and reception are always paramount. For anyone interested in feminist cultural politics, such considerations will necessarily inform any assessment of the place and the political usefulness of popular genres aimed at, and consumed by, mass audiences of women.

NOTES

First published in *Screen*, Winter 1984, vol. 25, no. 1, pp. 18–28.

1 Muriel G. Cantor and Suzanne Pingree, *The Soap Opera*, Beverly Hills, Sage Publications, 1983, p. 22. Here 'soap opera' refers to daytime (US) or early evening (UK) serials, not prime-time serials like *Dallas* and *Dynasty*.
2 See Jean-Louis Baudry, 'Ideological Effects of the Basic Cinematographic

Apparatus', *Film Quarterly*, 1974–5, vol. 28, no. 2, pp. 39–47; Christian Mctz, 'The Imaginary Signifier', *Screen*, Summer 1975, vol. 16, no. 2, pp. 14–76.

3 Laura Mulvey, 'Afterthoughts on "Visual Pleasure and Narrative Cinema" . . . Inspired by *Duel in the Sun*', *Framework*, 1981, nos. 15–17, pp. 12–15.

4 Laura Mulvey, 'Visual Pleasure and Narrative Cinema', chapter 1, pp. 22–34 in this volume; originally published in *Screen*, Autumn 1975, vol. 16, no. 3, pp. 6–18.

5 Pam Cook, 'Melodrama and the Women's Picture', in Sue Aspinall and Robert Murphy (eds), *Gainsborough Melodrama*, London, British Film Institute, 1983, p. 17.

6 Tania Modleski, *Loving with a Vengeance: Mass Produced Fantasies for Women*, Hamden Connecticut, Shoe String Press, 1982, p. 105. See also Tania Modleski, 'The Search for Tomorrow in Today's Soap Operas', *Film Quarterly*, 1979, vol. 33, no. 1, pp. 12–21.

7 Cook, op. cit.

8 Methods and findings of social science research on the social audience for American daytime soap operas are discussed in Cantor and Pingree, op. cit., chapter 7.

9 Modleski, *Loving with a Vengeance*, op. cit., p. 88.

10 Charlotte Brunsdon, '*Crossroads*: Notes on Soap Opera', *Screen*, Winter 1981, vol. 22, no. 4, pp. 32–7.

11 Cook, op. cit., p. 19.

12 John Ellis, *Visible Fictions*, London, Routledge & Kegan Paul, 1982.

13 Brunsdon, op. cit., p. 32.

14 A similar model is also adopted by Dorothy Hobson in *Crossroads: The Drama of a Soap Opera*, London, Methuen, 1982.

15 Cook, op. cit.; E. Ann Kaplan takes a contrary position in 'Theories of Melodrama: a Feminist Perspective', *Women and Performance: a Journal of Feminist Theory*, 1983, vol. 1, no. 1, pp. 40–8.

16 Modleski, *Loving with a Vengeance*, op. cit., p. 87.

16

THE OTHER QUESTION: THE STEREOTYPE AND COLONIAL DISCOURSE

Homi K. Bhabha

To concern oneself with the founding concepts of the entire history of philosophy, to deconstitute them, is not to undertake the work of the philologist or of the classic historian of philosophy. Despite appearances, it is probably the most daring way of making the beginnings of a step outside of philosophy.

Jacques Derrida: Structure, Sign and Play

I

An important feature of colonial discourse is its dependence on the concept of 'fixity' in the ideological construction of otherness.[1] Fixity, as the sign of cultural/historical/racial difference in the discourse of colonialism, is a paradoxical mode of representation: it connotes rigidity and an unchanging order as well as disorder, degeneracy and daemonic repetition. Likewise the stereotype, which is its major discursive strategy, is a form of knowledge and identification that vacillates between what is always 'in place', already known, and something that must be anxiously repeated . . . as if the essential duplicity of the Asiatic or the bestial sexual licence of the African that needs no proof, can never really, in discourse, be proved. It is this process of *ambivalence*, central to the stereotype that my essay explores as it constructs a theory of colonial discourse. For it is the force of ambivalence that gives the colonial stereotype its currency: ensures its repeatability in changing historical and discursive conjunctures; informs its strategies of individuation and marginalization; produces that effect of probabilistic truth and predictability which, for the stereotype, must always be in *excess* of what can be empirically proved or logically construed. Yet the function of ambivalence as one of the most significant discursive and psychical strategies of discriminatory power – whether racist or sexist, peripheral or metropolitan – remains to be charted.

The absence of such a perspective has its own history of political expediency. To recognize the stereotype as an ambivalent mode of knowledge and power demands a theoretical and political response that challenges deterministic or functionalist modes of conceiving of the relationship between discourse and politics, and questions dogmatic andmoralistic positions on the meaning of oppression and discrimination. My reading of colonial discourse suggests that the point of intervention should shift from the *identification* of images as positive or negative, to an understanding of the *processes of subjectification* made possible (and plausible) through stereotypical discourse. To judge the stereotyped image on the basis of a prior political normativity is to dismiss it, not to displace it, which is only possible by engaging with its *effectivity*; with the repertoire of positions of power and resistance, domination and dependence that constructs the colonial subject (both colonizer and colonized). I do not intend to deconstruct the colonial discourse to reveal its ideological misconceptions or repressions, to exult in its self-reflexivity, or to indulge its liberatory 'excess'. In order to understand the productivity of colonial power it is crucial to construct its regime of 'truth', not to subject its representations to a normalizing judgement. Only then does it become possible to understand the *productive* ambivalence of the object of colonial discourse – that 'otherness' which is at once an object of desire and derision, an articulation of difference contained within the fantasy of origin and identity. What such a reading reveals are the boundaries of colonial discourse and it enables a transgression of these limits from the space of that otherness.

The construction of the colonial subject in discourse, and the exercise of colonial power through discourse, demands an articulation of forms of difference – racial and sexual. Such an articulation becomes crucial if it is held that the body is always simultaneously inscribed in both the economy of pleasure and desire and the economy of discourse, domination and power. I do not wish to conflate, unproblematically, two forms of the marking – and splitting – of the subject nor to globalize two forms of representation. I want to suggest, however, that there is a theoretical space and a political place for such an *articulation* – in the sense in which that word itself denies an 'original' identity or a 'singularity' to objects of difference – sexual or racial. If such a view is taken, as Feuchtwang argues in a different context,[2] it follows that the epithets racial or sexual come to be seen as modes of differentiation, realized as multiple, cross-cutting determinations, polymorphous and perverse, always demanding a specific and strategic calculation of their effects. Such is, I believe, the moment of colonial discourse. It is the most theoretically underdeveloped form of discourse, but crucial to the binding of a range of differences and discriminations that inform the discursive and political practices of racial and cultural hierarchization.

Before turning to the construction of colonial discourse, I want to discuss briefly the process by which forms of racial/cultural/historical otherness have been marginalized in theoretical texts committed to the articulation of 'difference' or 'contradiction', in order, it is claimed, to reveal the limits of western representationalist discourse. In facilitating the passage 'from work to text' and stressing the arbitrary, differential and systemic construction of social and cultural signs, these critical strategies unsettle the idealist quest for meanings that are, most often, intentionalist and nationalist. So much is not in question. What does need to be questioned, however, is the *mode of representation of otherness*.

Where better to raise the question of the subject of racial and cultural difference than in Stephen Heath's masterly analysis of the chiaroscuro world of Welles's classic, *A Touch of Evil*? I refer to an area of its analysis which has generated the least comment, that is, Heath's attention to the structuration of the border Mexico/USA that circulates through the text affirming and exchanging some notion of 'limited being'. Heath's work departs from the traditional analysis of racial and cultural differences, which identify stereotype and image and elaborate them in a moralistic or nationalistic discourse that affirms the *origin* and *unity* of national identity. Heath's attentiveness to the contradictory and diverse sites within the textual system, which *construct* national/cultural differences in their deployment of the semes of 'foreignness', 'mixedness', 'impurity', as transgressive and corrupting, is extremely relevant. His attention to the turnings of this much neglected subject as sign (not symbol or stereotype) disseminated in the codes (as 'partition', 'exchange', 'naming', 'character', etc.), gives us a useful sense of the circulation and proliferation of racial and cultural otherness. Despite the awareness of the multiple or cross-cutting determinations in the construction of modes of sexual and racial differentiation there is a sense in which Heath's analysis marginalizes otherness. Although I shall argue that the problem of the border Mexico/USA is read too singularly, too exclusively under the sign of sexuality, it is not that I am not aware of the many proper and relevant reasons for that 'feminist' focus. The 'entertainment' operated by the realist Hollywood film of the 1950s was always also a containment of the subject in a narrative economy of voyeurism and fetishism. Moreover, the displacement that organizes any textual system, within which the display of difference circulates, demands that the play of 'nationalities' should participate in the sexual positioning, troubling the Law and desire. There is, nevertheless, a singularity and reductiveness in concluding that:

> Vargas is the position of desire, its admission and its prohibition. Not surprisingly he has two names: the name of desire is Mexican, Miguel . . . that of the Law American – Mike. . . . The film uses the border, the play between American and Mexican . . . at the same time it seeks to hold that play finally in the opposition of purity and mixture which in turn is a version of Law and desire.[3]

However liberatory it is from one position to see the logic of the text traced ceaselessly between the Ideal Father and the Phallic Mother, in another sense, seeing only one possible articulation of the differential complex 'race-sex', it half colludes with the proffered images of marginality. For if the naming of Vargas is crucially mixed and split in the economy of desire, then there are other mixed economies which make naming and positioning equally problematic 'across the border'. To identify the 'play' on the border as purity and mixture and to see it as an allegory of Law and desire reduces the articulation of racial and sexual difference to what is dangerously close to becoming a circle rather than a spiral of difference. On that basis, it is not possible to construct the polymorphous and perverse collusion between racism and sexism as a *mixed economy* – for instance, the discourses of American cultural colonialism and Mexican dependency, the fear/desire of miscegenation, the American border as cultural signifier of a pioneering, male 'American' spirit always under threat from races and cultures beyond the border or frontier. If the death of the Father is the interruption on which the narrative is initiated, it is through that death that miscegenation is both possible and deferred; if, again, it is the purpose of the narrative to restore Susan as 'good object', it also becomes its project to deliver Vargas from his racial 'mixedness'. It is all there in Heath's splendid scrutiny of the text, revealed as he brushes against its grain. What is missing is the taking up of these positions as also the *object(ives)* of his analysis.

These objectives have been pursued in the January/February 1983 issue of *Screen* (vol. 24, no. 2), which addresses the problems of 'Racism, colonialism and cinema'. This is a timely and welcome intervention in the debate on realist narrative and its conditions of existence and representability – a debate which has hitherto engaged mainly with the 'subject' of gender and class within the social and textual formations of western bourgeois society. It would be inappropriate to review this issue of *Screen* here, but I would like to draw attention to Julianne Burton's 'The politics of aesthetic distance: the presentation of representation in *São Bernardo*'. Burton produces an interesting reading of Hirzman's *São Bernardo* as a specific Third World riposte of dualistic metropolitan debates around realism and the possibilities of rupture. Although she doesn't use Barthes, it would be accurate to say that she locates the film as the 'limit-text' of both its own totalitarian social context *as well as* contemporary theoretical debates on representation.

Again, anti-colonialist objectives are admirably taken up by Robert Stam and Louise Spence in 'Colonialism, racism and representation', with a useful Brechtian emphasis on the politicization of the *means* of representation, specifically point-of-view and suture. But despite the shift in political objectives and critical methods, there remains in their essay a limiting and traditional reliance on the stereotype as offering, *at any one time*, a *secure* point of identification. This is not compensated for (nor contradicted by) their view that, *at other times and places*, the same stereotype may be read in a contradictory way or, indeed, be misread. What is, therefore, a simplification in the process of stereotypical representation has a knock-on effect on their central point about the politics of point-of-view.

They operate a passive and unitary notion of suture which simplifies the politics and 'aesthetics' of spectator-positioning by ignoring the ambivalent, psychical process of identification which is crucial to the argument. In contrast I suggest, in a very preliminary way, that the colonial stereotype is a complex, ambivalent, contradictory mode of representation, as anxious as it is assertive, and demands not only that we extend our critical and political objectives but that we change the object of analysis itself.

The difference of other cultures is other than the excess of signification or the trajectory of desire. These are theoretical strategies that are necessary to combat 'ethnocentricism' but they cannot, of themselves, unreconstructed, represent that otherness. There can be no inevitable sliding from the semiotic activity to the unproblematic reading of other cultural and discursive systems.[4] There is in such readings a will to power and knowledge that, in failing to specify the limits of their own field of enunciation and effectivity, proceeds to individualize otherness as the discovery of their own assumptions.

II

The difference of colonial discourse as an apparatus of power[5] will emerge more fully as this paper develops. At this stage, however, I shall provide what I take to be the minimum conditions and specifications of such a discourse. It is an apparatus that turns on the recognition and disavowal of racial/cultural/historical differences. Its predominant strategic function is the creation of a space for a 'subject peoples' through the production of knowledges in terms of which surveillance is exercised and a complex form of pleasure/unpleasure is incited. It seeks authorization for its strategies by the production of knowledges of colonizer and colonized which are stereotypical but antithetically evaluated. The objective of colonial discourse is to construe the colonized as a population of degenerate types on the basis of racial origin, in order to justify conquest and to establish systems of administration and instruction. Despite the play of power within colonial discourse and the shifting positionalities of its subjects (for example effects of class, gender, ideology, different social formations, varied systems of colonization and so on), I am referring to a form of governmentality that in marking out a 'subject nation', appropriates, directs and dominates its various spheres of activity. Therefore, despite the 'play' in the colonial system which is crucial to its exercise of power, colonial discourse produces the colonized as a social reality which is at once an 'other' and yet entirely knowable and visible. It resembles a form of narrative whereby the productivity and circulation of subjects and signs are bound in a reformed and recognizable totality. It employs a system of representation, a regime of truth, that is structurally similar to realism. And it is in order to intervene within that system of representation that Edward Said proposes a semiotic of 'Orientalist' power, examining the varied European discourses which constitute 'the Orient' as an unified racial, geographical, political and cultural zone of the world. Said's analysis is revealing of, and relevant to, colonial discourse:

> Philosophically, then, the kind of language, thought, and vision that I have been calling orientalism very generally is a form of *radical realism*; anyone employing orientalism, which is the habit for dealing with questions, objects, qualities and regions deemed Oriental, will designate, name, point to, fix what he is talking or thinking about with a word or phrase, which then is considered either to have acquired, or more simply to be, reality. . . . The tense they employ is the timeless eternal; they convey an impression of repetition and strength. . . . For all these functions it is frequently enough to use the simple copula *is*. [my emphasis][6]

For Said, the copula seems to be the point at which western Rationalism preserves the boundaries of sense for itself. Of this, too, Said is aware when he hints continually at a polarity or division at the very centre of Orientalism.[7] It is, on the one hand, a topic of learning, discovery, practice; on the other, it is the site of dreams, images, fantasies, myths, obsessions and requirements. It is a static system of 'synchronic essentialism', a knowledge of 'signifiers of stability' such as the lexicographic and the encyclopaedic. However, this site is continually under threat from diachronic forms of history and narrative, signs of instability. And, finally, this line of thinking is given a shape analogical to the dreamwork, when Said refers explicitly to a distinction between 'an unconscious positivity' which he terms *latent* Orientalism, and the stated knowledges and views about the Orient which he calls *manifest* Orientalism.

Where the originality of this pioneering theory loses its inventiveness, and for me its usefulness, is with Said's reluctance to engage with the alterity and ambivalence in the articulation of these two economies which threaten to split the very object of Orientalist discourse as a knowledge and the subject positioned therein. He contains this threat by introducing a binarism within the argument which, in initially setting up an opposition between these two discursive scenes, finally allows them to be correlated as a congruent system of representation that is unified through a political-ideological *intention* which, in his words, enables Europe to advance securely and *unmetaphorically* upon the Orient. Said identifies the *content* of Orientalism as the unconscious repository of fantasy, imaginative writings and essential ideas; and the *form* of manifest Orientalism as the historically and discursively determined, diachronic aspect. This division/correlation structure of manifest and latent Orientalism leads to the effectivity of the concept of discourse being undermined by what could be called the polarities of intentionality.

317

This produces a problem with Said's use of Foucault's concepts of power and discourse. The productivity of Foucault's concept of power/knowledge lies in its refusal of an epistemology which opposes essence/appearance, ideology/science. '*Pouvoir/Savoir*' places subjects in a relation of power and recognition that is not part of a symmetrical or dialectical relation – self/other, master/slave – which can then be subverted by being inverted. Subjects are always disproportionately placed in opposition or domination through the symbolic decentring of multiple power relations which play the role of support as well as target or adversary. It becomes difficult, then, to conceive of the *historical* enunciations of colonial discourse without them being either functionally overdetermined or strategically elaborated or displaced by the *unconscious* scene of latent Orientalism. Equally, it is difficult to conceive of the process of subjectification as a placing *within* Orientalist or colonial discourse for the dominated subject without the dominant being strategically placed within it too. There is always, in Said, the suggestion that colonial power and discourse is possessed entirely by the colonizer, which is a historical and theoretical simplification. The terms in which Said's Orientalism is unified – the intentionality and unidirectionality of colonial power – also unify the subject of colonial enunciation.

This is a result of Said's inadequate attention to representation as a concept that articulates the historical and fantasy (as the scene of desire) in the production of the 'political' effects of discourse. He rightly rejects a notion of orientalism as the misrepresentation of an Oriental essence. However, having introduced the concept of 'discourse' he does not face up to the problems it makes for the instrumentalist notion of power/knowledge that he seems to require. This problem is summed up by his ready acceptance of the view that 'Representations are formations, or as Roland Barthes has said of all the operations of language, they are deformations.'[8]

This brings me to my second point. The closure and coherence attributed to the unconscious pole of colonial discourse and the unproblematized notion of the subject, restricts the effectivity of both power and knowledge. It is not possible to see how power functions productively as incitement and interdiction. Nor would it be possible, without the attribution of ambivalence to relations of power/knowledge, to calculate the traumatic impact of the return of the oppressed – those terrifying stereotypes of savagery, cannibalism, lust and anarchy which are the signal points of identification and alienation, scenes of fear and desire, in colonial texts. It is precisely this function of the stereotype as phobia and fetish that, according to Fanon, threatens the closure of the racial/epidermal schema for the colonial subject and opens the royal road to colonial fantasy.

Despite Said's limitations, or perhaps because of them, there is a forgotten, underdeveloped passage which, in cutting across the body of the text, articulates the question of power and desire that I now want to take up. It is this:

Altogether an internally structured archive is built up from the literature that belongs to these experiences. Out of this comes a restricted number of typical encapsulations: the journey, the history, the fable, the stereotype, the polemical confrontation. These are the lenses through which the Orient is experienced, and they shape the language, perception, and form of the encounter between East and West. What gives the immense number of encounters some unity, however, is the vacillation I was speaking about earlier. Something patently foreign and distant acquires, for one reason or another, a status more rather than less familiar. One tends to stop judging things either as completely novel or as completely well-known; a new median category emerges, a category that allows one to see new things, things seen for the first time, as versions of a previously known thing. In essence such a category is not so much a way of receiving new information as it is a method of controlling what seems to be a threat to some established view of things. . . . The threat is muted, familiar values impose themselves, and in the end the mind reduces the pressure upon it by accommodating things to itself as either 'original' or 'repetitious'. . . . The orient at large, therefore, vacillates between the West's contempt for what is familiar and its shivers of delight in – or fear of – novelty.[9]

What is this other scene of colonial discourse played out around the 'median category'? What is this theory of encapsulation or fixation which moves between the recognition of cultural and racial difference and its disavowal, by affixing the unfamiliar to something established, in a form that is repetitious and vacillates between delight and fear? Does the Freudian fable of fetishism (and disavowal) circulate within the discourse of colonial power requiring the articulation of modes of differentiation – sexual and racial – as well as different modes of theoretical discourse – psychoanalytic and historical?

The strategic articulation of 'coordinates of knowledge' – racial and sexual – and their inscription in the play of colonial power as modes of differentiation, defence, fixation, hierarchization, is a way of specifying colonial discourse which would be illuminated by reference to Foucault's poststructuralist concept of the *dispositif* or apparatus. Foucault stresses that the relations of knowledge and power within the apparatus are always a strategic response to *an urgent need* at a given historical moment – much as I suggested at the outset – that the force of colonial discourse as a theoretical and political intervention, was the *need*, in our contemporary moment, to contest singularities of difference and to articulate modes of differentiation. Foucault writes:

the apparatus is essentially of a strategic nature, which means assuming that it is a matter of a certain manipulation of relations of forces, either developing them in a particular direction, blocking them,

319

stabilising them, utilising them etc. The apparatus is thus always inscribed in a play of power, but it is also always linked to certain coordinates of knowledge which issue from it but, to an equal degree, condition it. This is what the apparatus consists in: strategies of relations of forces supporting and supported by, types of knowledge.[10]

In this spirit I argue for the reading of the stereotype in terms of fetishism. The myth of historical origination – racial purity, cultural priority – produced in relation to the colonial stereotype functions to 'normalize' the multiple beliefs and split subjects that constitute colonial discourse as a consequence of its process of disavowal. The scene of fetishism functions similarly as, at once, a reactivation of the material of original fantasy – the anxiety of castration and sexual difference – as well as a normalization of that difference and disturbance in terms of the fetish object as the substitute for the mother's penis. Within the apparatus of colonial power, the discourses of sexuality and race relate in a process of *functional overdetermination*, 'because each effect . . . enters into resonance or contradiction with the others and thereby calls for a readjustment or a reworking of the heterogeneous elements that surface at various points'.[11]

There is both a structural and functional justification for reading the racial stereotype of colonial discourse in terms of fetishism.[12] My rereading of Said establishes the *structural* link. Fetishism, as the disavowal of difference, is that repetitious scene around the problem of castration. The recognition of sexual difference – as the precondition for the circulation of the chain of absence and presence in the realm of the Symbolic – is disavowed by the fixation on an object that masks that difference and restores an original presence. The *functional* link between the fixation of the fetish and the stereotype (or the stereotype as fetish) is even more relevant. For fetishism is always a 'play' or vacillation between the archaic affirmation of wholeness/similarity – in Freud's terms: 'All men have penises'; in ours 'All men have the same skin/race/culture' – and the anxiety associated with lack and difference – again, for Freud 'Some do not have penises'; for us 'Some do not have the same skin/race/culture'. Within discourse, the fetish represents the simultaneous play between metaphor as substitution (masking absence and difference) and metonymy (which contiguously registers the perceived lack). The fetish or stereotype gives access to an 'identity' which is predicated as much on mastery and pleasure as it is on anxiety and defence, for it is a form of multiple and contradictory belief in its recognition of difference and disavowal of it. This conflict of pleasure/unpleasure, mastery/defence, knowledge/disavowal, absence/presence, has a fundamental significance for colonial discourse. For the scene of fetishism is also the scene of the reactivation and repetition of primal fantasy – the subject's desire for a pure origin that is always threatened by its division, for the subject must be gendered to be engendered, to be spoken.

The stereotype, then, as the primary point of subjectification in colonial discourse, for both colonizer and colonized, is the scene of a similar fantasy and defence – the desire for an originality which is again threatened by the differences of race, colour and culture. My contention is splendidly caught in Fanon's title *Black Skin White Masks* where the disavowal of difference turns the colonial subject into a misfit – a grotesque mimicry or 'doubling' that threatens to split the soul and whole, undifferentiated skin of the ego. The stereotype is not a simplification because it is a false representation of a given reality. It is a simplification because it is an arrested, fixated form of representation that, in denying the play of difference (which the negation through the Other permits), constitutes a problem for the *representation* of the subject in significations of psychic and social relations.

When Fanon talks of the positioning of the subject in the stereotyped discourse of colonialism, he gives further credence to my point. The legends, stories, histories and anecdotes of a colonial culture offer the subject a primordial Either/Or.[13] *Either* he is fixed in a consciousness of the body as a solely negating activity *or* as a new kind of man, a new genus. What is denied the colonial subject, both as colonizer and colonized, is that form of negation which gives access to the recognition of difference. It is that possibility of difference and circulation which would liberate the signifier of *skin/culture* from the fixations of racial typology, the analytics of blood, ideologies of racial and cultural dominance or degeneration. 'Wherever he goes,' Fanon despairs, 'the Negro remains a Negro' – his race becomes the ineradicable sign of *negative difference* in colonial discourses. For the stereotype impedes the circulation and articulation of the signifier of 'race' as anything other than its *fixity* as racism. We always already know that blacks are licentious, Asiatics duplicitous. . . .

III

There are two 'primal scenes' in Fanon's *Black Skins White Masks*: two myths of the origin of the marking of the subject within the racist practices and discourses of a colonial culture. On one occasion a white girl fixes Fanon in a look and word as she turns to identify with her mother. It is a scene which echoes endlessly through his essay 'The Fact of Blackness': '*Look*, a Negro . . . Mamma, *see* the Negro! I'm frightened. Frightened. Frightened.' 'What else could it be for me,' Fanon concludes, 'but an amputation, an excision, a haemorrhage that spattered my whole body with black blood.'[14] Equally, he stresses the primal moment when the child encounters racial and cultural stereotypes in children's fictions, where white heroes and black demons are proffered as points of ideological and psychical identification. Such dramas are enacted *every day* in colonial societies, says Fanon, employing a theatrical metaphor – the scene – which emphasizes the visible – the seen. I want to play on both these senses which refer at once to the site of fantasy and desire and to the sight of subjectification and power.

The drama underlying these dramatic 'everyday' colonial scenes is not difficult to discern. In each of them the subject turns around the pivot of the 'stereotype' to return to a point of total identification. The girl's gaze returns to her mother in the recognition and disavowal of the Negroid type; the black child turns away from himself, his race, in his total identification with the positivity of whiteness which is at once colour and no colour. In the act of disavowal and fixation the colonial subject is returned to the narcissism of the Imaginary and its identification of an ideal ego that is white and whole. For what these primal scenes illustrate is that looking/hearing/reading as sites of subjectification in colonial discourse are evidence of the importance of the visual and auditory imaginary for the *histories* of societies.[15]

It is in this context that I want to allude briefly to the problematic of seeing/being seen. I suggest that in order to conceive of the colonial subject as the effect of power that is productive – disciplinary and 'pleasurable' – one has to see the *surveillance* of colonial power as functioning in relation to the regime of the *scopic drive*. That is, the drive that represents the pleasure in 'seeing', which has the look as its object of desire, is both related to the myth of origins, the primal scene, and to the problematic of fetishism and locates the surveyed object within the 'imaginary' relation. Like voyeurism, surveillance must depend for its effectivity on 'the *active consent* which is its real or mythical correlate (but always real as myth) and establishes in the scopic space the illusion of the object relation'.[16] The ambivalence of this form of 'consent' in objectification – real as mythical – is the *ambivalence* on which the stereotype turns and illustrates that crucial bind of pleasure and power that Foucault asserts but, in my view, fails to explain.

My anatomy of colonial discourse remains incomplete until I locate the stereotype, as an arrested, fetishistic mode of representation within its field of identification, which I have identified in my description of Fanon's primal scenes, as the Lacanian schema of the Imaginary. The Imaginary[17] is the transformation that takes place in the subject at the formative mirror phase, when it assumes a *discrete* image which allows it to postulate a series of equivalences, samenesses, identities, between the objects of the surrounding world. However, this positioning is itself *problematic*, for the subject finds or recognizes itself through an image which is simultaneously alienating and hence potentially confrontational. This is the basis of the close relation between the two forms of identification complicit with the Imaginary – narcissism and aggressivity. It is precisely these two forms of 'identification' that constitute the dominant strategy of colonial power exercised in relation to the stereotype which, as a form of multiple and contradictory belief, gives knowledge of difference and simultaneously disavows or masks it. Like the mirror phase 'the fullness' of the stereotype – its image *as* identity – is always threatened by 'lack'.

The construction of colonial discourse is then a complex articulation of the tropes of fetishism – metaphor and metonymy – and the forms of narcissistic and aggressive identification available to the Imaginary. Stereotypical racial discourse is a four-term strategy. There is a tie-up between the metaphoric or masking function of the fetish and the narcissistic object-choice and an opposing alliance between the metonymic figuring of lack and the aggressive phase of the Imaginary. A repertoire of conflictual positions constitutes the subject in colonial discourse. The taking up of any one position, within a specific discursive form, in a particular historical conjuncture, is thus always problematic – the site of both fixity and fantasy. It provides a colonial 'identity' that is played out – like all fantasies of originality and origination – in the face and space of the disruption and threat from the heterogeneity of other positions. As a form of splitting and multiple belief, the 'stereotype' requires, for its successful signification, a continual and repetitive chain of other stereotypes. The process by which the metaphoric 'masking' is inscribed on a lack which must then be concealed gives the stereotype both its fixity and its phantasmatic quality – the *same old* stories of the Negro's animality, the Coolie's inscrutability or the stupidity of the Irish *must* be told (compulsively) again and afresh, and are differently gratifying and terrifying each time.

In any specific colonial discourse the metaphoric/narcissistic and the metonymic/aggressive positions will function simultaneously, strategically poised in relation to each other; similar to the moment of alienation which stands as a threat to Imaginary plentitude, and 'multiple belief' which threatens fetishistic disavowal. The subjects of discourse are constructed within an apparatus of power which *contains*, in both senses of the word, an 'other' knowledge – a knowledge that is arrested and fetishistic and circulates through colonial discourse as that limited form of otherness, that form of difference, that I have called the stereotype. Fanon poignantly describes the effects of this process for a colonized culture:

> a continued agony rather than a total disappearance of the preexisting culture. The culture once living and open to the future, becomes closed, fixed in the colonial status, caught in the yolk of oppression. Both present and mummified, it testifies against its members. . . . The cultural mummification leads to a mummification of individual thinking . . . As though it were possible for a man to evolve otherwise than within the framework of a culture that recognises him and that he decides to assume.[18]

My four-term strategy of the stereotype tries tentatively to provide a structure and a process for the 'subject' of a colonial discourse. I now want to take up the problem of discrimination as the political effect of such a discourse and relate it to the question of 'race' and 'skin'. To that end it is important to remember that the multiple belief that accompanies fetishism not only has disavowal value; it also has 'knowledge value' and it is this that I shall now pursue. In calculating this knowledge value it is crucial to consider what Fanon means when he says that:

> There is a quest for the Negro, the Negro is a demand, one cannot get along without him, he is needed, but only if he is made palatable in a certain way. Unfortunately the Negro knocks down the system and breaks the treaties.[19]

To understand this demand and how the native or Negro is made 'palatable' we must acknowledge some significant differences between the general theory of fetishism and its specific uses for an understanding of racist discourse. First, the fetish of colonial discourse – what Fanon calls the epidermal schema – is not, like the sexual fetish, a secret. Skin, as the key signifier of cultural and racial difference in the stereotype, is the most visible of fetishes, recognized as 'common knowledge' in a range of cultural, political and historical discourses, and plays a public part in the racial drama that is enacted every day in colonial societies. Second, it may be said that sexual fetish is closely linked to the 'good object'; it is the prop that makes the whole object desirable and lovable, facilitates sexual relations and can even promote a form of happiness. The stereotype can also be seen as that particular 'fixated' form of the colonial subject which *facilitates* colonial relations, and sets up a discursive form of racial and cultural opposition in terms of which colonial power is exercised. If it is claimed that the colonized are most often objects of hate, then we can reply with Freud that

> affection and hostility in the treatment of the fetish – which run parallel with the disavowal and acknowledgement of castration – are mixed in unequal proportions in different cases, so that the one or the other is more clearly recognisable.[20]

What this statement recognizes is the wide *range* of the stereotype, from the loyal servant to Satan, from the loved to the hated; a shifting of subject positions in the circulation of colonial power which I tried to account for through the motility of the metaphoric/narcissistic and metonymic/ aggressive system of colonial discourse. What remains to be examined, however, is the construction of the signifier of 'skin/race' in those regimes of visibility and discursivity – fetishistic, scopic, Imaginary – within which I have located the stereotypes. It is only on that basis that we can construct its 'knowledge–value' which will, I hope, enable us to see the place of fantasy in the exercise of colonial power.

My argument relies upon a particular reading of the problematic of representation which, Fanon suggests, is specific to the colonial situation. He writes:

> the originality of the colonial context is that the economic substructure is also a superstructure . . . you are rich because you are white, you are white because you are rich. This is why Marxist analysis should always be slightly stretched every time we have to do with the colonial problem.[21]

Fanon could either be seen to be adhering to a simple reflectionist or determinist notion of cultural/social signification or, more interestingly, he could be read as taking an 'anti-repressionist' position (attacking the notion that ideology as miscognition, or misrepresentation, is the repression of the real). For our purposes I tend towards the latter reading which then provides a 'visibility' to the exercise of power; gives force to the argument that skin, as a signifier of discrimination, must be produced or processed as visible. As Abbot says, in a very different context,

> whereas repression banishes its object into the unconscious, forgets and attempts to forget the forgetting, discrimination must constantly invite its representations into consciousness, reinforcing the crucial recognition of difference which they embody and revitalising them for the perception on which its effectivity depends. . . . It must sustain itself on the presence of the very difference which is also its object.[22]

What 'authorizes' discrimination, Abbot continues, is the occlusion of the preconstruction or working-up of difference: 'this repression of production entails that the recognition of difference is procured in an innocence, as a "nature"; recognition is contrived as primary cognition, spontaneous effect of the "evidence of the visible" '.[23]

This is precisely the kind of recognition, as spontaneous and visible, that is attributed to the stereotype. The difference of the object of discrimination is at once visible and natural – colour as the cultural/political *sign* of inferiority or degeneracy, skin as its natural '*identity*'. However, Abbot's account stops at the point of 'identification' and strangely colludes with the *success* of discriminatory practices by suggesting that their representations require the repression of the working-up of difference; to argue otherwise, according to him, would be to put the subject in 'an impossible awareness, since it would run into consciousness the heterogeneity of the subject as a place of articulation.'[24]

Despite his awareness of the crucial recognition of difference for discrimination and its problematization of repression, Abbot is trapped in his unitary place of articulation. He comes close to suggesting that it is possible, however momentarily and illusorily, for the *perpetrator* of the discriminatory discourse to be in a position that is *unmarked by the discourse* to the extent to which the *object* of discrimination is deemed natural and visible. What Abbot neglects is the facilitating role of contradiction and heterogeneity in the construction of authoritarian practices and their strategic, discursive fixations.

Although the 'authority' of colonial discourse depends crucially on its location in narcissism and the Imaginary, my concept of stereotype-as-suture is a recognition of the *ambivalence* of that authority and those orders of identification. The role of fetishistic identification, in the construction of discriminatory knowledges that depend on the 'presence of difference', is to provide a process of splitting and multiple/contradictory belief at the point of enunciation and subjectification. It is this crucial splitting of the ego which is represented in Fanon's description of the construction of the colonised subject as effect of stereotypical discourse: the subject primordially fixed and yet triply split between the incongruent knowledges of body, race, ancestors. Assailed by the stereotype, 'the corporeal schema crumbled, its place taken by a racial epidermal scheme. . . . It was no longer a question of being aware of my body in the third person but a triple person . . . I was not given one, but two, three places.'[25]

This process is best understood in terms of the articulation of multiple belief that Freud proposes in the essay on fetishism. It is a non-repressive form of knowledge that allows for the possibility of simultaneously embracing two contradictory beliefs, one official and one secret, one archaic and one progressive, one that allows the myth of origins, the other that articulates difference and division. Its knowledge 'value' lies in its orientation as a defence towards external reality, and provides, in Metz's words,

> the lasting matrix, the effective prototype of all those splittings of belief which man will henceforth be capable of in the most varied domains, of all the infinitely complex unconscious and occasionally conscious interactions which he will allow himself between believing and not-believing.[26]

It is through this notion of splitting and multiple belief that, I believe, it becomes easier to see the bind of knowledge and fantasy, power and pleasure, that informs the particular regime of visibility deployed in colonial discourse. The visibility of the racial/colonial Other is at once a *point* of identity ('Look, a Negro') and at the same time a *problem* for the attempted closure within discourse. For the recognition of difference as 'imaginary' points of identity and origin – such as Black and White – is disturbed by the representation of splitting in the discourse. What I called the play between the metaphoric-narcissistic and metonymic-aggressive moments in colonial discourse – that four-part strategy of the stereotype – crucially recognizes the prefiguring of desire as a potentially conflictual, disturbing force in all those regimes of 'originality' that I have brought together. In the objectification of the scopic drive there is always the threatened return of the look; in the identification of the Imaginary relation there is always the alienating other (or mirror) which crucially returns its image to the subject; and in that form of substitution and fixation that is fetishism there is always the trace of loss, absence. To put it succinctly, the recognition and disavowal of 'difference' is always disturbed by the question of its re-presentation or construction. The stereotype is in fact an 'impossible' object. For that very reason, the exertions of the 'official knowledges' of colonialism – pseudo-scientific, typological, legal-administrative, eugenicist – are imbricated at the point of their production of meaning and power with the fantasy that dramatizes the impossible desire for a pure, undifferentiated origin. Not itself the object of desire but its setting, not an ascription of prior identities but their production in the syntax of the scenario of racist discourse, colonial fantasy plays a crucial part in those everyday scenes of subjectification in a colonial society which Fanon refers to repeatedly. Like fantasies of the origins of sexuality, the productions of 'colonial desire' mark the discourse as 'a favoured spot for the most primitive defensive reactions such as turning against oneself, into an opposite, projection, negation'.[27]

The problem of origin as the problematic of racist, stereotypical knowledge is a complex one and what I have said about its construction will come clear in this illustration from Fanon. Stereotyping is not the setting up of a false image which becomes the scapegoat of discriminatory practices. It is a much more ambivalent text of projection and introjection, metaphoric and metonymic strategies, displacement, overdetermination, guilt, aggressivity; the masking and splitting of 'official' and phantasmatic knowledges to construct the positionalities and oppositionalities of racist discourse:

> My body was given back to me sprawled out, distorted, recoloured, clad in mourning in that white winter day. The Negro is an animal, the Negro is bad, the Negro is mean, the Negro is ugly; look, a nigger, it's cold, the nigger is shivering, the nigger is shivering because he is cold, the little boy is trembling because he is afraid of the nigger, the nigger is shivering with cold, that cold that goes through your bones, the handsome little boy is trembling because he thinks that the nigger is quivering with rage, the little white boy throws himself into his mother's arms: Mama, the nigger's going to eat me up.[28]

It is the scenario of colonial fantasy which, in staging the ambivalence of desire, articulates the demand for the Negro which the Negro disrupts. For the stereotype is at once a substitute and a shadow. By acceding to the wildest fantasies (in the popular sense) of the colonizer, the stereotyped Other reveals something of the 'fantasy' (as desire, defence) of that position of mastery. For if 'skin' in racist discourse is the visibility of darkness, and a prime signifier of the body and its social and cultural correlates, then we are bound to remember what Karl Abraham says in his seminal work on the scopic drive.[29] The pleasure-value of darkness is a withdrawal in order to know nothing of the external world. Its symbolic meaning, however, is thoroughly ambivalent. Darkness signifies at once both birth and death; it is in all cases a desire to return to the fullness of the mother, a desire for an unbroken and undifferentiated line of vision and origin.

But surely there is another scene of colonial discourse in which the native or Negro meets the demand of colonial discourse; where the sub-verting 'split' is recuperable within a strategy of social and political control. It is recognizably true that the chain of stereotypical signification is cur-iously mixed and split, polymorphous and perverse, an articulation of multiple belief. The black is both savage (cannibal) and yet the most obedient and dignified of servants (the bearer of food); he is the embodi-ment of rampant sexuality and yet innocent as a child; he is mystical, primitive, simple-minded and yet the most worldly and accomplished liar, and manipulator of social forces. In each case what is being dramatized is a separation – *between* races, cultures, histories, *within* histories – a separ-ation between *before* and *after* that repeats obsessively the mythical mo-ment of disjunction. Despite the structural similarities with the play of need and desire in primal fantasies, the colonial fantasy does not try to cover up that moment of separation. It is more ambivalent. On the one hand, it proposes a teleology – under certain conditions of colonial domi-nation and control the native is progressively reformable. On the other, however, it effectively displays the 'separation', makes it more visible. It is the visibility of this separation which, in denying the colonized the capaci-ties of self-government, independence, western modes of civility, lends authority to the official version and mission of colonial power. Colonial fantasy is the continual dramatization of emergence – of difference, free-dom – as the beginning of a history which is repetitively denied. Such a denial is the clearly voiced demand of colonial discourse as the legitimation of a form of rule that is facilitated by the racist fetish. In concluding, I would like to develop a little further my working definition of colonial discourse given at the start of this article.

Racist stereotypical discourse, in its colonial moment, inscribes a form of governmentality that is informed by a productive splitting in its consti-tution of knowledge and exercise of power. Some of its practices recognize the difference of race, culture, and history as elaborated by stereotypical knowledges, racial theories, administrative colonial experience, and on that basis institutionalize a range of political and cultural ideologies that are prejudicial, discriminatory, vestigial, archaic, 'mythical', and, crucially, are recognized as being so. By 'knowing' the native population in these terms, discriminatory and authoritarian forms of political control are considered appropriate. The colonized population is then deemed to be both the cause and effect of the system, imprisoned in the circle of interpretation. What is visible is the *necessity* of such rule which is justified by those moralistic and normative ideologies of amelioration recognized as the Civilizing Mission or the White Man's Burden. However, there coexist within the same apparatus of colonial power, modern systems and sciences of government, progressive 'western' forms of social and economic organization which provide the manifest justification for the project of colonialism – an argument which, in part, impressed Karl Marx. It is on the site of this coexistence that strategies of hierarchization and marginalization are employed in the management of colonial societies. And if my deduction from Fanon about the peculiar visibility of colonial power is acceptable to you, then I would extend that to say that it is a form of governmentality in which the 'ideological' space functions in more openly collaborative ways with political and economic exigencies. The barracks stands by the church which stands by the schoolroom; the cantonment stands hard by the 'civil lines'. Such visibility of the institutions and apparatuses of power is possible because the exercise of colonial power makes their *relationship* obscure, produces them as fetishes, spectacles of a 'natural'/racial pre-eminence. Only the seat of government is always elsewhere – alien and separate by that distance upon which surveillance depends for its strategies of objectification, normalization and discipline.

The last word belongs to Fanon:

> this behaviour [of the colonizer] betrays a determination to objectify, to confine, to imprison, to harden. Phrases such as 'I know them', 'that's the way they are', show this maximum objectification successfully achieved. . . . There is on the one hand a culture in which qualities of dynamism, of growth, of depth can be recognised. As against this, [in colonial cultures] we find characteristics, curiosities, things, never a structure.[30]

NOTES

This article is a revision of a paper given at the Sociology of Literature Conference, Essex University, 1982 and published in Francis Barker, (ed.), *The Politics of Theory*, Colchester, University of Essex, 1983. I would like to thank Dr Stephan Feuchtwang of City University for providing the critical and companionable context in which it was written, and Terry Eagleton for inviting me to speak on the subject at Oxford University and for his comments afterwards. The article was first published in *Screen*, Winter 1983, vol. 24, no. 6, pp. 18–36.

1 Realizing that the question of woman's relation to castration and access to the Symbolic requires a very specific form of attention and articulation, I chose to be cautious till I had worked out its implications for colonial discourse. Second, the representation of class difference in the construction of the colonial subject is not specified adequately. Wanting to avoid any form of class determinism 'in the last instance' it becomes difficult, if crucial, to calculate its effectivity.

2 Stephan Feuchtwang, 'Socialist, Feminist and Anti-racist Struggles', *m/f*, 1980, no. 4, p. 41.

3 Stephen Heath, 'Film and System, Terms of Analysis', Part II, *Screen*, Summer 1975, vol. 16, no. 2, p. 93.

4 For instance, having decentred the sign, Barthes finds Japan immediately insightful and visible and extends the empire of empty signs universally. Japan can only be the Anti-West: 'in the ideal Japanese house, devoid or nearly so of furniture, there is no place which in any way designates property; no seat, no bed, no table provides a point from which the body may constitute itself as subject (or master) of a space. The very concept of centre is rejected (burning frustration for Western man everywhere provided with his armchair and his bed, the owner of a domestic *position*)' (Roland Barthes, *L'Empire des Signes*, trans. Noël Burch as *To the Distant Observer*, London, Scolar Press, 1979, pp. 13–14). For a reading of Kristeva relevant to my argument, see Gayatri Spivak, 'French Feminism in an International Frame', *Yale French Studies*, 1981, no. 62, pp. 154–84.

5 This concept is discussed below; see p. 325.

6 Edward Said, *Orientalism*, London, Routledge & Kegan Paul, 1978, p. 72; emphasis added.

7 ibid., p. 206.

8 ibid., p. 273.

9 ibid., pp. 58–9.

10 Michel Foucault, 'The Confession of the Flesh', in *Power/Knowledge*, Brighton, Harvester Press, 1980, p. 196.

11 ibid., p. 195

12 See Sigmund Freud, 'Fetishism' (1927) in *On Sexuality*, vol. VII, Pelican Freud Library, Harmondsworth, Penguin Books, 1981, p. 345ff; Christian Metz, *Psychoanalysis and Cinema: the Imaginary Signifier*, London, Macmillan, 1982, pp. 67–78. See also Steve Neale, 'The Same Old Story: Stereotypes and Differences', *Screen Education*, Autumn–Winter 1979–80, nos. 32–3, pp. 33–7.

13 Frantz Fanon, *Black Skin White Masks*, London, Paladin, 1970; see pp. 78–82.

14 ibid., p. 79.

15 Metz, op. cit., pp. 59–60.

16 ibid., pp. 62–3.

17 For the best account of Lacan's concept of the Imaginary see Jacqueline Rose, 'The Imaginary', in Colin MacCabe (ed.), *The Talking Cure*, London, Macmillan, 1981.

18 Frantz Fanon, 'Racism and Culture', in *Toward the African Revolution*, London, Penguin Books, 1970, p. 44.

19 Fanon, *Black Skin White Masks*, op. cit., p. 114.

20 Freud, 'Fetishism', p. 357.

21 Frantz Fanon, *The Wretched of the Earth*, Harmondsworth, Penguin Books, 1969.

22 Paul Abbot, 'Authority', *Screen*, Summer 1979, vol. 20, no. 2, pp. 15–16.

23 ibid., p. 16.

24 ibid.
25 Fanon, *Black Skins White Masks*, op. cit., p. 79.
26 Metz, op. cit., p. 70.
27 J. Laplanche and J. B. Pontalis, 'Phantasy (or Fantasy)', in *The Language of Psychoanalysis*, London, Hogarth Press, 1980, p. 318.
28 Fanon, *Black Skins White Masks*, op. cit., p. 80.
29 See Karl Abraham, 'Transformations of Scopophilia', in *Selected Papers*, London, Hogarth Press, 1978.
30 Fanon, 'Racism and Culture', op. cit., p. 44.

INDEX

Abbott, Paul 325–6
Achetez des Pommes 142–3
Adam's Rib 234
'address' 120; address in pornography 177
advertisements 131, 136, 137–9. 151, 156, 168; and feminist campaigns 152, 169n, 170n, 204; for *Not a Love Story* 211
Ai No Corrida (*Empire of the Senses*) 167
Akerman, Chantal 84–5, 86–7, 89–90 98
Aliens 1
All About Eve 225, 249, 250–3, 256
alternative film practice 23, 85, 96
Althusser, Louis 116–17
Apollo Belvedere 139–40
apparatus 319–20
artist, the 176
Arzner, Dorothy 85
L'ssassin musicien 56
audience 43; look of the 33; social 305, 306, 309, 310

Ball of Fire 70, 73
Barthes, Roland 38, 248, 318, 330n
Bazin, André 82
Bellour, Raymond 10, 225, 246, 247, 277
Ben Hur 286
Benviste, Emile 118, 119, 120, 124n
Berger, John 136, 139
Beyond the Forest 237
Bhabha, Homi vii, 9, 10, 11, 293–4, 312–31
Birds, The 9
bisexuality 122; female 223

Black Skins, White Masks (Fanon) 321–2
Blonde Venus 223
body 74, 77, 78, 79–82, 96, 113, 116, 232; in advertising 152; art 142; as evidence 200–1; female 5, 29, 140, 239; in feminist cinema of fictionality 218; in language 75; male 5, 163, 261, 271–5, 281, 285, 286; in pornography 164, 177, 212, 217
Bogart, Humphrey 275
Boetticher, Budd 27, 173
Border Incident 281–2
British Board of Film Censors 148, 155, 157
British Independent film production 146; *see also* alternative film practice; counter cinema
Brown, Beverley 184, 185
Brownmiller, Susan 204
Brunsdon, Charlotte 308, 309
'buddy movie' 27
Buñuel, Luis 173
Burch, Noël 229, 231
Burton, Julianne 315

camera: look of the 33, 159, 173–4; in Hitchcock, subjective 31; technology 23, 28; *see also* look
Camera Obscura collective 86, 98
Carter, angela 165, 191–2, 204
castration 9, 16, 18, 22, 49, 60–1, 74, 77, 78, 79, 86, 96–7, 330n; anxiety/fear 78, 104n, 159, 163, 189; blinding 78; complex 17, 41, 49, 79, 160; symbolic 62–3, 64–5, 187, 188, 193; threat 29, 44, 190–1, 233, 247, 269

Caught 248
Cecilia, La 93, 94
censorship 148, 157, 168; and the Arts
   Council (GB) 140–1; calls for 179,
   206, 207; and the child 190; of the
   female gaze 237–40; film 155; sense
   of 174
Chomsky, Noam 71, 112
cinema 23–4, 25, 43, 82–3, 92–3, 96,
   111, 159, 278; counter 45; early
   silent 229; and ideology 42, 70;
   pornographic 157, 166–7, 175; and
   psychoanalysis 39, 68, 213; radical 33
cinematic: apparatus 229, 246, 247;
   codes 33, 229; institution 42
Cixous, Hélène 61, 75, 105n, 232, 234
classic narrative cinema 3, 6, 172, 173,
   237, 278; *see also* classic realist text;
   Hollywood; mainstream narrative
   cinema; narrative film
classic realist text 10, 134, 292, 297,
   314
Clift, Montgomery 266
Collector, The 94
colonial: discourse 293, 294, 312, 313,
   316–7, 318, 319, 322–4, 326–8;
   subject 266, 313; *see also* difference;
   fantasy; other; power; stereotype
Coma 88
Cook, Pam 34n, 185, 297, 303, 304,
   310
Crossroads 308
Cowie, Elizabeth 10, 185
criticism 40, 41, 45

Dance, Girl, Dance 85
Dark Victory 237, 240
Daughter Rite 299
daydreams 213–4
death, representation of 190
de Lauretis, Teresa 224, 249–50
Delon, alain 280
Derrida, Jacques 312
desire 38, 58, 83, 212, 225, 256;
   homosexual 194, 261; male
   homosexual 263–4; Lacanian notion
   of 296; representation of 249;
   woman's 4, 22, 245, 246
Desperately Seeking Susan 225, 249,
   250, 253–6
Deux Fois 85
diegesis 38–9

Dietrich, Marlene 27, 29, 30, 223, 235,
   285
difference 112, 115–6, 122, 291, 313,
   315, 316, 326, 327; theory 3, 10–11,
   225
discourse 96, 99; *see also* colonial
Dishonoured 30
Doane, Mary Ann vii 9, 223, 224–5,
   227–42, 246–7, 248–9
Dr Jekyll and Mr Hyde 181
Doisneau, Robert 207, 239, 240
Dora 52
dreams 7, 227
Duel in the Sun 9, 17, 248, 282, 302
Dworkin, Andrea 204, 205, 209
Dyer, Richard vii, 5, 17, 186, 262–3,
   265–76

Eastwood, Clint 279–80
editing 28, 32, 121
ego 26, 32, 37, 77; ideal 280, 294
Ellis, John vii 131–3, 146–70, 171, 184,
   186–7, 191–3, 194, 195, 278, 284
Empire of the Senses (*Ai No Corrida*)
   167
Encore (Lacan) 47–8, 53, 55, 56, 61, 65
enunciation 118–9; in Hitchcock films
   246; in pornography 158, 176; in
   rude jokes 180
eroticism 284, 285
eye 76–8; contact 265, 267; as phallus
   77

Fall of the Roman Empire, The 285
family in psychoanalysis, the 97
Fanon, Frantz 318, 320–1, 322, 324,
   325, 327, 329
fantasy 9–10, 130, 134, 179, 181, 213,
   214–15, 217; colonial 327–8; female
   218; *see also* phantasy
female 56; homoeroticism 225;
   protagonist 225; representation of
   the 165
female pleasure 47, 159–61, 167,
   211–12; in feminist cinema 216–7; in
   pornography 164–5, 176, 192
female spectatorship 235; possible
   pleasure in 225; theories of 230, 233,
   241n, 244–8
feminine 73, 91, 113
femininity 16–17, 51, 66, 80, 81, 227–8,
   229, 234, 235, 240, 241, 247, 261,
   263, 286

feminism 195, 197, 200–1, 207–8;
  backlash against 203; and
  pornography 198–9, 205; and sex
  and violence 209–10; and writing 71
Feminism and Cinema Event
  (Edinburgh 1979) 291–2, 295, 296
feminist 91; writing 129
feminist critique: of cinema 3, 5, 98,
  197, 292; of pornography 134, 146,
  151–3, 163, 165, 211; of television
  29, 305
feminist film 93; culture 295; practice
  212, 297–8; 299; theory 211, 212,
  249, 292, 296, 299, 302
feminist theorist(s) 17, 19, 20, 110, 247
femme fatale 8, 225, 235
Festival of Light 148, 149–50, 151, 153,
  154, 207
Fête de la Raison, La 87
fetish 162–4, 188, 320
fetishism 41–2, 43–4, 76, 79, 121, 132,
  133, 159, 160–3, 172–3, 175, 177–8,
  187, 191, 192, 193, 196n, 246, 284,
  285, 319, 320; post-Lacanian
  understanding of 187
fiction 39, 134, 214, 215–7; film 90
film 83, 88, 95, 154–5; debates 1, 134;
  education 39, 45; history 24; studies
  2, 15; text 15
film noir 8, 29, 172, 284
film technology 23, 24
film theory 2, 35, 36, 39, 110, 184,
  188–9, 212, 213–14, 245, 262, 302,
  202
films by women 91
Flash Gordon 280
fort/da game 6, 81, 124n
Foucault, Michel 119, 123n, 214, 318,
  319–20, 322
frame, the 172, 175
Freud, Anna 194
Freud, Sigmund 3, 6, 8, 9, 18, 24, 26,
  37, 38, 42, 43, 44, 47, 49, 50–2,
  56–7, 58, 59, 64, 66, 68, 76, 77–8,
  79, 98, 99n, 101n, 121, 124n, 161,
  162, 163, 169n, 173, 180, 188–91,
  194, 213, 223, 227–8, 233, 234, 239,
  246, 248, 261, 269, 320, 324, 326
Freudian account of women 17, 43

Gauguin, Paul 143, 144
Gay Movement 277
gaze 24, 171–2, 225, 236–7; female 223,
  224, 230, 237–41, 262, 263; male 6,
  9, 27, 32; woman's 162
'Gaze' 185, 193
gender identity 1–2, 133, 193, 249, 279;
  representations of 20
Gidal, Peter 86
Glanz 43–4, 162
Gledhill, Christine vii, 35–46, 291–2,
  295, 296, 297
Goodbye Girl, The 88
Guns in the Afternoon 283
gynocentric genres 293, 301, 306

Haskell, Molly 3, 27, 233
Hawks, Howard 70, 280
Heath, Stephen vii, 18–19, 20, 40–1,
  42, 47–106, 113, 121, 167, 297, 314
Heine, Heinrich 227–8
Henley, Nancy 262, 265–7
hero 278–9; in Hitchcock 30, 32
heroine 27, 229
heterosexual 1
heterosexuality 192; male 269
Hitchcock, Alfred 10, 16, 29, 30–2,
  246, 278, 284, 285
Hollywood 89, 245, 246; *see also* classic
  narrative cinema; classic realist text;
  mainstream narrative cinema;
  narrative film
homosexual 1; eroticism 27; pleasure
  244; pornography 133, 185; woman
  225
homosexual desire, repression of 5
homosexuality 52, 249; female 248
horror film 236
Hotel Monterey 84
Hudson, Rock 286
Humoresque 237
hysteria 50–3, 62, 77, 103n; male 6, 51,
  166

identification 10, 25, 26, 225, 245, 256,
  278–83, 325–6; female 224;
  representation of 249
identity 71, 78; colonial 323
ideology 116, 298; dominant 41; and
  rape 202, 203
image 26, 85, 240, 241n, 244–5
images of men 267
'Images of Women' 135, 136, 142, 144
Imaginary 23, 117, 322; in
  pornographic cinema 212; and the
  symbolic 109–12

imaginary 25, 67–70, 77, 78, 88
imaging, practices of *see* cinematic codes
Irigaray, Luce 66, 75, 102n, 112, 188, 231–2, 233

Jeanne Dielman, 23 Quai du Commerce, 1080 Bruxelles 84
'Jeune Parque, La' (Valéry) 69
Johnston, Claire vii, 3, 11, 34n, 82, 104n, 130, 142, 159, 242n, 291, 292, 295–300
joke(s) 180–1, 239, 240
Jones, Allen 178
Jones, Ernest 51, 189, 190
jouissance 47, 48, 49, 54–5, 58, 61, 63, 65, 71, 76, 194; *du voir* 84
Julia 88
Juliet of the Spirits 69
Junior Bonner 286

Kaplan, Nelly 167
Klein, Carola 91
Klein, Melanie 194
Kristeva, Julia 188, 248
Kuhn, Annette vii, 1, 4, 292–3, 301–11

Lacan, Jacques 3, 8, 11, 18, 19, 20, 25, 36, 37, 38, 45–6, 47–50, 55–6, 60, 61, 64, 65, 68, 69, 70, 73, 74, 76, 78–9, 80, 83, 84, 86, 99n, 100n, 107–10, 112, 113–16, 124n, 174, 188, 189, 190
Lacanian: approach 3; psychoanalytic theory 9, 15, 17, 18
Lacanian theory 107, 111–2, 117–20, 123n; and cinema 120; of the subject 6, 15, 16
lack 10, 44, 49, 54, 57, 58, 60, 62, 76, 78, 90, 160, 161, 231
Lakoff, Robin and Mary Ritchie Key 72–3
language 18, 19, 20, 23, 25, 37, 40, 41, 57, 70–4, 111–12, 115, 117–18, 120, 124n, 184, 280, 295; alternative 212; Amazonian Cocama 72; American English 72; English 72; hieroglyphic 228–9, 241n; masculine 99; and pornography 180; the subject in 107–9; Thai 72; woman's 162, 174–5; women's 72–3, 89
langue 71
Leave Her to Heaven 237, 240

Lemoine-Luccioni, Eugénie 61–5, 67, 190
Leone, Sergio 279–80, 284, 285
Lesage, Julia 35, 41, 42, 43
lesbian: desire 225, 261; pornography 130; *see also* homosexual; homosexuality
Letter From an Unknown Woman 88
libido 26, 32, 59, 76
light on the eyes 169n, 171–2, 173, 174
linguistics 107–8, 109, 111–12, 120
Lippard, Lucy 142–3
Longford Report 149, 150, 151
look 16, 26, 27–30, 32, 75–6, 78, 82, 85, 86–7, 172, 175, 177, 178, 179, 188, 217, 240, 244, 245, 247, 261, 262, 263, 265, 269, 273–4; fourth 132–3, 174–5, 177, 178, 180, 181; -s 33, 159–60, 173; voyeuristic-scopophilic 33; *see also* to-be-looked-at-ness
looking 76–8, 278, 283–7; pleasure in 24–7; 211, 245, 247; voyeuristic 263; woman 236

Maccheroni, Henri 81
Mad Max 280
magazines 13, 136, 141; pornographic 154, 156, 157, 163, 166; women's 262, 267
Magritte, René 79
mainstream narrative cinema 4–5, 27, 33, 45, 132, 263; *see also* classic narrative cinema; classic realist text; Hollywod; narrative film
Major Dundee 283
male 5, 56; as erotic object 245; sexuality 6, 181; *see also* body, power
male pin-up 262, 263, 267, 269, 270; black 271, 272; white 271, 273
male subjectivity, representation of 5; *see also* subjectivity
man 28, 119, 140
Mann, Anthony 281, 284
Man of the West 286
Man Who Shot Liberty Valence, The 282–3
Marnie 30
'Marxist film' 93
masculinity 16–17, 130, 261, 263, 264, 267, 276, 278, 279, 286–7; as action

269–70; heterosexual 277; images of 282; as sexual spectacle 257n
masochism 7, 310; male 5–6, 130; in *Vertigo* 31
masquerade 234–5, 240, 242n
meaning 15, 16, 19, 211
Mekas, Jonas 92
melodrama 292, 301, 303, 304, 306, 308, 309, 310; Gainsborough 303, 304
men: American 198; feminist 195
Men Against Sexist Violence 205
men's sexualities 195
Merck, Mandy 11, 291
Metz, Christian 41–2, 44, 82, 110, 170n, 191, 224, 231, 297
metalanguage 195
m/f 186, 204
Michelangelo's Moses 269
mirror phase 1, 25, 41, 42, 44, 109–10
Mirror Phase 91
misrecognition 117
Mitchell, Juliet 43, 188
Modleski, Tania 303, 310
Montrelay, Michèle 64, 65, 66, 68, 69, 71, 75, 232, 235
Moral majority 207, 210
Morgan, Robin 204
Morocco 30
Mulvey, Laura vii, 2–4, 5, 7, 9, 16–17, 22–34, 41, 42, 43, 82, 85, 86, 98, 104n, 121, 129–30, 132, 142, 159–60, 163, 169n, 176, 178, 189–90, 223–4, 225, 229, 230, 234, 244, 245, 246, 247, 248, 261, 263, 277, 278, 279, 281, 282–3, 284, 285, 302, 303; and Peter Wollen 66–7, 85
muscularity 273–5
musicals 182
musical numbers 27
Muybridge, Eadweard 270

narcissism 25, 68, 225, 231, 240, 278–9, 282
narcissistic: male image 281; phantasies 279
narration and pornography 176–7
narrative 29, 162, 214; pornographic 151, 163, 177; realist 315; soap opera 301
narrative flm 84, 90, 93, 95; conventions 25, 33; mainstream

27–8, 32, 89, 236, 245; popular 16; and spectacle 27
National Organisation of Women (US) 205
Néa (*A Young Emmanuelle*) 167
Neale, Steve vii 5, 17, 263, 277–87
Newman, Paul 269
News From Home 85, 86
North by Northwest 277–8
North Sea, The (Heine) 227–8
Not a Love Story 211, 212
Now Voyager 229–30, 236
nude: female 138, 157; male 139–40

Oedipus 65, 249–50; complex 96–7, 114, 187, 189, 303; structure 190
Only Angels Have Wings 28
Ophelia (Millais) 52
'Other' 10, 54–5, 57–8, 59, 79, 83, 195, 235, 326
otherness 313, representation of 314

Pajaczkowska, Claire viii, 133, 184–96
paranoia 193, 194
Pat Garrett and Billy the Kid 283
patriarchal ideology 3, 18, 142, 202
Peeping Tom 25, 77, 79, 82, 132, 229
Peeping Tom 236
penis 22, 24, 62–3, 161, 188, 192, 196n, 262, 274, 275; in Hitchcock films 31; -phallus 74; -phallus distinction 50
Penthouse 80, 129, 141, 142
phallocentric theory 4, 7, 11, 262
phallocentrism 22
phallus 18–19, 20, 22, 49, 60–1, 64, 79, 81, 100n, 112, 113, 114–15, 122, 161–2, 189, 192, 262, 274; eye as 78; and *jouissance* 54–5; Lacanian notion of 297; and the penis 5, 16, 18, 19, 20, 50, 161, 163; in pornography 164–5, 192; woman as 163
phantasy 134, 213–14, 215, 217, 218; male 28; of masculinisation 224, 302; in *Rear Window* 31; sexual 213; world 26; *see also* fantasy
photograph(s): in body art 142–3; as case records 52–3; of women 135, 136, 137, 142; *see also* Robert Doisneau; Henri Maccheroni; Eadweard Muybridge; *Un Regard oblique*

photography 80–1, 239–40, 270; realist 130
pleasure 6, 24, 26, 27, 32, 33, 190, 211, 320; male 166, 167, 178, 211; a politics of 212, 217; *see also* female pleasure; *jouissance*; looking; woman's pleasure
Point Blank 286
Pollock, Griselda viii, 130–1, 135–45
popular culture 292
pornographic 156; text 10
pornography 5, 80–1, 89, 129–34, 146–59, 160, 163, 164, 165, 166–9, 171, 179–80, 195, 197–9, 200–10, 212, 217–18; campaigns against 197, 199, 203, 204–6, 210, 215, 217; conference on (ICA/SEFT) 184, 185, 193, 195; and feminism 146, 181, 186, 218; feminist writing on 205; and health 150; industry 147, 212, 216; and the law 148, 149, 152, 153, 154, 155, 156, 157, 158, 167–8, 185, 204, 206, 207; lesbian activities in 163, 164; masturbation in 142, 163, 164, 180, 216, 217; nineteenth century 76, 142–3; and the phallus 164–5; and representation 158–9, 176, 208–9; woman's sexual pleasure in 164–5, 178; *see also* cinema; Festival of Light; Williams Committee
power 269; black 271; colonial 322; and knowledge 318, 319, 329; male 19, 211, 265, 270–1, 274
pre-Oedipal phase 68, 184, 223, 224, 233, 247
primal scene 83, 179, 188, 321, 322
projection 194
Propp, Vladimir 282
proximity 231
Psycho 236
psychoanalysis 15, 18, 22, 35–6, 37, 39, 41, 42, 44, 45, 47, 50, 53, 64, 97, 98, 99n, 297, 302, 303; and the cinema 22, 35, 53; feminist work in 188, 292, 296–7; as theory 191–5; and women 35
psychoanalytic theory 3, 15–16, 43, 121–2, 187, 188, 291, 194; *see also* Freud; Freudian; Lacan; Lacanian
Pursued 172, 179

rape 201–3, 204, 206–7, 208

reader 298
reading 297, 298; against the grain 5
realism 28, 121, 214; and fiction 216
reality 26
Rear Window 30, 31, 236
'Reclaim the Night' 152
recognition 25
Reeves, Steve 280
Regard oblique, Un (Doisneau) 237–9
Renaissance space, illusion of 27, 33
representation(s) 74, 75, 79, 84, 85, 86, 95–6, 105n,111, 146, 152–3, 176, 211, 212, 229, 262, 263, 302, 318; fetishistic 33, 43, 44; system 44
representational techniques 121
Revolt of Mamie Stover, The 34n, 297
Riddles of the Sphinx 66–7, 68, 87, 93, 98
Riefenstahl, Leni 92
Right to Life slides 208
River of No Return 27
Riviere, Joan 224, 234–5
Rodowick, David 245, 281
Rose, Jacqueline 110, 113
Rothman, Stephanie 85, 185

sadism 29, 190, 194, 283–4
Safouan, Moustafa 65, 235
Said, Edward 316–9
Saint Teresa (Bernini) 8, 18, 47–8, 56, 76, 84, 98
Samourai, Le 280
Santoro, Suzanne 140
São Bernardo 315
Saussure, Ferdinand de 108; *see also* linguistics; sign; signification
Schaulust 84
Schreber case history 193–4
Schwarzenegger, Arnold 268, 273
science 35–6, 37, 39
scientific theory 188
scopic: drive 77, 84, 160, 174, 322; regime 229
scopophilia 24, 25, 26, 28, 77, 239; cinematic 82; fetishistic 29, 285
scopophilic: eroticism 30; instinct 32
Screen 17, 22, 35, 36–7, 38, 39, 41, 42, 43, 45, 46, 261, 291; Brecht issue 35; on pornography 129, 130; Racism, Colonialism and Cinema issue 315; and *Screen Education* 184; *Screen Readers* 2
screen-spectator relationship 2, 4, 224

seeing 76
sex and violence 206–10; and the Right 210
sexism 134, 199–201, 209
'sexist' 91
sexist ideology 207
sexual: phantasies 213; relation 53, 59, 65
sexual difference 3, 10, 11, 18, 19, 32, 47–99, 113, 122, 124n, 142, 160, 161, 184, 188, 190, 193, 218, 231, 232, 236, 246, 291; physical 164
sexual subject 1, 11; and cinema 3; cinematic theories of 4
sexual violence, campaigns against 202–3
sexualities: for feminism 207, 217; men's 195
sexuality 56–60, 63–5, 66, 92, 113, 132, 134, 147, 208, 213, 218; discourse of 163; female 65–7; healthy 150, 208; portrayal of 146–7, 151; representation of in pornography 164, 166, 167; representation of in public places
shine on the nose 174; see also Glanz
sign 19, 107, 111, 229, 330n; Saussurian notion of 19; -signified 228
signification 37, 38, 108–9, 112–13
signifier 20, 111, 115
sopa opera 232, 292, 301, 303–4, 306–10
Song of the Shirt, The 298
Spartacus 285
spectator(s) 16, 42, 44–5, 82, 93–5, 244, 246, 279, 280, 305, 306, 309, 310; female 9, 17, 130, 132, 223, 224–5, 228, 240, 247, 248, 306; masculinization of 245; in pornography 164, 165; -text relations 302, 307–8; women as 43
spectatorship 7, 129–30, 132, 190, 223, 231, 248; film 192; gendered 292, 302, 303, 307; see also female spectatorship
specular 69–70
Spender, Dale 265
sphinx-woman 66
sport 271
Stacey, Jackie viii, 9, 11, 223, 225, 244–257
Stam, Robert and Louise Spence 315

star 28, 160; male 281; system 25
stereotype 293, 294, 312–13, 315, 318, 320–8
Stern, Lesley viii, 9, 10, 133–4, 197–220
Sternberg, Josef von 16, 29, 30, 223, 285; and the screen 30
story 39
structural/materialist film practice 86
structuralism 2, 123n; see also linguistics
Student Nurses 185
subject, the 3, 4, 15, 37, 38, 42, 65, 69, 73, 78, 83, 90, 95, 103n, 111, 114, 116, 118–9, 123n, 186, 320–1; in fantasy 9–10; female 4, 7; feminine 303; feminine in the narrative 245, 246, 250; Freudian theory of 232; Lacanian theories of 1, 4, 6, 19, 107–9, 110, 123n; male 4, 6–7; material 7–8; social 308, 309; and the spectator 4; in the text 295; see also colonial subjectivity 4, 10–22, 25, 114, 116, 120, 246; in the cinema 3; and the text 295
Superman 2 280
Susan Slept Here 182
suture 74, 95, 165, 172, 215, 316
Symbolic 19, 20, 23, 29, 330n; and the Imaginary 109–112; pre-symbolic 18
symbolic 60–1, 62, 79

Tahitian Woman with Mango Blossoms (Gauguin) 143–4
Taking a Part 299
'taking place' 85
television 305
text 2; -context 293, 303, 308, 309, 310; feminine 303; -subject relations 297
text-reader: circuit 192; relationship 11, 292
textual strateies in film 298–9
theoreticism 296
Théories du symbole (Todorov) 180
theory 195
Three Women 88
T-Men 281–2
to-be-looked-at-ness 27, 172, 173–4, 177, 244; see also look
Todorov, Tzvetan 180, 229
To Have and Have Not 27, 28
Touch of Evil 39, 40–1, 88, 314–5
transvesticism 234–5; transvestite 240

Turning Point, The 88

unconscious, the 47, 59, 61, 65, 66, 67, 97, 113, 114, 214; female 4, 7; feminine 67; and language 109; male 9, 16
unpleasure *see* pleasure

vaginal imagery 132, 140, 142, 159, 163, 165, 178
Varda, Agnès 92, 94
Vertigo 30, 31–2
vision 75
'Visual Pleasure and Narrative Cinema' 22–34; *see also* Mulvey, Laura
voice, the 53, 74; in feminine writing 103n
voyeurism 29, 41, 43, 75–7, 79, 82, 121, 160, 175, 231, 236, 283, 284–5; in early silent cinema 229; in Hitchcock 30, 31
voyeuristic desire 231
voyeurs 25

Wayne, John 283
Ways of Seeing (Berger) 136
Wenders, Wim 175
Whitehouse, Mary 149
Wild Bunch, The 283
Willemen, Paul viii, 132–3, 171–83, 184, 194, 217, 281–2. 284, 297
Williams Committee 146, 153, 158, 166, 167, 185; Report 147, 149, 153–5, 168–9, 176
Williams, Linda 236, 270
woman 4, 6, 8, 23, 54–6, 61–9, 79, 89–90, 101n, 113, 142, 165, 193, 225, 228, 229, 232; and castration 8–9, 22; cinematic image of 9; as difference in nature 63; in jokes 180, 239; the look of 87–8, 133, 162, 174–5; as main protagonist 34n; as not-all 54; as nude 144; as object of the male gaze 16, 27, 28, 29, 151; as other 63; and the phallus 164–5, 192; as phallus 163, 232; and representation 18, 26, 105n; as screen 229; as sexual difference 29, 160; as sexual subject 9; as spectacle 244, 249; *see also* desire; language; subject; writing
womanliness 235
woman's picture(s) 233, 301, 307, 309
woman's pleasure 184, 191, 194, 195
women: artists 142; in cultural production 90–1; as objects of male anxiety 153; in psychoanalysis 35, 43; as spectators 85
Women Against Pornography (WAP) 203, 204, 205, 206, 207, 208, 212
Women Against Violence Against Women (WAWAW) 205, 212
Women Against Violence in Pornography and Media (WAVPM) 192, 204
Women's Art History Collective 136, 142, 145
Women's Movement, the 134, 140, 142, 153, 179, 197–8, 201, 202–3, 213, 265, 272, 296, 297
writing 70–3, 121, 184; feminine 74–5, 121; and pornography 157

Young Emmanuelle, A (*Néa*) 167
Young Mr Lincoln 40